FOUR TIMES A SCAPEGOAT

Captain Douglas Harvey

Published by

MELROSE BOOKS

An Imprint of Melrose Press Limited
St Thomas Place, Ely
Cambridgeshire
CB7 4GG, UK
www.melrosebooks.com

FIRST EDITION

Cover designed by Bryan Carpenter
The front cover depicts the author's favourite ship, the LPGC Quentin, in drydock.
The back cover shows The Greem Flash. A rare phenomenon that occurs just before the Sun
sets. Its rays are refracted in the atmosphere into the green part of the visible spectrum. This
effect generally shows emerald green and lasts for only one second. It is also possible for the
rays to turn blue.

ISBN 1 905226 15 2

Printed and bound in Great Britain by:
Bath Press Limited, Lower Bristol Road,
Bath, BA2 3BL, UK

Four times a Scapegoat
But I can hold my head up!

Captain Douglas T. Harvey
Master Mariner

Scapegoat / skeipgout / noun 1, someone made to take the blame or punishment for the errors and mistakes of others.

To my daughter Morag, and my son Graham, without whom the world would be a very dull place.

For Hazel, my fiancée, who thinks she understands me.

Finally, the ladies of Cadham Library, Glenrothes, Fife (where most of this was written), Marilyn & Lysbeth for their patience, support and understanding. A smile goes a long way.

Thank you.

<u>Acknowledgement.</u>

I am indebted to

Reverend Archie MacMillan and the congregation of Glenrothes Baptist Church for their fellowship on the Lord's day, my non-writing day, and their prayers and support on the other 6 days, especially when recounting the difficult times.

I will forever remain in the debt of Mrs Sheila McBride, who told me that my sixth sense was God looking after me, and I therefore remain His most humbled servant.

Captain D.T.Harvey. 3rd November 2004. Glenrothes, Scotland.

FOREWORD

It is not a pleasant experience, being used as the scapegoat, particularly as you seemed to be the only person in the company who was doing any work. That was the first time, and the second time.

The third time was just plain stupid by the company who tried it, particularly as they tried to use the second time to their advantage. They themselves ended up in a deep mess. It is revealed here for the first time. I learnt later that my efforts were worthwhile.

The last time was just plain criminal on an international scale.

The saddest thing of all, is that for all the companies that I have worked for, all over the world, in each case, these companies were British, which probably does not say a lot for their standard of management. Most certainly in the third case, as you are about to get your eyes opened.

Most people will, at some time in their lives, have stood on a river bank and watched ships going by, or stood on cliff tops or beaches and seen them passing by at sea. Perhaps they have crossed the channel by ferry, and that will have been as close to a ship as they are ever likely to get.

Oh, ships hit the headlines occasionally, when there is a collision, or a fire, or worse, run aground, with all the pollution. Then they sit up and listen, but invariably, don't really understand.

But what about all the pollution that you cannot see? All the gas blown off by tankers as they go about their daily business, in an industry where theft and fraud go hand in hand, and most days somewhere.

The aim of every aspiring deck officer is to sail as master. I just happened to have been in the right place at the right time, when I was promoted from a highly experienced chief officer, with more tricks up his sleeve in operating gas tankers, than anyone. Since then, I have perfected the art of being in the wrong place at the wrong time gaining this unique knowledge that I choose to share with you here.

I do not wish to be alarmist, but the standard of deck officers, especially in their understanding of gas tanker operations, has fallen terribly to the stage that a lot of them just do not know what they are doing. These are the people who are operating around our coastlines.

By the time you have read and understood this book, then you, with no previous knowledge beforehand, will probably know more than they do. But remember, a little knowledge is a dangerous thing.

Did you think that ships being piloted into port make them safer?

Wrong! I will also share my experiences as a pilot on the River Forth.

Then, for the absolute experts only, join me in the wonderful world of delivering ships around the globe.

This may look or sound easy, but believe me, it is anything but. What you are about to read, is a true story, with a bit of humour thrown in, just to keep it interesting.

If at times, it appears too technical, be patient, there are two good reasons for this.

1) So you will understand Part 5 better.

2) You'll need this knowledge as you unravel the puzzle in Book 3.

PART 1

I was 31 when I first took command of a small gas tanker in Scapa Flow, *MV Quentin*, 1600 tonnes, a ship that I helped build in 1977, had worked on many times a chief officer, and was now in command of on 1st July 1986.

I'd worked for Gibson Liquid Gas from 1978, starting as second mate, and worked my way up, gaining my masters' certificate in 1984. This was a terrific company to work in, everyone was the best of friends, there was very little 'oil and water' between mates and engineers, virtually everyone had a nickname, and although we worked hard, there was usually some practical joke or 'mickey take' going on somewhere. Even the office staff in Leith joined in, or at least until *Mack the Knife* (managing director) joined, but even he had trouble with all us mavericks. Their ships were all small gas tankers running mainly in North West Europe, although occasionally we would trot off world wide. We carried virtually every type of liquid gas in all sorts of different ways. Chemicals occasionally as well.

The best practical joker was a chief engineer with a wicked sense of humour, described by the late actor, Fulton Mackay, as a *sloe-eyed Mancunian*, although I wasn't far behind.

It was not unusual for you to leave a ship with your suitcase, full off clothes etc, only to arrive home and discover that you now possessed the contents of the engine room rag bag, plus various lumps of scrap to make up the weight. Your 'gear' was always forwarded on a few days later, and there was not a lock that he couldn't pick. One of his favourite tricks was to rewire your cabin lights, so they wouldn't switch off, and its very difficult trying to get to sleep with all the lights on. He would glue the bulbs in too.

I suckered him a beauty one day in retaliation and he has never forgiven me.

If you take a 2 gallon foam mix for a fire extinguisher, and take the 'A' compound, the brown one, and pour it into the toilet cistern, then sprinkle the 'B' compound, the white one, into the toilet bowl, then it looks like Harpic. When it's flushed, the chemical reaction is a sight to behold, and there is nothing you can do to stop it, as it fills the bowl in about 5 seconds, and doesn't go round the bend too well. I got him before he had his trousers up. It smells odd too.

When I took over as master, I had to try to be a little more responsible, well a little more at any rate, as my first chief officer was 'Blunderman,' and you don't get a name like that for nothing.

Although an extremely pleasant fellow, he was terribly accident prone in anything that involved tools or machinery, and on a gas tanker, there is an awful lot of both.

His ship was once in Zeebrugge tank cleaning, at the same time, undergoing survey. There is always a lot of survey work to do, so any opportunity is taken to wade through it. It has actually got out of hand now, and something is going to have to be done to at least try to curtail it. I'll comment on this later.

On this particular day he was bulling the surveyor as only he could do, but this surveyor was getting fed up with it, by the time they came to test the fixed dry powder installation. These are very powerful pieces of equipment for putting out fires, and are not something that you mess around with if you do not know what you are doing which off course, he didn't. It comprises a high pressure tank containing 750 kg of dry powder, and 4 nitrogen cylinders charged to 250 bars pressure. Some are bigger. It is designed, to discharge completely in 40 seconds, which equates to the powder flying out the 50 mm barrel of the gun at 20 kg per second, and that's a lot. There is a valve you can shut to control it, but this one was stiff. There is also a small nitrogen cylinder to get it going. It's automatic.

The surveyor was less than impressed with his explanation of the test procedure, and told him that he was "going for lunch, so find out how to do it properly by the time I come back". Then promptly went up the gangway to his car which was parked beside the ship, about 10 metres away. Opening the driver's door and putting in his briefcase and helmet, he then started to take off his boilersuit, when *Blunderman*, 'accidentally' set off the dry powder system. The entire charge shot out of the nozzle, across the dock and into his car, the better part of 700 kgs going inside, the balance covering him. He was completely white and in shock. If you know how difficult it is to try to clean up spilt talcum powder, then you can imagine the crew trying to clean out his car. They used shovels, and were at it all day, but to no avail. They just had to give up and buy him a new car.

He spent 3 days in hospital being treated for shock, most of the time being spent in the shower, and swears that it was 'done deliberately'. Writing the letter to the company was extremely difficult.

Now I've got him on the *Quentin* as chief mate. When I was chief mate, obviously, we never sailed together, thank goodness. I would have had no hair left. Precious little even now.

We had two ships operating out of Scapa Flow, the other being the *Borthwick*, a name that came to haunt me for years. This ship was the last ship built in Robb Caledon's yard in Leith, and for everything that is good about the *Quentin*, is bad about the *Borthwick*. There is an old saying, "if it looks right, it probably is," and there is nothing that looks right about this heap of junk. We used to joke that it was built out of the bits left over from all the ships built previously by this yard. But we still had a lot of 'fun' with it anyway.

The idea from Gibsons was that these two ships would be operated by three masters, who would alternate between both ships with 1 being on leave at some time. The other two masters were '*Gale Force Gordon*,' and '*The Fang*.'

GFG got his nickname by being able to find a gale to steam into, even on a flat calm day. He held the record for the slowest passage to Norway, usually 1 day, by taking 9 days to get there, steaming into an Easterly gale. It wouldn't be so bad, but the wind changed into a Westerly gale for him to come back into, and he took 10 days to get back. A lot of people just wouldn't sail with him. He was also the worst speller in the world with terrible grammar, but had a penchance for writing endless letters to the company which were a continuous source of mirth.

He came from Esso, and I think rather fancied that he ran a VLCC.

The Fang was the dirtiest, scruffiest, most awful person in the world, His middle name was avarice. He got his nickname from the one top tooth to one side of his mouth, which was fine until he failed his medical, and had to have it out. We were stuck for a name for him then, until he let it slip that he had joined the Masons. He then became known as the *Leith Arab*. *Leith* because he came from there, and *Arab* for his love to screwing you out of your money, but secretly his other name was *Sheik Mahandy* (shake-my-hand, for his affiliation to the Masonic Lodge). I have nothing against The Masonic Lodge.

For breakfast every day, he would sit down to a huge plateful of All Bran, but not with milk on it like everyone else. Nope. Grapefruit Juice! I do not have to describe how this affected the olfactory organ.

He was also a terribly dishonest seaman, and screwed me up terribly with his smuggling activities which I'll describe later. He's dead now, and is not missed. At least not by me.

Both the *Quentin* and *Borthwick* had to be converted from their original design to carry the gas out of Flotta, Scapa Flow, and it was not easy stuff to carry, even for expert gas men. The terminal was owned and operated by Occidental, the gas coming from the ill-fated Piper Alpha platform. The tanks were designed to handle down to -48 degrees Celsius, and 6.5 bar pressure. LPG is normally only carried to one of these parameters, ie either propane at -42 degrees Celsius and zero pressure, or at 6.0 bar pressure and about +10 degrees Celsius. Out of Flotta it was a mix of propane and ethane, with some hydrogen sulphide and carbon dioxide as well. The net result was this was carried at up to 6.85 bar pressure, with modified safety valves to 7.05 bar and also at about –46 degrees Celsius, leaving little room for error, either way. On top of this the mixture ratio changed all the time. It was fine when you got the hang of it, but getting the hang of it was tricky. We had a few close shaves with this stuff, and remember, I had *Blunderman*.

The reason I was promoted at this time, was that we had all just been made redundant, and then offered contracts with a manning company, with the ships being re-flagged to the Isle of Man. There was an awful lot of ill-feeling as everyone had taken a pay cut of around 25%, but my promotion meant, financially, I didn't lose out. Gibsons retained the technical management in Leith, but they set up Denman in Douglas IOM, with of all groups, Denholms of Glasgow. They could not have chosen a worse company.

In Gibsons, we were used to being honest with everyone, we told the truth, no matter how much it hurt. Now we were dealing with a bunch who were indeterminate in being truthful, and that is being diplomatic. They promised us that they had a solid core of gas men to draw from, but gas qualified officers are as rare as hens' teeth. After they had the contract, they then set about advertising for men to fill the gaps. So much for their solid core.

But we are all mavericks, and after seeing their adverts from their Aberdeen office, which were spread around the company, we all 'applied to join'. In short, we applied for our own jobs, but in code. When we asked where all these 'extra' men were, we were told that they had 45 applications and would interview shortly. It took them 6 weeks to work out, that they already employed these 45. They were not pleased until it was pointed out that they had had a salutary lesson in being honest, and they were not to mess us around.

Before we went with Denholms, we had our own crews, and many excellent ABs. Very few went over to Denholms. They must have known something we didn't. Now we were getting Denholms' 'men'. Most were the dregs of the Merchant Navy, about as much use as dirty ballast.

Of the six that I engaged on the first day, one walked off after 12 hours, as he couldn't have his 'wife' (hooker) with him, ran up a load of bills in Kirkwall, then got arrested at the airport in Kirkwall. I had to go ashore to sort out the mess. One was caught smuggling tobacco, so was sacked.

How he got caught was interesting, and serves to explain the standards of men we were getting rather admirably.

I received a 'phone call from the agents in Kirkwall, when we were alongside in Porsgrun, Norway. Our usual discharging port. I was asked to come ashore next time back, as a delicate matter had arisen, so delicate that they could not discuss it on the 'phone. Curious.

Next time back, I went to see the boss of our Agents. It transpired that this AB had posted off his tobacco allowance when ashore in Kirkwall. This is illegal.

Unfortunately, he 'forgot' that he had moved house, and sent it to his old address. The new occupants had no forwarding address, so opened the letter, got the agent's address, and posted it back with a covering letter.

How is that for being just plain dumb?

The agents off course wanted nothing to do with this, so I had to get rid of him.

The others though were also joining in and two more were sacked for drugs offences, and the other 2 lasted 3 weeks. They caused a near riot in Leith, as both managed to get a doctor to 'sign them off', claiming they were affected by 'the gas leaking from the ship'!

One of the 'druggies' after being advised that he would be discharged in Scapa Flow, gave ample proof that he was on a 'high.'

After he left my cabin, he went downstairs where I heard a bit of a commotion, and then a 'smack'.

The mate, *Blunderman* appeared, looking a bit stunned, and said, "that wee so'n so just smacked me in the mouth. I never said a word."

"It's okay Jim, he's leaving in Scapa Flow as soon as we get back."

However, about 15 minutes later, with my door closed, there is a sudden pounding, and it was thrown open. It is very unusual for my door ever to be locked. The code was that if it was open, I was available, if shut, then I was asleep. There standing outside it was this AB, without a stitch of clothing on, stark naked! A very brave man indeed as my chief engineer lived opposite, and was now standing behind him.

Now JC, my chief is normally a very easy going guy. We'd sailed together before and many times since. I go along and see him occasionally since he retired.

He is also very distinctive, dressing in exactly the same way today. A blue shirt in that new material, 'crumplene,' a pair of jeans, held up by a leather belt, with 6 inches sticking out after the buckle, somewhat hidden under a large and expanding paunch, occasionally a uniform jersey of indeterminate vintage, topped by the 'face'.

Distinctive? Not the sort you forget easily, with big bushy eyebrows, a greying beard, blue eyes, and hair that definitely looks as though he has shares in 'Grecian 2000 for Men'. Ever seen 'Blackbeard', well just about the same, only with bigger hands.

This AB starts mouthing off, until, 'tap tap tap,' on his shoulder from JC followed with "away yeh go sonny, afore ah help yeh."

The transformation was amazing, as he slunk off.

JC said, "he had nice wee cheeks on his bum though." We both had a dram and a good laugh.

I made it very clear that as fast Denholms could send me rubbish, I would send them back, irrespective of the cost.

It took them 3 months to latch on to this, but I was not going to compromise my standards. I maintained this stance until I walked off the *Borthwick* in 1989, and I'll explain why later in the book. I did eventually get quality crews as they couldn't afford to send me inferior staff.

The *Quentin* was built in rather an unusual way. She was designed by a Dutch Naval Architect by the name of Jaap Windhouer, and the hull was built in a yard in Aalst, Holland that built Rhine barges. From then on, everything else was sub-contracted out. She was then finished in Lips-Kellers yard in Rotterdam, a yard that only fitted propellers and rudders to, yes, Rhine barges. It all worked out perfectly, and strangely enough, took exactly the same time to build as the *Borthwick*, which was built in a shipyard, the difference being that the *Quentin* was a quality ship, the credit being mostly due to the innovative ideas of a Mr James White, who also owned Liquid Gas Equipment, and was the new owner.

She was originally named *Pentland Crag*, but this had to be changed before she was commissioned into *Pentland Moor*, as the Dutch had trouble pronouncing *Crag*. She only became *Quentin*, when she was bought by Gibsons some time later.

So crewed up, re-registered, and loaded, we continued our regular trade to Norway. I'd done this for 4 years as mate. It was summer and pleasurable.

Ship handling is one of these things that you can either do or you can't. It isn't as easy as it looks. There is not a simulator yet built that is of any use other than for giving you the basics. Off course, everyone else on the ship is an 'expert', the scale of expertise being on a sliding scale from the captain (who has to do it), being at the bottom end, to the crew on the fo'c'sle at the top end, and their chances of getting a go are NIL.

Then there are the super-experts. Those ashore. And the super-duper experts. Those with hindsight and a crystal ball. (You can include some of the press in this category.)

When I first came to sea, a chief officer told me: "There isn't a book yet written that tells you how to pump with a pump that won't pump, through a pipeline full of holes." Nothing beats experience.

Now I have to do it, and it's a steep learning curve.

There is no bow thruster on the *Quentin*, but she is so beautifully built that you don't need one.

Going alongside in Porsgrun was, as you may expect, nerve racking. But I made it. It was only later, as I got more confident, that testing the fenders became the name of the game.

It was when we were alongside and discharging that the 'phone rang. We had a telephone on board, which we plugged into a socket on the jetty. And no, I did not steam off one day and forget to un-plug it. That was *GFG*'s sole domain, and more than once too.

It was from Leith, to tell me that my old mentor had died. Captain Tom Mitchell. We sailed together many times, and I learnt more from this man, than any other at sea. On his final voyage, I sailed with him, when he had a heart attack on board. Fortunately, we were alongside a lay-by berth at the time in Moerdijk, in the Netherlands, and got him off to hospital in minutes. He had a total of 10 months in retirement, and all of his plans came to nothing. He would be sorely missed, and not only by me.

An amusing part though, and I know he would like me to tell this tale.

The captain who came out after he was taken to hospital was *Ivor the Engine*.

He asked me what he could send to the hospital. "Scotch," I suggested, but no, "did he like chocolate?"

"I'm not sure, I think he does," said I.

"Oh, well then, I'll not send anything," said *Ivor*.

He is so tight and mean that I'm not letting him off with sending nothing, so retorted with, "he likes milk chocolate as opposed to plain. Yes, he likes chocolate."

So a few bars were sent to the hospital. Tom hated the stuff, so gave it to the nurses, who ended up with rather a lot, as in an awful lot. Why?

Our only communications on the lay-by berth was by VHF, which just happened to be on the channel for 'Maas Approach,' the signal station for one of the busiest ports in the world. However, in times of need, I called them and asked for an ambulance. It was there alongside in less than 5 minutes, and this place is 'out in the sticks'.

But then again, everybody knew Tom, he'd been coming in and out for years.

So everybody sent chocolate, in all shapes and forms.

He said to me at a private dinner in an Edinburgh hotel, set up by Gibson's to give him his retirement gifts, "I'd like to meet the guy who said I liked chocolate. I can't stand the stuff. The nurses ate the lot. I'd have preferred a dram."

I though it best to remain silent on this rather delicate point.

After sailing from Norway, early one evening, off the Norwegian coast, we came across a small boat adrift, about 9 feet long, red in

GRP.

Nobody in it, so we picked it up, and reported this to the Norwegian Coast Guard. It was landed to the care of the Police next time back in Porsgrun. We even got a receipt, as we could claim it back after 6 months, if nobody claimed it. It was ideal as a jolly boat as our inflatable was past it. *GFG* tried to claim it back after 6 months, only to be told that it had been 'stolen out of the police station'. A likely story as some copper just fancied a new boat. Whenever we picked up anything after this, we just kept it, and we amassed a fair old fleet.

One day, my chief engineer came to the bridge, and said "have you seen what *Blunderman* has done?"

"Oh no, what is it this time?"

I knew it was too good to last after 10 days.

"He can't have blown the safety valves as I didn't hear them going off." (They sound like a Howitzer firing a shell.)

"Go on, surprise me."

(One thing about him was that he never had the same 'accident' twice, but boy, did he have a fertile imagination.)

"He decided to change the bolts on No 2 cargo pump at the non-return valve, as they looked a bit rusty."

"But chief, they are stainless steel, and anyway, they're not bolts, they are studs, I remember fitting them when we built this ship."

"Oh you know that, and I know that, and now he knows that, as he has just sheared two of them."

They were 20 millimetre stainless steel, and hard as anything.

"So he'll have to drill them out, and re-tap them before putting in new studs. That's a big job!"

"Yep, but look and see how he's doing it."

I looked, amazed at how anyone could be so dumb.

There he was with a hand drill, fitted with an 18 mm drill bit, happily turning away.

"He'll be there till next year at that rate chief."

"Yep, but it stops him breaking anything else in the meantime."

After 2 hours he was knackered, having drilled to a total depth of zero millimetres, but never mind, only another 300 millimetres to go.

"Whatever you do, don't tell him we have diamond tipped drills or a heavy duty air drill."

"Don't worry captain, they're hidden."

We had to help him, and the engineers spent the whole afternoon drilling them out. He was warned not to pick up any more tools. The concept of redundancy before I took over led to a certain amount of neglect, not least of all in the on-going battle with survey work, so my first three port calls in Norway meant I had to clear the backlog. The ship, when I left was back up to standard in all respects despite the many crew problems. This later became a major irritant, as you will soon see.

The company decided at this time to fit Cellular 'phones to all four of their coastal vessels. Good idea this, as on the VHF in Orkney there is no such thing as privacy. When a local gets his first paycheck, the first thing he does is to buy a VHF scanner and listen in. Why? Apart from being nosey, they love to have 'informed' gossip. I say 'informed', as this can be dead handy when you want to tell someone what you think of them, only you don't tell them, you tell someone else, knowing that they are listening in.

This being Gibson's however, buying the 'phone is done on the cheap.

The two ships operating out of Scapa Flow can only tune in to the North of Scotland area, it doesn't work anywhere else. The two ships on the south coast can only use it on the south coast.

I had the *Quentin*'s 'phone installed in the chartroom, so that we could, if necessary fold out drawings etc to discuss a problem when on the 'phone. Seemed logical.

On the *Borthwick* however, the master choose a different logic. There, it was installed in the bridge toilet. Why? you may ask, as did a lot of people. Because, in the past whenever the company 'phoned the ship by VHF, he was invariably sitting on the loo, so he reckoned if it was in there that would save him getting up.

Now this 'phone was supposed to be scanner proof. Normally it would be, but this is Orkney, and it took them less than a day to re-tune all their scanners to the new frequency.

After 6 weeks, I left to go on leave having had my baptism. The *Leith Arab* could have *Blunderman* all to himself.

It was my turn for the *Borthwick* which I joined on the 1st of October 1986 in our happy hunting ground of Scapa Flow.

The reason that the *Borthwick* is such a bad ship, is not the fault of the shipyard. Her original design on paper was quite good, but it was hacked about so much, that the end product bore little relationship to the original. She was built to a standard known at the time as IMCO 2/2, but this was never ratified. In order to squeeze in as much cargo as possible and still come under the 1600 gross tons rules, her accommodation block was reduced from three decks to two. During the inclining experiment, it was then found that she has *too much* stability, so had upper hopper wing tanks added. Not over the whole length, they missed out the 2 in the middle to keep the freeboard within the 1600 ton rules. To keep the costs down, they were filled with fire hoses and drained by drop valves. Does this sound rough? Yep!

It was also found that if the chain lockers had no doors fitted into the forecastle space, as this then counted as an exempt space. Her cargo tanks were modified in design, and they managed an extra 300 cubic metres over the *Quentin*, built at the same time.

I cursed them later for not fitting doors to the chain lockers.

Her underwater hull form resembled a brick, but the hull plating was reduced to save weight, and frequently cracked, big style. Her propeller was too big. It went on and on, and you'll discover more as you read more.

My Chief Engineer was a man I had not sailed with before, but he was a legend in the company. In truth he should have retired when made redundant as he was rather past it. When we joined Denman, our cabin steward was removed permanently, so we had to clean our own cabins, make our own beds and so on. To the chief, this was not really a problem, as he would have lived quite happily in the Black Hole of Calcutta, and set about doing so. On one particular occasion, he came in moaning to me, the conversation going something like this:

"Hey cap'n, these duvets are a pain."

"Oh, I'm as warm as toast, and a lot better than sheets and blankets."

"Well I'm not, when I pull it up to my chin, my feet shoot out the bottom, when I tuck my feet in, it only comes halfway up my chest."

I should point out that he was about 5 feet tall but built like a ball with legs.

"Well just think of the mountain it has to get over in the middle chief."

"Come and have a look, and less oh yer cheek young ain."

"Only after you get the vacuum out."

This was a sore point with him, as I had been on at him to do a spot of 'cleaning'. In fact he never did it at all, and when my next chief

JC joined, set about cleaning up the cabin. When HE got the vacuum out, there was so much dust kicked up, that he set off the internal fire alarms.

"You daft clot, that's not how you put a cover on a duvet."

"I wrestled with that for 2 hours and that's the best I could do."

He had the quilt a quarter turn out, inside the cover, and to take up the slack, had a row of staples down one side.

We laughed for weeks.

I'll stop for a minute while I tell you about his rather wicked, sly sense of humour. This was in the days when Gibson's was still a 'fun' company.

In the early 1970s, a new product came on the market, called 'Foss'. This was just phosphoric acid, but when brushed onto ships' paintwork, removed all the rust stains. It was for the time, magic stuff.In later years it became known as 'Metalbrite'.

Carefully cutting the full page advert out of the magazine, and pasting it onto a piece of paper he added the words, 'Under no circumstances is this product to be supplied to *MV Lanrick*, as after application, there will be no ship left'!

Then he posted it off to the office. Try doing that in a shipping company nowadays!

I got on well with the chartering manager of Occidental, and as he had no time for the *Leith Arab*, plus only needed one ship for the next 3 months decided to send me 'round the houses', ie, anywhere but Flotta or Porsgrun.

So we set off for Teesport, but first had to get rid of our vapour from the cargo tanks. In recent years I have objected to this, as the amount of gas which is blown into the atmosphere is colossal.

I will go into this in greater detail in Part 5. It will horrify you.

But for now, we have to blow down the *Borthwick*, and get rid of 20 tonnes of NGL (gas) which has traces of hydrogen sulphide. (This smells like rotten eggs).

This takes up to 12 hours. It could normally be achieved in about 6 hours, but we are so close to our limits, that it has to be done more slowly, than with straight LPG. No terminal wants hydrogen sulphide in its product, so getting rid of that is the priority. A lot easier said than done.

I tried it both ways, blowing down from the top of the tank as opposed to the bottom. From the bottom got rid of most of it, with just trace elements left. A dreadful waste though.

One of the great advantages of getting off our regular run, was that we could stock up our bond and beer lockers with different and plentiful fare. We could also get a change from our usual food stores. Storing a ship in Orkney is different from any other port. It involves the supplier going to the local supermarket, and tends to be a bit more expensive, as well as, always the same.

The *Leith Arab*'s smuggling in Norway, had left both ships 'tarred with the same brush'. Such was his greed, that in order to maximize his profit, a bottle of spirits or a case of beer was sold for 100 Kronar, the equivalent then of £10, a huge hike when it was bought for about £3, often less. To stop his crew eating into his profit, he would double all the prices on board, and so, take a cut from them.

It wouldn't be so bad, but he was using the company's money to buy the stuff in the first place. The Norwegian Customs knew it was going on, but just couldn't catch him although they came close a few times.

The British Customs also knew, but again couldn't prove it.

To curtail him, both ships were only allowed to carry a maximum of 1 month's supply at the time, which worked out at 0.185 litres of spirits per man per day, ie 0.185 x 12 x 30 = 66 litres. More than enough, even allowing for ships representation. This is a clause in a charter party which allows for the charterer to cover gifts and 'entertainments' to port officials etc, and is usually in the region of USD($) 100 per port call. You rarely need it in NW Europe, even nowadays, but by jove, do you need it in South America or Africa!

So into Teesport to load for Le Havre, lovely cargo of easy to load butane. Its like pouring water in, it's that dormant.

You might not know this, but there is more than one type of butane, in fact there are many, and a lot of them are made specially to order by the oil refineries. They do all however fall into the temperature range of 0 deg C to –13 deg C, so are easy to carry. The stuff you get in camping gas bottles is all the rubbish mixed up together.

It is also odourless, no smell, until it is injected with traces of isobutyl mercaptans (so you can tell when you have a gas leak).

You do not want to get downwind of a ship injecting this stuff in concentrated form. If you are in the UK, the closest you want to be if it leaks is Hong Kong! It leaks frequently too.

I had been in Le Havre on the *Melrose* as chief mate just before I was promoted, so knew what type of beer/goodies to buy.

The captain at that time was also accident prone, but not as bad as *Blunderman*, close, but not quite. He only managed to run into the lock gate, by virtue of not being able to stop in time, and closed the entire port for 24 hours while they repaired the gate.

I gained a reputation over time of being able to buy the cheapest bond of any master, not as I am considered mean, but because chandlers do tend to rip ships off and it's nice to keep them in their place.

Also, it screwed up the *Leith Arab*. So, 250 cases of 'Pelforth Lager' (trying saying that after a few) was crammed into the spare cabin, much to the chagrin of the crew, but when they saw the price and tasted it, changed the minds. I sold everything at cost.

Coming out of Le Havre, we had a small incident. Clearing 'Le Grand Ecluse,' the big lock with the repaired gate, the pilot asked to blow the whistle, and he duly pressed the button.

The one good thing about the *Borthwick* is that she had a decent whistle. It would do the *QE2* proud, the bridge shakes as it goes off. Unfortunately, it jammed on, and stayed on for nearly 3 minutes until we managed to find the valve to turn the air off. It was 5 o'clock on a Sunday morning. Sorry Le Havre. (Actually, having such a loud whistle can sometimes be useful. You have to test it before each sailing. So if someone from shore side has annoyed you, just wait until he has his back turned before you do.)

After this we popped up to Flushing to load for Shellhaven where I had my first big prang. But first we had to get there. *Biggles*, our 2nd mate, so called because he was studying for a private pilots licence, managed to 'break' both radars, so we had to go up the Dover Strait without our electronic eyes. Never again, it was beautiful visibility, but we just couldn't judge distance. A fact not appreciated by the uninitiated is that radar does not tell you where you are going, it can only tell you what has already happened, and it takes a lot of skill in order to operate it properly. A skill that a lot of today's junior officers just do not have. Believe me, this is a worrying trend that is getting worse, not better.

When the *Borthwick* was built, *Fergus*, the original master considered himself an expert ship handler. Big mistake. Huge. He had so many bent or holed plates in the hull, that the ship was virtually re-hulled. The problem was when the propeller was put over to astern pitch, it was anybody's guess where the bow would go.

Normally, a right-handed propeller, one that turns clockwise when viewed from astern, when going astern, cants (swings) the bow to starboard, and you use this when berthing. The *Borthwick* has such a poor underwater hull form however that even setting up a starboard swing before going astern doesn't always work.

This is what happened in Shellhaven, no wind to speak off, no current in the River Thames off the berth and as soon as the pitch came on astern, she swung back violently to port. She does not have a bow thruster. We landed with a terrible thump onto a mooring hook built for a big tanker, which decided to have a look inside our forecastle space and adjust the frames at the same time. Oops!!!

Fortunately, the hole could be patched up, but not before Shell had charged us £ 750 for 'damaging' their mooring hook, and about 6 hours were used up writing various letters to the company.

With a huge grin, the loading master confirmed our orders for the next cargo, Flushing back to Shellhaven.

"See if you can get the one on the other end captain, we could do with replacing it, but can't afford the 25 Grand just now." A great boost to my confidence this.

Next time I came in there was enough current to land as light as a feather, but my worst nightmare was standing on the jetty.

Blunderman was back to haunt me.

The weather by now was heading into winter which in the North Sea is not very nice, but was still fine as we headed for Slagenstangen, which is about 20 miles south of Oslo. When we got there it had deteriorated to a full gale. In the first anchorage we dragged anchor.

The *Borthwick* is not good on her anchors and drags everywhere. I managed to re-anchor in pitch darkness just off the berth, and went to bed.

During the night I kept hearing this intermittent clang, but nobody could find out why. Found out at first light. There was a great big mooring buoy with no light on it, which wasn't on the chart right alongside and we were swinging into it, then swinging off it. Even the pilot didn't know it was there.

In Scapa Flow, there is unofficially, a spot slap bang in the middle, and carefully worked out, called 'Rab's Hole'. This captain anchored there every time, on the premise, that if the *Borthwick* dragged anchor, then no matter what direction the wind was from, he was always the same distance from land.

The rest of us had our own favourite places.

A small aside. Where at sea is the nearest land?

Usually, right beneath you.

From Slagen we tried to get to Immingham, but the weather was terrible, and after clearing the Oslo Fjord, were virtually hove to for the night. In the morning, when it became light, it was clear that something was wrong. The bow seemed to be terribly heavy, so after laying her off the wind and sea, I sent *Blunderman* to investigate.

Thanks to having no doors on the chain lockers, during the night, the seas coming over the fo'c'sle had swept off the chain locker covers, filled up the chain lockers, and then three quarters filled the fo'c'sle space. When it was pumped out, this took some 6 hours, we then had to set about sorting out the mess. All the mooring ropes which are 200 metres long were tangled up together, but joining in the fun, was about 300 litres of paint, 2 tons of salt and a chair. Exactly why there was a chair, I do not know. It took ages to unravel, but at least the weather was moderating.

The chief was getting off in Immingham, and was less than impressed to discover we were going alongside the long jetty at South Killingholme, It's a good mile, and he wasn't overly fit. He also had a great affinity for Vodka, and it tasted 10 times better if it was someone else's, usually the Captain's representation bottle, which as soon as we were alongside, he started to demolish. My new chief was the one from the *Quentin*, so handover was a 10 minute affair, if that. He got through a complete litre, without any apparent effect, and then talked the customs into letting the captain get another from the locker to replace it. Not that it bothered me, I can't stand the stuff. What he didn't know was that the bottle in his suitcase, plus the bottle he got out for me were both full of water with the top glued back on. He went off home in the knowledge that he had got one over the new master. The customs were in on it as I knew them from old. Oh, did I catch it next voyage.

From Immingham, or as seamen know it, 'The People's Democratic Republic of Ming Ming,' it was back to Flotta for one cargo to Norway.

Going up the Frierfjord to Porsgrun in Norway, and at the narrows, where the rocks are close on each side, the steering gear started playing up. This is not good for the heart. I switched straight over to the secondary system, and pulled her straight again, narrowly missing ripping out the port side. No sooner was she straight, than she swung the other way, as the secondary system also failed. Straight into emergency, avoided taking out the starboard side.

The pilot was as white as a sheet, so to lighten people up, when we passed the narrows, I decided to tell of another occasion, when I was mate on the *Traquair*, some years previously, when her steering gear had locked at hard a starboard going up The Minches in Scotland at 18 knots.

To demonstrate how fast she turned I swung my arm round in a fast arc, and caught *Blunderman* full in the face. Only he could be in the wrong place. I can remember the look on his face to this day.

"I'm not sailing with you again. Every time I do, I get thumped," he said.

Life got to be even more exciting after discharge in Porsgrun, as it was Slagen to Ming Ming again. Yet another 20 tonnes of gas to be blown off first though. The terminal in Porsgrun, just could not handle our vapour, as this would have been infinitely more preferable to blowing it into the atmosphere. Most terminals can handle vapour.

Now you would think that after warning *Blunderman* on the *Quentin*, not to pick up any more tools, that he would have heeded my warning, or at the very least, taken a little more care. Nope!

The conversation between the chief engineer and myself went something like this.

"You didn't notice a blue flash from the deck just now did you captain?" This is a gas tanker remember.

"No, I was in the chartroom, why?" (emphasis on the y)

"Remember that electric motor that was ashore for re-building, the one from the void space fans? The one that only came back last port?"

"You didn't give it to Blunderman?"

"Not quite, he pinched it and has re-fitted it."

"Well there's nothing hard in that, even he should manage it," I said.

"He connected up the cables as well."

"He hasn't got the phases crossed?" It was a three-phase motor.

"He's blown out the starter box as well!"

"I think we'll see if we can arrange a transfer at the end of the voyage to the ethylene ships, everything there is stainless steel."

"He can break that as well remember."

It was about this stage that we noticed something quite unusual was happening with the *Borthwick*, she started sinking. For some reason, her void tanks started filling up. These are the tanks above the double bottoms, but below the upper wing hoppers, and do not have an alarm system in them. Cost saving in the building yard again. It only became apparent when she started to heel over with a list, so we started the ejector to pump out the one that was filling, then went in for a look, but could find nothing wrong. While we were scratching our heads, another one would fill up on the other side, and so it went on, until we had 3 suspect tanks. Then it stopped.

After Immingham, we went to load butane at Karstoe, SW Norway for Coryton. We had 2 days in the anchorage here, so set about putting on lists with ballast to see if the hull welding was intact. It was. Curiouser and curiouser. But it had stopped.

In Karstoe, my chief wanted a pipe fitter to attend, and make a new length of pipe. Normally, our engineers would make their own, as we had all the equipment for this, but this was one of these pipes that goes here, there and everywhere, and had to be done in one piece. The Norwegian pipe fitter, not overly endowed in the common-sense department, dipped his fingers in the residue of the pipe after it was sprung, and tasted it.

"Diesel?" He asked.

"No, sea water," said the chief, with a queer expression.

"Oh, right," or whatever they say in Norwegian. And off he went.

Afterwards, I said to the chief.

"By the way, what is that pipe for?"

In between guffaws of laughter, he said, "Sewage tank overboard discharge to sea."

(Years later, I was back in Karstoe on another ship. The agent recognised me, and said, "that pipe, I never forget it, I tell everybody.")

This next voyage is indelibly imprinted on my mind, as it was on this passage that I nearly lost the *Borthwick* in a hurricane. If I knew how much trouble the ship was going to cause me in later life, then I wish that I had let her sink at the time. Such the value of hindsight.

The passage out from Karstoe was in December, and the sea was moderate. Chugging along quite nicely, at lunchtime, when the engine room fire alarms went off. One of the main engine exhaust pipes had fractured so we had to stop and put on the spare. The engine is a B & W Alpha diesel in a V 14 arrangement with twin turbochargers, one at each end driven by one bank of cylinders each.

Of course, sod's law came into play, as it was the bottom exhaust pipe which had fractured, so the three on top had to come out first. When it was time to start up again after changing the pipe, the engine was barred over, but found to be full of water. Oh no!!!.

At first a cracked cylinder head was thought to be the reason, So the two that supplied the cracked exhaust pipe were changed. Barred over again, now the *entire engine* was full of water.

The only other place to check were the turbochargers, which was the cause, the forward blower had collapsed. There was no way this was going to work again. Normally you could pull out the rotor and fit blanking gear. Well you could, but our cost cutting company didn't go to that expense as we didn't have any.

So, It's 'toot toot tug time', for a tow into the nearest port which was Esbjerg in Denmark. This was ideal as B & W Alpha are Danish anyway.

Unfortunately my superintendent, *Carrot Top* wasn't in the office in Leith, he and *Old Baldy* were at Unigas in Rotterdam.

The relationship between Unigas and Gibsons was never that good, as both tried to screw the other out of as much money as possible. Unigas operated a pool system.

The more points a ship accrued, the more it got paid, and this was abused to hell and back. We had all sorts of ways of making a ship appear better (at least on paper) than it really was. You'll see a few examples as you read on.

If they could have got away with it, then Unigas would never have found out that the *Borthwick* had broken down, and so was 'off hire.' The delay would have been explained away as 'sheltering for weather.' I'd seen the *Traquair* divert to Zeebrugge, tank cleaned, had a cargo pump pulled and repaired, the ship re-inerted and sailed, and Unigas never having known a thing about it.

A tug was duly hired, a boat by the name of *Mercur*, call sign DEDY, and was coming from Hamburg.

It was at this point that the weather got bad and I *mean bad*. At the height of the storm, wind speed in excess of Hurricane Force 12, that is way in excess of 64 knots, our estimate was nearer 100 knots, the seas went up to at least 70 feet, and we had no engine. As the seas built up, our rolling became increasingly violent and it was apparent that I had to do something, so I decided to sacrifice an anchor, and got the mate to put the port anchor on the bottom, the water was 3 shackles deep,

270 feet.

As soon as it hit the bottom, the cable jumped over the winch and pulled out to 6 shackles. We may not get this back, but it pulled the bow 2 points off the wind, and the mate just managed to clear the fo'c'sle before the first sea came over, a minute later and he would have been lost.

At the height of the storm (which lasted for about 12 hours), the wind would undercut the crest as the ship came to the top of a wave, causing aeration/turbulence. The ship would then come rushing down into the trough, landing with a terrific shudder, slide into the turbulence, and shudder even more. On the way up the next wave the anchor cable would suddenly bite jerking the bow round, and the height of the bow would fly higher than the bridge.

Try to imagine a cork on a string, thrown into a fast running river. That was us.

Why that anchor cable did not break, I have no idea. The second anchor had been cleared, but it was doubtful if men could have got it out in time if the port one did break, before the ship capsized.

We dragged that anchor going backwards for 29 miles, and then it fouled on something. Even going backwards, the rolling was still 20 degrees each way every 10 seconds. All we could do was hang on.

Then we started sinking again, but couldn't get on deck to do anything about it.

During this time I had to 'phone the office twice per day.

Stonehaven Radio knew we were in trouble and kept frequencies reserved just for us. You would not get this service today. My frequencies were to transmit on channel 10, and receive on 1856 KHz. (It is amazing what you remember when your life is on the line. The tugs call sign as well for example.)

To 'phone in, I had to wedge myself in between the radio and the battery charger, then back round to operate the controls. At the absolute height of the gale, *Blunderman*, the mate was on the bridge with me, he was hanging onto the central stiffening pole, and when I was on the 'phone, the port bulkhead gave way with the bookcases coming clean off and a set of breathing apparatus.

This started sliding violently across the chartroom, and the mate tried to catch it, but couldn't quite time it.

"For goodness sake mate, jump on it."

He did, only to utter "Aaiiiiiieeeeeeeeeeeeee," as the combination flew across the chartroom, landing in a tangled mess on the other side. "I'm not listening to you again," he said, a tad upset I think.

One dope from the office asked, "have you any idea what the anchor has fouled on Captain?"

My reply was something like, "Who the f--- cares as long as it f------ stays there."

I think I made my point.

We got on deck as soon as we could to sort out the sinking problem, four tanks had to be pumped out, different ones from before, then it stopped again. This was getting silly. We never did find the reason.

The weather had moderated by the time the tug arrived, but it was dark, about 6 at night. The tug master came on the VHF with, "I think it's too dangerous to take up the tow tonight Captain, I think we'll wait till the morning."

Ah ha, he's on an hourly rate. You really need to know what you are doing to be captain.

"No problem, come as close as you can and we'll send a line on a rocket."

Now it's one thing firing a rocket, it's another thing entirely, trying to catch it.

"Don't do that captain, the line might tangle in my Voight-Schneider gear." (A type of propulsion equipment).

"Well if you've got Voight gear you can come close enough for a heaving line."

Gotcha.

"Okay, we'll try."

My crew were all ready up forward when he approached. There were four German crew on this tug ready to connect up, three had safety helmets on. My Bosun threw the most perfect throw, and bonked the helmet-less one beautifully.

Now connected, we had to try and get the anchor up. The windlass was engaged and run with cold oil, this increases the power. Fortunately, we did recover all the cable and the anchor, but the last two shackles and the anchor were polished silver, from being dragged so far.

On tow next day, the weather was almost flat calm, when the tug master came on the VHF with.

"*Borthwick*, my Decca Navigator has broken down, can you tell me your position please?"

30

The mate's reply?

"We are 250 metres behind you."

I think, he wanted a latitude and longitude mate.

I was the most relieved master in the North Sea to be safely tied up alongside in Esbjerg that night.

Unfortunately I discovered when we got in, that the company had declared 'General Average'.

This is declared, when there may be a danger in losing the ship, or the cargo, or both.

What it effectively means, is that anyone with an interest in the voyage, will suffer a loss in proportion to their investment. Everything is taken into account, before the claim goes to the loss adjusters. In this case, with GA being declared, although the ship and cargo were saved, the towage and repair bill are split in the same way, roughly 13/15ths to the owners, 2/15ths to charterers, and there can be a lot of them.

What it means at this stage, is that the captain has an awful lot of paperwork to get through, as well as extensive reports to make. You daren't miss out anything.

On my way back from the agent's office, I was collared by a ship-chandler, who offered me what I thought at the time to be a pretty good deal. After discharge in Coryton, we were going back on our regular run to Norway.

"I've got a special offer on a select brand of Scotch Whisky captain, would you be interested?"

"Not really, I've been filling my bond locker for the last 2 months and it's now nearly full."

"It's only £20 a case. That ship there, the *Ashington* took 20 cases". I took eight cases, my locker was *now* full and should last at least 12 to 15 months. It was called King of Scots. With a name like that, it must be good.

We repaired the engine in 48 hours and got on our way, everyone including three engineers from B & W Alpha worked round the clock on it. For engineers, eight complete units, plus a new turbocharger. The company bought everyone a bottle of Chivas Regal in appreciation. I should add, that the crew I had now, were as good, as the first crew I had on the *Quentin* were bad.

I still had a pile of paperwork to get through, but I had 3 days' grace in Scapa Flow to finish it, as it all had to be typed, and I could use the agent's secretary there.

So we trotted off to Coryton, in the Thames arriving on Christmas Eve and parked the boat alongside. (This is about 1 mile further downriver from Shellhaven.)

2 o'clock on Christmas morning, the engine room fire alarms went off. Jumping out off the bed, the accommodation was full of smoke. What now? The generators on the *Borthwick* are V8 Dorman Diesels. High speed diesels which run at about 1800 rpm. There are four of them in two sets of two. Being numbered from the port side, as engineers do (on deck everything is numbered from starboard, and I have no idea why it is this way.)

The excitation coil of No 1 generator, not the engine bit, had gone on fire. No 2 generator had taken the entire load, and was overheating.

One of the engineers put out the fire with a fire extinguisher, while another started No 4. They are air started. However, when it was spun up, one of the valve stems sheared, dropped down to meet the piston coming up, got buried in it, before blowing off the cylinder head, which flew across the engine room narrowly missing everyone, before hitting the excitation coil of No 1 and setting it on fire again. That left No 3, which fortunately started okay. In the space of 2 minutes our generating capacity had been halved. Happy Christmas.

Guess how we all spent Christmas Day?

"Never mind boys, we're on our way back up to Scapa Flow, and we aren't loading before the 3rd of January."

We did however have a serious incident going into the pilot station to enter Scapa Flow, which started off a long battle with the pilot service in this backwater.

The pilot boarding area for Scapa Flow is just south of the entrance of Hoxa Sound, so for ships to get there, they first have to pass through or across the Pentland Firth. Effectively, all the awkward or tricky navigation is done *before* the pilot steps aboard. A lot of ports are like this.

There is an awful lot of false concern about the Pentland Firth. It is in fact one of the easiest stretches of water around the UK. The people who voice the loudest about it are the ones who understand it the least.

I learnt most of it from my old mentor, Captain Tom Mitchell.

A few years ago, there was a newspaper article written by a Scapa Flow pilot, advocating the need for a pilot service for ships transiting the Firth. Had this come from anyone but him, then it may have had just a hint of credence, but this particular pilot needs to get the chart out, to go in a straight line, inside Scapa Flow. He was kicked off my bridge on more than one occasion on later voyages.

Setting up a pilotage service here, or even extending the jurisdiction of the Orkney Harbours area would be *extremely dangerous*.

In the days of sailing ships, and this is before radar, or even engines were invented, masters had a very simple way of getting through, and it works to this day.

They would approach the entrance, say the eastern entrance for going westwards, at slack water, just before the westerly going stream, and take down all of their sails. The tide would then carry them through, until they were well past Dunnet Head, then put them up again and carry on, knowing that the current would carry them clear of the islands in the middle.

The very same works in reverse going the other way.

The greatest misconception is that the tides flow through at up to 12 knots. True it does, but not all of the water is going in the same direction.

There are countercurrents, which if you know where they are, you can utilize.

I tried one, after *GFG* told me about it (this was one I didn't know about), but on the Easterly going stream, there is a counter current very close on the Lother Rock, which is just off the tip of South Ronaldsay, which sweeps you up in towards the entrance to Scapa Flow, and hence the pilot station. *GFG* used it all the time, and I must I add, so did I occasionally, from then on.

Similarly on the south side, if you stay close on the shore, there is a countercurrent from Duncansby Head which takes you clear of Dunnet Head, and will even allow you to pass inside the white water when the Merry Men of May are running.

I should add however that these are small ship routes. If you are on a big ship, then you just go up the middle, and even against the tide, you can still make way over the ground.

Modern concerns though, from people who do not really know what they are talking about, have to a point, put an end to this traditional form of navigation, and the world is a poorer place for it.

We were coming in for our pilot at about 4 in the morning, and apart from myself, the mate, second mate and the lookout were on the bridge. The tide was flowing Easterly, at about 8 knots. To get in, all we have to do, is head towards the eddy behind Swona (without going into it if possible), and then head on up for the pilot.

Orkney Harbour Radio are *supposed* to give navigational warnings for ships leaving Scapa Flow, but on this morning he didn't. Just as we got to the critical point, we noticed the navigation lights of a tanker coming out. They are hard to see against the lights of Flotta terminal. Radar is not a lot of help due to sea clutter, hence so many people on the bridge. Modern radars are much better in this respect. We had a combined closing speed of 30 knots. I had to go into the eddy to miss him, we passed at less than 100 metres. *That is too close*!

The point is, is that had I known he was coming out, I would have slowed down until he was clear, then gone in.

I was less than impressed with that folically challenged ass (he was completely bald), and complained accordingly, not that it did any good, because he did it again to me about 2 months later. After that I refused to have him on board as a pilot, which did not go down well.

The first 2 days were mostly spent ashore, attending to the paperwork associated with General Average being declared.

However on Hogmanay, we had a great laugh as we all tried to loosen up a bit.

I had sent flowers to the personnel manageress at Denman for Christmas. *GFG* on the *Quentin* hadn't, so after lunch ashore, we all embarrassed him into buying her a Christmas gift. (There were four others from the two ships.) We decided for him that flowers wouldn't do, as she already had some, it would have to be something personal, such as a negligee set, black fishnet tights and bra and so on. He just wanted to go back to his ship! But, he was hauled round various shops in Kirkwall. After all, *he* was paying.

There was only one small teensy weensy problem, a minor matter really.

None of us had actually met her, so had no idea what she looked like, what size she was, or even how old she was. All we had to go on was the sound of her voice on the 'phone.

That should be enough.

To cover all possibilities, we went for a range of sizes, and *GFG* was so embarrassed, he parted with about £40 just to get out. The girls in the shops were amazed. So were we that he actually paid. Then we took him to the Post Office, just to make sure it was all sent. Next year, he sent flowers.

When I got back to the *Borthwick*, one of my crew, a teuchter (an Outer Hebridean) came up and said, "hey cap, you know that King of Scots whisky?"

This was a seasoned campaigner and knew his stuff after 40 years at sea.

"Well, I've tried it straight, I've tried it with water, I've tried it with Coke, I've tried it with lemonade, I've even tried it with custard, and it's still f------ awful."

"Only seven and a half cases to go then."

New Year came and went, and we went off to load at Flotta jetty and set off for Norway once again.

Going round the southern tip of Norway at Lindesnes, or 'The Naze' as it is often known, plus at night, I started to get the feeling that something was seriously wrong, and so went up to the bridge. Putting on all the floodlights revealed nothing amiss, but the ship was starting to get sluggish. At first light, we found out what it was.

We were starting to accumulate ice on the deck. This can be very dangerous, and some ships have capsized because of this.

The problem was what to do about this. Slow down, but spend longer in it, or push on and get into port. All the double bottom ballast was in, so I ordered extra fuel for delivery immediately on arrival, and pushed on.

By the time we were alongside, we had 200 tonnes on the foredeck, and getting the cargo pumps started was going to be fun, as they were under 3 feet of ice.

Going alongside was taken very carefully, as she was getting rather 'tender', that is, getting a bit short of positive stability.

The fuel was loaded and we had our stability back.

We then bored into the pump with steam hoses, the crew were all busy getting the high ice down. It was so cold that no sooner had we bored out No 1 cargo pump, that it re-froze as we lined up to pump out the cargo, so had to start again. Such is life.

GFG was due in about 3 days behind me, so I 'phoned him and warned of the danger, he could at least rig ice warps. But *GFG* being *GFG*, wasn't going to listen to a "junior" master, did nothing about it, steamed straight into it and had to divert into Kristiansand with 350 tonnes to come off. Some people never learn. He could have lost the *Quentin*.

So we went back to Scapa Flow where I was relieved by *Ivor the Engine*. Welsh off course and as tight as a ducks ****. The lengths he went to save money, and it always cost him dear. One day he asked the agents by VHF (call is free) to send his wife £5 worth of chocolates for her birthday. They sent 5lbs weight and he got a bill for £43. He was still not forgiven for the bike in the bus episode but that's another story for another book. Or I might tell you it at the end of this one. My next book is just stories of things we used to get up to. Educational for aspiring deck officers too.

My chief told me later, that he spent the first day, after I left, taking over 200 cases of beer out of the locker, just to count them, in case he was being 'cheated'. You'd think he could have found something better to do.

Six weeks later, I was back in Scapa Flow to relieve *GFG*, this time, back to the *Quentin*. Only 6 months before, I had left this ship in as near a perfect condition, as it is possible to get. Although we were due in dry dock in about a month, I was down to only one radar, which was temperamental to say the least. During handover from *GFG*, I said, "what's that banging Gordon?"

"Oh, I'm coming to that, the rudder is loose."

"What do you mean loose?" Horrified. Normally they are dead tight.

"Oh, the pins on the hydraulic rams are a bit worn."

It wasn't the pins that were a bit worn, it was the whole assembly! This was serious damage. The entire rudder blade was floating about. Somebody has gone and hit something hard, and not reported it.

Although we were due in dry dock in about a month, it is doubtful if we were going to make it, especially as it is still winter.

We can only try.

Meantime, my chief engineer, the ball shaped one, is having a go about his missing Vodka, and seeks restitution. He was retiring at the end of his voyage, so sought solace ashore in Kirkwall.

Eventually, I could take more of his whinging, and said, "Right, get your gladrags on and we'll go ashore."

Of course, when push came to shove, he couldn't be bothered, but said, "when you are ashore, get me some magazines, you know the type I like."

His 'type' were ones kept on the high shelves, the more blue the better. I can't stand them, but as he didn't specify, he's going to pay for all the junk of the day. £20 for *The Beano*, *The Dandy*, *Farmers Weekly*, *Good Housekeeping* and so on. Plus a bottle of Vodka. The cheapest I could find of course, gosh it was rough.

After loading, we set off for Norway once again, three cargoes to deliver before we go off to dry dock, *if* the rudder holds together that long.

Before *GFG* left, he warned me that there was sea ice off the coast of Norway, not particularly thick, but enough to reduce speed for, especially when entering the ice field.

There was right enough, but during the time we were discharging, the wind got up from the south-east, and blew all the ice from The Kattegat across to the Norwegian coast, where it started to layer up.

Although we didn't know it at the time, it was reckoned to be up to 18 feet thick. It also snowed all night like there was no tomorrow, and before we could sail, we had to dig the ship out. My first trip chief mate decided to speed things up by running the deck spray water system. Nice idea if you are in sea water, but up the fjord, it is fresh, so although he got rid of the snow, he replaced it with ice. What do they teach these people at nautical college? He'd have learnt more in the pub.

When we got down to the outward pilot station, the extent of the sea ice became apparent. There were three ships stuck in various places, and I was advised to head out down a lead and get as far out as possible, as the BIG icebreaker was coming down from Oslo.

The *Quentin* has 2500 BHP on her main engine, and has her own cooling water pumps geared off this engine. To prevent ice gumming up the generators cooling water, they were shut down, and the emergency generator which is air cooled was started up. All non-essential services were also shut down to reduce the load.

Steaming in ice isn't easy, as you have to go where the leads are, and they are not always going where you want to go. I managed to go about half a mile before getting stuck, or more correctly, beset. By backing up, and slamming in the power again with the rudder hard over did not free us very far, and remember, the rudder is badly damaged.

At this stage it was announced that the icebreaker from Oslo with 16 000 horsepower, was also stuck, and didn't think it would be able to clear a 'roadway' until next morning. Although the ships are beset, the icefield in its entirety is moving on the current, so to stay where we were was foolhardy. The icebreaker from Brevik was on its way out to free us so we could get back to the anchorage. He needed all of his 10

000 horsepower to break us out, and get us turned round, and it was apparent from the size of the ice flows just how thick this ice was.

Running in to the anchorage needed full power just to force our way through, and when the anchor was dropped, it weighs 3 tonnes, it just bounced on the ice and lay there. Such is life. At least we were not going to move much during the night.

Next morning a roadway had been cleared, just by breaking up the floes, but it took the big icebreaker on wires running ahead of us, at full power, us at full power, plus another icebreaker pushing on the stern at full power, in all nearly 30 000 horsepower, for us to make 1 knot. We did this for 5 hours. The transom is bent to this day.

When a ship moves through broken ice, the hull growls and bangs. It can be rather disconcerting. Going through this, apart from the terrible vibration from so much power, our hull squeaked. In dry dock later, we found that the ice had taken off every bit of growth from 3 years at sea, every barnacle, and every bit of loose paint. I knew that as the ice behind had a red tinge.

We dropped the icebreakers 5 miles out, when our speed started to increase, but we still had to go another 4 miles to find open water. *Next time back, the whole lot had disappeared.*

The company wanted us to delay our dry dock by another month, but I had to put my foot down on this, as I could not guarantee if we would have any rudder left by then. I was totally vindicated when we saw the extent of the damage, but I was not very popular. On top of this, I was down to half a radar.

So, off we went to drydock in Sunderland, all our ships went there, as it was at that time a great wee yard, scruffy and filthy, but still great.

GFGs version of what was wrong with the rudder bore no relationship to what we found.

The stock bush, that is made from phosphor bronze, which is very hard but self-lubricating, had gone oval. It is jacked into the hull under enormous pressure, and usually lasts the life of a ship. It fell out. The stock which connects the steering gear to the palm of the rudder, that is the bit above the blade, which contains six enormous bolts each about 3 inches in diameter, had also gone oval, and fell out. Usually it takes some persuasion to get it out for survey. Of the six bolts, only two were left, the other four long gone, and of the two left, one of those fell out, narrowly missing the fitters down below. The palm itself, was cracked about 50% of the way round, and there was a crack in the leading edge of the blade about 10 feet long. Oh, and *GFG*, the hydraulic pins were worn too. This was serious damage, and Gibson's tried to blame me, calling it 'ice damage.' Get stuffed boys and grow up. It was damaged before I joined.

All told we were in dry dock for 12 days.

A constant battle with ship's staff and the office, is the 'extent' of the dry dock list. The ship wants everything fixed that can't be done in service, and the office wants it done as cheaply as possible. This is a common denominator with *every* shipping company in the world. So, to get the extra bits done, the bits that the office cancelled, the ship has an 'unofficial' list, paid for in cases of beer, which goes down as 'representation'. Scotch occasionally as well.

We got through 60 cases, and it came to the attention of the yard owner.

He said, "this is the last time I pay my men to work on a Saturday. I'm paying them, but they're all working for the captain!"

I was at the time having my coffee table in my cabin extended to a useful height. Before the welder came, the cut portion was just balanced on the bottom bit, when the yard owner decided to sit on it. It was murder trying to keep a straight face, especially after the chief came out with, "look what you've gone and done, you've broken it!"

There was however one rather amusing episode concerning the chief, the dirty ball on legs.

The first night in the hotel, (we had rooms with no facilities), at 3 o'clock in the morning, he got up, dressed only in underpants, and set of down the corridor in search of the toilet, but couldn't find one, so he went down a floor. On his way back, he forgot that he had changed floors, and managed to get into the wrong room, which unfortunately was occupied by a rather elderly lady, who was not overly impressed and screamed the place down. We *all* had to leave that day and find another hotel.

Back in dry dock, with the extra delay, Gibson's decided to survey the propeller. This is a variable pitch unit with four blades. They broke the seals taking it apart, and off course hadn't thought about buying any spares beforehand. The nearest set, *Esberg, delivery 4 weeks*. Somebody managed to conjure up some alternatives, but it still delayed us further.

3 years before, after the previous dry dock, I was the chief mate on board, and had the task of gassing the ship up in Flotta. This is not an easy task, as trying to get the balance right for starting loading is tricky.

The pressure has to correlate pretty roughly with the pressure, ie about –45 degrees Celsius and 6.5 bar. If the pressure is too low, the temperature will go below the minimum of –48 degrees Celsius, and it is possible to damage the cargo tanks, ie crack them. Not good.

On this particular day, I was down to temperature, but only at 5.5 bar so had to make vapour to bring up the pressure.

This is done using the cargo heater as a vapourizer, ie changing liquid gas into a vapour. Now this heater was designed for LPG, but it can be used as an NGL vapouriser, if you are careful. Seawater is used as the heat source.

The shell pressure is carefully brought up to 7bar, and liquid dribbled in, while *slowly* bleeding off the vapour to the cargo tanks, and it is slow. There is frankly, no other way of doing it.

It was working a treat, until *Miss Piggy,* the second mate thought he could speed it up by throwing open the vapour bleed valve.

I heard the most terrific bang, and couldn't believe what he had done. All my careful work gone in a few seconds.

What happens is without the pressure over it, the liquid temperature goes straight down to about -60 degrees Celsius, the seawater freezes, and the tubes explode, big style, all 300 of them.

So in dry dock the heater has to come out, it weighs 7 tonnes, is nearly 10 metres long, and has to go to Rotterdam for re-tubing. A big job, as the bolts haven't been off in 9 years. Why Rotterdam? Because although it only takes a few days to re-tube, it takes 6 weeks for the coating to cure, and the only place to do this work is in Rotterdam.

Gibsons were not impressed when they saw the damage, but they were warned 3 years before, so had no excuse for not knowing. (It was even entered on their copy of the 'goody' form. This was a form sent to Unigas every month, detailing the state of the ships equipment. If you entered anything other than 'good', then the ship lost pool points, and income. In reality, you filled in this form well in advance and dated it accordingly. A waste of time really.)

It wasn't possible to get a new stock bush in phosphor bronze, so it was replaced in stainless steel. Expensive? Very.

It is 1 metre long, 90 cms in outside diameter, with a wall thickness of 100 mms. It was jacked in with 300 ton jacks, the inside then being lapped (ground out) to take the built up stock. Not easy.

We eventually got out of Sunderland, and went back to Scapa Flow, complete with carpeted bridge, lovely, two new radars, one angled to a height so that *The Poison Dwarf* would have to stand on a box to see into it (he hates me, but not for this. Another reason which is explained in Part 3), the propeller and rudder repaired, all bright and shiny again and fully surveyed (I, as usual copped for all the survey work.) Time to take the mickey out of *GFG*, who is now on the *Borthwick*. So we just added a few extra bits on.

The old radar scanner from the first replaced radar was bolted onto a barrel, fitted above the bridge to become a computerized automatic plotting radar. Known as an ARPA. We now 'had' three radar scanners.

The engine room rag bucket was turned upside down, glued to a brush, and painted white to become a radome for a satellite communications system. And the empty paint drums made ready on ropes.

This is an awful trick. Good fun, but awful. If you ever get the chance though, try it.

GFG was anchored at the North end of the flow, so we went up close such that he could have a look, then we anchored 4 miles away. Sure enough, he is coming over in a lifeboat.

There is only one thing more useless than a harpsichord in a lifeboat, and that is *GFG*. When he came aboard on the starboard side, my crew were hiding on the port side, armed with the empty paint drums, ready to tie them on to the bottom of the boat where they can't be seen. The *Borthwicks*' lifeboats are slow anyway, but with all this extra drag, they are now really dead slow. It's going to be a very long trip back, plus tough to steer. 3 hours in fact with frequent checks to the propeller. He didn't speak to me for days, which was great.

He was not impressed with the bridge, especially the new radars, which were in fact perfectly okay, and said he would write to the company in his own inimitable style. I wish I had kept the letter, it was hilarious, and if you ever read this Gordon, radar is spelt *radar*, not *raider*!

Before gassing up, I had a 'phone call from the charterers, Occidental in London. The conversation went like this, "Doug, how long would it take for you to heat up about 1000 tonnes of propane from –40 to say zero?"

"Off the top of my head Ken, I would say 6, possibly 7 weeks."

"Don't muck me around, I'm serious, why?"

"Because although the ships' in Scapa Flow, the cargo heater is in Rotterdam."

"Nobody told me," with a laugh, "you *are* having me on?"

"Nope."

"I'm going to 'phone Gibson's."

"Good luck, it's about time someone gave them a hard time."

Oh, did the gravy hit the fan, as charterers are supposed to be kept fully informed. This was enough to put us off hire for 6 weeks at least. But we got away with it, and went off to Grangemouth for butane instead, for sunny Dordrecht, up behind Rotterdam.

It was here that I met an ace ship chandler, he could get *anything*.

So I filled up my bond locker with some good stuff, plus a load of rubbish for the *Leith Arab*.

We discharged into barges, and it was all very pleasant.

Thence to Teesport where my chief engineer retired.

The poor man died about a year later, and was missed by many.

His replacement was my usual chief, who I had come to know rather well. I visit him to this day, as he just lives along the road, so he'll *not* forgive me for relating this little story about our time in Amsterdam.

We both have a penchance for prawns, not the little tiddly ones that you get in this country, no, the big ones from the Far East. They are rather pricey, but I was getting 2 kilos or so from the chandler in Rotterdam/Dordrecht, and sharing them with everyone on board. He couldn't get enough of them.

In Amsterdam later, the ship was waiting for cargo space and was shut down. A rare chance, so we both went ashore for a few hours.

Walking along this street in the city, he spotted some in a fishmonger's window. In he goes and orders 100 grams worth. Last of the big spenders eh! He didn't notice but I did, as to how many he got, but 'they' were wrapped up into a big parcel, and off he goes.

"You going to share 'them' with me Jim?"

"Naw, get yer own," as he unwrapped the parcel.

"Heck, I only got 1!"

He hates me telling this story, but I take every chance I can get.

Then it was back to Flotta for our usual trade until the end of the voyage.

One thing though, we seemed to be getting through was an awful lot of cook/stewards. (Denholms, were a bit of a rough company). Most were okay as cooks, but as a steward, they didn't want to know. Until *Tufty* arrived.

Now *Tufty* and I had sailed together before, and I knew most of his foibles. Such as when his cabin door which was usually left open, was then locked. He had company, of the female variety.

One night, he decided to go ashore in Kirkwall.

Every three days, a boat was laid on, leaving the ship at 1830, and returning at 2330 from Scapa Pier. There is, after all, not a lot to do in Kirkwall, after you have walked the streets, which takes roughly 30 minutes. So you tend to arrive in a pub. This particular night, *Tufty* did. Then missed the boat back.

The agreement, was that if you missed the boat back, then you either paid for another boat, at £150, or, if you were lucky, cadged a lift back as it went to another ship, or swum.

Nobody swims in Scapa Flow, unless they are Orcadian.

He arrived back on board at 11 am next morning.

It was no big deal. Technically, I should have 'logged' him, but I knew this was out of character, so let it go.

This ship after all was only lying at anchor, waiting to load.

I was on the bridge, keeping anchor watch, when he came to see me.

"Okay *Tufty*, what happened?"

"Sorry Cap. I missed the boat, and I've spent the night in that little concrete hut at the end of Scapa Pier. You know the one."

Indeed I did, as everyone, who ever joined a ship in Scapa Flow will tell you. (If there is only ever one place colder to spend a night, then that is the Royal Hotel in Kirkwall. If you are unlucky enough to spend a night here, take 15 hot water bottles with you, and that is for one leg. One chief engineer in Gibsons, took the entire oil filled electric radiator.)

"Okay then this time *Tufty*, but the crew had to make their own breakfast, so I would suggest a fairly decent dinner tonight in recompense."

And that I thought was the end of it, until Thursday, the day, the local rag (newspaper) arrived on board.

Most Orcadians have a pretty good sense of humour. You would need to have, living in a place like that. It must be the only place in the world that the Forestry Commission grows trees horizontally. To do it vertically, would mean being answerable for unguided missiles landing in Norway. Gosh, can it be windy.

There are, however, quite a few people in the Orkney Islands who have no sense of humour. It is a very select few, who include the Police, the Sheriff, the owner of our agents, 'John Jolly' (and he is anything but Jolly), and anyone connected with the church. Frankly, there are not many left. However, their highlight, is reading the local paper, especially the bit entitled, 'Around the Courts'.

On this particular Thursday, we were loading, and in the morning, I was reading the paper, whereby I came across the following,

"From custody this morning, the following persons were brought before the court... First up was a Mister Alastair Mac..., who gave his address, as c/of *MV Quentin*, At Anchor, Scapa Flow."

Oh ho, I knew nothing of this, but read on.

To the charge of 'urinating in a shop doorway', he pleaded guilty.

However to the charge of 'assaulting a policeman', he pleaded not guilty. He was admonished, after the court accepted his explanation (which brought great hilarity), that, "when a polis turns you round mid pee, then ye just cannae turn it aff like a tap". He was fined £50.

This was the guy, who told me he spent the night in the concrete hut! This was just 'too good' an opportunity to let go, as my crew were just as much a 'mickey taker' as me. I called a safety meeting.

"Good afternoon Gentlemen, there is only one subject to discuss. (Curious looks) That is, where we are all going to hide after the cook starts throwing his knives about. Now Alastair...

You could have fried an egg on his face. He is still trying to get me back, but he never will. I don't even know where he is now, but then, he might.

After a trip ashore in Norway, two of the crew came up and asked me how you managed to 'talk' to the women? Now remember, I'd been coming here for years, and knew a lot of people, but felt a bit of a joke coming on.

"Oh, you have to learn a bit of the language," and then taught them a phrase, which in reality is about the absolute worst thing that you can say to a Norwegian, but told them that it meant, "you have beautiful eyes."

Next time back, they tried it, but with no success, as one came back with a black eye.

"What happened to you?" I asked.

"I don't think we got the dialect quite right captain. Can we come with you next time?"

They had no chance of doing that.

Once again, a perfect ship was handed over to the *Leith Arab*.

His only concern was what I had in the bond.

"Why? I left you a good selection last time".

"Oh, I had to sell that, it was too difficult to count." (For sell, read smuggle.)

"What, *all* of it?". (About £2500 worth at cost, that's £7000 to his pocket, plus £2500 to the safe as it was Gibsons money.)

"The beer as well." By the way, "what type of beer have you got? None of that Pelforth stuff I hope."

I was stunned at the sheer audacity of it.

"No, there are ten cases of Royal Dutch," I said, still stunned. I decided not to tell him about the 50 cases of Orangeboom. This stuff makes you fart. I'm going to fix him next time.

So it was back to the *Borthwick* 6 weeks later, and I lost my rag at *GFG*. Not only was the ship filthy, but there was a pile of overdue survey work and a lot to repair. I told him if this happened again, I would not take over. He went home in the huff.

I found out later that he had had his son with him for a voyage, the kid was 9. At the bottom of the captain's bunk in the bedroom was a full size poster of Samantha Fox, semi-nude, and his son had told his mum who was waiting to give him a rocket when he got home. So it was taken down, rolled up, and posted off to *GFG*. He might as well get a proper rocket. It felt rather satisfying.

It was during this voyage that Gibsons really started going downhill, and where a lot of my problems started. I was not going to break the law for them, or anybody else.

I got the job of 'going round the houses' again and we were everywhere. The factory in Porsgrun, Norway shut down for 3 months, and a political argument between Occidental and Unigas started. The *Quentin* was returned to Unigas to trade for Occidental, who had chartered it, and wanted it traded during the next 3 months. Occidental would run the *Borthwick*. In that Unigas were getting paid anyway, saw no point of going out of their way to find work for the *Quentin*, so she lay at anchor for 3 months, while we worked our butts off. Suited me.

One cargo that we carried was 1-3 Butadiene from Antwerp to Fawley. This is nasty stuff, and carcinogenic. Although it is effectively an LPG cargo, it requires to be stabilized with a chemical inhibitor which in this case was Nalfloc 27, which is effectively 4-tetryl butylcatechol with a few additives. It sticks like anything, and gets everywhere. Where LPG is in most cases, dry, this inhibitor is wet.

After it was discharged, Occidental fixed us up with 3 cargoes of VCM, vinyl chloride Monomer. *This is the real nasty stuff, and highly carcinogenic.* I had had a bad accident with it in 1982 on the *Traquair* going to Australia, and was ill for the next 10+ years.

When the cargo tanks were opened up, (we were due to load in Rafnes, Norway, opposite Porsgrun), the inhibitor from the butadiene remained. This is a common problem, but it can only be cleaned off one way, other than dilution by a low cost LPG. High pressure washing with methanol, and all the associated safety measures, then steam cleaning, then high pressure fresh water washing. (At that time anyway.) We got a shore cleaning team in, as we just didn't have the gear.

Gibsons did not help much here, in fact they were rather obstreperous, and as usual, the captain was at fault. Ho hum.

After cleaning, and re-inerting with nitrogen, we were ready to load. Plugs were blowing out from the loading line when we started loading, so we had to stop and put them back in. Trying to get people to use breathing apparatus was scoffed at, so if they fell ill, it was their own fault. Prolonged exposure to VCM causes cancer to the liver. Nasty.

One plug came out with such force, that it whistled past the mate like a bullet, and it took me to bang in a tapered plug before the liquid gas followed. We always kept these things handy on this ship.

This is a high value cargo, at that time it was $1100 per tonne. It is also extremely heavy with a density of 0.93 at fully refrigerated temperature of −13.8 deg C. We carried it at ambient, about +10.

The Bills of Lading were prepared using ship's figures, not an uncommon matter as gas tankers' cargo tank calibration tables are normally ultra accurate. The tank ashore that we were loading from was filling up from their process as we were also taking it out.

The first cargo was discharged in Teesport, but this was a part cargo.

Then it was back to Rafnes to load for Rotterdam. This was a maximum lift cargo which had never been done before on the

Borthwick. We lifted 1950 tonnes, and she was even keel, at 19 feet 6inches. Remember that I described the underwater hull form as resembling a brick. Well now it was a brick. Totally impossible to steer at under 8 knots. This was going to be fun going up The Maas in Rotterdam. I didn't trust that ship enough, so I put tugs on each end.

That was a wise move, but the dolphin mooring hook that 'fell over' going alongside didn't think so. More damage, but as it was dark and nobody seemed to notice, I hit upon a rather different approach to writing the inevitable letter, and calling in the P & I Club. (Insurance.)

We'll give the damaged area a quick touch-up, and if anybody asks where the dent came from, we'll just say it was one of *Fergus's*, the original master. He'd left the company some years earlier, but this was a minor detail.

Then back to load at Rafnes, this time for Aviero in Portugal, but there is a draft restriction there of 17 feet, so we short load.

Now however, there is some concern, about the amount we discharged in the previous two ports. They are short, 40 tonnes in the Tees, 34 tonnes in Rotterdam.

It might not sound much but in dollar terms that's $81 400. So where was it? We simply didn't know at that stage.

So we set off for Aviero which is about halfway between Oporto and Lisbon.

Going down the Dover Strait, and it was as busy as anything, the bridge 'phone rings. It was daytime, and I was navigating.

"*Borthwick*, captain, sorry we're very busy just now, so we'll call back," and hung up

It was Gibsons.

It rang again, so it was switched off. It was that busy with ships.

Northforeland Radio came on the VHF on Channel 16 about 15 minutes later with urgent traffic for us.

I had to get the mate up, hand over the watch, and take the call. It was Gibsons, and they were angry, as in more than just a bit.

"How do you expect to get into Aviero at 17 feet maximum draft with 1950 tonnes of VCM? And don't hang up."

"Because I've only loaded 1500 tonnes, which makes 17 feet."

I hung up. Engineering superintendents dabbling around in things they don't understand. That was *Old Baldy*. He could be a pain.

Aviero is a dump. A backwater in salt marshes, but the people are nice. There was even an apology telex from *Old Baldy*. But 70 tonnes were missing on discharge. All told now, 144 tonnes, $158 400.

During this discharge, I had the mate put the reliquefaction plant on.

This is unusual during a discharge, reliquefaction is normally done either on loading, to convert the vapour into liquid, and increase the amount of cargo lifted, or on passage, either just to contain it, or cool it down for a receivers specification. When a cargo such as propane is carried fully refrigerated, a part of the plant will run all the time, as a holding unit.

Quite often cargoes such as Butadiene are loaded ambient, say +20 degrees C, in say Antwerp, and cooled down to –3.5 degrees C, while the ship crosses the Atlantic for the US.

So why during discharge?

Remember, this is a carcinogen, and I for one do not want to blow it into the atmosphere. Unigas couldn't care less, as long as someone else does it.

By reliquefying No 1 tank first as it is only half full, and returning the liquefied gas to No 2 tank, then the tank pressure falls to zero, until the pump has finished pumping out all the liquid. But then the pressure will continue to fall as the tank goes into vacuum. The *Borthwick*'s tanks can go down to 50% vacuum, that is 0.5 bar absolute, or another way, -0.5 bar on the gauge. Then reliquefy No 2 until it is empty as well.

When the vapour space is equallized, then both tanks will be about 25% in vacuum. As a liquid gas cannot exist in a vacuum, then all that remains is 75% of the ships total volume. It started at 2500 cubic metres, but now is in effect, only 1875 cubic metres. Complicated?

Just remember, that *none* of it has been let loose into the atmosphere, where it has the potential of doing considerable harm.

From the ships point of view, the absolute maximum has been discharged, and the ship is in all respects ready to load another cargo, earning maximum freight.

All it took was a little effort, but knowing what you are doing counts for a lot as well.

Unigas and some other less scrupulous charterers prefer Filipino crews, or other third world crews, as they don't argue. If they are told to blow off 30 tonnes of VCM, then they blow off 30 tonnes. Why should they care, they live on the other side of the world, and don't give a hoot anyway, just as long as they get paid.

They, Unigas, don't like me at all, but then I care, whereas they don't. I'll come back to this later, with a vengeance.

So we went to Sines, south of Lisbon to load Raffinate 1, ie,rubbish. Who should be there in Sines, none other than *Carrot Top* trying to find the missing cargo.

Even by recalculating it a different way, we were still short, so there had to be something else wrong. After all, three different ports receiving cargo into empty tanks had less chance of being wrong than the ship.

When I looked back through the ship's records, I noticed an anomaly that no-one had picked up on before. There was always a large discrepancy when she was part loaded. When she had been running Flotta to Porsgrun, part loaded, the discrepancy ran at about 5 tonnes, which normally would not be of a great concern due to the fluctuations in the mixture of propane and ethane, that is, obtaining an exact density.

So, armed with the discrepancies, I managed to calculate that somewhere around the 52% level (half full) in No 1 cargo tank, the calibrations were too high by some 85 cubic metres, which would account for all the VCM losses. Recalculating other cargoes with this as a constant could account for these losses as well.

Reporting this back to Unigas, they agreed to set up a survey on the next discharge, where we would stop discharging at regular intervals, measure the ship, and the shore tank, and compare figures. Nice and simple, bit of extra work for us, but we could then find out if the cargo tank had to be re-measured.

I received confirmation of this in a telegram, which I have kept in my diary to this day. It reads: Tuesday 6th October 1987. 51words, channel 81, from GNI(Niton Radio), time 1631GMT. "Master GWIM/ GNI. During next discharge Antwerp. Draft survey will be done on behalf Gibsons/Unigas by Depauw. Product will be discharged into isolated shore tank for verification purposes. Please maintain same ballast conditions before/during/after discharge. Please render max. cooperation. Regards. Unigasinter."

You may ask, why be so precise with this?

Because this was never done, it was cancelled, and has been used against me ever since, featuring highly in why I became the scapegoat, not only in Gibsons, but also partly by Forth Ports, when I stopped piloting.

For the rest of this voyage, I was told by Unigas not to offer 'Letters of Protest', or 'Letters of Deadfreight', or 'Letters of Exception'. These are documents which are issued when there are discrepancies between ships figures and shore figures after a cargo is loaded. There are nearly always differencies, so are routine. In the meantime, Gibsons are checking their records on how the tanks were calibrated. They got the curves for the tanks out of the Scottish Records Office, but didn't know how to interpret them. All ships built in Scotland (and presumably the rest of the country too,) give a complete set of drawings etc to the local records office archives. Anyone can get them out providing they are not for legal purposes. So if you are interested in any ship for any particular purpose, all you need to know is its original name, when it was built and where it was built, and for a small fee, bingo.

For ships built in Leith, they are in Edinburgh, for the Clyde, Glasgow, and so on. Forget anything built for the RN, that's more tricky, but still possible, as they are in London.

However, Gibsons records threw up a surprise. The first time the tanks were calibrated, by an Independent Firm, when they were back calculated to check them, the 98% level in No 1 tank came out at 2 metres above the top of the tank. (Somewhere out on the deck). So these calibrations were ditched. Then another Independent Firm was brought in. Same thing, although this time, the 90% level was at the 98% level, and the 98% level 1 metre above the top of the tank. So they were ditched as well.

In the end, the shipyard did it. But then another surprise. When the *Borthwick* was converted, another set of tables were produced, for the NGL trade, only by now, nobody knew which were which, or which to use for the LPG trade.

Confused? So were we, totally.

How do I know all this? *Old Baldy* told me.

To resolve the issue of the VCM financially, Unigas agreed to pay the difference in the freight back to Norsk Hydro (the shippers), through Occidental (the charterers).

In effect, they were admitting that there was a problem, and Unigas International do not like this one little bit, mostly because I have a very long and very good memory. How this works to the owners/Unigas' benefit is rather convoluted, as not every cargo will show a plus, for something that isn't there, but never will it show a minus, so they can't lose.

The loser is who pays the bill. Then ultimately, you.

If the Bill of Lading is based on 'shore' figures, then the ship will show a higher figure, and a Letter of Protest will be issued, along with a claim for the difference in freight. Then, if the cargo is discharged on 'ship's' figures, it will appear that the receiver, has in fact received more than he has 'paid for', further reinforcing the claim for 'loss of freight'. If the cargo is discharged on 'shore' figures, he gets what he has paid for, but the ship then has a claim for freight. If the Bill of Lading is based on 'ships' figures,' then the ship is being paid for cargo that isn't on board. If this is a known factor, then this is fraudulent. Then the receiver gets less than he has paid for, plus has paid freight on something that wasn't there in the first place. It's a win, win situation for the ship, or at that time, Unigas International, but not for the cargo receivers.

The ship was supposed to have been recalibrated in the next dry dock, but never was, and as you read on, you'll find out all that has been done to keep it covered up, and why I was the scapegoat, only now, with this book, it's coming out in the open. So, we went to Ming Ming to load for a port I hadn't been to before. Brofjorden in Sweden. It was somewhat uneventful, until it came time to sail for Scapa Flow once again. I had been watching the glass (barometer) falling all day, but it was falling too fast to be normal, plus, it kept on falling. The clouds coming over the sky seemed to be going even faster, and coming from the south, which meant the sea on the beam all the way to Scapa. I decided to stay alongside until the weather moderated. The berth was free anyway.

The terminal weren't pleased and insisted that I sail. A red rag to a bull that one with me, so I put out extra moorings, and stayed put. *A very wise decision it proved to be.*

You will recall the hurricane that came through the South East of England and did so much damage. Well this was the same one that was now coming up to hit Norway and Sweden, and it howled just as much through these two countries as it did further South. I sailed next day, and the sea was nearly calm, but with a slight swell. I can recall this, as we added a small inflatable to our growing flotilla.

However, worse was to come.

After loading in Flotta, we headed back to Porsgrun, and on the way across we passed the *Quentin. GFG* told me to watch out for *logs* of all things.

When the hurricane came through Norway, at a pulp mill at Skien, which is about 6 miles up the fjord from Porsgrun, 30 000 cubic metres of logs had floated away when the water level in the fjord rose 2.5 metres in 2 hours. The hurricane pushed the water level up.

For once, *GFG* was to be taken seriously, you could hardly move for logs. There was a logjam at Porsgrun town which had to removed with explosives, but in the fjord, we had to go up at dead slow to avoid damage. Remember, the hull on this boat ain't very good. My chief officer at this time was a super Irishman I had known for at least 7 years, but his logic was rather Irish at times. In the anchorage waiting to go alongside, I looked up the deck to see a boathook from the well-deck holding a log alongside. Peculiar, so I went to have a look.

"What are you doing mate, holding a log alongside?"

"Oh, I've caught it, now I'm trying to think of a use for it." Mmm!

The poor guy was lost at sea under very odd circumstances off the coast of India 4 years later. By then he was a captain too. The *Leith Arab* relieved me again, but by now we were all ready for him.

The bond had been sub-divided into 12 bond lockers, each member of the crew had their own, and had filled it up with what they could use for the rest of the voyage, plus what they could legally take home, all paid for at cost prices. This is all perfectly legal, as I had come to know the Customs in Kirkwall quite well, and had consulted with them first. The ship's locker No 13, was filled up with Portuguese Brandy, from Sines. However the bottles were rather thin, and they did have the unfortunate tendency of exploding at random. Who said No 13 wasn't unlucky? Furthermore, in Rotterdam, I bought two 'special offers,' from the chandler, two cases of Whyte & Mackays Scotch, plus 10 000 Raffles cigarettes, just to get a presentation wooden barrel of 12-year-old Malt. One for me, and one for the chartering manager at Occidental. Boy oh boy, was that Brandy rough. He'll have trouble flogging that in Norway.

It was so bad, the Norwegians who tried it, brought it back for a refund. The *Leith Arab* had to write it all off out of his own pocket. Did this cure him? Did it heck, but I cured him properly next voyage, but only after he dropped me right in it.

So home for leave, after a very demanding trip.

For some reason, I did not join the *Quentin* in Scapa Flow, but flew to Skien via London and Oslo, and joined her in Porsgrun. *GFG* wasn't taking any chances in not getting off, and for once, I was joining a ship that seemed to be as near good as it gets. He was still moaning about the radars, but that went in one ear and straight out the other.

This was also the only trip (3 months) I did as master in Gibsons where we did not go off our designated run, Flotta to Porsgrun.

During the flight from London to Oslo, with lunch I had a beer, called 'Polar Beer.' The name really appealed to me, so I stocked the ship up with it. Everybody else agreed that this was very pleasant, until, one night lying at anchor, it was one of the crew's birthdays, so had an extra case of beer available.

Next morning, he came to see me, and said, "Captain, that Polar Beer there is something wrong with it. We drank two cases of it last night, but we didn't even get to the happy stage. Is it by chance alcohol free?"

Dammit, found out, but the joke had lasted 6 weeks!

However, on the second trip back, we ran into weather which was worsening, and although I thought I could push on hard and get into Scapa Flow before it broke, it just wasn't possible so I had to slow down to prevent damage. The sea is a powerful foe.

About 50 miles out, I hit a rather big wave at about 6 knots (it was dark) and was slowing her down further, when we hit an almighty wave following. The bow went completely under, so did the deck and compressor room, then it came over *the top* of the bridge. For a few seconds or so, we were a submarine. The *Quentin* shook herself up and in doing so, blew almost every fuse on the bridge. We had open lifeboats, and they were full.

Irresponsible? Going too fast? Well consider this, the *St Sunniva*, the ferry from Aberdeen to Shetland was on her maiden voyage that night and was in the same area, and hit the same wave, which blew in her bridge windows, she had to return to Aberdeen. You do occasionally gets these super waves, and this was one of them. The wave itself is not the problem, it is the trough caused by the wave before it. We did eventually get into Scapa Flow, and did a very careful inspection. Fortunately the only damage was to my nerves.

I had for some time been having trouble with the pilots in Scapa Flow. The other two captains and my predecessors had become somewhat complacent and lackadaisical in their dealing with the pilots, to the extent that the service they were providing was poor in the extreme. By 2004, little has changed, it is still poor.

The one thing that must never exist on the bridge of a ship, particularly when there is a pilot on board, is doubt. The pilot is *never* in command, he is only there to advise the master. If the master declines this advice, or has reason to doubt the accuracy of this advice, then that is the master's prerogative. Some pilots however resent this, and those are the ones referred to as 'Prima Donnas'. These are the one's that every master and *thinking* bridge officers watch like hawks. (I'll refer to the term 'thinking bridge officers' later.)

I *never allowed* a pilot to steer, or operate any equipment other than the VHF. Up to this point in my time at Scapa Flow, two pilots had been 'kicked off' the bridge for incompetency, a point that did not go down well with the harbour master, who took this as a personal affront.

What really annoyed him was a complaint that I tendered, about his pilots being late for the sailing time. He was of the opinion that as we were regular runners, and spent so much time at anchor anyway, that an hour here or there didn't matter much anyway. That is not the point, pilots are here to serve ships, ships are not here to serve pilots. On the previous voyage, before the plant in Norway shut down for 3 months' maintenance, we had a 'latest time of arrival' for Porsgrun. Because we were an hour late in leaving Scapa, as the pilot was late, we in turn were an hour late in arriving in Porsgrun. For this, Norsk Hydro would only accept half the cargo, so the balance, some 450 tonnes went to the flare stack in Rafnes. A total waste of energy. Captain Ronald Johnston, the author, and previous master on the *Quentin*, when the trade was set up, wrote "the standard of pilotage in Scapa Flow varies between average and dangerously incompetent." That was in 1980. By 1988, little had changed, other than two of the 'dangerously incompetents', had left to be replaced by two more.

On this particular loading, we had taken our first parcel, of some 700 tonnes, but we did not have time to take the balance, up to a full cargo, being some 100 tonnes short as Occidental needed the berth. So we went back to the anchorage to wait.

Just before berthing for the balance, I received a call from the terminal manager, advising me that one of the vice-presidents of Occidental was on Flotta for a tour, and would it be okay for him to make a ship visit when we were alongside? This is something that is always welcome, and the *Quentin* was a good ship for him to see.

However; The pilot that night was not playing fair. (I know he was set up for it by the harbour master.)

"I know you don't like doubt on your bridge captain, so who is doing this tonight, you, or me?"

By 'me' doing it, he meant, I'll tell you what to do, and you will do *exactly* as I say. In reality this means that, if I (the pilot) prang it, or do any damage, however slight, then it will still be your (the masters) fault.

I didn't trust this guy anyway, so told him that I would do it. I then signed his bill accordingly, This again, is master's prerogative.

He then announced by VHF that the master would be berthing the *Quentin* that night. What was he up to I wondered?

Later, when ashore, he endorsed the bill with 'captain berthing tonight having declined pilots advice.'

That is *very, very, naughty*, and backfired on him.

I waited East of the berth, until the tanker coming off was clear, then made my approach to go port side alongside. Although I say it myself, it was the most perfect piece of ship-handling ever. We stopped exactly in position 3 inches off. My crew threw the ropes out, and that was that. Even the pilot was impressed. But then the fun started.

Although I didn't know it at the time, the vice-president from Occidental commented with. "Well, if that's how the captain does it, why do we employ pilots?"

By the time this got back to the harbour master, after we had sailed, it had changed into.

"The master berthed his ship without a pilot." And that is against the law. Also, totally untrue.

The vice-president had a very satisfactory visit, and everyone left happy.

Three hours later, we sailed.

There was a message for me on arrival in Norway, "urgent, 'phone the Leith office."

I got *Old Baldy*, who said somewhat angrily.

"I've had a report from the agents in Kirkwall, who tell me that you berthed your ship on xx date, and quote "without a pilot being on board. Is this true?"

"No (heart in mouth), I had a pilot, it was Mike M-------, his name is entered in the bridge movement book."

"Are you sure?" (He always was a bit slow.)

"Of course I'm sure. Do you want confirmation from the chief who was with me on the bridge?"

"I'll need to check on this."

Off course, the story being passed down the line, had got all mixed up, and now, with everyone washing their hands of it, the harbour master ended up with the blame. (He could be as slow as *Old Baldy*.)

From then on, my name was mud with the harbour master, but then, what was new?

Arriving back in Scapa Flow again, after discharging in Norway, the weather blew up again, this time from the South East, and boys, oh boy, did it come up, at least 70+ knots. The Pentland Firth was a bit bouncy, the Easterly stream running against the wind. I didn't close on the Lothar Rock on this occasion, but approaching the pilot station, it was clear that we were not going to get the pilot on board safely, so elected for an escort. Fortunately, it was one of the better pilots. We got him on board inside Scapa Flow, and went to the anchorage close on the island of Hunda, which is the South East corner. There is a bank here that you can trip the cable over, that is, put the anchor on one side, and let the ship lie on the other. This improves the holding power of the anchor.

Contrary to popular belief, it is not the anchor that holds the ship at rest. It is the weight of the anchor cable, called the 'catenary'. The more cable you have out, the more 'secure' will be the ship. However, you swing about more as well. It is a juggling act, getting it right. Sometimes the second anchor just on the bottom helps.

A very rough 'rule of thumb' is to allow for between two to eight times the depth of water, but most masters do it by experience. Just guess! The only way I could get the pilot off again (he only came to get his bill signed), plus the agents on, was to steam on the anchor to make a lee. So hard a starboard (it was the port anchor that was out), and a kick ahead, and all change.

She wouldn't come back to her cable however, that is, come back head to wind. I sent the mate forward, who came back with,

"the anchor cable has broken, we've lost an anchor and 6 shackles of cable."

What a way to start a day.

So, it was back over the bank and put the starboard one out.

After 'phoning the office, with the bad news, I obtained permission to try and find it, failing that, we would need a new length of cable sent up by road, and a crane to put out the spare(anchor).

My pal Charlie, who ran the launch obtained a creeper, which is just a lump of iron with hooks, a long rope, and a diver, and after the weather moderated, set off to try and find it. After all, it's 540 feet long, stretched out in a straight line, and is over a bank. Shouldn't be too hard to find? Should it?

He found five before he found ours, but by that time we had to go and load our first parcel, so it was buoyed off.

What do you think happened next?

The pilot bringing the tanker off the berth, anchored the tanker on top of the buoyed cable!

He had the whole of Scapa Flow to choose from, but had to choose the same bit. Told you my name was mud. Or rather, he was a fool.

Fortunately, he didn't get it tangled up, and after loading, we came back to hook the ends of our cable back together, then recover the anchor. We even got back the broken joining shackle, which showed why the cable had parted.

Years of swinging around at anchor had worn the steel away on the joining shackles, so I had 12 more flown in, and replaced the lot.

Total cost, recovery and repair, £1000.

Cost of 6 shackles of cable plus transport £20 000.

Gibsons didn't even say thank you, but then I was dealing with another superintendent, *Snow White*, who you will hear a lot about later.

Ah, but the harbour master. He came out in a tug, circled the ship, just to make sure that I had in fact, two anchors in the hawse pipes.

Why you may well ask?

I got it from his secretary later.

If I was going to sail short of an anchor, then he was going to report me to the Department of Transport for sailing in an un-seaworthy condition, and that is a definite no-no.

He'll have to do a lot better than that with me. Tough luck Mr B---
-.

So we trotted off back to Porsgrun, where I really came unstuck, thanks to the Leith Arab. I resigned over this.

We berthed in Porsgrun at about 2 in the morning, and the agent boarded on arrival, took my papers for inward clearance, and gave me the cash that I had previously ordered, which went into the safe. Then I went to bed.

At about 0430, there was a knock on the door. It was the Norwegian Customs. Peculiar hour I thought at the time. It transpired that my ship was accused of selling bonded goods to the tug *Frier*. This was our escort tug on many occasions, but on this particular trip inwards, we had the *Bulldog*.

How much, I enquired?

15 bottles of whisky, and 7 cases of beer.

At the *Leith Arab's* prices, NKr 2200.

No chance with it being this ship, here is my 'Outward Clearance Declaration' from Scapa Flow, and here is my 'Inward Declaration' for Porsgrun. Let's go check the locker.

One of the Customs' officers was extremely officious, the other, somewhat embarrassed.

Everything tallied up exactly. It had to. I checked it all before I came in.

He wants *all* the crew up, to check that what they had tallied with the Crew Declaration. It did, and he became very angry.

I remember his words well,

"The captain on the *Frier* says it came from here, so I am detaining your ship until the Police have completed their investigation. All cargo operations must cease immediately."

This was getting out of hand. *Quentin's* hire rate was $800 per hour.

Off-hire for even 1 hour was twice the value of that 'sold'.

I 'came to an agreement with him,' that I would 'hand over' NKr 2200, what he determined was made from the 'sale.' I would claim it back from the P & I Club later. (This happens a lot, particularly in South America.)

Big mistake on my part, huge. I trusted him. Never again.

"Ah ha," he said, as I got the cash from the safe, "it was you, you've got the money in the safe."

I showed him the receipt for taking 'Cash to Master' from the agents only that morning. I needn't have bothered. Ignorant twit.

That however, wasn't the end of it. The other Customs officer stayed on board all day, and let me into a few secrets.

They were after the *Leith Arab*, and knew it was him, but he had sailed, on the *Borthwick*, and they had to 'pin the blame' on someone, as their boss was demanding it. He was almost apologetic. Too late for that now, I'm getting the blame for someone else.

The skipper on the *Frier* was so drunk that he would have said anything. When he sobered up, and realised what he had done, he was deeply ashamed and sorry. That was a lot of use to me. His company sent him to a clinic to dry out, and then to Haugesund in South West Norway, away from temptation.

Fortunately, the *Leith Arab* had sent me a letter, such a rare occurrence, that I had kept it. Foolishly for him, he assumed that as he was selling the bond, so was everyone else. I don't think *GFG* was, but I certainly wasn't.

In this letter, he advised that he was putting his prices up to NKr 110 per bottle/case. I used this later to rub his nose in it. Meanwhile, the first Customs' Officer had gone to the Police with the NKr2200, and made a complaint. Two weeks later, I got a letter with a further 'fine' of NKr 5000, or 21 days in pokey.

I hit the roof, not only am I now Nkr7200 (£685) out of pocket, as the P & I Club would not pay, as another company ship was involved, but I have a record for something that I have not done. Plus Gibsons in Leith were now involved.

Old Baldy, who *knew* it was the *Leith Arab,* told me to 'get it sorted,' so I 'phoned the *Leith Arab* at home.

He agreed to 'phone the office, and 'sort it all out.'

Fine, was my reply, you can recompense me when you relieve me.

About 30 minutes later the 'phone rang. It was *Old Baldy*.

"Captain **********, says he knows nothing about this."

I hit the roof again, only higher this time.

"Right, that's it, you'll have my resignation within 24 hours, and I will sort out that man when he gets up here to relieve me.

I will consult with a solicitor when I get home." Then put the 'phone down.

The brown soup really hit the fan then.

Believe it or not, the *Leith Arab* was due to relieve me on the following Monday, this was Friday.

Fortunately for him, the superintendents stepped in, the gist of what I heard later was that it would not be prudent for the *Leith Arab* to board, as 'Doug'll go for him.' Too true I would.

Next day, *The Poison Dwarf* (who had been temporarily promoted) relieved me. The *Leith Arab*, had been suspended indefinitely. I spent the weekend in a hotel in Kirkwall, calming down, and flew home on the Monday.

It was eventually sorted out. What upset Gibsons was that I took my solicitor into the office with me. I did, after all, work for Denholm's, Gibsons were only the 'technical managers.'

I sent the *Leith Arab* a copy of his letter, and received a cheque from his wife, of all people, by return. I didn't resign, but I should have, it would have saved me a lot of hassle later, but that is the value of hindsight. *So I was the scapegoat. That was the first time.*

It was my intention to clear my name with the Norwegian Customs. My solicitor advised that although I had a good case, and would probably win, I should take into account that the next time I went to Norway, then I would be targeted, and it would be twice as bad. So I very reluctantly let it go, but it left a most disagreeable taste.

A further thing that came out in the office, however, finally sealed the fact that I would not be staying in the company for much longer was this from the managing director, with a copy of the 1987 Pilotage Act.

He said, and he was never a seaman, or even sensible,

"in future, you will do *exactly* as the pilot says, irrespective of whether you think it is wrong or not. If the ship knocks down the jetty, or incurs damage, then we have insurance to cover that. I do not want to hear any more on this subject. Do you understand Captain?" "Quite frankly sir, *no*! What happens when someone gets hurt?"

I have never heeded his instruction, nor would I ever do.

That was in 1988, I still await an answer, but I don't think I will get one now.

This job, as master, is hard enough, *without* going around with one hand tied behind your back, so to speak.

The 'officious' Customs' Officer was sacked shortly afterwards, not only as was stated for being 'over zealous,' but for serious infringements of safety regulations on gas tankers. A lot of people in Norsk Hydro hated him.

Comment:

I have gone into how this man was eventually caught in some detail, not with the specific intention of trying to disgrace him, he could manage that by himself, or to tarnish his name now that he is deceased, and cannot therefore defend himself, but to illustrate what I think is lacking in the UK today.

Since the early '90s, a change in EU legislation, did away with a lot of the paperwork for ships trading within the EU. Similarly, at that time, we saw the disappearance of many Custom's Officers from our ports. True, there is still a presence, but it is very rare for a master to see a Customs visit in a UK port. (With the exception of the ferry terminals.) This I think is where the start of many problems lies.

A lot of the highly skilled boarding officers and 'black gangs' were shifted sideways into the VAT section. This is the sort of work that could be done by any 'licensed' firm of accountants, indeed, a lot of it could be done by 'house-persons' (I hate that term), working from home, thus releasing the skilled personnel back to the ports.

There is no point blaming The Police, for the worsening drug culture/problem in this country. They, after all, have only got the mess to sort out *after* the drugs are in this country. It needn't only be drugs, there are off course other undesirable elements smuggled in.

Customs & Excise should be the first line of defence, with a significant *visual* presence in ports and the ever growing number of marinas.

A sharp eyed Customs' officer with his 'nose and ear to the ground' is far more valuable than any bank of computers, or information lines. The dress tie of the Customs, shows a Red Ensign with an overhand knot in it. How many people know that this means, "we want the Customs," when flown from a ship? Or more to the point, where are the Customs Officers to see it? Or even a British ship?

It was well known in Norway, in the 1980s, that the Customs often sat on the hills around the ports with a powerful telescope, and sought the evidence, before they went on board. Knowing that, in itself was a deterrent.

The British 'black gangs' could get into places on a ship, that the crew couldn't. That was also a deterrent.

I, personally, and I don't know of any other master who does this, will call in the Customs and have them search my ship, irrespective of flag, and I've done this in many ports around the world. This achieves two things; my crew know that I will not tolerate anything illegal. Everyone knows that my ship is clean. No doubt the term 'productivity' will be voiced, but this is one group who should not have targets set, as long as they stop anything being brought in illegally.

The average individual, returning from abroad will no doubt grumble about paying duty for being over their allowance when returning to the

UK, so I would say this to them. What do you prefer, having Customs stop drugs etc coming in, or coming back to a house that someone has broken into, to get the money to buy more drugs?

I know which I prefer.

I delivered a tug from Hong Kong to the UK (you'll read about this in Part 6). We were asked to stop in the middle of the Dover Strait by a French Customs launch, and were searched. Frankly, I welcome this, especially after I saw some of the detection equipment they have nowadays. Let this be known publicly, and the temptation to smuggle in by yacht, even small quantities, will be reduced. Finally, I know they are costly, but we need more Customs Launches. Crew to run them? Try using the Royal Navy, they need the training, and they have the men who after all, are already getting paid. Plus more Customs Officers on board as well.

They can do one more important thing, but read Part 5 first.

To let things 'cool down', my next trip was to the ethylene trade, with the *Melrose*, a ship that I had re-built in dry-dock immediately before being promoted. I'd traded here, Baglan Bay (near Swansea) to Moerdijk (behind Rotterdam) for some years, and knew it as well as the Flotta/Porsgrun run. It would be interesting to see how the others were getting on with the Denman set-up.

They weren't. If anything, the moaning, and grumbling still went on.

The *Melrose* was built in 1972, but with it being a Gibsons' ship, was screwed up at the start. She was supposed to have been built under the 1600 gross tons rule, but mistakes were made, and she ended up over this. She then ended up according to the 1999 gross tons rule, the difference being that she now had to carry an extra deck officer (third mate), and a radio officer.

To try to minimize the additional costs, a deck tank was added. This tank caused more problems over the years, than it was worth, mainly because in further saving costs, Gibsons didn't put a pump in it. To discharge this tank, a cargo compressor was run to overpressure the liquid into No 1 port cargo tank. This ship was in fact many years ahead of its time. She (and her sister ship, the *Heriot*, less the deck tank), were built as pressurized LNG tankers, a concept only developed further in 2003.

The tanks were built from an aluminium alloy, and were rated down to -162 degrees Celsius, but at the same time, the safety valves were set for 5 bar. The main engine was a Sulzer, 6 in line diesel. The reason, that they were never further developed, was that the technology at the time, hadn't kept pace with the idea. LNG tankers, because the cargo is always 'boiling', use the 'boil-off' in the boilers of a steam turbine ship for propulsion. (More on this later.)

In the case of the *Melrose*, however, after three attempts, in which they set fire to the engine room three times, the project was shelved. The *Melrose* then spent most of her life as an ethylene carrier, until, even then, technology took over once more in the mid '80s.

She eventually 'fell to bits', but then, anything that Indians' get their hands on always does. The cargo tanks at this time were as good as the day they were built. They just fell through the bottom of the hull.

There is currently, in 2003, an LNG tanker getting built with a diesel engine, but, and this will be watched by many, is also a small pressurized ship of some 1200 cubic metres, and safety valve settings of 250 bars. The company doesn't have any gas tankers, or has ever had, and as such no experience whatsoever, which should make this interesting. The intention is to load 'straight out of the ground in the gas field', and deliver it 'raw' to the user. If it works, and I have serious reservations about this, then it would certainly solve a lot of environmental problems. See Part 5.

Now, who should be at the top of the pilot ladder, when I joined by launch in Margate Roads, which was where the *Melrose* was anchored. None other than *Blunderman*.

And more to the point, whose idea was it to send him to the ethylene tankers? I know, mine. So, I'm stuck with him.

Typical of the morose attitude in Gibsons at this time, I had a whole pile of survey work to get through. The same excuse from 'up north' prevailed,

"Oh we were going to do it, but we've never had the chance." Now, in Margate Roads, you are not going to get anything done, and as the ship is waiting to go back on her usual trade of Baglan Bay to Moerdijk with ethylene, we might as well take the opportunity to bring everything up to date.

Unigas were reluctant to let me move her, but eventually agreed, so we trotted off to The Isle of Wight, and anchored in St. Margarets Bay.

This is dead handy for a surveyor to come out from the MCA, or as it was known then, the Department of Transport. Not only can I get all my statutory certificates updated, I can get all my visas 'Off Class' as well.

Nice plan. Pity we had *Blunderman*, who excelled himself. The surveyor, was the most senior surveyor in Southampton. Great, this guy will really know what he is doing. So I very carefully warn him to keep well out of the way of *Blunderman*. *All the time*!

Everything went well, until the end, when the surveyor wanted to test some fire extinguishers. No big deal really?

We set off from the master's cabin for the poop deck, collecting extinguishers as we went.

The first one was 'water', and had been mounted on a bracket in the alleyway, which had been welded on many years before. As soon as *Blunderman* picked it up, the bracket fell off the bulkhead. An ominous warning perhaps? but worse was to come. He set the CO_2 one off in the engine room, 'by mistake' and engineers were flying out all over the place, gasping for air. "*We*, Jim, will get the rest." Now having gathered four extinguishers (Water, Foam, CO_2, and Dry Powder), on the poop deck, we are ready to start. *But*, "hold on a minute, we'll just go up behind the funnel (two decks)."

That was the chief engineer (the *sloe-eyed Mancunian*), and me.

"Why?" said the surveyor.

"Because, we know what he is like!"

"Nobody can be that bad!"

He was.

Got the surveyor straight in the ear, then down his entire right side with a Foam Extinguisher, before pointing it over the side. *We 2 were now 3.*

"You're right, he is *that* bad."

"Told you. Just think yourself lucky that you haven't got your car."

"Why?"

"I'll tell you when he's left for leave, if we have any ship left by then." "Good luck Captain." Boy, were we going to need it. Earlier, on the *Borthwick*, we had a surveyor who came up to Scapa Flow from Aberdeen. Where the Department of Transport found this guy, is anybody's guess.

Scruffy? To say the least. The exact opposite of the one we had just had. His boilersuit was obviously one that had been washed many times, that the pockets had fallen off, but, it had not *all* fallen to bits yet, so was repaired, but with what? Towelling bar mats! The one on his right rear still had 'ents' printed on it, suggesting that it may have originally been from 'Tennents'. The only story of note, was when he walked into the officers mess, and asked to see the safety manual. This is a loose leaf file that has instructions relating to the safety equipment on board. Nobody ever reads it. It was in a drawer, so was duly pulled out.

"Captain", he says, "this should be left out where everyone can see it, not kept hidden away in a drawer."

Fair enough, so when he gave it back, I duly threw it under the table.

"Why did you do that captain?" asks he, with a horrified look.

"Because when this ship goes to sea, and starts moving, that is where it will end up, so it might as well start off there."

It went back in the drawer.

However, fully certificated once again, we set off for Swansea Bay, and got tangled up, with of all things, *a powerboat race*, just as we went to pick up our pilot. Now, it has been said of me, that I do not suffer fools gladly. If that is true, then the pilot in the River Neath, who was also the Harbour master, General Factotum, and Uncle Tom Cobbley, didn't suffer fools at all.

Regrettably, he died a few years ago, on the day he retired.

The Powerboat race was around Swansea Bay, but the organizers didn't bother to check with *all* the port authorities before they laid out the course. Neath wasn't really considered a 'port authority'!

Believe it or not, and you probably won't, but one of their turning marks was the end of the River Neath Channel, which, just a mite coincidentally, just happens to be the pilot boarding position as well.

And *yes*! We all arrived at the same time.

One 2500 ton ethylene tanker, (in very restricted water), one pilot boat, and 35 power boats, doing the best part of 70+ knots, and an anchored yacht, which was the turning mark. *All at the same time.*

He would have been the *turning mark*, if he had stayed put, but as he is in the channel, has decided to move before he was sunk. *Wise precaution.* Thinking at last, eh? Not really, as none of the power boats know where to go next.

As my memory serves me, two of the power boats ended up on the beach. This was not at the high water mark, but *well up*, i.e. on the dunes, beside Swansea Golf Club. Some just gave up. The race was finally abandoned, and I don't think the organizers were on the pilots' Christmas Card List either.

To load in Baglan Bay, the *Melrose* had to be modified, as the ship sits on the bottom on a prepared layerage of asphalt. You could if you were brave enough, walk around the ship at low water.

Insurance criteria demanded that the ship 'takes' the bottom, and 'comes off' the bottom within 3 inches of even keel, and is upright. This is not as easy as it sounds. To help, get the bow down, No 1 Double bottom, was filled with drilling mud, which has a density of 2.000, as opposed to sea water, which has a density, of 1.025. On top of this, the forepeak tank is kept full by taking a supply from the shore main. This becomes the generator cooling water, which is piped aft to the engine room. At this stage, the after peak is empty.

The cargo condensers also take a supply from the shore and there was always a race to get this pipeline on. Then the loading arm is attached, so we can get about 100 tonnes into No 1 cargo tanks. This all has to be achieved in about an hour, before she sits on the bottom.

Traditionally, she would load over two tides, so after she would sit down the second time, the after peak tank would be filled. Then the fore peak shut down about 5 hours before she came off the second time.

This was tricky to say the least, until you got the hang of it, as the heights of tide are changing all the time, as was the loading rate. The deck tank was the problem, as we didn't always have time to fill it, but I used to top off No 1 & 2 tanks, and then consider anything that I could get in as a bonus. With some mates, and *Blunderman* was one of them, if they got within 18 inches of even keel, then that was a 'good day'. If they could get the ship upright as well, then party time!

Our main discharge port was Moerdijk, in the Netherlands, although we could head for Stade in Germany, about 4 hours steaming up the Elbe. There is not a lot to choose between them, it's only an end of a pipeline after all. However, one day, and it was a Saturday, we were heading up The Oude (Old) Maas to Moerdijk, I thought we would have a little fun.

There is a long bend in the river, where the reeds come down to the water's edge, and it is in amongst this that some of the locals 'take the sun' by lying naked in it.

We are not going particularly fast at this point, so head out from the middle of the channel, towards the reed beds. Not much, but why?

Because this sets up a wash, which moves the water away from the bank initially, before coming back with a vengeance, so they all get wet, unless they can move out the way fast enough, which is only if they can see through the reed beds. It gets them mad, but then, they're Dutch. Unigas country.

Then our steering gear locked out to starboard, so it was switched to Emergency, and the engine thrown astern. There were unfortunately, a herd of cows wallowing in the mud, and one was not just quite quick enough in getting out of the way before it was biffed by the bulbous bow. Stangely enough, we did not go aground, so reversed the engine to ahead and carried on as though nothing had happened.

Just on the point of sailing after discharge, a rather irate farmer came down. With the Police. Fortunately I knew the policeman.

Seemingly he had just managed to catch his cow, which ended up some nine farms away. He was suitably 'rewarded' from the bond locker, and left with The Police who thought it rather funny.

There was a terrific customs officer who also came on board most times in. His name was Cees (pronounced case), and had roughly the same sense of humour that I do. Hard to believe I know. One day, he had a huge grin on his face as he came into my cabin, and said.

"Doug, you'll love this story, I've just come from an Italian ship, and when I saw his Customs Declaration, I thought, oh no, this can't be right, he must have made a mistake."

"Yeah, go on Cees."

"Well, I checked his bond locker, and do you know he hadn't made a mistake. He did have 480 000 cigarettes."

"That does seem to be rather a lot. How many crew were on board?"

"Ten. So I asked him why he needed so many, and do you know what he said? Because we are very heavy smokers sir."

"Let me guess, was his next port Naples by any chance?"

With a stunned look, he said, "how did you know that?"

"Just figures. It just happens to be where most of the smugglers keep their fast boats, that's all."

Calling in to Moerdijk, sometimes twice a week, meant we got to know people rather well. One of these people was a loading master by the name of Harry Smit. I should imagine he is dead by now. If not, then he should be. He was also known as 'unbelievable.' When you consider that this place was run by Shell, it is hard to imagine how he got away with what he did. This man could drink whisky faster than the Scots could make it.

Harry, however, did have a rather fascinating 'party trick'. I've never seen anyone else do this, anywhere, and I've been around a bit.

He could write with both hands at the same time. Totally legibly, the only difference was that his left hand produced a mirror image of his right. To read it, you had to hold it to a mirror. It was fascinating, as it was also fast.

One morning, about 6 o'clock he came into my cabin, when I was signing off the cargo, and signing a few odds and ends. He was always welcome, as he was an old Dutch captain.

"Good morning Doug, I'm afraid to tell you that I was at a party last night, and I'm a bit thirsty."

"Cup of coffee then Harry?"

He looked at me aghast, "do you have anything stronger?"

"Oh, strong black coffee then?"

"I was thinking more like a wee dram."

Now to Harry, there was no such thing as 'a wee dram'. I did however have a secret weapon that I kept for these situations. I had a litre bottle of a Scotch whisky by the name of 'Lord John'. Most people used it as paint stripper. After you had one, you didn't normally ask for another. It was horrible, but it did have one advantage, it was cheap, at £10 per case. People at sea can get things people ashore have never heard of.

After getting the bottle out, and filling a tumbler for him, I went back to signing various odds and ends. I signed my name once when I heard "ah...h" followed by a clunk, as the glass was laid down.

Not to be outdone, I suggested, "another perhaps?"

"Very gracious of you Doug, I think I will."

Signed my name once more and heard, "ah...h" followed by another clunk, as the glass was laid down once more.

"I'll tell you what Harry, let's dispense with the glass. Just keep the bottle okay?"

How he ever survived I'll never know, but there was one certainty. Even with the best constitution, drinking Scotch like that led to only one conclusion, an early visit to the undertakers.

We called him 'unbelievable', because when he regaled a story, it would either start or finish with the words 'I tell you captain, it was quite un...*believ*...able.'

Then there was another loading master, they were both about the same age, who we knew as 'incredible'. Same thing.

It was going to be a long day when both 'unbelievable' and 'incredible' came on board together.

I dare say, that standards at Moerdijk have now changed somewhat. About this time, Marpol 3 came into force. All ships garbage had to be landed ashore for proper disposal. This was great news for us, as getting rid of ships used equipment is a major nightmare, such as old mooring ropes, engine parts for example. If they get chucked over the side, fishermen get them in their trawls, which for some strange reason, just annoys them. But mooring ropes float, being polypropylene, and if you get one round the screw, suddenly find yourself stopping. Getting them off is murder and they bind up akin to a steel bar.

'Unbelievable' with due accord announced that there was now a steel skip on the jetty for our garbage. Oh goody, we can have some fun with this!

Under cover of darkness, we filled it up. In went four old engine liners, three cracked cylinder heads, 3 x 200 metre long ropes, most of the engine room scrap box, and a load of old oil in drums.

All up weight, about 10 tons! They are going to have trouble picking that up. We then sailed.

They did, their little truck wouldn't look at it. Oh, did we catch it next time back.

Not long after joining, I asked the Chief, why we were running around at only 400 rpm on the main engine, when her full speed should have been 480 rpm.

"It's to reduce the vibration. If we go up past 460 rpm, then the cylinder head bolts shear."

That was a new one on me. "Has anyone checked the propeller?"

So we had a close look at in Baglan. Sure enough, she had been aground somewhere as all the tips were bent over, and ragged.

Although I put it on the drydock list, Gibsons tried to blame me for it. Obviously, with the company going downhill fast, it would have been more prudent not to say anything. But I, for one, still have my pride, even if they don't.

We used to anchor, either for weather to improve or for the tides at Baglan, by anchoring in the lee of Lundy Island, in the Bristol Channel.

If you can get in close, the holding ground is excellent, so we used to hang around here rather than go up to Swansea Bay.

On this particular Summer's Day, that was where we were, and it seemed like a good idea to have a lifeboat drill.

No matter what you see in the cinema or on television, launching lifeboats is a hazardous matter, unless the sea is *absolutely* flat calm. We try to get the boats into the water for a run every 3 months or so. It's just a matter of where.

Blunderman, has been suitably briefed of what to do and more importantly, what not to do.

Off course, he manages to get the only piece of rope round his propeller, and ends up, washed up, on the only bit of beach on Lundy, on a falling tide, with wait for it, no bottom left in the boat. How am I going to explain this away? But he isn't finished yet is he. Oh no! He actually manages to borrow a tractor, and sets about putting, what's left of his boat, end over end, back into the water, thus incurring more damage. The company accepted it was an accident, I could still talk *Old Baldy* round, but the boat had to be landed in Moerdijk for repair.

This episode reinforced my point that *Blunderman* was a danger, not only to himself, but to anyone nearby.

He left the *Melrose* later that day, and I have never seen him since. The last I heard of him was that he had been promoted to Master, on a small gas tanker where his wrecking spree continued, only now, he has to write his own letters. I should imagine that there is quite a pile by now.

I only found out about this story by chance. I was picking up a tug in Cobh (pronounced Cove) in Southern Ireland for delivery to The Philippines. I was telling the agents about him when I was in their office, when the agent said, "I don't suppose his name was Jim ...?"

"Why yes, do you know him?" I replied.

"Oh yes, *we* know *him* all right, whenever he comes here now, everything else stays tied up or at sea, until he is stopped and finished."

"That bad, eh?"

"No, Doug, *worse!*"

His ship is fitted with a Becker rudder. This is a type of rudder which will go over past the normal 35 degrees, sometimes as much as 85 degrees.

In port, it gives a ship terrific maneuverability. At sea, it is generally locked to no more than 35 degrees. Normally that is, for anyone else, but this is *Blunderman*.

He was coming up the river towards Cobh, with another ship following, when his steering gear locked out going over to 80 degrees, which set him off in a tight circle, still at full speed. He got all the way round, before correcting it, and then carried on. Unfortunately the other ship, who until this time was still minding his own business, altered to avoid a collision, and ran straight aground. Four tugs to get him off.

Now you see why he is dangerous. Especially to others.

I'll put this little tale in here. I was going to keep it for Book 2, but you might as well have a proper chuckle. I've got a good stock yet.

When I was chief mate on the *Traquair*, in Zeebrugge, I could inert with nitrogen from air to inerted at −25 degrees C dewpoint, oxygen, less than 0.3%, with about 18 000 cubic metres on N_2. Just under 3 volumes. It hasn't been bettered, by anyone.

Blunderman came in under air, to inert, connected the N_2 line to his System 2 manifold, and started off.

A first check after 6 hours should have alerted him that something was wrong, but no, he just carried on.

It was only after using 100 000 cubic metres of nitrogen, and the tanks were still full of air, that the chief engineer spotted that he hadn't taken the manifold cross line bend out.

The nitrogen had been coming in the port side, tracking through the manifold cross line, and straight out the starboard side, *without* going anywhere near the tanks.

For this, he truly earned the name of *Blunderman*!

A few weeks later, we are back at Lundy, when the Clovelly lifeboat dropped by. This was the only lifeboat with a paid crew, and we often had them on board for a meal and a few jokes when the weather was kind. This particular fair evening, the coxswain asked if anyone wanted to go ashore on Lundy. There is a hotel with a pub, but it's a heck of a climb up from the beach.

Now by the time you get to Chief Engineer, you would think that a little common sense would prevail. Not with my new chief, but then I had sailed with him many times before, and knew what he was like.

Six took up the offer and went for a beer or six.

Only five came back though.

"Where's the chief?"

"Oh yes cap, he's spending the night with 'Sexy Sue.'"

"Is he indeed? We should be able to have some fun here then."

Next day he is back, courtesy of the lifeboat, and thought nothing was wrong until the coxswain suggested a blood test might be a good idea in about a week or so. His face fell to his boots.

One more practical joke successfully under way!

After Moerdijk, we were going to the Tees. This is working out admirably. But first we have to get there.

The Dover Strait causes some people a lot of worry, as it can be busy. Actually, as long as you obey the rules and plan it all in advance, it is really straight forward. We were through 4 times a week, so were familiar with it.

I came through one night on the *Heriot*, and we were in a group of 16 ships, all within a 2 mile radius of the ship in the middle, and all doing different speeds, when a ferry poked its nose out of Dover. This is one to watch, as if any of us are on a collision course, then we must either alter course to starboard, to pass his stern, or slow down. Altering course is preferred to slowing down, but there are 15 others in this group, so extra care is needed.

Fortunately the ferry was prudent, and stopped until we had all passed, but stopped sufficiently early to waylay any doubt as to his intentions. Well done that man. It doesn't happen nowadays though.

One thing I kept drumming in to my officers was not only to keep a lookout, but to watch behind you as well.

On this particular warm but dark night on the *Melrose*, it was relatively quiet with traffic when I heard this whistle blowing.

The lookout came in and reported a ship flashing a light on our port quarter, and estimated that this was the ship that was also blowing its' whistle.

Sure enough, he comes on the VHF with,

"Little ship on my starboard bow, you are in my way. This is 25 000 ton tanker overtaking you. Get out of my way, as I am coming to starboard." This was on Channel 16, the International Call Up and Safety channel. Not a working channel as it should have been.

The VHF is to be avoided, as you cannot identify the actual ship it is being transmitted from. There have been collisions by VHF, known as VHF assisted f----ups.

"Little ship, get out of my way."

He is the overtaking ship, so it is *his* responsibility to keep clear, *not* mine. The rules are very clear on this point.

So, I countered with, "ship on Channel 16, if you are blowing your whistle, and flashing a light at me, please go to Channel 80."

On Channel 80, he repeats everything, so I countered with,

"Dover Coastguard, did you get all that on tape?"

"Confirmed *Melrose*, do you wish to register a complaint?"

"Affirmative on that, written complaint to follow."

When I related all this later to *Old Baldy*, he said.

"What did you do then?"

"Oh, I took a round turn to starboard and came on his stern."

"But you had right of way."

"I know, but a round turn is easier to execute, than dealing with a collision."

In the event, Port State Control got a hold of him in Rotterdam, and he was detained for a week. Not bad considering all he had to do was keep clear in the first place.

Arriving to anchor off the Tees, I decided to book an appointment for the Chief by VHF to the agents on an open channel. In the Tees, everybody knows everybody, and all listen in to their VHFs. Ch 69.

It's a bit like Orkney, but in England. Still weird accents though.

"Good morning *Melrose*, what can we do for you?" It was the agent.

"One man for the doctor, can you get him an appointment?"

"Surgery or hospital captain?"

"Better make it the hospital, STD clinic if there is one."

A distinct chuckle, before "what is his name?"

The chief is listening in, and came on with "don't you dare tell him my name!"

"Sorry, but the chief doesn't want me to tell you his name."

"Oh, right, well we'll see you when you are alongside then."

Just to make sure he went to the doctor, we all went with him.

But there was more to come. The fake 'fax.' Transmitted to coincide with our arrival in Moerdijk.

"Chief engineer to 'phone this number ----------------- asap."

His face was pure white, until he realized that he was speaking to the talking clock.

That'll teach you to mix it with Sexy Sue then Geoff. He never to my knowledge saw her again. But then, you never knew. The agents still talk about it. So did most of the Tees. He of course, doesn't.

The day I left the *Melrose* was also interesting, as we were bound for Fawley, which is just South from Southampton. As we came into the Solent, there was not a thing to be seen, not even a yachtsman.

Why?

Because it was the start of the Spithead Race, which even the pilot had forgotten about, or we would have anchored somewhere else, rather than in the middle of their first beat.

It was hilarious, by 10 o'clock there were over 1000 yachts, or as they are known by professional seamen, WAFI (wind assisted flaming idiots.) There is also a rude version of WAFI, better too.

By 12 o'clock, there was no wind, but didn't stop them having a *go* at the *Melrose*. One came so close on the quarter, that he tore his spinnaker on the log bracket, then suggested that *we* should pay for it, as we were 'in his way'. I just ignored him, as there were others now having a go at the anchor cable. By 2 o'clock pm, most had given up, and were paddling or even rowing back, from whence they came.

Not to worry me, next trip I'm heading back to the *Quentin*. Most regrettably, the production platform of Piper Alpha, had blown up, with a severe loss of life. We carried the gas across to Norway from this field.

Here is a little known fact to the general populace. When the crude oil comes ashore in Flotta, it is stabilized, before being shipped out. That is, the methane, ethane, and propane is taken out.

The bulk of the propane is shipped out as propane, the balance which is mixed with the ethane, we used to ship to Norway, as NGL (natural gas liquids). This was a British Government instruction to reduce unnecessary flaring. The receivers were happy, as they were getting a feedstock at half the price of propane. Plus, it kept us employed.

But the methane? Occidental paid a set amount per barrel of crude oil to Orkney Islands Council. They had also, when they built the terminal, installed a gas turbine generator to run on methane, the intention being to plug this into the Orkney Electricity Grid, and provide *free* power to the islands. It was never utilized. Why?

Because Orkney Islands Council, wanted to be paid a tariff on this as well. Getting paid for something that was free. So, all the methane has gone to flare.

Not only has fuel had to be burnt in their own power station, but fuel has been used shipping the stuff up there for it. One does wonder about some people's logic.

By now, both the *Borthwick* and *Quentin* had been handed back to Unigas, and were both tramping around North West Europe. I had never worked so hard before, or since then. We were everywhere, even carrying some of the *Borthwick*'s cargoes when she was delayed.

One of the ports we went to discharge at was Shellhaven, in the Thames. My ship handling by now was rather good, although I say it myself.

Approaching the jetty, we had just a touch of the ebb tide left, which was handy, as we were going starboard side alongside. About 50 feet and going nicely, in rolls a fog bank. I could barely see the compressor room, far less the bow, but my second mate was an old friend who talked down the distance off. About 10 feet off, I started to straighten her up, and landed very gently forward, then alongside. We backed her into position, and made fast.

When I was clearing the ship in, the second mate was hanging around my door. After the agent left, he said with a smile,

"How do you think you came alongside, Doug?"

"It was okay I thought, why Ian?"

"Because, about 20 tons of concrete fell off the end."

How am I going to explain this?

Just then, the loading master came in, with,

"I remember you. You had a go at a mooring hook last time you were in. Have you seen the end of our jetty now?"

Quick as a flash, I said, "well, what do you expect, there are no lights on your jetty, how am I supposed to judge distance?"

He conceded that I had a point. Seemingly in the October hurricane, a barge had got loose, then got stuck underneath the jetty on a rising tide and had destroyed all the cabling. This time, Shell paid us for our damage.

Just out of curiosity, next morning I had a look at the mooring hook. Sure enough, the black paint from the *Borthwick* was still there on the mooring hook.

There was rather an amusing incident coming out of Antwerp one day, we were bound for Le Havre, with one of the *Borthwick*'s delayed cargoes.

It was a lovely calm day, dead still, clear sky, sunny etc. One of these days that you enjoy.

We came off the berth, slid astern into the channel, and then stopped.

"Eh, pilot, why are we just sitting here?"

"Oh, you are turn No 3 for the lock, we are waiting for the other 2 ships."

I looked around, and there was absolutely *nothing* moving, anywhere.

"Why don't we just take turn No 1, pop her into the lock, we'll tie up, and you can get off home?"

"Okay, I'll check first with Port Control."

So, it was agreed and that was what we did.

You can often spend up to 12 hours in Antwerp locks, waiting for enough ships to fill them up, they are that big. A river pilot boards here to take you down to either Flushing, or to the Waandelar Sea Pilot Station. It's a good service.

After about 2 hours, a small coaster, who was turn no 2, comes in and parks beside, but on the other side of the lock. *Then*, turn No 1 arrives, only now he is turn No 3, a ship called the *Atlantic Cartier*. A massive great big container/RoRo ship. Now I know why he was turn No 1. He is in a hurry to get to Southampton for the tide and his schedule. But we are now in the way.

The lock floods down to river level, and my river pilot comes on board, only he is not MY pilot, he is for the *Atlantic Cartier*, and has come all the way up from Flushing specially for it. My pilot was stuck in a traffic jam in Antwerp.

By this time, though we have slipped our ropes and are heading into the river, which fortunately for us had just started to ebb. So we went flying down the River Scheldt.

Just as I was dropping my pilot off at the Waandelar, the *Atlantic Cartier* came past, going like a bat out of hell, best part of 26 knots +. He came on the VHF to the Pilot Boat with,

"Some b-----d pinched my river pilot, and I'm late, so I'm over-carrying my pilot to Southampton. I don't have time to slow down."

Oops. Was that us perchance?

We had a number of cargoes to collect from Fawley, just down from Southampton, but not like everybody else, who got the easy berths on the river side. Oh no, I have to get the tricky one on the inside. But it was here that my knowledge of anchors came in handy. An anchor is often also referred to as a poor man's tug.

You can dredge them to work your way into an awkward corner, or you can turn on them if there is a tide, and you can also use them to stop in an emergency, although this is not recommended.

You do rather tend to lose them, or set fire to the brakes. Or both. Not good for a gas tanker.

In Fawley, it was the second option, but this is not for the faint hearted, as it all tends to happen rather fast.

The second time I came in, we were going just a little bit too quickly, when I gave the signal to drop the starboard anchor. A toot on the whistle. My old pal was up forward and knew what to do. I then came full astern, the tide caught the ship, and we swung round and straight alongside, bang in position, and tied her up.

There was another ship ahead of us, and their captain came along.

"Do you always do it that way captain?" he asked.

"Oh yes, every time." (You need to lie a bit in this game.)

"Well, that was very impressive, I must try it that way next time I come in. How much anchor cable did you use?"

"Oh, anchor on the bottom, and say 20 feet of cable," nonchalantly.

Next time back, I said to the pilot, "what happened to the end jetty?"

"Oh," he says, "some German captain came in the way you do, but got it all wrong and knocked a fender off. He's away getting his ship repaired now."

Oh, dear, dear, dear. How sad.

I had always reckoned that the *Quentin* was capable of more speed than her customary full ahead speed of 12.5 knots, but my previous chief engineers were rather old and would not, or could not balance the main engine, such that all 12 cylinders were putting out the same power. Now I had a chief engineer who was prepared to try. It took him several weeks, and in the meantime, I was experimenting with the trim, which I always thought was excessive. Some ships prefer a heavy trim 'by the stern', some prefer to 'run by the head,' occasionally, you get a ship that has to be run 'even keel'. So for the *Quentin*, her best setting seemed to be less 'by the stern'.

Towards the end of my time on board, we took over a charter from another Unigas ship, which was going to dry dock. It was to carry propane and butane from Sines in Portugal, to Lisbon. This was hectic, as it is only 4 hours steaming time between ports. Loading was not a problem, as it was done one grade at a time, and it was always from the same berth. However, discharge in Lisbon was at any one of four berths, and very often all four were used. Initially I had instructions for the first five cargoes, which we soon got through. Everyone concerned agreed that the *Quentin* was more efficient than any other ship, particularly as our experiments in bringing up the speed, were now producing results, and loaded, we ran at 14.5 knots, in ballast, 14.9 knots.

Gibson's benefited to the tune of £25,000 per quarter knot over her charter speed of 12.5 knots. For the sixth cargo, I had no written orders, so jokingly suggested that I would take one tank of propane, and one of butane. To my surprise, they agreed, so that is what we did. The orders came through the next day.

On one occasion, after leaving Lisbon, I was anchored in Sines, before the agent in Lisbon got back to his office through the traffic.

Just before heading south to take up this charter, one of the *Quentin*s' generators blew up. These were V10 Mercedes diesels, and really more suited as a truck engine. Generators on gas tankers take an awful pounding, and we roughly got through an engine every 10 months. In this case, a piston had come through the side of the block, so we really needed a complete new engine, which was duly ordered. It's an insurance claim. Routine for us by now.

It arrived in Lisbon, having been flown out from Germany, at 10 o'clock at night, in the back of a truck to a jetty which had no crane. Wonderful. I asked the agent to put it on a tug, or barge, and we would pick it in the river with our own crane. There was no sign of it when we sailed, but as we would be back the following day, weren't overly concerned. We did not know at this stage, that they, the agents had now gone and lost it!

It took them a week to find it, but how they delivered it was spectacular.

My chief engineer, came into my cabin as I was clearing the ship in, in the anchorage with the comment,

"Doug, come and *see* this, and bring your camera."

The engine, which weighs only 800 kg, is suspended from a hook of a floating crane, which can lift 150 tonnes, and is being towed by two tugs. And everyone on board both tugs wants to be Captain. We eventually got it on board. The gesticulations were magic.

About the same time, I had a message from the agents in Sines,

"You have to go to the Police Station when you get back to Lisbon."

"What for?" I asked.

"For *not* reporting in to Lisbon Port Control (LPC) when you sailed last time." I had a vague recollection of this, as I had given up trying when they would not answer.

"Oh, and you have been fined 200 000 Escudos." (About £800)

That was a new one, being fined for *not* doing something.

Next time back, I trot off to the Police Station, with my agent to translate, if need be. It was, plus it was a public holiday, and the only person in for the day was an inspector.

I had to make a statement, to the effect that LPC would not answer, whereupon, the inspector came out with rather a thick book of local byelaws.

The rule he referred to said that, 'if there was no response by VHF, then the ship should hoist signal flags indicating her call sign, or pass her call sign by Aldis Lamp in Morse Code.'

I could only apologize, that I knew nothing of this, and would notify the Admiralty accordingly. I did. It's still in the book we use.

The statement was typed out, and duly signed, my copy of course being in Portuguese. The fine was more of a bond, in case I skipped the country in the meantime, which was very likely, me being in command of a ship.

But it didn't end there.

Next time back, I had a visit from the Portuguese Navy, a fairly high ranking officer, who, when he was in my cabin along with the other officials, came out with.

"My brother works for Lisbon Port Control, and I know you not report in when sailing. If you make trouble for him, then I make plenty for you."

I replied with,

"By the way, this thing on my desk is a voice activated tape recorder, and I have every word on tape. Now get off my ship, and don't come back."

But who is sitting next door with the chief engineer? None other than the Police Inspector.

It transpires that he has managed to type out the entire statement, without including my name, or the ship's name, and would I be good enough to sign a new statement, so that *he* would not get into trouble?

"Only if you tear the first one up first."

It was and the new one duly signed.

After he left, I retrieved all the bits out of the bin, fitted them back together, and sent it with an explanatory letter to the P&I club. The 'fine' was paid back within a week, and I never heard any more about it.

It was the mate who noticed it. The Shore figure was almost exactly the same as the ship's figure, every time. Now, this is unusual.

I had become friendly with one of the loading masters, and asked him about this.

"Oh Doug, it's easy really. All we do is wait until we have the ship's figure, then we go ashore, have a cup of coffee, and think of a number between 2 and 200 (kilograms), then add it on, and call this The Bill of Lading Figure. We never have any problems that way."

I'm not surprised. I wish everyone did it that way!

For the last two loadings, my pal Jim, my chief from before was back. I explained to him that we had a system for signing for the cargo, which on average, was 250 signatures (mine) per grade.

I got a pile of papers from the agent, signed about 30, and then passed them to him, where he would stamp them with the ships stamp, and then pass them onto the agent, who would sort them out. The system had been infallible up till this point.

Off I go then with the first 30 passed over, and as I continued, I heard the familiar 'thump, thump' as the stamp passed between the pad and the document. It's *working*.

A few minutes later the agent said, "excuse me captain, but….."

No stamp.

"Hold on a minute Jim. First of all, you have to open the lid of the stamp pad."

"Aw! I wondered, but I've no got my glasses on see."

Mmm. We came off this charter a few days later, having run through 38 port calls in 21 days, sometimes 3 a day, and headed off for Slagenstangen at our new revised speed of 14.5 knots.

To this day, only I know completely how this was achieved, and it was not 'flogged'.

And, I'm not telling, especially Unigas!

This is the *true* story of what happened on the *Borthwick* on my final voyage with Gibson Liquid Gas. It is not the one told by a certain Tees Harbour Pilot, or the one told to Forth Ports by *Snow White*, an ex-superintendent of Gibsons who had joined Forth Ports plc, when I stopped Piloting on the River Forth.

I'll use nicknames only here, although I would really love to expose them. By the time you read Part 3, you'll understand why I'm a bit fed up with litigation. But I got my own back anyway. How later.

I joined the *Borthwick* on the 9th February 1989 in Carrington, which is in the Manchester Ship Canal. The master I relieved on his previous voyage had had a collision with a dredger coming out of Lexioes, in Northern Portugal, which very nearly sank. Seemingly as well, as I digested the ships history since my last time on board, *Ivor the Engine* had had a collision as well in Le Havre, when a ship coming in, had 'lost' her steering gear, and walloped her up the stern.

The relieved master just couldn't wait to get off, complaining of a 'bad back', so my handover information was minimal.

I knew as soon as we let the ropes go, that there was something seriously wrong with the *Borthwick*.

She was unstable, and one thing that this ship did not lack was stability.

After sounding round, we found nearly 350 tonnes of loose water in No 1 hold. This is where the cargo tank sits. It should be bone dry.

The damage was enormous, after we pumped out *all* the water. A large proportion of the insulation cladding had come off the tank, and scraped away a lot of the insulation.

The insulation is polyurethane foam, 6 inches thick. The cladding is galvanized steel, riveted together forming a shell.

So where did the water come from?

It was as a result of the first collision, when the ship should have been not only inspected, but dry docked as well. She wasn't.

As such I found a 7 foot crack in the collision bulkhead, which had the fore deep tank on the other side of the hold. This tank was pumped out for loaded passages, and filled for ballast ones. So every time it was filled up, it was draining through into the hold. This had been going on for nearly 6 months. I even found in the ballast record book, a reference on six occasions (the monthly check), that there was water in there, but *nobody* had bothered to find out why.

It didn't end there though; the *fore peak* tank also had a hole it, and to rub insult into that, the after peak tank was also open to the sea, the result of the second collision.

This was just the ballast, practically none of the gas plant was working as it should. Even the cargo compressors had the wrong oil in them. Then there was the bridge, one radar out of operation, a huge Earth fault on one of the VHFs, and the Gas Analyser out of commission.

What had they been doing? Very little!

Sailing was delayed until she was properly stable, and we set off for Dover Roads For Orders.

In the meantime, we all set to fixing the gas plant, so that we could at least load. Then we started hauling out all the scrap from the hold.

This was going to be a major repair. Tricky too.

Just as we arrived at Dover, we get orders to head for Stanlow, about 3 miles down the Manchester Ship Canal from where we had started. As the cargo wasn't ready, we were to go to a lay-by berth and wait. Right, we'll weld up the collision bulkhead, and see if we can fix the peak tanks.

No sooner had we finished welding, than it came to lunchtime, and as the chief engineer and myself, still filthy from welding, discussed the afternoon in my cabin than a Bureau Veritas surveyor walked in.

"What are you doing here?" I asked.

"I've come to do your change of registry."

"First I've heard of it." I was captain.

"You are changing from Isle of Man to Hong Kong Registry."

"I'll need to phone the office first," but my superintendent, *Snow White* wasn't in the office, and nobody really knew where he was. I found out an hour later at 13 30 when he walked in as well.

"What's going on *Snow White*?"

"Oh we were going to tell you it would be in the next fortnight, but with this delay in your cargo, we decided to bring it forward." *Liar*.

However, it got worse, as at 1430, in walked a certain *Gonzales* of Denman with the personnel manageress.

He was away 15 minutes later, after his famous phrase.

"Pay off all your British crew by 5 o'clock, your Filipinos will be here at 6 o'clock. You will need to change all of their contracts, as you are getting the *Quentin*'s crew."

"Right, where are my set of articles? (crew agreement, and Official Log Book).

"Oh, we haven't got them yet, just sign them on to your IOM articles."

"Get lost pal, that isn't legal."

And with that he was gone.

Am I worried about *Gonzales* suing me? Not at all, as you'll soon find out why, plus, he has made so many enemies in the Shipping Industry that they will quite happily, 'rub his nose in it'. He's retired now anyway, and not before time I can tell you. Three hours to sign a crew off, close accounts, change registry with a full survey that normally takes 3 days, then engage a new crew who aren't meant to be coming here at all, and nothing to work with. Great.

My first mistake was not walking off there and then, but I tried to maintain a positive attitude, trying to believe that I could make this work.

We set about getting the ship surveyed, but one thing was missing and of vital importance, the Carving Note. This is an official document which gives you permission to change the Port of Registry on the stern, as well as changing all the lifebuoys and lifeboats etc. It would just have to catch up later.

Snow White is meanwhile covering his tracks, as the ballast book went missing. He was also trying to steer the surveyor away from No 1 hold.

During the afternoon, we received orders to shift berth at 06 00 next morning to load for Lisbon.

Wonderful, a complete new crew, of indeterminate quality to shift berth in a canal. It could only get better, but off course, it didn't.

The six British crew left at 5 o'clock, quite happily as they were going to other ships. At least the cook left us a meal.

The surveyor had taken re-survey as a paper exercise and would return next day to complete it.

At 6 o'clock, I went to collect my new crew who arrived in a minibus. What a motley bunch. At this point, I was under the impression that they had just flown in from the Philippines, so settled them into their cabins, with instructions that we would be shifting to load next morning. Let then recover from the flight and so on.

It transpires, that they had been sitting in a hotel in Rotterdam for 2 weeks, waiting to join, but because of visa requirements in the UK, had been waiting for their respective ships to go to Continental ports.

After shifting, and we went extremely slowly, they all trooped up to my cabin with their contracts. Their first question?

"Captain, when are we transferring to the *Quentin*?"

"You aren't, I've to change your contracts to *Borthwick*.'"

They were not happy with this at all, and who could blame them.

The one appointed Cook/Steward came out with,

"Sir, where is my messman?"

"You aren't getting one."

"But Sir, I *must* have a messman."

"Read my lips. You aren't getting one." An AB would help out in the meantime until he was settled in.

"I am very good cook sir, I work in hotel in Manilla, but I need a messman."

Obviously, he cannot lip read. Denholm's excelled themselves next, by sending me a new chief mate, without telling anyone. A certain *Ratters*. Now a Tees Pilot. You will soon find out why he is hated. Not detested. *Hated*!

Now the ship has had a complete change of officers and crew within a week. Thankfully, all the officers were familiar with the ship. I decided to go for breakfast, nothing fancy, just eggs and bacon.

After waiting for nearly an hour, in came my 'breakfast', delivered with a grin.

"Here is your breakfast sir."

I kid you not, I received 'a piece of fillet steak fried in herbs, some cabbage, a potato hash cake, and some cornflakes, *all* on the same plate.' At least, I think that was what it was.

It was disgusting.

It was only after sailing that we discovered that he was a lift boy in a hotel in Manilla, and had never ever been a cook, but thought it looked easy enough. Perhaps it would have been. Ashore. But this is a bucking little gas tanker in a gale in the Bay of Biscay, in winter. The cargo was duly loading at the phenomenal rate of 30 tonnes per hour. It transpired it was a special type of butane, which was being made, and then immediately loaded.

Nobody on board was happy about anything.

"Right mate," says I, "we'll start the crew off with a guided tour of the ship's safety equipment, explaining how it works, etc, then show them the safety videos." We had a lot of safety equipment.

During this, it transpires that the motorman (engine room cleaner, etc) doesn't speak a word of English, or more correctly, doesn't want to.

I decided to pass on lunch, but the chief engineer went.

"How was it John?"

"Oh, it was the meal the British cook left for us, Spaghetti Bolognese, but for some reason, the new cook added some raw eggs."

Meanwhile, the 'cook' was up at me again, still marthering on about having no messman, with a request.

"Sir, I do not have any French fries."

"Yes you do, come, I'll show you."

Opening the vegetable room door and pointing at some paper sacks with "there you are".

"Oh no sir, these are potatoes, I need French fries." Hmm.

"Well, you peel them first, then cut them up in long squares, then put them in hot fat."

I could tell by his bemused look that this was foreign to him.

It went on and on, but then Unigas joined in the fray.

The cargo was desperately need in Lisbon, so we're just to sail with what we had on board.

You've guessed it, No 1 cargo tank hadn't been recalibrated, and so, up came a 40 tonne difference again.

How Gibsons managed this was really quite clever from their point of view. They had changed their superintendents around in the office, but didn't tell the new superintendent of the problem, when I was on the *Melrose*. They just covered it up, and hoped for the best.

I however, am faced with a dilemma. I know that this difference doesn't exist, so if I issue a Letter of Protest, or a Letter of Deadfreight, then it could be conceived that I was committing fraud, and this I will not do.

Tough Unigas, you'll just have to lump it. They weren't pleased. So we sail. Going down the canal, the pilot declined lunch. What did he know that I didn't? Rather a lot actually.

"How was lunch chief?"

"Roast Chicken, not bad after you scraped off the strawberry jam." After clearing the locks we head down The Mersey for sea. Three days at sea, we should be able to sort something out. Nope!

The chief mate came to the bridge, "we've lost a pilot ladder."

It transpires he had told one of the AB's in seaman's jargon, to 'throw' the pilot ladder over the port side. This means secure it on the port side for the pilot going off. The AB took him literally, and threw it *completely* over the side.

The pilot got off, using the spare, and we set off for Lisbon.

"Right mate, we will concentrate on safety training only. We'll start with a fire and boat drill."

It was all explained to them beforehand what to do, and where to go. The alarms were rung, and they all came to the bridge-wing, the muster point. How the motorman managed it, I do not know, but he had his lifejacket on *upside down*. This, is, going, to, take, a, lot, of, patience! We *all* spent the rest of the day on instruction in safety equipment.

But, then I got a weather forecast, *and* it was not a good one.

There was a dumbbell depression building in the Atlantic, and the barometer was falling fast. (This is where one low pressure tries to overtake the previous one, and can, if it swings to the south, lead to high winds, much more than gale force.) We watch them carefully.

The chief engineer came to me with, "have you been in the galley?"

"What is it?"

"You better look."

Not only was there smashed crockery everywhere, but there was a smoking chip pan on the range, and nobody in sight.

Asking the cook to explain turned out to be a waste of time.

"Right chief, pull the fuses after every meal. If we don't, we'll end up with a galley fire."

Then suddenly, the ship blacked out, and as I went to the bridge, the chief ran down below.

On the 'phone after we got going again, the chief explained what had happened.

The motorman had been sent to clean the plates, but didn't like this idea, so set about stripping down the generators cooling water pump, to see how it worked. Unfortunately, it was running at the time. If you think I'm making this up, believe me, I'm not, *it gets worse*.

The weather meantime has deteriorated to the extent that I have to make a choice, either to run for shelter, or press on. The second low *had* swung to the south. The *Borthwick* isn't good on her anchors, and as we were still making 10 knots, and every hour was getting us further away from the low, decided to press on. Later it transpired that this was the correct decision. (The ships sheltering in Mounts Bay, off Penzance, took quite a battering.)

But for one other thing. *All* the new crew suffer from seasickness, and boy, did they suffer.

By this time we were in the Bay of Biscay, and although it was February, wasn't too bad really. The wind and sea were on our starboard quarter.

Then the chief came to the bridge,

"We've flooded out the steering gear compartment."

"How? we've secured for heavy weather."

"The 'crew' have opened the hatch leading on to the poop deck."

I went down, and asked why. All I got were blank stares.

Then it was hammered shut, with instructions, *do not* open it.

The steering gear was pumped out, only for it to happen again, worse this time, we nearly lost one of the steering motors. The hatch was open.

The bosun volunteered with "we need air."

This time it was 'dogged' really hard shut.

Needless to say, with the ABs also suffering from seasickness, the lookouts were the engineers.

There was however one rather humorous moment, but I only found out about this much later, after I had left.

One of the 'ABs' eventually struggled up to the bridge and said to the mate.

"Sir, is it always as bad as this?"

"Oh no" says the mate, *Ratters*, "it is usually far worse."

To cut a long story short, the cook managed at the fifth attempt to actually set fire to the galley. He was fired and told that he was leaving in Lisbon.

The poop deck hatch was open again.

This was getting serious. "Who opened it?"

No response, right, "you are all leaving in Lisbon."

If it had been possible with the weather, I would have diverted the ship and put them all ashore, but no deviation ports were open.

This time, the hatch was welded shut, plus the engine room door, to the steering flat, and the officers were doubled up until Lisbon. I, and no-one other, trusted what they might do next. We duly arrived in moderating weather in Lisbon, after I had 'phoned Denman for a complete new crew, seamen this time, as I had discovered that five of the six had not actually been to sea before.

They had 'bought' their qualifications just before leaving Manilla. Only the bosun had been to sea, and that was on a 40 000 ton bulk carrier.

Not ideal on a 1600 ton gas tanker in the North Sea in winter time.

Did I get a new crew? Do pigs fly?!

What I got, was *Snow White*, and *Gonzales* (tosspot).

He broke convention by not coming to the master first, but went to see his *crew*, who gave him a load of complaints, then he came to see me. By this time we had berthed at an island offshore.

I will never forget his opening remarks,

"*You* do not have the right to sack the crew for anything, as it is too expensive to fly them back to the Philippines." What I did not know at the time, was that, *he had told the crew as well*!

It was at this point that I decided enough was enough. I still had no crew agreement, or Official Log Book, but he tried to fob me off with some sarcastic remarks. He was told to get off the ship immediately, and never to come back. In none too pleasant a tone. If we had been alongside, I would have been on the first 'plane home. But there was more to come. After discharging, we awaited the tide for sailing, when at 06 45 in the morning, there was a bang, a rumble, an even bigger bang, the ship shook, all the lights went out, and the fire alarms went off.

A generator, a Dorman V8 had exploded, with an engine room fire.

The engineers put the fire out. There wasn't enough left of the engine to dismantle, it was just swept up into buckets. The governor linkage had broken, and the engine went to overspeed.

But *where were the crew*?

In bed of course!

I asked them all, "Did you hear the fire alarms go off?"

"Yes captain, but 'Captain' *Gonzales* says you cannot sack us for anything, so we stayed in our beds."

To say I was stunned is a gross understatement. Even writing this today, I find difficult to comprehend that anyone could be so stupid.

But there was more to come from *Gonzales*, only it came out a long time later. I totally refuse to this day to address him as Captain, or Mr.

I eventually sailed from Lisbon, heading for Teesport.

Every one of the officers had their heads down. Stunned.

. Going across the Bay of Biscay, the 'crew', were washing down on top of the compressor room. We had long since given up on safety training, we'll just shut everything down after we use it.

The mate however goes off to liquid free the cargo tanks, opens the manifold to blow it away, when unfortunately, the French Concorde goes over the top. There was the double bang, from the sonic boom, which scared the life out of the crew. It took hours to get them out of their cabins, but then, they refused to go on deck.

I tried to get a 'phone call out using the MF/HF radio equipment, to advise Denmans that I was going no further than the Tees. No sooner had I raised Schevingen Radio, than both sets of batteries went down. Brilliant, now no long range communications. From the second collision, the after mast had also been bent to the extent that the aerial was now earthing up against the funnel.

Going up the English Channel, I did however get a call out to Unigas, by VHF, concerning one of their ships showing incorrect navigation lights. One of the 'Happy' boats who are anything but.

Also by VHF, I had a chat with *Blunderman*, who informed me, that not only had the *Quentin* got the *Borthwick*'s crew and vice versa, *but* the *Heriot* had the *Melrose*'s crew and vice versa. To all intents and purposes, they were all pretty useless. No-one was happy.

Going up the coast off Cromer, we had managed to get the crew back on deck. Unfortunately, an RAF Tornado had just gone supersonic when it went over us. A double bang again, and an almighty roar. We never saw the crew on deck again.

My final 'phone call to Denman went like this.

"Good morning June, captain of the *Borthwick*." I had no gripes with her, she was just the one caught in the middle. She was actually a very pleasant person.

"Good morning Captain."

"We will be in Teesport tomorrow morning about 01 00. You will need to get another Captain, as this one is going no further."

"Oh dear, would you like to speak to Bob (*Gonzales*)?"

"I will never speak to that idiot again." And hung up. I was rather angry, and at times like these, it is better not to say too much.

We berthed on arrival, my last radar, on its last legs, my last VHF had given up, and all I had left to communicate with was the cellphone. No longer in the bridge toilet though. In a useful place.

I put her alongside, and went to clear the ship in.

The Customs officers, who I knew, were astonished by what they found, and fortunately gave me their full support. They could not believe that this was a Gibsons ship. I then had to shift the ship to another jetty, which I did. I packed my suitcase, and went home.

I was to be used as the Scapegoat. This was the second time. I went, a few weeks later, to see *Old Baldy* in Leith. *Gonzales* had tried a few times to call me at home, but was totally ignored.

I resigned shortly after. I never regretted it.

As a result of this, the *Borthwick* went to dry dock a few weeks after I left, and was in for a month. It should have been in 6 months before this. But that is *Snow White* for you. Tosspot No 2.

The Filipino crew from the *Borthwick*, were sent home. From the other ships, the rest soon followed.

The contract between Gibsons and Denholms was torn up, and Gibsons set up Fort Shipping in Rotterdam, run by one their surviving masters. *Gonzales* very nearly lost his job. Not a single officer elected to stay with Denholms. Do you wonder why? But evil minds were at work, *Ratters*, *Snow White*, and *Gonzales* changing the story round to suit themselves.

A very stupid thing to do, as you will find out later. Gibsons continued with their desire to get to the bottom of the sewer, achieving this 2 years later, before they were bought out by a Swedish company. To this day, the company still exists, but I should point out, that it is only the name that is the same. The current Gibson Gas Tankers is not connected in any way with the one I left in 1989.

PART 2

You will all be familiar with the saying, if you can't beat 'em, join 'em. Well, after all the hassle that I had with the 'pilots' in Scapa Flow, I decided to apply to join the Forth Pilots, was interviewed, and placed on the waiting list, exactly where, I found out only later.

Very interesting too. After resigning from Denman, I went job hunting, and found myself a position with VShips Norway, after an interview in Oslo. As *Master*. Of an NGC (Norwegian Gas Carriers) ship, Unigas' competition.

The company was only set up from the 1st of May 1989, and I was their first appointed master.

Following the interview, I was taken out for dinner by the managing director and a gentleman who was to be my superintendent. I say gentleman, as not many associated with ships are, but Einar was the exact opposite of *Snow White*. This guy actually knew what he was doing, and honesty, the best way, was to the fore. The MD, you'll also hear about later, but he was a truly absolute gentleman as well.

I kept this tale in reserve, in the hope that I could remind the MD of it sometime, but an occasion never arose. So here it is Eric.

We went to this rather pleasant Chinese restaurant in the centre of Oslo, just off Kirkevien, if you want to go there. That's if it is still there of course. It might have changed since 1989 perhaps.

The menu was in Norwegian and English, and I can honestly tell you that 'chop suey' is spelt exactly the same in both languages.

Eric, the MD suggested that we each order something, and then place it in the middle of the table, and we all sample each others. Fine idea, but. Who can't read? The meal was ordered by numbers.

The table warmers arrived, extra cutlery arrived, two plates arrive one for me, one for Einar, but none for the MD.

Curious.

Then the food starts to arrive, and it looked delicious, but the MD still had no plate, until a sizzling noise was heard. The MD, by mistake off course, had ordered number 11 (I remembered the number just in case an opportunity arose to 'embarrass' him later).

He got a 'T bone steak.'

His face was almost the same colour as Tufty's, and was so apologetic.

It did however break the ice, and we all got on famously.

I flew back next day, and got ready for my next command.

But first, I had obtain a Norwegian Master's Certification. This did not prove as difficult as I first thought.

In Oslo, I was given three tomes of rules and regulations pertaining to ships under the NIS flag. This is the Norwegian Offshore Register. Rather like the IOM to the UK.

These books were about 5 cms thick, and every paragraph started off with the words, "The King decrees that ..."

There were hundreds of paragraphs. He must have been a very busy King. I was also told that I *may* be questioned on this when I went to the Norwegian Consulate in Edinburgh. I ploughed my way through them, and trotted off to Edinburgh, armed with all sorts of forms, and certificates for my CRA, (Certificate of Receipt of Application). The only question I was asked was,

"do you take sugar in your coffee?"

Ho hum. Well, at least I knew their rules.

The CRA covers you until the qualification document comes through, backed up off course by my British Class 1 Masters, about 3 months later.

I flew out to join the *San Francisco*, soon to be re-named *Norgas Challenger* in Houston, Texas, USA. *Talk about out of the frying pan and into the fire!*

Whoever dreamed up calling this Norgas ship *Challenger* had a good sense of humour. This was some challenge.

Therapeutic. Yes.

The *San Francisco* was 5 years old, and owned by Ivarans of Oslo. She was known within that company as the 'party' ship. To be fair to them, they were a container ship/cargo/passenger company, and were at a loss with their one gas tanker.

She was built at Kleven in Norway, and started off for her first year with an all Norwegian crew. She was very well built, but looked a bit lop-sided, as her funnel on the port side, was to all intents and purposes, a funnel. On the starboard side though was only half a funnel. It stopped short, just level with the top of the accommodation block. It was after all, just the inlets for the fans to the engine room. A shame really, as she was a smart ship in all other respects. I did actually consider extending it with a dummy, but had no time.

The only company that comes close to building ships to this standard is Bergesen, which incidentally is also a Norwegian company. You'll hear more about them in Part 5. More eye-openers I can assure you.

After a year the *San Francisco* changed to an all Filipino crew for the next 3 years, and then they went back to a Norwegian master and gas engineer, with Filipino officers and crew, to try to bring her back up to standard. They failed miserably. I was supposed to get a 7 day handover, but the master I was relieving was not pleased at losing his job, so banned not only myself, but my British Chief Engineer, and German Chief Officer from doing or seeing anything.

Fortunately, my chief engineer, was as switched on as much as I was, and we did see an awful lot. It wasn't good.

From Houston, we went to Port Arthur, where I was to take over. We anchored offshore for a day or so before this, and I was intrigued by the chief officer (Filipino), who was leaving, when he went to bring in the anchor. I know a lot about anchors, but this was a new one on me. When an anchor clears the waterline, it is then brought up as far as it will go, into the hawse pipe, and then, with power still on the winch, the brake is pulled up tight, then the winch disengaged, before the chains are put on (if seaward bound), and tightened. Not so in this case.

Oh the anchor was pulled up to its limit in the hawse pipe okay, but then, he put some slack back in the cable(chain), then put the brake on, then after disengaging the winch, put the chains on, but left them slack.

"Why?" I asked.

"Oh sir, you see, the stock on the anchor is bent and it jams in the hawse pipe." The stock is 9 inches square, and it's bent?

"If I leave some slack, and leave the chains slack, then a sea will come along, and knock it free. Then it is ready for dropping next port."

"Yes, but the next port might be 10 000 miles away!"

"It will still be ready for dropping sir."

That's if it's still there. (Anchors have been lost this way.)

I could see that I was going to have to wary of some of their logic.

How right I was to be wary.

We also had an underwater survey done, and filmed on a video camera. Particular attention was paid to where she incurred damage. How she incurred this damage will be explained in full later, when we get her down to South America. Watching the video afterwards I can assure you, is a lot less exciting than watching paint dry. The chief engineer fell asleep!

The plan was, that when I took over, the remaining officers and crew would stay for a period of 3 months, for evaluation. VShips were going to need crews for other ships in the future. Then I had the option of replacing all ranks with Indian Officers and Crew, or sticking with Filipino's. Nice plan, but it didn't quite work out that way, as in, not at all.

Totally without warning, four Indians showed up, two were Third Engineers, 1 was an Electrician, the other, an AB.

The Electrician was a Sikh, one of the Thirds was Hindu, the other Catholic, and the AB was Moslem. The Filipinos were all Catholic. Bearing in mind that the Chief Officer is German, and the Chief and myself British. The gas engineer was Norwegian, with eyes that looked like 'Cyclops', and a terrible penchance for anything alcoholic. We are going to have fun getting this to work.

Eventually, the day came when I took over, *but*, the ship had been delayed *not*, as the charterers suspected, to allow the sale to go through, but due to the ineptitude of the Norwegian master. The ship was to sail to Coatzacoalcos, in Mexico to load ethylene for Stade in Germany. A trot for us across the pond (Atlantic) to find out what we needed to store in NW Europe, before heading to South America. That was the intention.

To load ethylene, we had to get the dewpoint in the cargo tanks down to –45 degrees Celsius. Not a big problem, we just keep purging dry nitrogen through, until we have removed all the moisture. But the Norwegian master had insisted in 'drying' the tanks with air first, by heating the air in the compressors. It may be hot, but it is also wet, very very wet, almost 95% humidity wet. Effectively, you are pumping water in. It totally defeats the object of drying the tanks. We are going to need an awful lot of nitrogen to 'undo' his 'good work'. It should be possible to purge this ship with 5 volumes, say 34 000 cubic metres of nitrogen. In the end, it took 168 000 cubic metres, just to get to –40 degrees Celsius, and the charterers were not pleased. That was a great start for me, but by 4 months, I had reversed that.

We had to go ashore in Port Arthur and buy some batteries. Believe me, this is far easier than ordering anything through a chandler, especially in the US of A.

We ended up in a Tandy store. I can never fathom out why they need your name and address, when it comes time to pay for anything with this group, but it did provide a laugh. Einar gave his address in Norway. Anyone who knows anything about America will immediately realize that a Norwegian address will not fit onto a computer set up for American addresses. Just so, here.

He lived in a town called Moss. It's a bonny wee corner of Norway, not far from the Swedish border in the south of the country.

"Oh," says the girl behind the counter, "Moss, Norway, do you have a zip code?"

"Yes," I said "about six inches and vertical. Holds the trousers up real well." I needn't have bothered, but she had another go.

"Norway, is that near New Orleans?"

"Sort off," says Einar with a strange look on his face. "You head for New Orleans and then keep going for another 6000 miles."

I don't think this girl was ready for the level 1 IQ test just yet.

What do they teach kids at school in America?

So, stored up, purged, and cleared, we set off for Mexico, with my little 'League of Nations'. We didn't see Mexico, until 6 weeks later. Yes, I know it is only a 2-day passage, but we had a little hiccup on the way. Just as I left my cabin next morning, bound for the bridge, before breakfast, there came from below, a noise that sounded like grrr! Then the engine slowed down and stopped. No fire alarms, so we'll see what my new chief comes up with.

We start drifting with the ship NUC (Not under command). It was actually, a very pleasant period of weather in the Gulf of Mexico.

After about an hour, he 'phoned me. It was not good news. There was white metal in the crankcase of the main engine. It was traced to No 7 bottom end bearing which had failed, plus there were scratches on the crankshaft. This is not just bad news, this is terrible news!

After 2 days of polishing the crankshaft by hand, we had come to the conclusion, that the crankshaft would need specialist engineers to fix it, as a set of bearings failed after 1 minutes running time.

During this time, I had been in touch with the office in Oslo. They were extremely supportive. What a change from working with Gibsons. In Oslo, they were professionals. It went like this by telex.

"Could you get the ship into a port Captain, or do you require a tug?" I'd been towed in on the *Borthwick*, so didn't fancy it again.

"My chief reckons that if we take out the running gear on No 7 unit, and blank off the lube oil ports, we should be able to run the engine, but we do not know what the vibration will be like."

"What is your nearest port?"

"Corpus Christi in Texas, we'll try for there."

"Let us know when you are under way again."

So, the unit was blanked off and the engine started. It was a Wartsila Vasa 46, medium speed diesel, which ran at 760 rpm. By jiggling the pitch with revs, we found a setting for minimum vibration, and ended up doing 10 knots. I say minimum vibration, in truth, it was terrible, but we *were* moving. The only downside, was that I could only use about 3 degrees of rudder, before the bridge started shaking itself to bits.

For port entry, I was going to have to steer with tugs, but not as you would suppose, one at each end, no, there is a better way of doing it.

One on each bow, at the shoulder.

VShips had worked through the night, setting up for our Port of Refuge, in Corpus Christi. Fortunately, we were under nitrogen, and weren't gassed up with LPG.

I took my pilot well out to sea, and explained the problem to him. He had never steered a ship with tugs like this, nor had I, but I read it in a book somewhere, probably at college in the library. It worked a treat. All the way to Cargo dock No 12 without a glitch. "I'm afraid pilot," as we got towards the port, "but your only engine movement is *stop*." "No problem Cap," and it wasn't.

So, safely tied up and relieved, we set about finding out just what *is* wrong with the main engine. It took a day, but the synopsis is not good.

We had only gone and *bent* the crankshaft on the main engine. To repair it, we need a new crankshaft. This is a *big* job, taking perhaps a month. Not a good start to a new job, but, as things worked out, was really a blessing in disguise.

I had, the time we were drifting compiled a list of everything else that needed fixing as well. It was a formidable list. I also discovered that we had 'Off-hire Insurance'. That will come in handy.

Under US laws, General Average has to be declared by the master. In practical terms, although he does it, it is really the owners that do it.

Fortunately, or perhaps unfortunately, this was going to be an insurance claim, and as you can't have both, GA was not declared. Saves me some paperwork perhaps? You should know by now that I don't get off that lightly.

But first things first, we need better communications with the Office in Oslo, and the Charterers, in both Oslo and Buenos Aires.

What we had on board at this time was only telex. A mobile 'phone supplied by the agents, was so complicated, that we gave that a miss. This left a 'phone box at the bottom of the gangway, but every time a truck passed you had to stop talking.

I had the agents get in touch with the 'phone company, and arrange to get two telephone lines run in. This was the start of many trying days, dealing with American companies. How they ever got a man on the moon, goodness only knows.

Waiting time for two lines, 1 month. I am not one to mess around, so, "Richard," he was the agent, "get in touch with South Western Bell, (the 'phone company), and tell them that if I don't have two lines run in by tomorrow at the latest, then I will take a hacksaw to the 'phone box pole, and run it in myself to my office."

"Are you joking Cap?" He was even slower than *Old Baldy*.

"Try me, but I want two lines in here tomorrow. Just do it."

Next day, we had two lines in.

"Okay, where is the handset?" I had a bare end of cable.

"Oh, that's A T & T," said the fitter who installed the 'phone lines, "we're SW Bell, *we* only do lines."

I went to a supermarket and bought two handsets. It was quicker.

If we were going to be in for a month, garbage was going to be a problem. MARPOL 3 had just been introduced. MARPOL is short for Marine Pollution, in effect, we don't chuck anything over the side anymore, it is all landed to skips, provided by the ports, and disposed of in landfill sites. Well, in Europe, and every other sensible country it is. But this is the US of A. So, I invited the harbour master and Port Director down to lunch, and discussed the problem.

"No problem Cap, we had a British ship in here recently, and shipped their garbage down to the Naval base for boiling."

'Boiling?'

"Oh yes, under state law, it has to be *boiled* to sterilize it." This was the start of a long battle. However, the British ship, happened to be an RN ship, but as we were merchant, the naval base would not do it for us, but the two invited to lunch when they found this out, didn't tell me for a week. By then, it was a problem.

It is the things that you do at the start of a major repair afloat, that saves oodles of time later, allowing you to concentrate on hiccups as they come along. And they will come along. Often!

I hired a car. Why? If you have ever tried to get a taxi in Corpus Christi, or have been in one, you would soon realize why.

Then set off to the US Coast Guard offices to arrange for the necessary permits for us to get the repair under way. This is a lot quicker than getting the agent to do it.

Dealing with the US Coast Guard is never easy at the best of times, and most gas tanker captains dread having to deal with them, they can be so dogmatic, but not so, as I found in Corpus Christi.

They were quite pleasantly human. Their boss however, a certain Lt. Cmdr Doug Cameron, became a close personal friend, but then, with a name like that, and a Scots Captain what else can you expect?

In the meantime, Wartsila engineers are arriving, as was my own superintendent. Poor man had only just flown back from Port Arthur to Oslo, when he had to about turn, and come back to Corpus Christi.

The chief and I set off for the airport to meet him, and it was here that we started to realize that driving in the USA is far from easy. Interstate Highway 37, according to the signs, runs North/South, but in Corpus Christi, it runs East/West. Confused? We were, and duly got lost. By the end of our time here, we all had intimate knowledge of almost every back street, and parking lot in the place. It must confuse the locals as well though, as every junction has a roundabout, or circles as they call them to get you going the right way. After the intelligence of one certain female in Port Arthur, 'roundabouts' must be too difficult for them to spell.

Planning a major job like this is a must, not only in logistics from the outside, which I would take care of, but internally as well.

To get the old 'bent' crankshaft out of the ship, and the new one in, we are going to have to cut a hole in the hull.

The crankshaft is 7 metres long, and weighs 5 tonnes. We cannot take it out the top of the engine room, as all the accommodation is in the way. There are no skylights, as most ships have. We are going to have to cut a hole. But before we do, the inert gas generator, and the oil/water separator have to be removed. They were in the way of where the hole would be.

Anyone who has ever dismantled a car engine will appreciate that you get an awful lot of bits. This engine is a 9 cylinder medium speed diesel, only this time, most of the bits are too heavy to pick up, so we had to install a few extra hoists. You don't just get a 'lot' of bits, you get bits that range from a nut, up to an entablature weighing 25 tons.

You daren't lose any. I was for once glad that the *sloe-eyed Mancunian* wasn't here. One of his tricks was to add a few extra bits in, when his own engineers had dismantled something, like pistons for example when a generator was stripped down.

The temperature, each day, didn't help. Even with all the fans going full speed, it got up to 60 degrees Celsius, or as the yanks say, 140 degrees Fahrenheit. Dehydration of people was a concern until we discovered 'Gatorade'. By the end of the repair, we had got through 160 cases of it. This is brilliant stuff. I just wish I knew where to buy it in the UK.

Everyone, with the exception of the three deck officers was working down below. They were starting on my list, such as getting the lifeboats freed-up. The port one was seized solid and took 3 days to get it to run. We couldn't test it in Port Arthur, as it was not allowed by the port authorities, but we were *assured* that it had been tested recently. It did not take us long to discover that most records were either falsified, or didn't exist. So, we'll just overhaul everything, and start new records.

My German Chief Officer, however was rather 'Teutonic' in his approach. This may work with other Germans, but it most certainly does not work with Filipinos, and he was taken aside and advised accordingly. He didn't listen, and the two junior officers duly 'lost face'.

Losing 'face' is not really understood by Europeans, but it is a serious matter to those from the Orient. It is only a matter of understanding how they work, that you can get round it.

If for example, something is 'dirty', you do not say, "that is dirty, clean it," but rather, you would say "I do not believe that (whatever) is as clean today, as it was yesterday." And smile. It takes no great effort.

This was too much for my chief officer, but he had to try. He didn't try hard enough though.

My galley crew, cook, and two messmen (not like in Gibsons) were superb. Any top restaurant in London, would have been glad to employ them. We really need this though as there were a lot of extra people to feed. Some days you may not have known what it was, but it was *always* good.

One day, I walked into the galley and asked what was for dinner that night. The reply I got was,

"Oh this (pointing at a pot on the range), this, (pointing at another pot), and that (pointing to a tray on a worktop)."

"Yes Crispin, but what is it called?"

"I dunno." At least he was honest.

It is important during this period, that people do not 'burn out', so although everyone worked hard, there was time to relax as well. With Filipinos, it does not take them long to find out where to go to find some fun. Fortunately, they took the Indians as well.

For my part, I had to report our progress back to Oslo every night. With the time difference, they had full reports each morning, and there was an overlap period in our morning when we were in touch by 'phone. Putting in 'phone lines was more than worth it. The bill at the end came to just over $3000. (For a month!)

The superintendent, stayed in a lovely hotel, just along the road, so we, the chief and myself, would spend an hour or two relaxing in the later evening with him. We started playing a wee game.

Texans are some of the nicest people you will meet anywhere, but they do have one drawback, they are *slow*, oh, are they *slow*.

'Taking the piss', is such a fundamental part of the British way of life, that it happens anyway. But with Texans, it becomes a wholly different ball game, as they don't think that anyone can be better than them. Facing us across the bar top in the hotel restaurant is a formidable array of just about every type of cocktail mixer you have ever seen. So, we'll see how many we can sample, without paying for them. 43, before the barman latched on. Not all in one night mind you, it was 14 nights in all, before he twigged. But, oh, did he get his revenge.

Out came a bottle of 'Everclear'. One sniff, told me this was something to steer well clear off. The chief agreed, but the superintendent is Norwegian, and tries it.

You could visibly see the colour drain out of his face, as he swallowed, followed with Wow!!eeee.

I had a close look at the bottle, on the label it had,

"It is dangerous to smoke near an open bottle."

A closer look revealed.

"At least 196 degrees proof." 98% pure alcohol, or more correctly, ethanol. You could run a racing car on this stuff.

I was glad I never tried it, as my friend could hardly speak for about 10 minutes. So, that was the end of that little bit of sport.

As we were in most nights we met quite a few people, so had left them with an open invitation, to 'stop by anytime you're passing and have a look round.' Most people have never been on board a ship. One particular Saturday, this couple did. After they had a look around the ship, and were duly impressed, I took them in for a late lunch.

Did you know that Americans don't know how to use a knife and fork at the same time? They cut everything up first, and then eat with the fork. It's amazing.

But not half as amazing as the comment the woman came out with.

"Gee Captain, this is the most delicious piece of chicken that I've ever had!' In that drawl they all have.

I couldn't help but respond with.

"That's very interesting, considering that it started of life as a duck!"

The new crankshaft was flown in from Finland. With my previous experience in Lisbon, I rather knew that it would arrive on a flatbed truck, with no crane to get it off. I had to arrange for a crane to come when the truck arrives. However, we might as well get our money's worth out of this crane when it is here.

The charterers, NGC, decide to fit the ship with satellite communications, and have ordered an Inmarsat A system. There is a whole rigmarole of paperwork that has to be done first, including getting approval of where to sight the radome. Rather like planning permission for a house, but the marine variety, which is 100 times more complicated that it needs to be. A 'radome' is the bit that looks like a sagging golf ball, and contains the antennae, which is gyro stabilized. When the ship is moving at sea, pitching or rolling or both, then the gyros compensate for this keeping the antennae pointing at the satellite. It automatically compensates for a change in latitude or longitude. Clever bit of kit really.

The radome sits on a mounting plate, which is built onto a mast. The radome itself, is not overly heavy, all up, about 100 kgs. But the mast should be stiff enough, not to vibrate, or wobble.

This was explained to a company engaged to assist with tools etc, who were appointed to assist with the main engine. The company were known as Coastal Iron.

We didn't know it at the time, but apart from being the only engineering company in Corpus Christi, they were also the worst in the United States. And that is saying something!

The ship, being built in Norway, is fully *metric*. Texas, is fully *imperial*, and nothing fits each other.

The drawing for the radome mounting plate, had its dimensions in millimeters, was photocopied, and passed to Coastal Iron. The remark I got was.

"Gee Captain, this is gonna be a big bit of steel!"

"No, hold on a minute, that's millimeters, not inches."

"What are they?"

I thought that he was having me on.

"Divide everything by 25.4."

Rather than take a chance, I did it for him.

"Now, I want it 2 metres high. Okay?"

Not okay, when it came down next day, the mounting plate was perfect, but the mast was only 2 feet high. It looked absolutely ridiculous. *2 metres* seemingly doesn't divide too well by 25.4.

It went off to be modified, and came back in time to coincide with the crane. It was just as well, as they had used 1 inch thick pipe (25 mms), and even with three of us, we couldn't pick it up. It went up to the deck behind the bridge on a 50 ton crane. It was so heavy, it was almost an insult then to weld it down. When that ship goes to the breakers, then that mast will be re-usable.

When the crankshaft was safely landed, we also used the crane to change the port anchor. Anyone, who has ever tried to fit a ships spare anchor, anywhere other than in dry dock, will know why a crane is a godsend. But sod's law came with us, as the top shackle on the spare is seized. Four bottles of acetylene later, it was free, and duly fitted. The one coming off, was kept as a spare, but as it was bent, and I do not know to this day, how anyone other than that crew could have bent the stock, but they did.

As bad as Coastal Iron were, there was another company that we used to get rid of the engine room bilges. This was an independent guy by the name of Pierre. He couldn't do enough for us.

When the cooling water is drained from the engine, it drops to the bilges, but in order not to cross the US Coastguard (you've got to keep them on your side), we had it disposed off properly ashore. Costs a bit, but really worth it. The costs all go down to Insurance.

One of the couples we met ashore, invited the chief, my superintendent and myself to a mid summer celebrations party, 'up state' as they say.

Being in command of a Scandinavian ship, rather pressurised me into going. Mid summer is celebrated, as we would celebrate the 5th of November. It was very pleasant, apart from there being an ulterior motive.

This was also the pre-opening celebration for the new Seamen's Centre in Corpus Christi, to which we all were invited to attend next day.

However.

Next day, was a Sunday, and we're all having a quiet day, as we await some tools coming in from Finland.

I was sitting in my office after lunch, tidying up some paperwork, when all of a sudden, in bursts the mission padre, with,

"you have to come quick, we are opening the new Seamen's Centre, and we don't have any seamen!"

The chief and superintendent legged it, and hid, leaving me 'holding the baby' so to speak.

I had completely forgotten about it.

"Okay, I'll throw on a clean shirt and be right with you," grabbing the car keys as I went.

Now, I thought that all I would have to do, would be stand at the back, and at most, give a wee wave.

Nope! I don't have that easy a life as you may have gathered.

When I arrived and got out of the car, my heart sank to my boots.

There was a crowd of at least 10 000, four sets of TV crews, and umpteen reporters.

Sneaking onto the back of the crowd, I kept my head down.

Not far enough though.

I was summoned with,

"we are delighted to have Captain Doug Harvey with us, the captain of one of the ships in port just now (that was a bit strong, we were the only ship in port just now), would you just like to come up and say a few words Captain?" No.

But then every head turned to look, and there was nowhere to run to.

Now, I don't like speaking in public at the best of times, and this was not one of those times, but there is nothing else for it, I have to. I had nothing prepared, so it all came off the top of my head and went something like this. After a few big gulps.

"Thank-you sir, for the opportunity to speak with you all, today. It is of great comfort to us at sea, to know that there are facilities like this for us to relax in when time permits when we are in port." (Utter bull I know). Then I had a flash of inspiration.

"There is a saying in Scotland, where I come from; it is 'Cued mil Failte', which is Gaelic, and means, a hundred thousand welcomes and that is what we receive from seamen's centres around the world, and so, on behalf of seamen everywhere, I thank you." Rapturous applause and cheering as I stood back, mouth dead dry, and in need of refreshment. Of the beer variety preferred.

The tape was cut, and in we all went. I was looking to escape, but I was cornered, by the newspapers, and had to give yet another story, and how do you spell 'Cued mil Failte'. Even now, I still don't know how to spell it, or even pronounce it properly. I eventually escaped, and went back to the ship in search of my 'friends', who thought escaping was hilarious. I'll fix them later.

Later that night, I was again in my office preparing the report when the crew burst in.

"Captain, you're on television, on the news!"

Oh no! Why me?

Later in the hotel, having shaken just about everybody's hand, with my new found 'celebrity' status, my superintendent said quietly,

"I didn't know you spoke Gaelic."

"I don't."

"Well, how do you know that much?"

"Easy, it used to be written above the ticket office in Edinburgh Station, but don't you dare let on." For days afterwards, I daren't venture ashore.

I also got my own back on my two escapees, as we elected to have dinner in the hotel. This is really sad when you consider the combined intelligence and qualification levels of us three.

We change tables after every course. You can only do this with waitresses who have a good sense of humour, which fortunately they did. They knew us after all.

It got out of hand though, when the Americans started doing it as well. It was all change every 10 minutes or so.

The waitresses would come out from the kitchen, laden with food, arrive at a table to find a set of completely different people sitting there, and then say, somewhat exasperated. "Where have they gone this time?"

By the end of the night, the waitresses were so confused they didn't know where they were. My two companions decided they were not going for a meal with me *ever* again, as embarrassment took on new meaning. Serves you right for deserting me in my hour of need.

The waitresses got a decent tip from everyone. Then we all celebrated with champagne. All of us, the Americans too.

The things you do for a laugh eh!

Now during all this time, we are accumulating garbage, and it is getting rather smelly, as in, more than just a bit.

The port are obviously not going to comply with International Law, so I put the Norwegian Consulate in Houston onto the problem. It was, after all, a Norwegian ship, but then, I could always call on the British Consulate, the German Consulate, the Indian Consulate, and the Philippines Consulate, as being their representatives of my crew. My little League of Nations.

It didn't take him long to find out that while every other country in the world is complying with MARPOL 3, the USA, has an exemption till August.

They are signatories, but don't yet have to comply. Interesting.

We still have to comply, however, with state law.

Enter, the Department of Agriculture.

For a ship?

Seemingly, we can buy foodstuffs, and export it, ie take it with us, but, we cannot land any garbage to shore, unless it has been out of the country for more than 2 years. With the correct paperwork of course. And who ever thought of keeping track of that? Even empty tin cans (from Gatorade) cannot be landed without being sterilized.

"Right, where is your plant so we can get it sterilized?"

"We haven't built it yet." (Hence the dispensation till August.)

"How about a mobile rig?"

"If you can get one, Captain, then it will have to be supplied with steam.' It has to be boiled for 30 minutes.

It was seemingly, quite okay to sterilize it on the quayside, before trucking it off to the dump.

Oh, I got two in fact, took a bit of doing, and it came in from Mississippi, along with a 'mobile steam generating station' or for British readers, a boiler.

"Sorry Captain." Dept of Agriculture, "Your steaming rig won't do."

"Why? pray tell?"

"It's the wrong type of steam."

"You're taking the mickey!"

"No, that puts out wet steam, you need dry steam."

And I am not joking either.

Now where am I going to find a source of dry steam?

"The oil refinery!" And I just happened to have met the chief chemist at the Seamen's Centre.

Would he oblige?

"No problem Captain, we have all the steam you need."

So two containers complete with steam injection rigs, and 2 cubic yards of extremely smelly garbage were loaded onto flat bed trucks, and taken to the refinery.

Most masters would have given up by now, but whenever someone tells me that something cannot be done, I just dig in my heels and come up with a way of doing it. It's a sort of game.

The area we were allocated was away from the main refinery, which was very fortunate.

The steam was connected, the containers filled with water, and lime, (Dept of Agriculture reckoned lime was a good sterilizing agent, and who am I to argue), and off we went, bringing this concoction up to 100 degrees Celsius, or for Americans, 212 degrees Fahrenheit.

The smell was indescribable, so we all retired seriously upwind.

Suddenly, just as it came to the boil, one of the containers exploded, blowing the lid some 200 feet, followed by a load of old tin cans. (Gatorade no doubt).

It had to be shut down, while all the cans were swept up, and put back in, as "it is not sterilized yet."

From the sidelines, this was great sport, you couldn't pay for better entertainment.

So off we go again, only this time, after it was boiling for about 10 minutes, the drain plug blew out. We never did find it, but again we had to stop while the hole was plugged, and the 'soup' had to be shovelled back in.

By now though, there is a veritable crowd of spectators, giving all sorts of 'advice'.

Try again.

Just before we had completed the due 30 minutes, it blew its top once more! The crowd of spectators seeking hurried cover as cans and bits of this awful mess flew in all directions. And then it was done.

Unfortunately, the containers which started of roughly cuboidal, were now nearer spherical, and there was no way the lids were going to go back on. But it was duly dumped, all nicely sterile.

Everyone was happy until I chipped in with.

"So same time tomorrow then?"

"What do you mean?" they all asked, in a horrified tone.

"Oh that was just last week's garbage, there is a whole lot more to go yet, the *really* smelly stuff from the start of the repair."

Only this time, I arranged for the newspapers to come down, and the photographer had us on the front page of the *Corpus Christi Caller Times*, with the headline "Stinker of a problem piles up in city Port." I think it may be some time before the harbour master makes any more promises to captains about how to dispose of garbage. This time, *everyone* was well upwind, *and* out of range, which was just as well, as I now discovered what my chief officer had smuggled into the containers when no-one was looking. All the old ships' pyrotechnics that I found in a wardrobe, when I joined. (Distress flares, smoke floats, rockets, etc.) There was an almighty whoosh, as a distress rocket flew out at an angle, last seen heading for town, closely followed by another one going in the opposite direction. Was nowhere safe? Apparently not.

Department of Agriculture shut it down early. He'd had enough.

I rather fancied Doug Cameron's solution. Just put it in shopping bags captain, leave it on the front seat of your car, and somebody is bound to come along and steal it. Why didn't I think of that?

During the days, as we continued to work on the main engine, a never ending stream of Independent Surveyors showed up. When one came out from the UK, then the last threads of our charter were beginning to be revealed. Each surveyor had to have a set of reports of how the crankshaft was damaged plus a set of reports from the repair. This was developing into a major full time job on the Photocopier, for the Radio Officer.

When I had it finally unraveled, it went like this:

Ship owned by Laboremus of Oslo, chartered in the first instance to NGC (Norwegian Gas Carriers), chartered on to Cheminter in Buenos Aires, Argentina. Operated under cabotage laws on coasts of Argentina and Brazil, so secondary owners, Global in Rio de Janeiro, with sub owners/charterers, Interfrete in Brasilia, and sub chartered again to Interfrete in New York.

However, intended cargo at breakdown, ethylene to Stade. Sub chartered to Pemex in Mexico City, with further charterers of Mitsui in Brussels, and Mitsui in Tokyo. Somebody in London also got involved.

And they all had to be kept informed. After 3 weeks in Corpus, the charterer finally decided that after the repairs were completed, we would be loading somewhere in the US Gulf are for Argentina, possibly Bahia Blanca.

So, we are not going to be able to store up in Europe after all. In Europe, you can get anything, and more importantly, everyone who deals with ships, speaks the same 'language'. I was asked by VShips Oslo, to try to get a price for new mooring ropes. A ship's mooring rope is a standard item, that is, it is 100 fathoms long, or 600 feet or 200 metres, give or take a wee bit. Eyes spliced in both ends, comes all rolled up, all you need to specify is the size, 6 inch, 7 inch, 8 inch, 10 inch and so on. Strangely enough, the size is always measured in inches. For an 8 inch rope £600, or $1000 at that time.

I asked the chandler to get me a price for an 8 inch rope (and remembering this is Texas), 600 feet long with eyes spliced in both ends. Fairly simple task I would have thought. Look up a book perhaps? Nope. Next day, he came back with,

"I've got a price for that mooring rope that you wanted captain."

"Right, fire away."

"It will cost $1 and 13 cents per pound."

To this day, I still remained stunned. We didn't order any. With us not now going to Europe, I had to store up my ship for South America. I was pre-warned about what you cannot get there, which is just about anything. (For a ship that is.)

At best, as I found out, Argentina was a 'fag' country, and Brazil was a 'spirits' country. They were both 'beer' countries.

This is the 'representation' that featured in the charter party, which allowed me $100 per port call. Taking stores in Corpus was out of the question, they were used to coastal traffic. So I'll store in Houston, hopefully, if we go there.

But taking beer was easy.

The chief and I set off one evening for the local supermarket, and collared the manager with, "we need some beer please."

"How much do you want?"

"Oh, a car full."

"How much is that?"

"Don't know yet, so let's find out."

In went 300 half cases. It was down on its springs, but then it was a hire car.

Then the manager chipped in with.

"How about my truck?"

"Right, pile it on."

In the end we had 800 half cases. That should be enough.

Thus we go to the checkout, where the brain of Corpus Christi sat. She scans a box, then enters x 800. The till won't accept that. So tries again. Still won't accept it. I couldn't resist it, and said, "Just pass it over the reader 800 times." She actually started to do it. "Look dear, let's do this by calculator." We did, and paid the bill.

Buying it this way was cheaper than going through the 'official' track, even allowing for State sales tax.

Better beer too. During rebuilding of the main engine, and this was done with Wartsila's engineers supervising, they hit upon a snag. The camshaft had to be drilled. This requires what is known as an *in situ* drilling machine. One specially designed to do the job with high precision, inside the engine. But it is in Helsinki, Finland. The guys from Wartsila had long since worked out, that if they needed anything, then they just saw the captain, and it was as good as considered done.

I got straight on the 'phone to Helsinki, explained the problem, and Wartsila made the arrangements. It was at the airport within an hour. These guys work at *my* speed.

It was due to arrive in Dallas at 11 o'clock at night, and my agent was briefed to get it cleared by customs as soon as it came off the 'plane.

He then excelled himself with laid back laziness, by informing me that it was booked on a flight for Corpus Christi at 10 o'clock next morning. *That will not do at all.*

"The ship is held up Richard, we need it *asap*."

"No other way Captain, that's the best we can do."

"No it isn't, hire a plane and get it straight on it, now." He had long since decided that arguing was not a good idea.

Remember I said we had 'off-hire insurance'. Well, this has a very useful clause, and is known roughly as the 20% of the hull insured value, divided by 365 (days per year), per day saved proven pro rata. Effectively, I can spend up to $8767 per day if I can prove that I have saved a day. With the ship losing $21 000 per day in lost earnings, then this is worth doing and more than covered the cost of hiring a plane. It need not all be spent, hence the pro rata clause added on. The hull insured value? 16 000 000 US Dollars. The drill was on board by 2 am, some 12 hours faster than the agent had arranged. I used this clause again, later in the voyage.

Now one day, a huge box arrived, was opened by the chief engineer, and then left. Unfortunately, in the middle of the office, where we all had to go round it.

"What's in the box chief?" I so innocuously asked.

"That's your paperwork Captain."

"What? *All* of it!"

"Yep. Have fun."

There was masses of it. Not only that, but most of it was yonks out of date. How am I going to find time to do all of this? Simple solution really. I won't.

"Right chief, here is what we will do. We'll take out all that we really need, and chuck out the rest. Then if anyone says, 'where is such and such,' then we'll plead ignorance, and say, what is that? By the time, it is delivered, we'll be long gone. (It is amazing what can be lost in the mail.) I know. I'd worked for Gibsons. And Denholms.

It worked. Apart from one thing. The victualling record. This was a massive book, all to be kept in triplicate, but no carbon paper. Fine when ships had Chief Stewards, but now I have to do it. There is nothing more boring.

When in doubt, delegate.

"Crispin, this is for you. Have fun." I gave it to the cook. He looked at me, totally aghast.

"Do I have to fill this out?"

"Yes, and as it works on a 3-month cycle, here's another one to go with it." He was not overly enchanted. As in, not at all.

How do ships know which direction to go in, to arrive at their next port? Silly question? They use a compass, right?

Not exactly, in our case.

Oh, we had two, a magnetic compass, and a gyro compass. Ships never really got round to Inertial Navigation Systems, as used on aircraft, mostly because the Department of Transport in the UK is 25 years behind the times, and a lot of other flags just copied whatever they did.

Every magnetic compass has to be corrected, after which a 'Deviation Card' is produced. Proper calibration by a compass adjuster, will at most give a deviation of 1 degree, either East or West. It is a complicated subject, and needs a book all to itself, just to explain, so, you'll just have to take my word for it. It is also a really boring subject, best avoided if you can.

The Deviation Card for the *San Francisco* looked like a roller coaster on its side. For 090 degrees, 11 degrees West, for 100 degrees, nil, for 110 degrees 13 degrees East.

Something obviously far wrong here! But. The second mate, our 'navigating' officer, has fixed it. Tipp-Ex! Just change the ship's name, that'll be enough. No it won't. I had a look at the compass more closely. By now, I'm getting used to the fact that nothing is as it should be.

"Eh, Romero (second mate), there seems to be a few bits missing from the compass."

The Flinders bar, and spheres (soft iron correctors), and magnets (hard iron correctors) just were not there. As well as this, the compass had a huge bubble in it, and was 7 degrees out of line anyway.

He was giving me that vacant look of someone way out of his depth. To think that the previous master wanted to promote him to mate too.

"Right, take the compass out of the binnacle, and bring it down to my office, I'll get it sent for repair."

Now for the gyro compass. This was in the chartroom, but behind a steel panel, held on with about 40 screws. I took it off, and was just reaching in, when the second mate said,

"Oh captain, we don't touch that," as I reached for the latitude corrector. This has got to be worth hearing.

"If we adjust that, we get big errors, so we leave it on 25 degrees North. This gives us an error of 1 degree low."

"Do you mean to tell me that you have just come up from Argentina at 40 degrees South to the US Gulf at 30 degrees North, without adjusting the latitude corrector on the gyro compass?"

"Oh yes sir," we do it all the time.

Not any longer you don't! I went to find the switch to shut it down. This was below the bridge, in a room the full width of the bridge, but only about a metre high.

When I found the correct switch, and shut it off, I turned, banged my head, and fell back onto a box, cursing just a little. Well, a lot then.

Divine Providence! What was in the box? All the bits for the magnetic compass. The day is beginning to look up.

Both were put back together, and were corrected after we sailed by a compass adjuster. At least, we knew which direction we were going in now. *But*. There is always a but on this ship.

How about the charts, to navigate with? The second mate was getting that 'grey look', that Filipinos get when they know something but don't want to tell you. He wasn't getting off that easily. I teased it out of him. The only charts that had been corrected were the ones they had used between the US Gulf and Bahia Blanca. The rest had not been corrected in 4 years. Totally useless. It was going to cost around £50 000 just to bring this up to scratch. Better get started then, so I did.

One day, I went to look at the emergency fire pump. I must have been bored, or sought a place to hide, as this was down a ladder from the fo'c'sle space, in a compartment about 4 feet square and 3 feet high, 50 feet down. Equipment such as this has a counter indicating the running hours. The ship mind is 5 years old, total running time since new, 8 minutes! Believe me, it gets worse yet. A lot worse.

Something with this amount of running time can suffer from 'Brinnelling' of the bearings. They go flat if they stay in the one place for too long. Yes, they had. So I changed the bearings. On test it ran for longer than it had from new. It will now be run weekly.

This reminds me of another story that you may find interesting.

Some years before, when I was chief mate on the *Traquair*, we were coming up to the ships' guarantee dry dock, when she was a year old. We had just come from Priolo in Sicily with a cargo of propylene. It's just like propane in a way, but has a distinct smell to it.

Sitting in the masters dayroom, this guy I knew from LGE (the company that designed and built the gas plant) asked me how often I ran the cargo compressors. On this ship they were big affairs, that took about 400 horse power each, just to start. More to run.

"When and as required," I replied, "on this passage, for about 3 hours one morning."

Ten minutes later, he came back with,

"I calculate that your ships tanks were 99.998% full when you arrived here in the Tees."

Every head turned to look at me, with daggers in their eyes, as that figure is dangerous. We should not go above 98% in any circumstances.

"Well," says *Old Baldy*, "explain yourself."

I hated that look he had when he was annoyed. His top teeth came over his bottom lip, and I'd been on the sharp end before.

"I presume that you based your calculation on the ship being 98% full on sailing, and the cargo has heated up by 4 degrees on passage."

He answered in the affirmative.

"We only loaded to 86% as they ran out of product, and as it is a heater discharge, saw no point in cooling it down, just to warm it all up again."

He was looking for a hole to swallow him up. The old saying, 'people who dig holes for others, invariably fall in them themselves'.

Back to the *Norgas Challenger*. Our time in Corpus Christi is rapidly drawing to a close, and this ship is a whole lot better than when it came in, as now, *all* of our safety equipment had been overhauled, and a lot of the gas plant as well.

I did, however, have one niggling problem. It is strange, but when you know something should be where it is supposed to be, but then isn't, your mind's eye tells you that it is actually there. Such was the case with our life raft hydrostatic releases, and bear in mind, this ship is 5 years old, has been surveyed by just about all and sundry, including the US Coast Guard, and Det Norske Veritas no less.

It came as rather a shock to find that the hydrostatic releases had never been fitted.

"Chief. Do you know why I cannot find the certificates for the life raft hydrostatic releases?"

"I know you've been searching for them, so why?"

"Because they haven't been fitted, and this ship has been going around for 5 years without them."

"You're joking of course."

"No, and I think we better get some."

Our charterers, Cheminter of Buenos Aires, wanted the ship back in South America, as soon as possible, to resume the ship's 'Normal Trade'. I highlight this for reasons that you will soon realize.

I therefore have to 'store' my ship for a prolonged period in South America. This is not as easy as it looks. I have to ensure that I have enough cash on board to pay my crew. (In cash, and in US Dollars). I have to ensure that, of this cash, I have enough USD in small bills to pay for anything that the ship needs, as I cannot get USD in Brazil.

I need to make sure that the ship has enough Lube Oil and of the correct grade, for ALL of its' equipment, as this is not available in South America. And as I discovered in Houston, enough paint as well. Here is where I will let you into a little secret.

The amount of cash carried on board ships is frightening. This is also the reason that piracy had again become a serious problem. To pay my 'crew' on this ship, I need to have about $28 000 cash, *every* month, just to keep a clear balance. Nothing other than 'clean' US Bills in denominations of $100 will do, the slightest tear or mark, renders them 'unacceptable'. I will refer to this later in Part 5.

Into the safe goes $100 000. That should be enough. It wasn't, but at least it was a start. Did you know, that all US currency, is exactly the same size. And your hands get 'black' just counting it. So why do the call it the old greenback?

We trot to Houston, Texas to load.

Our orders were to load three tanks of Butene 1 (effectively low grade butane), and three tanks of ethylene. 2 000 tonnes of each. The ethylene to be loaded in Coatzacoalcos, in Mexico. Nice. Little trot up the coast to Galveston perhaps?

Nope. After clearing the pilot station in Corpus Christi, we set off. About 1 hour later, the 'phone rings, just as we are coming through the trial program to build up to full speed. It's the chief engineer.

"Doug, we have to shut down the main engine, no power from No 3 unit."

"Right, shut it down." I had long since discovered that something my old chief said on the *Quentin*, was in fact true. It was a quote that went like this, from the chief engineer,

"You'll be glad to know Mr Lundberg, that I have saved the main engine, unfortunately, the Captain, has lost the ship."

I swung the ship out of the designated lane, and anchored.

"Right Chief, what is the problem?" Bearing in mind the engine has been re-built under the auspices of Wartsila, the engine builders.

"Bent pushrods on the inlet valves."

"Why?"

"Let's just get it fixed." (I knew why, but my chief didn't need my interference at this point). "Okay, but remember, after it's going again, I have to take this ship up the Galveston Channel to Houston, and I *need* a reliable engine." 6 hours later we were on our way, picked up our pilot, at Galveston, and headed inwards for Houston. Nearly had a collision picking up the pilot. But that's another story.

We arrived alongside our berth in Houston without further ado, apart from one thing. Coastal Iron hadn't been paid in Corpus Christi, a small matter of some $45 000. They are now on the 'phone to me. They would have been paid, if they had sent down a decent invoice. Their 'bill' was written on the back of an envelope, and tendered thus. It took several weeks for them to get the message that we only paid on 'properly' declared invoices, including timesheets etc. They went out of business shortly afterwards.

Just think USA, they might just have been involved in your space program. Look at what we saved you from.

Our arrival coincided with the first of the seasons tropical storms. These pre-date the hurricane season, which runs from September to December, but whereas they do not include high wind speeds, they also bring extreme amounts of rain, as in big style rain, lots and lots of it.

This one was no exception, and very soon, Houston started shutting down for flooding.

It didn't bother us, we just kept on loading, even although the jetty had long since disappeared, under water.

Unfortunately, the US Coast Guard had paid a visit, in 'Wellie' boots no less.

"Right Captain, Your sub-chapter 'O' endorsement has expired. I need to inspect your vessel." This is a statutory document that the US Coast Guard require for all gas tankers calling at US ports. I thought we might have got away with it, but no. Exactly what happened to the main chapter 'O', and all letters before 'O' is still a mystery, even *they* don't know. If you want to wade your way through US Coast Guard Rules and Regulations, then book now for your plastic surgery. You will need at least 40 fingers on each hand, just to hold the pages, as each one in its subroutine form says, "refer to page 42, subsection 21, para 89, which will take you to page 296, subsection 194, para 37, then onto Chapter 8, page 542, chapter 91, refer to page 7, subsection 98, para 19, sub-sub section ii) a or b, and so on, until you are as confused as everybody else. Then can't remember what you were looking for in the first place. Do what *all* captains do, plead ignorance, it always works. But will he inspect my vessel? "Yes."

"Right off you go then, let me know if you need anything." Normally, he would be escorted, but as I have no desire to get wet, everyone else is tired, and I still know what is wrong with this ship, I decided to let him get on with it. Fortunately, he didn't like the idea of getting wet either, probably because most of Houston was cut off by now, and the chances of getting dry again were slim.

So I used him.

Surreptitiously off course. I've done it since too, it works a treat.

Within the hour, using our new Inmarsat A system, he had been in touch with Washington, and re-issued a new "sub-chapter O endorsement." But then again, it's amazing what you can achieve with a colour photocopier, and a bottle of Tipp-ex.

Beer in Corpus Christi, then bond locker in Houston. The cheapest that I ever got Scotch, was £10 per case from a chandler in Teesport, and yes, it was *rough*. Ah! But Houston, now that is cheap. Scotch? 'Legacy.' It comes in boxes, which looks impressive, but then, there it ends. Only $10 per case. We'll have some of that.

Cigarettes, 'Brahma'. Ever heard of them? Neither had I, but then, I don't smoke, and if you are daft enough to set fire to something that you put in your mouth... Only $2 per carton, yes *carton*. We'll have some of that as well. 200 000 should be enough. It wasn't.

Ah, but the best was the Chinese White Wine.

'Ming Palace'. Product of the Peoples Democratic Republic of China, it said on the label. Export only.

Neither wonder. It was Rufff.

Not long after the coast guard left, I had a visit from NGC (Norwegian Gas Carriers). I was left with two rather awkward questions to answer.

"Why is your ship the wrong colour Captain? And why is the funnel back to front?" I should point out that the ship had been painted red, except that the accommodation block was white. It should have been orange and white. I rather suspected the previous chief officer may have been to blame here, and I wasn't far wrong. I eventually got the truth out of the second mate.

It transpires that he was colour blind, had looked up the paint book, and ordered 8000 litres in what his eye told him was orange. It was red. He then painted the entire ship in red, still unaware of his 'mistake'. And they let this guy loose on the bridge? At sea? The funnel should have had a blue NGC on a white band. We had a white NGC on a blue band. Oh well, if you are going to make a mess of something, you might as well make a complete mess of it.

We sail from Houston, a further day late, as somebody has been silly enough to lose a barge in the Houston Ship Channel, and then been even more silly, in letting it sink, without actually knowing where. This kept *all* the US Coast Guard busy. Unfortunately, you should not count your chickens before they have hatched, so to speak, as having just cleared the melee with the barge, the bridge telephone rang with.

"Doug, chief, air start valve on No 5 cylinder has blown its joints, it's glowing red now, we have to shut down the main engine."

"Can you give me 15 minutes to anchor chief?"

"Perhaps 5, at most." Great.

Only place to anchor out of the channel, was a cut coming up fast on the starboard bow.

We went for it, my second officer was a rather nervous chap, who had lost his confidence under the German Chief Officer, so suitably briefed, rushed forward with the crew, to 'throw' out the port anchor. That is the new port anchor, the un-tested one.

It was risky, but there was nothing else to do, as I swung with what was left of my main engine power, into this 'cut', and dropped the anchor, holding at two shackles. It was out in under 30 seconds. The current then took charge and swung us clear of the channel. There were sparks flying off the winch, as the anchor bit, and the cable jumped the gypsy. I knew the second mate wouldn't do anything stupid as he has already run away, narrowly beating the crew in the process.

I was asked afterwards why I used the port anchor, as opposed to the starboard one, which was after all, on the side I was heading, and the ship would then lie clear of its anchor.

It's very simple, a ship sitting on top of its cable acts as an extra brake, and puts the catenary at a smaller angle to the bottom, increasing the power of the anchor. You have to think quickly in this job. It may dredge a bit, but it all helps.

The pilot was one of these extremely arrogant types, who came out with.

"Captain, tell the chief to get his asbestos gloves on and get that valve changed quick before the Coast Guard get here."

"Pilot, I'm sure my chief knows what he is doing."

"Aren't you going to call the chief, captain?"

"I've told you already pilot. No. If my chief needs to be told what to do by a Houston Pilot, then he is no use to me as a chief engineer." In a rather frustrated tone.

"If you talk to me like that again, Captain, I will call the Coast Guard."

"Can you swim pilot, because, if you threaten me, you will discover just how cold the water here really is? I trust that you brought your lifejacket." He hadn't.

"Right pilot, call the Coast Guard, and when they get here, I will report you for having no lifejacket." I don't have a lot of time for this type of arrogance.

Sensibly, he kept quiet, fuming a bit, but quiet.

We upped anchor, carried on our way, and swung the compass.

In Houston, my German Chief officer, despite many warnings, had caused the crew to lose 'face.' The first I knew of it, was a note on my desk, which had been signed by every Filipino on board, requesting a relief.

When I winkled the truth out of them, which is never easy, it transpired that the third officer, who was also, first trip third officer, had been suffering a lot of verbal abuse from the mate, and had had enough. With Filipinos, if one loses 'face', then they all lose 'face'. What is easier, replace 1 German, or 14 Filipinos?

All I got out of the mate was "I cannot work with these people, they are stupid, all of them." He wasn't overly bright himself.

He's leaving then.

This of course means, that not only am I now master, but chief mate as well, and I have to load ethylene in Coatzacoalcos. And it's been a few years since I did a cool down and load. Ho hum, such is life.

One thing that we were short of, was fuel, and the charterers were not overly keen on buying any, particularly with the extra delay, and a cancelled cargo under our belts.

Normally, we operate with a safe margin of consumption, 5 days in reserve, only, we were now going to have to go into our reserve, and it would be a pretty close call to make Bahia Blanca with what we had on board. The passage time was 24 days, and we had fuel for 26. If push came to shove though, the charterers had agreed that *if it was necessary*, we could divert into Rio Grande de Sul, Brazil for fuel.

During cool-down to load in Mexico (we cool down the tanks at 6 degrees per hour, by spraying in liquid ethylene, and later, re-liquefying like mad to take out the heat. So from +30 to -100 takes more than just a wee while), it was time to get the laundry done.

We had equipment ordered for the ship to do its own, but like everything else, it was still in Germany. So this lot goes out to tender.

There were four quotes, three in the region of $30–$40, but one at $120. Either this was a deluxe laundry or a ? It was an a ?

The laundry owner, had brought his 'assistant', who would 'entertain' the captain while the laundry was cleaned. Boy was she rough, and ugly too, especially when she smiled, reminded me of the *Leith Arab*, when he was known as *The Fang*.

Needless to say, he and she didn't get the job.

Cargo on board, fully cleaned up, fully stored, and more than just a bit, short of fuel, we set off for Argentina, muggings here, not only having a ship to run, but keeping a watch as well.

One of the big differences between Gibsons and VShips, was that crew wages were calculated, and paid, on board. Almost every ship does it this way nowadays, but this was alien to me at the time. It still is in some respects, especially trying to get it to balance. Only in this case, I have one Indian crew member mixed up with my Filipinos, and he is not a happy chappie.

I felt a little for him really, as although Mulla (his name) is doing the same job as the others (give or take a bit for speed), he is receiving less pay.

I agreed with VShips, that we would, temporarily, bring him up to Filipino rates, and pay him out of what we were saving, by not having a chief officer. This kept us within the budget. However, Filipinos pay some $15 each month in Union Dues, and this is deducted on board. Yes you guessed, Mulla doesn't want to pay this, as he is Indian, not Filipino. But if I don't deduct it from him, then the rest of the crew won't want it deducted either. In the end, I kept it in the safe, until we changed to Indian Crew, then gave it to him.

You will recall from my last voyage on the *Borthwick*, that safety training was a bit of a disaster. Then again, if you pay peanuts, as Denholms did, you get monkeys.

Safety training here had also been rather neglected. Eight of the crew had never worn the ship's breathing apparatus. All gas tankers have a lot of safety equipment. With this ship being Norwegian, there was more. Maritime & Coast Guard Agency, please take note.

On our first safety drill, it is BA (Breathing Apparatus) practice, but not just your normal 5 minute job. Oh no, I do things differently.

The only way to instill confidence is to put people under pressure when using this. When you have exerted yourself, you need a lot of air into your lungs, and BA sets allow for this. The temptation to pull the mask off though must first be overcome.

I had No 1 void space open, and the big fans were on, so we'll go in at the top wearing BA, crawl underneath the cargo tank and climb out at the aft end. It was perfectly safe, as if something went wrong, then the void space was under air anyway.

The Filipinos thought this was some big joke, but there was no way out of it, they all had to do it. I led, going first with seven others following me. It was exhausting, because it was also hot.

One of the mess men and one AB cheated, so were sent round again. The Mess man was sent round a third time, and then a fourth time. It was slowly dawning on the crew, officers as well, that safety training was paramount with this captain. All in all, we had safety drills for the first 14 days.

Back to the bridge then, and I am keeping the 4–8 watch with the deck cadet. He was hopeless, at anything, but we had at least to try.

After sailing from Coatzacoalcos, I set up the Satellite Navigator. This was the type before GPS.

When I next came on watch, all the settings had been changed, so I reset them.

"Abner (Third mate), did you adjust the settings on the Sat Nav when you came on watch?"

"No sir." Fair enough.

Next watch, same thing, all changed, so once more I reset everything.

"Romero (Second mate), did you adjust the settings on the Sat Nav?"

"Oh yes sir, because you did it all wrong."

"Please explain." This was going to be worth listening to.

"You see sir, you put in a pulse feed of 100, and it should be 200. See it says so here in the book."

Idiot.

"No, Romero, what it says, is that in the event of a power loss, it will defeat to 200, which equates to a DR speed of 28 knots. We are estimating 14 knots, so the pulse feed is 100. Okay?"

"Oh no sir, we don't do it like that. All we have to do is press this button every 30 minutes, and it's okay."

'Forced position update.'

"Do you mean to tell me that a piece of fully automatic navigation equipment is being used on manual mode?"

"We always do it that way sir."

"Not anymore you don't. Now I will reset it once again, and do not touch it again. Okay."

"Yes sir," as he went that grey colour.

Believe it or not, I have sailed with worse navigators than this.

I was asked afterwards how I could sleep at night. "With one eye open perhaps?"

One day, as I sorted through the days telexes, there was a cry for help, "Captain, come quick, Mulla has fallen."

Dashing outside, I ended up flat on my back in paint. Mulla has not only fallen, but he's brought his paint pot with him, and I am now in its contents. Ever tried to get a 2-part epoxy paint off your back? Don't.

The dope has not only rigged his bosun's chair on the end of a rail, but wasn't wearing a safety harness. I reckoned he landed on his head, as he wasn't hurt.

Before setting off from Coatzacoalcos, I received details of our agents in Argentina. This is routine for any ship, but in Argentina, they do things slightly differently. You don't have one agent, you have two. The primary is in Buenos Aires, and the secondary, is in the port of call. So my brief was: Agencia Maritima Robinson. (Marine Agents by the name of Robinson in Buenos Aires.)

Agencia Maritima Martin. Dr Guido Sin Numero, Pto Ing White, Bahia Blanca, Argentina. Looks fairly innocuous, so for 24 days, all my daily telexes were addressed to Dr Guido.

It was only after I arrived, that I got the translation, not being overly well endowed in Spanish. Dr Guido doesn't exist. It translates into 'the street called Dr Guido, and the house with no number'. Pto Ing White, just means, 'the port of Engineer White', named after the Scotsman who built the place.

One day out from 'Pto Ing White,' sitting at my desk at roughly 9: 30 in the morning, in walked the chief engineer, with,

"Sorry if you're busy, but we have only got 12 tonnes of water left."

"That's okay Mike. We only use 8 tonnes per day, and we'll be in port first thing tomorrow. I'll send the agents a telex, and book it for delivery as soon as we are alongside. Just to be on the safe side, let the cook know we are short, and to go easy on the water."

A ships' galley can get through more water than the rest of the ship put together. This was one of those days. At about midday, just as I was finishing the noon report, who should appear at the door, none other than the chief, with,

"You won't believe this, but we have run out of water."

"Nah, chief, less than 3 hours ago, we still had 12 tonnes."

"I've even taken the lid of the tank, it's empty. I think you should look in the galley. Be prepared to be amazed."

More than just a bit curious, I went for a look.

It was amazing. Everything you could imagine, was full to the brim with water. Even in the crews' cabins, the sinks were full, even the baths. Words failed me for a minute or so.

"Eh, Crispin, did the chief not tell you that we were short of water this morning, and to go easy on it?"

"Yes captain."

"How do you account for this?" I couldn't wait to hear the answer.

"Oh but captain, we *have* to do this, because when the chief runs out, then he won't have any, but we will." It took a while for his logic to sink in.

"Just get it back in the tank, *all* of it." Remember what I said about their logic. But there was far worse to come. We duly arrive at the end of the buoyed channel for Bahia Blanca. I was a little sceptical, about going here, as, at this time, diplomatic relations between the UK and Argentina, hadn't been resumed.

First of all, though, there was a smallish navigational problem to overcome, namely there were no lights on the buoys, and of course, we arrive after dusk.

Why were there no lights? Because, all the buoys are upside down. And why are they upside down?

Because they are covered in sea-lions. (They didn't cover this in all the books I had read on navigation.) And sea-lions absorb radar energy. The buoys don't show up on radar.

So, we anchor till the morning.

Next day, we went in.

Some of the most pleasant people, I have ever met, were Argentinians, and this place abounded with them.

If you have ever been to a gas terminal, then you can say, quite easily that they all look the same. This was no exception, except for the other side of the river. There is a huge mud bank that dries out at low water. It pongs a bit too, but is also covered by some the most scarlet flamingoes that I have ever seen. It was really quite cheering. My charterer came down, and gave us our schedule for the next 3 months. We would run ethylene from Santa Clara in Brazil, to Bahia Blanca in Argentina. To me, this was not a big problem, but it was for the ship. The previous management from Ivarans, were not the most competent, and instead of delivering ethylene, fully refrigerated at minus 103.8 degrees C, had in fact been warming it up. It is loaded at minus 98 degrees C, and it is getting that little last bit of heat out, that is so difficult. At least it had been, but now, we are running the ship somewhat differently. They were delivering it at minus 96 degrees C.

He, my charterer (I won't tell you his name because it came up in a case I was working on as a marine investigator, and this time, he was on the wrong side of the fence. I still keep in touch though), elected to take the chief and myself, plus the agent and his wife out to dinner that night in Bahia Blanca. His wife was there but had stayed in the hotel. Wise woman obviously.

The agent, Arturo, and I hit it off immediately, and he sent his driver to pick us up, which was an experience.

I said to the chief when we arrived.

"Mike, just what side of the road do they drive on in this country?"

"I was hoping you would know. Both sides seem fair game."

He was nicknamed 'Fangio.'

You can say what you like about Argentina, but I can tell you this, their beef is out of this world. Certainly on a par with the best in Scotland. We had a great dinner, each of us, just 'hitting it off'. Santa Clara is a devil of a place to get to. First of all, it's in to Rio Grande de Sul and anchor. Then masses of paperwork, to clear the ship in. Then up a river, which is full of tight bends, to Lagos dos Platos, which is a lake which took about 7 hours to cross.

Anchor at Porto Alegre, and once more, all the paperwork to clear the ship in. Again. Then through a bridge, for which the radio mast has to be lowered, and snake your way up yet another river, which in places is only slightly wider than the ship, then up a cut, which is 4 miles long.

The jetty is effectively in the middle of the jungle, which also hides the refinery.

On top of this, the lake is shallow at just over 17 feet, and because of 'squat,' anything over 8 knots, and the ship hits the bottom, which is not something you want to do.

This of course is where the damage came from that showed up on the underwater survey. Some of it at least. The bilge keels? Read on.

For loading, we can only load to even keel draft of 17 feet.

When I worked it out, I reckoned on loading about 2900 tonnes, but the records (which I read with some scepticism), showed that the ship was only lifting 2400 tonnes. There was something wrong here. It was only during de-ballasting, that I found out what it was. The Filipino second engineer came to see me.

"Captain, you're loading this ship all wrong. We never did it this way before, and you will not let us open the engine room hatch."

He was quite literally, terrified.

The engine room hatch had a ladder built up from the workshop space, and was it later transpired, the 'engineers' emergency escape'. Seemingly, the ship had a habit of going unstable during loading and on her way down to the sea. She was known locally as the 'floppy ship'. Crowds used to gather in Porto Alegre, just to watch if this time she *will* capsize. Apparently, 20 degrees each way was normal, and she had been over to 35 degrees on one occasion. Most frightening of all, was one occasion when she had gone from 20 degrees port to 20 degrees starboard, going through the bridge at Porto Alegre!

Not when I'm captain it won't.

That explains the damage to the bilge keels then!

The Filipinos carry all their money around with them, from Santa Clara, down to Rio Grande do Sul, just in case they have to abandon ship, and the ladder from the workshop was there for the engineers to escape on.

What were we 'doing wrong?' I now had a new chief officer.

After the main ballast had been pumped out, the tanks are stripped using an ejector, until they are dry. Seemingly, this is 'wrong', as they, 'the Filipinos', "never do it this way."

Ah ha! That explains a lot. That is why the ship is unstable, they leave about 20 tons of ballast in each tank. That accounts for the loss of stability, and the shortage of cargo lifted. There were 21 tanks. (This is known as the free surface effect. If the ship is slightly out of upright, the water will flow to the low side, thereby increasing the list, until the ships 'righting lever' balances out the tendency to list. The more free surface you have, the greater the loss in GM, and the greater the list.)

The Second Engineer was so convinced that he was right, and I was wrong, that he wanted to leave immediately, and fly back to Manilla at his own expense. When I looked around, the rest were in the dayroom, wanting to go as well. I'd never seen anything like it.

In the end, I had to place a bet with each one of them, that the ship would not list over, except when taking the bends in the river. They were not a happy bunch. By law, in the 1968 Load Line Rules, the minimum GM, (transverse metacentric height) that a ship may sail with is 15 cms. When I calculated out the GM, when she was 'floppy', it came out at just under 12 cms. When I then re-calculated (doing it my way), her new loaded GM, it came out at 40 cms. More than adequate, but try convincing Filipinos this.

A further worrying factor, was that of all the pilots here, only two were prepared to work the ship when loaded. They got paid extra as well. A lot of people are going to be disappointed.

In the end, I squeezed in 2950 tonnes to 17 feet even keel, and set of for Bahia Blanca some 4 days away.

We never listed more than 2 degrees, going round tight bends and as soon as we could passing Rio Grande, bashed in a load of ballast, just to keep the Filipinos happy. But they weren't all convinced. You will never get a Filipino to admit that he was wrong. Don't waste your time trying.

One other advantage of closing the engine room hatch, as it should be at sea, is that the engine room is now pressurized, which in turn, increases the power from the main engine, hence, more speed. The charterer was delighted with the 'improvement', not only in cargo capacity, but with the speed as well. He came on the 'phone one day with,

"Captain, we are going to put a claim in against the previous owners, for under performance. The case will be heard in London, and we want you to go as our expert witness."

This a definite no-no, and I don't want to become involved, but in the end, this was shelved, as we had another setback.

The chief came to see me on the way back to the sea, to discuss a 'notion'. He came out with,

"if we are going to have these long stand-bys, I think we should learn some 'Tagalog'". This is the language that Filipinos use, but there are about 70 different varieties to it. Most Filipinos just use English anyway, saves time.

I replied, "I've got enough to do, but if you want to, then go ahead." This should be interesting.

About 3 weeks later, after I had forgotten all about it, he came to see me, and came out with "gobbledegook, gobbledegook, gobbledegook, ah! ah! ah."

"What d'you think eh?" In English.

"Very impressive chief, but what exactly does it mean?"

"Oh," he says, "it means 'good morning my fellow engineers, how are you this fine day?' And they answer, 'more gobbledegook'".

"Well chief, that will come in real handy, the next time we're ashore and trying to get a meal in a restaurant."

He went off with a smug, self-gratifying look.

This went on every morning for about a week, before he came to me once more and said,

"You should try this Doug, my boys are ever so happy. It makes me feel ever so buoyant each morning now."

Mmm.

The radio officer, Francis, sidled up to me one day on the bridge, and said,

"Captain, you know that phrase the Chief has learnt, that he starts off every day now with. Well, what he thinks is what it means, isn't."

"Oh ho, tell me more." This was going to be good. "What does it mean then?"

"Well sir, it really means, 'my new helicopter is full of baby eels, and I wish today was Sunday'."

"You're joking, does it really? Better not tell the chief then. Leave it to me, I'll find the right time to tell him."

I never did get the chance, so if you read this Mike, you've been had.

The cargo was duly delivered, early, and fully refrigerated. Now that we had the gas plant sussed, the full potential of what the *Norgas Challenger* could do, was realized. She is a very powerful little gas tanker. The cargo plant is out of this world. But, after discharging:

We sailed from Pto Ing White, and having just overtaken a large bulk carrier, and increasing the main engine up to full sea speed, the bridge 'phone rang.

It was the chief. "Doug, we have fumes pouring out of the main engine!" In a rather agitated tone.

To me, this means only one thing, a crankcase explosion is imminent.

To this day, there is some argument, as to who hit the Emergency Stop first, the Chief or me, but the engine was shut down. Pronto. However I'm still doing 18 knots, but now with no power. Emergency action was needed to stop safely, without going aground.

Unfortunately, by the time I got her stopped, we were well in to the approaches to the Argentinian Naval Base at Puerto Belgrano, and there is off course, no diplomatic relations between Argentina and the UK.

No bloody brake left on the windlass either, after it went on fire. Another job to do.

As expected, the Argentinian Navy did not like the idea of a fully gassed up gas tanker in their approach channel, and demanded that it be removed immediately. There was however, a humorous end to this. Sad really, but still humorous. Fortunately, as we weren't very far down the river, we managed to get one of our sailing tugs to tow us to a lay-by berth. The news from the engine room was not good.

"I think we may have cracked the new crankshaft captain" explained the chief.

"Any other damage?" I rather knew what to expect.

"Yes. The cylinder head is cracked, the liner fell to bits when it came out with the piston seized in it, and the bearings have melted." Why? There is actually a design fault on this type of engine.

The connecting rod is fastened over the crankshaft, to the bottom end bearing and two bolts are stretched to hold it all in place. When the jacks are fitted to the bolts, then it is possible for one of them to foul on the block, so when you think you have the correct tension, you don't.

This in turn had allowed the bearing shell to start rotating, and was fine until it blocked the lubricating oil port, and starved the crankshaft of its lube oil. The only saving grace was that the engine had not exploded. But we aint going anywhere fast now. In fact we aren't going anywhere at all.

As soon as VShips knew that the crankshaft was cracked, they organized a team to fly out from Oslo, to see if the cracks could be ground out. It was another big insurance job. More paperwork for me!

The first people up the gangway, apart from my agent, were the Argentinian Navy, who wanted a full report. This was not a problem, in fact they were quite good about it, but they did have a rather unusual request, apart from actually liking the 'Legacy' Scotch, which was flowing quite well, and smoothed out a lot of the tension.

"Do you have any spare paint Captain?"

This was in addition to a load of ciggies. But why did they need paint?

It was that they were so short of money, that their coastguard cutter was getting a bit dirty. So they got our spare grey, which was the ship's colour, before it was painted red, and was after all, surplus to requirements.

Over the next few months, we got to know them a lot a better, and they were really rather friendly.

Our new crankshaft, from Corpus Christi, was one of only five ever made of a specially new type of hardened steel. And it was hard.

It took a full day, just to grind it down by 1 millimetre. The maximum that it can be ground down is 4 millimetres, and the cracks are a lot deeper than that. In the end, they were scalloped out, but bearings failed after 1 hour. We need another new crankshaft.

All in all, we were delayed by 10 days, to achieve nothing at all. The refinery in Brazil however is running out of storage space, the refinery in Bahia Blanca is running out ethylene, and I have the only ethylene gassed-up gas tanker in South America. The nearest one is 3 weeks away. It will take 10 days to get another crankshaft flown in, so, as we had already proven that we could run the engine, with only eight out of the nine cylinders, I elected to try and make the 1 500 mile round trip to Santa Clara and back on eight cylinders.

Furthermore, there was a barge, the *Formentera*, that could be loaded up with ethylene in the meantime, if we would agree to a transshipment in Rio Grande, after loading in Santa Clara. To say that I was put under pressure, is putting it mildly. We set off.

Unfortunately, the pilotage has been suspended for bad weather, so tough luck Mr Pilot, you'll just have to come with us. This is quite acceptable, he'll just fly back from Brazil. He gets paid for it, while enjoying a cruise at the same time, without the pretty girls though.

First night out at sea, it was bad. The vibration we could live with, except in my office, where it was intolerable. I had to de-camp to my cabin. The weather was atrocious which didn't help at all.

At about 11 o'clock, just before I retired for the night, my sixth sense kicked in. There was something wrong, and for a reason that I could not explain, I knew it was in the engine room. It has since being explained to me how I knew, by a Mrs Sheila McBride, and that is explained in 'Acknowledgements' at the beginning of this book.

As soon as I went through the control room, I could smell smoke. A drum of oil had got loose, and was lying over the top of the exhaust manifolds, and leaking.

"All hands to the engine room, now!" over the PA system. To give them their due, the crew were down in seconds, the crew being the opposite to that which Denholms supplied. Rather good actually.

Then, just after midnight, there was a terrific bang. The crane had got loose. The gearbox had vibrated apart and the jib was swinging round in circles. If you have ever tried to lasso a crane in a gale, you will know just how difficult it is. Even turning into the wind.

I explained to the crew how to lasso the end of the jib, and then when it swung inboard, how we could tie it off. What I forgot to say, was that if you successfully lasso it, then wait till it swings back in, before you apply weight to the rope. One managed to get his rope over the end, but stupidly, just held on. A few seconds later, he is dangling over the sea, about 30 feet out, terrified.

"For goodness sake, grab him when he comes back," I shouted over the howl of the wind. We got him back but he was very white (grey), for a long time afterwards.

Just then, as we were securing the crane with only a small amount of damage to the rails and spray pipelines, all hell broke loose on the poop deck. Down here, were 45 gallon drums of chemicals, which although well secured, had broken free. Now they were rolling about, and had broken open. Only one thing for it, get rid of them, quick, as there is a chemical reaction occurring which is starting to smoke.

"Get me a fire axe, quick," as Filipinos are not noted for their bravery. It took about an hour to get rid of them, by that time, there was no paint on the deck. It had dissolved. In the galley next morning, I said to the cook.

"Crispin, do you have that victaulling record book that I gave you at the start of the voyage, you know, the big one?"

I knew that he hadn't been doing it, as he had enough to do, but I thought I would wind him up a wee bit, to ease some of the tension.

Filipinos love knowing that one of their group has been caught doing something they shouldn't, as long as it is not them.

He, as he stood there wringing his hands, said,

"Do you remember last night, when the crane got loose, and then the barrels got loose, and you had to throw them over the side? Well, a case of eggs got loose in the storeroom, and fell onto my book, so I followed your example and threw it over the side as well." I could only smile, and replied.

"Do you think I came up the Clyde on a banana boat Crispin?"

"Sir?" That was lost on him. "I'll get you another one then." What else can go wrong?

You should never ask this question on a ship.

After clearing in, in Rio Grande, the charterers had elected to take us to Porto Alegre at night. For this, navigation is tricky, and it takes the combined efforts of two pilots to do it. This is the only time that I would allow two pilots to work together, as the opportunity for doubt, is now three-fold. Not good.

So what went wrong?

Just before we got to the lake, the chief 'phoned up with,

"We have to stop Doug."

"Why pray tell?" This no longer was taken as a surprise.

"Expansion bellows on the turbo charger has cracked on the exhaust side. We can hardly breathe down here."

"Can you just give me another 45 minutes?"

Stupid question, I should have known better. So we anchor in the channel, about 5 miles short of the lake. We were the only dafties (ship) moving.

It only takes a few hours to put the spare on, but off course, sod's law came into play. We had swung round in the channel, and by the time the anchor was up, we couldn't get turned round again so had to set off in the opposite direction until we could get to a bit that was wide enough. Another 50, bone-jarring vibrating miles.

Eventually, we arrive in Santa Clara, and load. The barge loaded some 4 days before us, which meant only one thing, the cargo would be heating up.

We vibrate back down, only this time the vibration is coming out in different places, and we have to further jiggle the revs and pitch, to get a satisfactory setting. For some reason, it still liked my office. The cargo, ethylene, from the barge, was not only warm, at -85 degrees, but was starting to bubble out of the tanks. We were just in time.

There is an old gas tanker trick, which works very well, but does set up rather a lot of vibration, and not many people use it, or are prepared to take the risk. It is perfectly safe though, as long as you know what you are doing. It's called throttling. Basically, you close in the main liquid loading valve, so the gas has to expand past it. This in turn cools it down, as every degree that you can remove here is a lot less work for the ship's reliquefaction plant. What it also did, was upset the barge crew. Tough, you let it heat up, not us.

There is an amusing story about this barge. The crew in charge of it are not at all happy that they are going to have to tow it to Bahia Blanca and back, while we are in getting our repairs done. On a previous occasion, they were towing it and lost it. It was there when it got dark. It was not there in the morning, when it got light. It took them 3 days to find it. The crew on the barge were close to mutiny, due to hunger amongst other things.

The last I heard of it, was that it was in Bombay, where the locals can play with it, as that is about all it is useful for.

We set off for Bahia Blanca once again. The new crankshaft has arrived in Buenos Aires, and eight engineers are getting ready to come out from Wartsila. The ships engineers would only assist. It's expensive, but we need this engine fixed properly. So far, the bill stands at about $4 million.

After discharging, we set off for Buenos Aires. But first we have to clean the cargo tanks. This is done with an inert gas. Nowadays, most ships have a nitrogen generator, but we still had the old type, which generates mostly carbon dioxide, and a little oxygen. The oxygen content, has to be less than 2%, but it generally hovers around 0.5%, by burning gas oil or diesel in a burner, then washing it. They are notoriously unreliable. Lovely big words to describe it though, great to slip in to the conversation at parties, makes you sound rather knowledgeable; stoichiometric combustion. All it means, is that it burns up all the oxygen. The inert gas is used to change the atmosphere in the tanks before we sweep them with air. The tanks being cold take a considerable time to warm up. From -95 to +25 degrees Celsius. Of course, our IG plant doesn't really work, but then, what did? After 12 hours' use, the thing blew up, and of course, out of all our spares, we didn't have the bit we needed. Only one thing for it, we'll have to tank clean the old way. Some masters have criticised me for doing it this way, but there was just nothing else for it. We have some sort of cushion at least with what was produced. We have to go straight in with air.

Fortunately, *Norgas Challenger* has a huge fan for sweeping out the void spaces, it produces 12 000 cubic metres per hour, which is just over 2 volumes per hour, so it was going to be quick, or put another way, less risky.

The tank lids are heavy things, held on with 24 x 25 mm bolts, and I will take them off. Keep the others out of the way, it's safer, especially with some of their logic.

I know that I am going to end up with rather a lot of ice, but what the heck.

It went okay, and by the time we arrived in Buenos Aires, everything was safe. We'll get the water out, when the tanks have fully warmed up. In about a fortnight.

Going up the river to BA, the pilot was just a tad awkward.

"If you can only do 9 knots, Captain, I will have to have a sleep after about 8 hours."

"Do you like Scotch, Pilot? We have some very good stuff, called Legacy."

My crew by now knew that when I referred to 'the good stuff', I meant the opposite. "I can get a case for you if we can just keep going." We did. After all, we are 'off-hire' and time is money.

Of course, our berth is in the middle of the city, at Cargo Dock No 3, and just to make it more interesting, this is in the middle of the Navy base.

Just before we arrived, I had told the chief, that I was intending to put the ship on shore power, *and* everything was going to be fixed once and for all. Some Gremlin must have heard me, as just as we went alongside, after coming through some gates which were only slightly wider than the ship herself, all the lights went out. You will not credit this, but No 3 generator, a six-cylinder job, also by Wartsila, had blued its crankshaft. Is there no end to this, that's yet another insurance claim. And just to make it interesting, the bridge vibrated to bits as well, so two radars need new tubes, the gyro compass needs to be relocated after it vibrated off, and the auto-pilot to overhaul. Not much really?

I've got to try and keep track of all this. There are going to be a few late nights.

Now that we knew what we were doing in replacing the main engine crankshaft, and still had a lot of our jigs, work went surprisingly quickly. The old, cracked one was out of the engine in 3 days. I however was working my crew at getting through my own list. Plus, at the height of the repairs, I had over 100 workers from the shipyard, working round the clock as well.

My suggestion of fitting a door in the hull, in order to remove the old and insert the new crankshaft was only meant in jest, but that is exactly what the shipyard did. It was quite clever really, as when it came time to weld it up, it was exactly positioned for the welders.

The crew were all looking forward to sampling the delight of Buenos Aires, but shore leave was cancelled until *all* the work was done. They were not a bunch of happy chappies, but work comes first. Mulla, the Indian AB, thought he could try it on.

This is an old trick, but for some reason, Indian crew still try it, thinking its a new one, or we haven't caught on yet.

Feigning illness, (you can spot it a mile off), he stands looking pitiful in front of my desk, and wants to see a doctor, complaining that when he fell down, he had really hurt his shoulder, and would need an X-ray. Now I know there is nothing wrong with him, but I cannot refuse.

"Okay, Mulla, I'll arrange for you to see a doctor." This would normally mean, a free taxi to the hospital, and back again, and if he plays his cards right, he can have a couple of hours ashore, which the company pays for. He'll show the captain!

Better still if he gets a prescription, then he gets his medicine free as well, and then he can sell it back in India, for a few buckshee Rupees. It used to be with Indian crews, that you could expect this in every port, different ones taking it in turn each time.

He should really have waited a bit longer before the 'pain' disappeared from his face, or told the rest of the crew. Now they all trooped in, with various ailments. So they all think they're going. But, I arranged for a doctor to come to the ship. He did, arriving 2 hours later.

"Right Mulla, the doctor's here for you. In my office." He nearly tripped over his bottom lip. Miraculously, the rest of the crew had 'recovered'. Filipinos are notoriously shy of Western medicine. Most bring their own 'medicine chests' with them when they join a ship. Invariably it doesn't do them any good, but they still do.

After examining him, the doctor agreed that he would need an anti-cortisone injection, straight into the muscle. It is as painful as it sounds. But even more so, when there is nothing wrong with it. It doesn't do any harm, but you don't ask for another one in a hurry. Next morning, the taxi arrives at 07 30 to take him to the hospital. He was back on board by 08 30, and in more pain than he set out with. He was in for another shock though, the mate turned him to for work, on the premise, "you've still got another hand Mulla, so use that." He was not a happy bunny!

At the same time as the main engine crankshaft is being replaced, we start on all three generators. No 3 needs a new crankshaft, but we reckon that we can save the crankshaft 'keeps', after they have been machined. The machine for this is in Helsinki. You couldn't get further away. The 'keeps' support the crankshaft in the engine, all up weight about 280 kgs.

Our agent in Bahia Blanca paid us a lovely compliment. He 'phoned our agents in Buenos Aires, and said,

"Watch yourself with these guys Mike, they can really move themselves." He was about to find out for himself.

In his office, with my superintendent, we explained that we wanted them on a 'plane tonight for Helsinki.

"Oh no, that's not possible, it'll take 3 days to get them out of the dockyard, then 4 days to get them passed Customs, and at least 2 more days for them to get there." During this time, the ship is losing $21 000 per day.

"Okay, forget it, we'll just order new ones."

The superintendent nearly had apoplexy.

"We can't afford that, Doug!"

"I know, so shut-up and come with me."

Back on board, it was arranged for them to be boxed up, two to a box, but kept in the shipyard, not brought back on board. We'll pick them up later. John Hampton of Cromwell Engineering sensed straight away, as to why. He and I got on famously. The family were originally British, and spoke impeccable English.

"Sparky" (the radio officer), "pack an overnight bag, and bring down your passport, you're going on a wee trip."

"Where am I going Captain?"

"I've not got the ticket yet, but it's not far. Trust me." Even I, at times, don't trust me, but he did.

We set off for the airport in a couple of taxis, stopping off at the shipyard on the way for our small 'boxes'. The taxis were well down on their springs.

After getting him a return ticket for Helsinki, which went via Rio de Janeiro, Geneva, Zurich, Heathrow, and Copenhagen, total cost $1750, it was time to pay the excess baggage, cost $ 4750, all paid in cash from my safe.

"Right then Francis (the R/O), here is your ticket, here are some expenses, here is a pro-forma invoice for the customs. You will be met at the other end, and put up in a hotel for the night. Have a nice trip."

"But Captain, you haven't told me where I am going."

"Oh didn't I? Rio de Janeiro for starters. Acht, the rest is on the ticket. Now if you hurry, you'll just make it," steering him towards 'Departures'.

With that we beat a hasty retreat, as in, smoke from our heels.

"He'll be mad when he reads that ticket," said the superintendent.

"Too late for that now."

The poor man got back two nights later, totally stunned and exhausted. "Next time", he says, "could someone else go?" But more importantly, the 'keeps' were machined. It was paid for out of the 'off-hire insurance clause', that I'd used to hire a 'plane in Corpus.

The R/Os next job was a bit more complicated, but it kept him and the second mate busy. It didn't achieve much, but it saved me from doing it.

All the ship's planned maintenance schedules were written in Norwegian. All you have to do "is translate them into English. Here are the dictionaries to help you."

A Filipino who speaks *no* Norwegian translating it into English.

Well, I suppose it was a bit much, but I remember his remarks well. "Captain, this is *awful* difficult, a lot of these words just aren't in the dictionary."

With the main engine being repaired, three generators being overhauled, four turbochargers being overhauled, one main cargo compressor, every pump in the engine room being inspected. The bridge getting re-built. What else was there? We didn't need to look far. There was a 'clunk' and a grrrrrrr from inside the starboard funnel. The engine room fans had fallen off.

This was rapidly becoming one of *those* days.

"Right Einar, come on, I've had enough of this."

The superintendent's head was as far down as my own. What could be left to fall off?

"We are locking this office, we are going to Paddy's Bar in BA, we are going to have a few beers, tell a few jokes, have some sandwiches and everything will look different when we get back. Oh and did I tell you that I've engaged a few painters to paint the hull?"

"No, you didn't! But I'll have a beer with you." Eyes rolling upwards.

It would most probably not be medically recommended as a way to cure disasters happening around you, but it was all I could think off at the time. Plus, I was getting thirsty.

About 2 pm, after blethering to the chandlers, and having had a few sandwiches, it is time to head back, but first I had an errand to do.

"Right, it's my wife's birthday coming up. I've seen this rather nice necklace in a shop window in town. Coming?"

We go into this jeweller, and I describe the one from the window, which is duly brought out. I hadn't twigged yet that this was a rather expensive jewellers. It was absolutely gorgeous, and I ask the price.

With a completely straight face, the guy says, "in United States dollars, sir, 167 000." Gulp, yes, what do I do now? My friend was already out the door and had disappeared.

"Do you have matching ear-rings?"

"No, sorry, then I'll just leave it, thank-you." And fled.

Back on board, all was calm, and nothing else had fallen off, so in a slightly flippant mood, I sent a telex off to Norway. They could do with cheering up as well. "You will be delighted to know sirs that we have now reached the stage, where we can weld things back on faster than they can fall off." It went down rather well.

It took a month to change the first crankshaft, it only took 18 days the second time, but we all going flat out.

A guy from NGC came aboard, and told me to clear the old Ivarans crockery from the ship, and replace it. I had so much spare cash in my budget, plus Insurance Claims (on this type of claim everything goes down, even the food and toilet rolls).

It's a logistical paperwork nightmare, but has to be done.

I engaged a friendly chandler, and we went shopping. I even managed silver wine buckets and stands, and after some effort grape scissors to go with the fruit dishes. I was struggling to spend all of my spare budget.

Did I hire a car in Buenos Aires? You must think I'm mad if I did, although we had now worked out that they drive on the right, which is the wrong side. Well most of them drive on the right. 'Fangio' being the exception in Bahia Blanca. The other thing, if you ever go there, and if you get the chance, do, as it really is a beautiful city, and I never once felt 'threatened', is take your training shoes. Why? You need them to cross the road safely as a pedestrian. As soon as the 'green man' comes on, accelerate as if you were in the 100 metres at the Olympics. You should make the other side before the next 'Grand Prix' starts. They start on every green light. Four abreast usually, on a three-lane road.

Norwegian Gas Carriers asked me to 'look after' our charterers, and to help me get started airmailed out six Norwegian sides of Smoked Salmon. We had Oysters from Chile, King Prawns from Uraguay, Lobsters from Peru and so on. The first dinner went down so well, that we were asked if we could do it again. No problem, just tell me when. All the big cheeses came this time. But the most important thing was that we kept the charter. They could see that we were putting in the effort. However, to return the compliment, they invited us out, and it was here that I finally decided that I would *never* drive in this country. Ever. Portugal is tame compared to this place.

We followed Captain ----------------, the charterer in John Hampton's car, and remembering that they drive on the right, were in the farthest lane to the right as we came to a set of traffic lights at red.

When they changed to green, he turned left! In front of all the others on the starting grid.

In the restaurant, we all started with a dram.

The meal was excellent. They then sent down to the ship, two cases of an Argentinian red wine. It was better than excellent.

Just after I got home from this trip, I tried to get some in the UK, but there had just been a ban imposed on Argentinian wines. Too high a 'sorbitol' content apparently. Pity, as it was good. Try some if you ever get the chance.

Everything at the end came together very suddenly. The cargo tanks had been dried out. Taking the water from the tanks accounted for about 1 200 gallons per tank, and were now being purged with nitrogen. There was some concern from the Argentinian Navy as to what we were doing, but a few thousand cigarettes soon sorted that out. (For our 18-day stay in Buenos Aires, I gave away close onto 230 000 cigarettes. Sparky had to take the ferry to Montevideo to get more. It's only as far as Montevideo for sure?) The ship had been painted, and looked rather resplendent in Orange (the correct shade of orange),the crane was repaired, the gas plant was now fully operational, two of the three generators were back in Class spec, the main engine was nearly finished, and I had done a full survey as well. The restaurant was resplendent. We were all knackered, but we'd had a few laughs as well.

In the crew budget, VShips paid $100 per month, for the crew's benefit. It had built up, so I asked the crew to think of ways of spending it. They suggested a few musical instruments. We already had a few, so what did they want? It was the third mate who was tasked with asking me. "How about a piano Captain?"

"Not on your life. Can you imagine the damage if *that* got loose? Think of something else."

When I was paying off some small bills, and getting discount for cash, John Hampton from the shipyard, who had done a power of a lot of work, enquired if he could get it paid in cash as well? Inflation was rampant in Argentina at the time, but it didn't affect the US Dollar.

"Well, if I get a decent discount, I don't see why not." It was all going down to Insurance anyway.

I got 50%, $88 000 for $44 000.

I got a little bit braver, and asked the guys re-building the ship's bridge. The same thing, discount of 45%.

In that I had to pay my crew, it came to close a $100 000. That's a lot of cash.

But then the Chief Engineer from Wartsila came into my office. He was rather wild. You don't want to get Finns angry. Trust me on this.

Seemingly, their hotel bill, in the Sheraton, for nine engineers, for 18 nights, came to $17 450, but as he was going to pay 'American Express', they had doubled it, to cover themselves for inflation for the 30 days it would take for them to get paid from Amex. That's $34 900.

"Okay, leave it with me. I'll see what I can do."

I 'phoned Oslo, and asked for $120 000 to be sent express, 'overnight'. I did explain why. My superintendent just scoffed.

Next morning in my fax tray.

"Be at the bank by 11 00 hrs, we have sent the cash as requested. I had my briefcase with me, but it was soon apparent, that it wasn't big enough. I had never seen $120 000 in small bills, but take it from me, it makes a big pile. The two main bills were paid in the bank, the cash going into their safety deposit boxes. The rest went with me in a bullet proof Mercedes, that at one time was owned by the Peruvian ambassador, to the agent's office, where $ 17 450 was handed over.

"I want the hotel bill paid now, and all the engineers' passports in my office by the afternoon." I was rather stroppy, but the agents had f-----d us about no end. I then went back to my ship, paid the crew, and put the remainder, about $500 in the safe. Took roughly an hour to spend the lot. Whew! When I had walked off the *Borthwick*, I was, according to my GP, on the point of a nervous breakdown. Because of this, I knew the signs and how to watch for them.

My chief engineer was rapidly heading that way. It was no disgrace to him, he had had a torrid time, and was just about worn out. I had a quiet chat with him, and suggested that he goes on leave. Privately, he agreed that he had had enough. He had been there for 4 months.

This can be a tricky problem in shipping companiess, where the view is often taken, wrongly, that if you cannot hack it, tough, you're out. It would certainly be the case in Gibsons and in Denholms, but then, they are a huge disgrace to the shipping industry anyway.

I gave this further thought, then 'phoned the Managing Director, and carefully explained. He could not have been more understanding, and said he would grant him extra leave, as they wanted him back. Leave it with him, and he would talk with personnel, both in Oslo, and Southampton.

This conversation restored my belief that there were humans in shipping, especially after the way I had been treated. My superintendent took over as chief engineer, and my old chief flew home that night, a breakdown having been avoided. He wrote a lovely letter to me later, and it was apparent, just how close he had come to having to give up the sea altogether. Good on you Mike!

For our last night, we went out to dinner where my superintendent let me into a secret.

VShips Norway, were delighted with the way I was operating. In fact, the way the whole company was operating, and were being awarded more ships to manage for NGC. But, thought I should know something.

It stunned me. Both Gibsons in Leith and Unigas in Rotterdam, had made representations to NGC, when I joined VShips Norway during which they made serious allegations as to my suitability of taking command of an NGC gas tanker. Unigas had gone as far as stating that they would not charter a ship that I commanded. This despite the fact that Gibsons had given me a favourable reference, although they subsequently denied this. Something of this nature could only come from those living in a sewer, or someone(s) trying to cover something up, and we know what that was. The *Borthwick*. The fraud in the No 1 cargo tank calibration. This was not the only time they both did this, but as you read on, you will find just how low, and how far they were both prepared to go, before they were well and truly stuffed (flattened).

Next morning, and I did not sleep well that night, we came to test the main engine. We had run it like this in Bahia Blanca, so knew what to do. The engine is run up to full speed and full load with maximum propeller pitch, until the telegraph is balanced electronically, and every test is done. Getting it up to full speed takes about 8 hours, to let all the new parts run in.

First of all though, we have to 'tie' the ship down, so it can't move. Six sternlines, and six forward springs all balanced out evenly to take the strain, and gangway in then, off we go. It starts off quite innocuously, but at full power is very impressive. What it also does, although you can't see it, is it moves the bottom mud, from one end of the harbour to the other. Rather a large crowd gathered as well, as this is something that is not often done. The engine test was complete. Back to Santa Clara then to cool-down and load. This would seem to be a good time to change the crew, who were up on their contracts anyway. I had already set this in motion in Buenos Aires, and we were after all going to change to Indian officers and crew, except master, mate, chief, and second engineer who would remain British or Norwegian.

Getting crew, ABs, messmen, cooks etc isn't difficult, getting qualified officers is, and to this day, is still a problem. Getting crews who know what they are doing, is harder. Especially in India.

My off-going Filipinos though *all* want to go home together. They are like children on their first flight, going home. But it is going to be a staggered changeover. It is better for the ship, but this lot were not pleased.

"*Please* captain", one after the other they trooped in, "*please* tell Mr Sundan to *try* harder to get my relief here for Santa Clara, I am *so* tired now", with baleful eyes. It's difficult keeping a straight face. In the end, they all left after about a 2 week staggered changeover, except for and second and third mate, who were still there when I left. Such was the difficulty in getting two mates, that I was even considering Brazilian/Argentinian mates, but they were equally elusive.

We ran Santa Clara to Bahia Blanca for the next 6 weeks, the ship performing magnificently, running now at 16 knots, as opposed to Ivarans 13.5 knots, and lifting now 3000 tonnes of ethylene every time. We still occasionally trans-shipped as well, either from that bloody barge, or from a small gas tanker they kept there. The *Tacosul* which was getting on for 40. Didn't look it though.

I had a new British chief and second engineer. The mate was staying on. Everything had been turned around, and the charterers were 'over the moon'.

One morning though, as we arrived alongside at about 1 in the morning, no sooner had I gone to bed, when about 4 in the morning, my telephone went, and it was the agent,

"Sorry to call you Doug, but the Customs are here. They want to search the ship."

Wearily going back down below, I found about 20 customs officials, with more Gold Braid than Pancho Villa, plus an enormous dog.

It was a sniffer dog, and I was in a devilish mood.

You will recall that I like having my ship searched, all of it.

We started at the top and worked our way down, every compartment and cabin. My crew had all been called and all got up, except one Indian AB, who decided to stay asleep. One big lick from the dog across his face, and he was out of that bunk like a rocket.

"Okay captain, we are happy," said the senior customs guy.

"But I'm not," says I, "what about the rest of the ship?" After all, they had gotten me out of my bed. "Let's go and do the rest."

The dog had no problem with the deck compartments, until. We opened the void spaces. These do not have to be kept inerted with type 'C' tanks which we had, and anyway, we still had checks to do down there anyway.

It was not overly pleased to be fashioned into a harness and then lowered 40 feet down into the darkness. It voiced its displeasure when it got back on deck, with bared teeth. The handler did the other three voids.

A clean bill of health once more then? Yes, after another 5000 fags were distributed.

Normally, after the ship was cleared in, the agents and so forth would disappear ashore until we sailed.

One day they all stayed, all of them. Why? I must admit I was a bit slow that day.

After I enquired, I was told,

"An agreement has been signed in Madrid between The UK and Argentina. Now we are officially all friends again."

As if we weren't before. "Right then Arturo, party time."

"Book a restaurant in town, get a hold of everyone we know and invite them to dinner tonight, on me. Cookie, get a few cases of beer in the fridge, and we'll celebrate this properly."

Generous? I'm still trying to use up my excess victaulling budget.

Eating out costs pennies in Argentina. We had a great time.

My decision to change to Indian crew was a good one, as this lot could graft under their bosun, or Serang as he is known. They were on good overtime though, but earned it. Plus I had more orange paint.

It was time for me to leave. I would have stayed on but there was a family matter to deal with, and I was expected in Oslo before Christmas to tidy up all the Insurance matters, which now ran, at a little over $6 million. This voyage, I could probably have done without, after the *Borthwick*, and Gibsons, but in a way, it was rather therapeutic. Plus, I had established myself in another company, where I was truly valued. My confidence had taken a hell of a battering on the *Borthwick*, but was now fully restored. In Oslo, I was very well received, especially as I had spent some time in Buenos Aires at night taking long exposure photographs of the ship, and gave them one, complete with frame, which turned out really well. Fortunately I had the negative with me, as they needed 12 more for NGC.

Then I was invited to join the Forth Pilots. I was in a quandary here, as I rather felt that I should have stayed, at least for another trip with VShips, but the invitation coincided with the birth of my son, and I had missed a lot of my daughter's early life being at sea, so with some reluctance on both sides, I left to become a marine pilot. It lasted 3 days before Gibsons and Unigas started again. Bastards.

The only difference now, was that I knew who it was. In both camps. One day, they will regret their actions. It is coming soon.

Comment:

How this ship was funded was rather good. It may be something for the UK Government to consider.

Tapping in to the Norwegian pride, everyday people were invited to take shares in building ships, providing they were built in Norwegian yards, and for the first year, by Norwegian crews.

This kept work in the yards, and employment for the crews.

Tax incentives were offered, the only pre-requisite was that the ships had to be run by Norwegian Companies.

I am not suggesting that in this country, we start off by building ships as expensive and complicated as gas tankers, but virtually every container feeder ship trading here is under a foreign flag. With the new 'tonnage tax' offered under the Red Ensign, should make a competitive target, especially with more modern tonnage. Not only would it keep the shipyards working, but it would give our junior officers being churned out from the nautical colleges, the proper experience they need to advance in their careers, and we are going to need 'experienced' officers for port positions etc in the future. They are not going to get this experience from the ships that work the North Sea.

It should not be difficult to set up such a scheme, especially with the current low interest rates, to offer say, tax exemption on all earnings from the ship for say 5 years. There would be no mortgage on the ship, as the money is put up in advance. Little loss to the treasury, as the amount of tax paid on interest, when the interest rates are low, is small. It also allows almost everyone interested in the country to enjoy the same privilege as Names at Lloyds. Spending the same money twice, and we all know how successful they are. Plus our exports are going out in our ships. Nice bit of kudos this.

All it needs is for someone to do it. If I was a politician, I'd be tripping over myself to do this. It is bound to be a vote puller.

The downside however is one thing that has rather reared its' ugly head in this country once more. For every person who has the will to do something, there exists about a hundred who will try to convince them of why they *cannot* do it.

I, however am a professional seaman, worked for Gibson Liquid Gas, use lateral thinking if the obvious doesn't seem to work, and can get round virtually every regulation. All it takes is the desire to beat the system, so would those hundred please shut up, and let those of us with the will just get on with it. The EU? Chicken feed to a thinking seaman.

PART 3

Since the introduction of the 1987 Pilotage Act, the standard of pilotage in the UK has shown a steady decline. There is only one other branch associated with the ports around this country, that has exceeded this decline, by declining further, and that is that small body known as 'Competent Harbour Authorities'.

Off course, neither group are going to agree with this. It is not in their interests to do so, and will blindly tell everyone of their 'important contribution' to Maritime Safety.

Pilots are *grossly overpaid* for what they do, and will be the first to blame someone else, usually the Master of the ship, or the weather, or the tide, etc in the event of an accident, which are far more common than you know about.

Rarely a day goes by in the River Forth, when there is not some incident or other. I know from experience, as I was there for 3 years. Let us not forget the Sea Empress going aground seven times! in Milford Haven, or the Havkong 'blowing off' the jetty in Braefoot Bay. There are many more that you, the reader do not know about, but you soon will. In the merchant navy, the rank of 'Captain' doesn't exist. The 'old man' as he is affectionately known, is called 'Captain', but he is in effect the Master.

To call yourself Captain, you should have held or hold a Queen's Commission. Army, Navy, or Royal Marines, etc. It's also possible in the RFA, but are a right bunch of Charlies, and don't really count.

You would be surprised at the number of pilots who call themselves 'Captain', who before becoming a pilot did not have any ship handling experience, or had even been in command of a ship.

So, how are pilots selected?

It's quite easy really. You, in the first stage, write a letter with your CV to the area that you want to work in. It matters not a hoot if you *actually* know anything about that area or not, if you have been in command of a ship or not, or if indeed you know anything about ships or not. There is a pilot on the Forth, who was in charge of an oil rig, which stood on the sea bed of the North Sea, before becoming a pilot. And a right wally he is too. He is not the only one on the Forth.

The area you choose will have a CHA. This stands for 'Competent Harbour Authority'. You should view the term 'Competent' with due care, as few, if any of them are.

So, having had your letter accepted, you attend an interview. There will generally be two or more pilots, maybe a Harbour Master, or an Operations Manager for the port(s) concerned. This was the case when I went up. The questions you will be asked will vary in the extreme, and need not make much sense. You are, after all, applying to join, 'an elite'. Remember, I had just walked off a gas tanker, and was going to join another shortly, as master. At the time, this was unheard of, and I made such an impression that I went straight to the top of their 'preference list'. It is not when you applied, or how long you were on the list that matters about you starting as a trainee pilot, as they will only ever take from the top of the list. This is supposed to maintain a 'high' standard. It's a mystery how the oil rig guy got in, but nepotism can prevail rather a lot here as well.

There is also a story, which I am assured is true, and I can rather believe it to be so, that one future pilot was asked if he had Athlete's Foot? No, he didn't, but why? "That's all right then, you'll be able to use the shower in the pilot station." Nobody, who cared about hygiene, ever used that shower!

Other questions can vary, depending on how good your CV is, or what you call yourself. Some are brave enough to call themselves Captain, not because they have taken command of a ship, but because they have a masters ticket. A lot of companies have been caught out this way, especially foreign ship management companies. Remember, I said ship handling looked easy and isn't. They are about to be found out, if they aren't arrogant enough.

The preferred age range for new pilots is 35 to 40 years. Get 'em in young eh? No chance, the first thing to understand about piloting, is that what you think may be reasonable logic, invariably isn't. The age range is exclusively, to enhance the Pilots Pension Fund. Not your own

Pension are they interested in, theirs. At your expense. It was agreed at the interview stage, with Forth Ports plc, that I could keep my own private fund going. Like a fool, I trusted them.

Rule No 1. Forth Ports plc *cannot* be trusted. *On any subject.* I speak from experience.

After I obtained my licence, I was summoned to see the Operations Manager (OM). He is supposed to represent a link between the CHA, and the pilots. He was really a contemptuous little rat, only interested in himself. You'll hear a lot more about him as we go on.

With him, was the pilot, who kept an eye on the PNPF (Pilots' National Pension Fund). Another two-faced rat.

"Right," says the OM. "You are not getting to pay your pension into a Private Fund. Forth Ports will not get involved in separate schemes. You will contribute to the PNPF like everyone else." Why? Because his father was a 'pilot', and from the pilot came.

"All your predecessors paid in for the ones who retired, so you can pay in for us when we retire. Then the others will pay for you."

There seemed to be some misplaced logic here, when you consider that the number of pilots now employed are considerably less than there was, even a decade ago. By the time, I came to retire, then there might not be enough left for me to retire on.

I countered with, "I was told at the interview stage, that I could keep my own private fund."

OM again. "Here is what we are going to do, Forth Ports instead of paying your share into the fund, will deduct it as usual, and give it to the pilots, where it can be shared out amongst the other pilots. You can then make your own arrangements.

I got rather angry. "What you are proposing, is theft of my money!"

"Take it or leave it." I had to join the PNPF, but I was determined I would take the first chance I could get, to get out of it. Apart from being illegal, there is more.

Pilots are supposed to be self-employed, but they have no direct personal say in how their Pension is run? I know this to be a fine line, but if the Inland Revenue, knew what really goes on, not only with Pensions, but 'expenses,' then there might just be a few questions asked. Then there are 'extra' pilots' rates.

About 3 days after I qualified, 1 senior ex-Grangemouth pilot, came up to me and said. "You will sign up with this firm of accountants in

Grangemouth, who have looked after us for years. We are not having you screwing up our 'arrangements.' "

"Get stuffed pal, I'll have my own arrangements if I want to." A few days later, a letter arrived from this bunch in Grangemouth, which went straight into the bin. Nobody, blackmails me.

While I am on the subject of paying pilots, I might as well tell you about 'expenses'. I bet the Revenue don't know about this racket. This is pilots' 'tax-free' income. It's quite a few thousand, each.

Let us say that a pilot is in Grangemouth at the start of his shift. He gets expenses to go from the Pilots' office to the ship. However, pilots are rarely there. There is an arrangement with the boatmen, that their cars are parked there, and they go to the ship with them. So 1 taxi fare (office to the ship) goes into their pockets. No costs actually incurred. Then he sails a ship from Grangemouth to the sea. Getting into the pilot boat, he finds that he is taking another ship up to Grangemouth, so joins that and goes back up the river. Now he has gained two 'freebies.' He is paid expenses for going back by road to Grangemouth, and then when he gets there, expenses for coming back again. But he transferred between two ships by boat, and never even got ashore. Then again when the second ship is docked, it's back to his car by boat, claiming yet another taxi fare back to his office. This goes on all the time, with the ship eventually footing the bill, until it is passed on to you of course, the final customer.

Expenses caused more arguments between pilots than they were worth.

1 pilot from Leith had it down to a fine art, and could argue, that if he was on 'this' ship, maybe 3 days ago, then if this, this and that changed, then he should have had the expenses for 'this' ship, which meant he would be £3 better off. On top of this, taxis are seldom used. Pilots use their own cars, which are infinitely cheaper. There is even a scheme to recompense a pilot, if someone else uses their car. £5 was left in the ashtray, or coin slot. Even the most stupid could work out that if you worked with the same people all the time, then the same fivers were going round and round. But try explaining that to some of the old diehards out of Grangemouth or Leith. Better not to even try.

The hardest part of being duty pilot, was ensuring that a pilot was matched with his own car, as he finished for the day. Dealing with ships was the easiest part of his job. During the night, one of the pilot boats crew, acts as duty pilot, and they are 100 times better than the pilots at it. Woe betide the duty pilot, if a pilot ended up in Methil, lived in Grangemouth, and his car was in Leith.

How are pilots trained? Well, in Scapa Flow, it doesn't take a genius to work out how to go in a straight line, with a bend either left going in, or right, going out. The skill of going alongside is assisted by tugs, or for the really adventurous, securing a tanker to a loading tower to load. A single point mooring really, all you have to do, is point the ship at it, and make sure that you stop in time. If you think I'm being facetious, I'm not, because the towers that are there today, are not the original ones, they were knocked over a long time ago.

With the resulting oil pollution which was quietly covered up. If you want to anchor somewhere in Scapa Flow, then there are plenty of places to choose from, after all, if the Royal Navy can do it, then a Scapa Flow pilot 'should' manage.

However, I'll limit the text now to the River Forth in Scotland, which is somewhat more difficult, but no less hairy. First of all, you need a license from the CHA (Competent Harbour Authority), for Grangemouth only. Grangemouth is about 22 miles up the Forth, and is the main port for ships up to about 30 000 tons deadweight predominantly tankers, but some cargo/container ships as well. Initially your license will limit you to handling ships up to 3500 Gross tons for 18 months.

Straight away, you will see that I refer to 'deadweight' tons, and 'gross' tons.

The difference is that deadweight is actually a useful way of measuring ships, this being the all up weight of cargo, fuel, stores, water and so on. Gross tons however is about the most useless thing ever devised, and is so complicated to calculate, that the rules are changed frequently.

When someone puzzles out, yet another way of 'getting round' them, as a bigger ship which can trade on a smaller tonnage, then the rules are revised. *Again*! Some ships lose out though. The *Quentin*, for many years was 1596 gross, but now as the *Avarro* is 1764 gross, but nothing in the ship has changed. But CHAs like them, because that is how they get paid. The more gross tons, the merrier. *But*. When the new rules are calculated, and ships assigned new tonnages, are the port dues adjusted accordingly? Come off it, this is a competent harbour authority we are talking about, reduce fees? Whoever heard the like.

45 trips to Grangemouth then and, they need not all be on the ships you will be expected to handle in the next 18 months. It was during this period, when I jumped on board one, that I soon found out that, even the most senior pilot on the Forth had little clue, as to how to take a tanker into the locks at Grangemouth. So thank- you Calumn, an ex Leith pilot, for showing me how *not to do it*.

This was on a French tanker of some 30 000 tonnes, in ballast, coming in to load. Lack of experience was the cause, as the ship incurred serious damage to her port side. The hull remained intact, but in her next drydock, there was going to be some major repairs to her framing, which were well bent. Who was to blame, the master off course, despite the fact that the pilot was controlling the tugs, which were well out of position, as the ship struck the entrance to the lock. Reinforced concrete is not terribly forgiving.

45 trips with a qualified pilot, in or out, it doesn't matter, and you can go up for the exam.

The exam is a farce, all you need is a good memory, as every question is either based on the Admiralty charts, the local bye- laws, the local tidal streams, or the drawings available from the Scottish Records Office. If you are really well in, and know who is on the 'examining board', you can even get a set of questions.

Here is an example: Over what angle of arc, is the light on Inchcolm Island obscured? Now apart from steering or piloting a ship by lights at night, we are also expected to know where there aren't any lights. The obvious answer, is where it is dark. Another perhaps? What is the characteristic of the light on Inchkeith? Answer, Flash white every 15 seconds. Not good enough, you need to know the height as well, and its range. Meaningless information, as the light is on top of a huge great big island, that even the blind could spot, and if its foggy, then you won't see the light anyway. Just one more ludicrous one. This is really kept for masters going up for an exemption, that the pilots do not want to pass. What is the boatman's name who takes the stern lines in Methil? It's a pretty safe bet to answer, Jimmy. (Actually, it's Ian).

After this, seven more trips to any of the other smaller ports, and another exam, and you have your license. The other ports are Methil (at that time, Kirkcaldy), Burntisland, Rosyth (we'll come back to this later), Inverkeithing, Longannet Power Station, Granton and Leith. I can assure you from experience, that these 'smaller' ports are a damn sight more difficult to get into, than Grangemouth.

It is really quite frightening to think that someone with *no* ship handling experience at all is treated in the same way as someone who does. And they are let loose on the same ships. There are a lot of pilots like this around the coasts of the UK. The Humber is still the worst.

Just think, if my last ship, the *Norgas Challenger*, had come into the River Forth, and at 5650 Gross tons, I would not have been able to pilot her, even although I knew that ship better than anyone. A pilot who had never seen her before could. The mind boggles!

Very occasionally, and as far as I know, it only happened once, someone comes along and buggers up the system, by wanting to go into, Anstruther! This is within Forth Ports jurisdiction, and pilots are supposed to be available. The pilot who got the job, had to consult a road map, to find out where it was.

Just prior to my joining the pilots in 1990, which is not that long ago, the Forth Pilotage Service changed. There used to be three separate services, Leith, Grangemouth, and Fife. It was as you can imagine, hopelessly inefficient. Not much has changed though.

Medicals for pilots were introduced, and a lot of them failed. The numbers fell from 55 to 39, and that included 4 new pilots. The rest 'retired'. Some were retired before the medical, and just went through the motions of working. One was so fat, he had trouble getting up the pilot ladder, so took all the small ships.

Leith pilots piloted ships into Leith, Granton, Hound Point, and any ship bound for Grangemouth, where a Grangemouth pilot boarded. Fife pilots, piloted anything to Methil, Kirkcaldy, Burntisland, Inverkeithing, and any ships bound for Grangemouth, where again, a Grangemouth pilot boarded. The two stations took ships bound for Rosyth, where a navy pilot took over at No 19 Buoy. (Just before the Forth Bridge.) Unless they were RFA ships, who didn't take pilots. Then Grangemouth pilots took all ships into Grangemouth, occasionally Longannet, and sailed every ship out.

As I said hopelessly inefficient, but you have to look on the mentality of pilots. They think they are doing every ship a favour while at the same time extracting as much money in pilotage dues as possible. The mentality that, ships serve pilots, is never far away, whereas it should be, pilots who serve ships. Don't argue with them, they've had years of grumbling and won't listen to you anyway.

It was decided, that all left would 'train' so that everyone could go to all the ports, and to do this, they all had to accompany pilots from their respective stations. To learn about them first hand.

You soon discovered, as a trainee pilot, that it wasn't learning the written rules and bye-laws that presented a problem, it was trying to find out about the un-written ones. It was 2 years before I found them all, and I was considered 'quick.'

A pilot's 'watch' or day was from 8 am to 8 pm, but was more likely to be 7:30 to, how soon can I get back to the golf course? But not for everybody. No, the ex Grangemouth pilots would only come on station at 10 am, but would, if there were any sailings from Grangemouth from 8 am, sail these ships, then try to get to the golf course. Why? The traffic going into Edinburgh, meant for an 8 am boarding, they would have to leave home at 6 am to avoid the traffic. The ex-Leith and ex-Fife pilots could sit in the traffic jams though. This caused no end of resentment, but it gets more complicated. Although most pilots boarded the pilot boats in Granton, it was also possible to board them in Burntisland. This was regarded as 'unfair' by the ex Grangemouth pilots. Don't even bother to think of the logic by the ex-Leith pilots. Just, like me, shake your head.

About 3 days after I started 'training', I was summoned to the OM's office, where two of the other pilots awaited me with faces like thunder. This was because Gibsons had been on the 'phone. Note, they weren't asked, they just did this out of spite.

Bearing in mind that I am a Master Mariner, and a highly experienced gas tanker master, I do not expect to be treated like a wee boy. But that is what they did.

From the OM. "We have heard that you didn't walk off the *Borthwick*, as you stated, but that in fact you were taken off. We have confirmed this with Denholms." (Refer to end of Part 1, where the true tale is.)

"I don't lie, I told you at the interview what happened on the *Borthwick*. I did in fact inform Denholms by 'phone the previous day, that I was going no further than Teesport. My chief officer can confirm this. He is an assistant harbour master in Teesport." So I went through the whole nasty event once again, even although it was *absolutely none of their business*. Gibsons were in fact trying to get me 'booted out' of becoming a Forth Pilot, so a solicitor's letter was sent to the managing director of Gibsons. This however was not the end of it, and was why I ended up as the scapegoat for the third time, but that was in the future.

My respect for the Forth Ports Operations Manager, fell to nil.

No, that's not fair, less than nil.

Getting back to 'training' the existing Forth Pilots.

Remember, they are all 'experienced ship handlers', so we'll start with a ship called the *MV Helen*. You've probably never heard of her.

The captain wishes he'd never heard of the Forth Pilots. The ship was going into Methil, so a little about Methil first.

Methil is an old coal port from the many collieries that used to come from this part of Fife. It was built by the Victorians, who *knew* how to build ports. Solid granite, the hardest they could find, and mooring rings that will rust away in about 2 million years. There used to be three separate docks, but No 3 was filled in as the pits closed down. The channel is still there, and goes off to starboard after the breakwater end with another granite peak at the apex of the channel to the entrance to Nos 1 and 2 docks, which are entered through a pair of gates. These open from 2 hours before high water, till high water. On the port side, there is a wooden wharf. The entrance is 50 feet wide. The breakwater is made from the granite that they couldn't shape for the port, and is even harder.

On this particular day, a Fife pilot was accompanied by six other pilots, 'doing their turns,' supposedly five turns to each port they weren't used to, but changed to two, when they ran out of ships to 'wreck'.

The weather was not kind, and if there was a sensible thing to do, it would have been to wait until it improved, but then seven pilots cannot be sensible, as they could be on the golf course.

The *Helen* hit everything it could, the breakwater, the port entrance wharf, the starboard entrance apex, both sides where the gates were, then the intended berth, 'big style.'

The ship was so badly damaged, that it was declared a constructive total loss, and had to be towed away for scrap. Methil itself, got hardly a scratch.

Logic would say that the 6 extra pilots couldn't learn anything from this, but they all claimed it as 'training.' When you see what they did to the other ports, you will appreciate, that what they learnt was, how *not to get into Methil*.

One of them trained another trainee and me later, how *not* to get into Methil, so he was well 'trained.' This was a German ship of 499 Gross tons, but was in reality, nearer to 2000 actual tons. The ship was the *Nordcarrier*. It was a Saturday, and I was only there as my wife wanted the car in the afternoon. I was still 'training' for Grangemouth at the time. It was also a filthy day, and not really suitable for coming into port. The ship wasn't working cargo until the following Monday, so there was no need to 'risk it'. If you met this pilot, it wouldn't take you long to work out, that he was an arrogant, I know it all, type. The same as the expenses 'expert.'

We go out in the 'Methil' pilot boat, which looked as if was ready to fall to bits, and jump aboard the ship. The captain was all for canceling it, but the pilot talked him into it. Up anchor then and in we go.

The golden rule for entering Methil is *never* to fight the swell. Just outside the port is a rig building yard, with a long flat frontage, and the swell used to bounce off this, which in effects cancels out the swell coming in. So, if the ship is set in, the next swell lifts you back out. It takes a bit of getting used to. On this day, the pilot tried to fight the swell, and when something goes wrong, it goes wrong very quickly, as the ship bounced of the concrete entrance to starboard, before flying hard round to port, with the engine trying to go full astern, to then go straight through a wooden wharf. There were lumps of old timber flying everywhere. The funny thing about this wharf, was that it was condemned some years before and was fenced off at both ends. Even if had all be knocked down, it wouldn't really have mattered. The most important thing was the ship wasn't damaged. Oh, it was scratched a wee bit, but that only needs a coat of paint. After extracting ourselves out of the wharf, we then made a pretty decent attempt of trying to demolish the entrance. I was embarrassed, and felt for the master, but the pilot just accepted it as one of these things.

For incidents like these, which happen most days, the pilot has to submit a report. This usually takes about 5 minutes, and an incident is invariably explained away with the pilots favorite line, 'master declined pilot's advice'. I'll come back to this at the end. In that the master is always responsible anyway, one wonders why he needs a pilot in the first place. If I can get away with not taking a pilot, then I don't.

But there is more to an incident than you would think, as this is where Forth Ports make even more money, as they will claim on the ship's insurance for 'damage'. Forth Ports don't need a budget for maintenance of the ports, as their pilots provide a plentiful amount anyway. Also in this case, as about a year later, a barge came along and repaired the hole in the wharf with new timbers. Now there is a perfectly good bit of wharf, with a condemned bit at each end. Later, I'll tell you of an incident near Grangemouth, where Forth Ports really came unstuck. In fact, I'll tell you now, as it has a humorous touch.

Shortly after I qualified, there came along a new chief harbour master, his predecessor had retired. This chappie was an ex Queens Harbour Master from Rosyth, who soon became known as *Ten Knot Tony* (*TNT*), for reasons which will become abundantly clear later. A more officious pain in the arse, would be harder to find. He thought he knew everything, when in fact he knew precious little, in particular, how to treat people. Or *anything* about ships and the sea.

One day, a tanker arrived from the Continent. A ship called the *Erika*, under the Danish Flag, and of some 8000 tonnes, bound for Grangemouth, and loaded.

Reporting in to Forth Navigation Service (FNS), as he crossed the port limits, he was asked if he had any defects?

"Yes, I lost an anchor in my last port," was the reply.

Straight away, *TNT*, who just happened to be in the FNS room at the time sensed a quick 'buck,' and replied with.

"In that case Captain, you will require an escort tug to accompany you."

Just what this tug was going to do, was anybody's guess. But, the charge was £1000, for a fuel cost of about £50. Nice little earner. The ship took his pilot, and went up to Grangemouth. A bright day, and a nice day for a wee jolly.

When it was time for the ship to sail, the master was asked,

"have you managed to fit your spare anchor Captain?" Fat chance he's only been in 12 hours, and we all know how difficult it is without a crane. (Re, *Norgas Challenger.*)

"No, I haven't had time."

"In that case you'll need an escort, we will arrange it."

The Captain wasn't unduly bothered. A delay and a shift to another berth, and a crane would have cost a lot more.

So the same tug, Forth Ports pride and joy, the *Oxcar*, was dispatched from Leith. The only problem now, was it was dark, and there was no ship to follow up the river to Grangemouth. The tug came round the Bo'ness Buoy, about 6 miles out from Grangemouth, and made a mistake. The tugmaster mistook the light on the end of the jetty at Longannet, for the 'Hen and Chicken' Buoy (both are green), and promptly ran hard aground on the Hen and Chicken rocks. And I mean *hard* aground, as in very.

Meanwhile the *Erika* is in the lock waiting to sail.

If VHF contact had been established between the tug and the ship, then the ship's insurance would have borne the costs of the tugs repair. (It's a vagary in Marine Insurance.) But as it hadn't, it was Forth Ports Insurance that had to.

Another tug, the *Seal Carr*, was dispatched from Leith to get the *Oxcar* off, and into a drydock in Leith. In the meantime, the *Erika* sailed (without an escort, as they had run out of tugs).

These tugs have Voight Schneider gear, and such was the force of grounding that both units had been pushed 1.5 metres up into the tug. This was going to be expensive, as nothing from Voights is cheap. I did hear an initial figure of £150 000, but the final bill came to nearer double that. The tug was out of commission for weeks. One should not gloat, but the increase in insurance premium next year, was a great deal more, than the £2000 (actually £1000) that *TNT* thought he could make. But wait, even the increase was dumped onto the tugs hire costs, so in the end, the end user paid, you and I. A salutary lesson for *TNT* perhaps? You must be joking. This man brings new meaning to the word 'thick'. However, the biggest surprise came out later. *None* of Forth Ports tug masters, had ever been further up-river than the 'bridges', but all had certificates for the whole river. It was very quietly conceded by the OM, that they should have had 'in house' instruction, but there had been an oversight. Bloody expensive oversight, but as you read on, you will find that this is typical of the CHA, being Forth Ports plc.

I actually wrote the above in February 2003, before the first draft went out to my proof reader. I was not aware at the time that there was a court case pending against Forth Ports plc, one part of which was 'failing to provide adequate training to their employees'.

When the case came to court on the 8th of May, they pleaded guilty, and were fined £200 000. A man lost his life after entering an oxygen-deficient space.

When I came to sea in 1972, at the same time as the Chief Harbour Master, who was previously Operations Manager, the Department of Transport even at that time were drumming it in to everybody at sea, the need to check if an enclosed space had sufficient oxygen. They have been at us ever since through every publication going. You cannot move on some notice boards with reminders.

Nobody that I have ever met at sea (with one exception when I worked ashore in Qatar) would enter *any* space without testing it first, and then when in that space, would either carry an OX82 meter or similar with him, and continuously monitor the atmosphere until he and any others had all left.

An OX82 meter is about the size of a Police radio, fits nicely into a top pocket of a shirt or a boilersuit, and if the oxygen content falls to 18 % sets off an alarm, by which everyone gets out. 18% oxygen is about the same as the average person breathes out at. Normal air is 21%, the difference in this case 3% being carbon dioxide. Any enclosed space can have a deficiency in oxygen for any number of reasons, the creation of ferrous oxide (rust) absorbs oxygen, fermenting grain (in this case,) absorbs oxygen and so on.

By pleading guilty not only displays this company's total ineptitude, but brings full credence to my comment later, 'nothing changes in Forth Ports without there being an accident first'. A lot of evidence to this follows. This is nothing new in this company. It is high time it is stamped out.

But there is more. By pleading guilty, covers up a lot of things that they would rather hide, or put another way, would prefer that you did not find out about. This displayed admirably by the amount of press coverage it got at the time. A small article, lost in the inside pages, and forgotten about next day. I rather think though, that by the time you find out just what is being covered up, they will be on the front pages and it will not be forgotten about next day. I trust the poor fellow's family will sue accordingly, as the amount of legislation is mind numbing, and the Chief Harbour Master has had it drummed into him for over 30 years. He should be held to account, after all, he calls himself Captain.

Back to the *Oxcar* then.

The other factor that was quietly forgotten, was the pollution caused by the tug. But the most serious of all, was that these tugs were part of an emergency plan known as 'Operation Clearwater Forth'.

Who was the author? None other than *TNT*. The chief harbour master. Was another tug chartered in to cover for the one being repaired? What do you think? Of course not. Covering up is a popular pastime with this company remember.

There was another incident later, at Grangemouth, but we'll come to that one in due course. And yes *TNT* excelled himself! Again!

The next port round from Methil, we'll visit them all for those un-familiar with the Forth, is Kirkcaldy, sadly no longer used.

If Methil was old, then Kirkcaldy is even older. I doubt if anyone knows for sure, but someone is bound to tell me. The one endearing thing about this place, is that it was designed with a bent ruler. Even the entrance doesn't line up with anything, as it is two points off the line of the channel to make it interesting, and to further complicate it, has a shallow patch as well. You could get more light from a candle, than you can get from the light on the end of the breakwater.

But hold on. It's not *all* bad, there are some 'navigational' features that you won't find in *any* book. Items such as the 'traffic lights', the 'Pelican crossing', the 'hospital' in the background, and the best of all, the 'black hole'.

By the early nineties, the only thing exported was fragmented scrap, which of course had to be loaded from the most inconvenient berth, the one round the corner from the entrance.

Taking advantage of a 'training turn', was the only time I was there, before becoming qualified. Unfortunately, the 'training' pilot, ex Grangemouth hadn't been there at all! He cribbed instruction from an old Fife pilot, the one who demolished a listed building getting a ship in. That's a good story too!

The ship was a small Dutch coaster, coming down in ballast from Grangemouth, the master fortunately being the very relaxed type, who had seen it all before. Finding this place at night is hard, until you line up the hospital, with the black hole, then it's easy, until you discover than the channel is not as long as it looks. It was at this point that the pilot lost his nerve, and banged the engine full astern. Fortunately, this was exactly the right thing to do, as the transverse thrust kicked in, and she slid beautifully through the entrance. Even the captain was impressed.

About 6 months later, I brought in my first ship, and tried it, without the panic. It was exactly the right thing to do. Then I never went back, as the trade was falling away, and export was transferred to Inverkeithing.

Kirkcaldy is now closed. It's a small, tidal, boat harbour, marina doesn't quite suit it. Forth Ports, however, having milked the place for all it was worth, have let it decay, to what is now, an ugly eyesore. For many years, it was possible to fish from the end of the breakwater, a pastime enjoyed by many over the years. You can't any more, as Forth

Ports plc have fenced off the access. It is considered unsafe. But wait. Are they not responsible for it? After all, it is part of their property, inherited from the Forth Ports Authority before Forth Ports plc was created. Why not repair it?

Now before you think, or hear them say, lack of money or funds, remember this. Executive flats are being built on the old dock sides and surrounding land. Land that they didn't pay for in the first place, but got for free, and have sold off to a building company at a huge profit, not at 100% profit, or even 1000% profit, but at infinite% profit. Even the most crooked accountant couldn't better this.

The rest of the dock area is fenced off by a temporary fence, thus adding to the eyesore nature of the place.

Remember, they were fined for lack of risk assessment?

It is not possible to walk on the breakwater, but what happens if some poor wee weekend sailor, happily chugging back in to his mooring within the harbour, that he is paying for, just grazes the breakwater enough for a coping stone say to fall on him or his boat?

There is an old saying at sea, if you say, that can't possibly happen, it invariably does.

Forth Ports plc therefore have a choice, either extend the fence denying access all the way round *including* the seawards sides, that should look really ugly, or repair it.

But I have a better idea. The breakwater is by its age, listed, as is the gate house and the gates themselves, most probably the harbour too. Let's get Fife Council to repair it, then hand its maintenance over to Historic Scotland, and send the bill to Forth ports plc in Edinburgh.

This will be considerably cheaper than the next fine, especially if the poor wee chap who had a coping stone fall on him is killed, and that is very possible.

Now to Burntisland. There are two docks, the East, and the West. I have never seen a ship in the West Dock, but was still examined on it.

The East Dock was used by lightering barges, which offloaded bauxite from Takoradi, for the aluminium works, which have regrettably, now closed. There is also a tanker jetty for the import of caustic acid.

But what a lot of people don't know about, is what lies on the bottom of the East Dock, apart from the pure copper cables, the Navy used for degaussing their minesweepers. Just get yourself a set of scuba gear, and go and have a look. It is a veritable treasure trove of marine relics. But remember, it is 'wreck', and should be handed over to the Customs, that is if you can find one.

Eh, but, a wee word of caution, it is actually against Forth Ports bye-laws to go diving within the docks, but as they break their own bye laws more than anyone else, then this should give you a suitable defence if caught. It's more fun at night too.

When you're at it, the Eastern Breakwater (seaward side) is the best place on the Forth for lobsters. If you have a close look at the barges, (they are non-powered), you will see that they have rather a lot of bumps in them. How did they get them in and out of port, well none other than Forth Ports tugs. But you guessed that already, hence all the bumps dents and folds.

On the Fife Coast, is a gas tanker terminal. Braefoot Bay. Why on earth this place was built where it is, is a mystery, but from the time it opened, until late in 1992, was a danger to all nearby. Not as you would expect from the ships using it, but mostly from its operators.

This is what happens when people make rules, who don't really know what they are talking about, and I regret to say, that even to this day, the Oil Companies are the worst, closely followed by action groups, the local Fife one in this case. Some pilots were on the 'committee,' but they were not gas tanker men, only pilots, and off course, Forth Ports. Say no more? but I will.

There are two jetties, the East and the West. The East is for ethylene, the West for propane and butane.

The East is for ships up to about 15 000 cubic metres (the maximum size for ethylene tankers anyway, but smaller ones too). The West can take the largest LPG tankers, but usually up to about 50–60 000 cubic metres. (Still big boats though.)

For many years, ships going to the West jetty, came in from the west, through a narrowish channel, loaded, and left by the east channel.

Logical? The ship is heading outwards perhaps.

You'd be wrong.

The west channel inwards, is deep water, the east channel outwards, has a shallow patch. Whenever a ship is heavy (loaded), it has more chance of grounding. Ah ha, but the local rule makers thought of this. The ship will have a minimum under-keel clearance of 2 metres. Great, this gives it a window of 15 minutes from high water, to get clear, otherwise it is either stuck until the next tide. Was this always the case? No, this is one of the pilots' unwritten rules.

"Well take it out anyway, 1 metre is enough." You will soon find that ignoring rules is a popular pastime with most of the Forth Pilots. They have been brain dead for years.

The other problem, with big gas tankers lying alongside the West jetty, is that they present their sterns, with accommodation blocks, straight across the prevailing wind. The maximum area possible, of windage. This puts a colossal load on the ships moorings.

I, and a few other pilots did in fact write to the OM in 1991, expressing concern about this, but in many matters concerning this man, were ignored. My letter, mysteriously, disappeared!

I took no particular pleasure in being proven right, when the *Havkong* blew off the West jetty, early in 1993. Very fortunately indeed, there was little damage, but the potential was of massive proportions. It is unbearable to think of another scenario worse.

I had just come back from India, having delivered the RFA Regent to the breakers, and considered giving evidence at the enquiry, but decided against it. By the time you read all of this part of this book, you will probably agree that this could have been viewed as vindictive. My decision I think, was the correct one as the MAIB (Marine Accident Investigation Branch) slated Forth Ports accordingly.

Now, who do you think was responsible for this? The jetty operators? The Pilots? Forth Ports? The local committee? No, the master of the ship. He is doing his best to comply with every daft rule in the place over which he has no say, and ends up with the blame. Not providing adequate moorings is the usual one. I've been on some odd berths and it's pot luck sometimes where you can find hooks or bollards for your ropes. Braefoot Bay is not the exception.

It gets even more stupid. As the ship is now only partly loaded, he cannot come alongside to finish loading (after replacing his moorings), because, according to the local byelaws, only 'empty' ships are allowed to berth. Gas tankers ready to load however, are *never* empty, so why did Forth Ports allow them alongside? It's their rules. When I was still a pilot on the Forth, we all received letters from the terminal manager, which included the clause:

"all pilots when transiting the jetty to and from ships will be required to wear fireproof boiler suits." This was withdrawn, after one pilot told him, that if their jetty was that unsafe, the pilots would not be going anywhere near it.

There was some discussion at the beginning of 1992, about changing the way that large gas tankers went in and out, which 'strangely' did not come out in the inquiry. (Not if you know Forth Ports it's not.)

The chief harbour master, *TNT* off course, came up with the idea, of bringing large gas tankers in by the West channel, as usual in ballast, then turning them round with tugs after loading, and exiting by the West channel.

This was very quickly dismissed, as there is not enough room to get them safely turned, plus at half way round, the ship is lying straight across the wind. It wasn't Forth Ports who dismissed it though, but the ships owners.

There is one other howler about the West jetty, and as far as I know, it is still there.

There are two leading marks (lights), for ships to follow, when coming through the West Channel. However, they are in the wrong place, and if followed, would put the ship *on* the rocks. When this was realised, they were very quickly changed from 'leading' marks to 'clearing' marks. Whatever use they are!

Now, on the East jetty, they have their own quirks. By coming in the East channel, and going alongside, starboard side alongside, then the ship has to turn round before going out by the East channel. These are smaller, more manoeuvrable ships, so it is less of a problem, turning them round.

Here however was a Forth Ports howler. If the tugs are made fast to the ship for going alongside, 'but not used', the wires remaining slack, then the operator paid towage dues at half rate.

What is the point of making fast a tug, and not using it? This was changed in 1990, by none other than Forth Ports. Why? Safety reasons perhaps? Local pressure perhaps? Oh no, they just weren't making enough money, so lumped the increase onto the Oil Company, who in turn, passed it on to you and me.

There is another quirk about this place. Shipmasters with Pilotage Exemptions for the Forth in general, cannot go alongside at Braefoot Bay, without a Pilot.

The passage through Mortimers Deep, where the jetties are, cannot be used if there is a gas tanker alongside. That seems sensible enough. But, if there is no gas tanker alongside, then masters *can* use the channel, even for going up to Grangemouth, and many times when the Royal Navy were at Rosyth, they did so, as navigation exercises.

162

You can go <u>past</u> the jetties, and there is no rule about how close you can pass them, but you just cannot stop at them. In any other industry, this would be known as extortion.

Between the two World Wars, the passage through Mortimers Deep, north of Inchcolm, was in fact the buoyed channel for going up river. One day, one of the scuttled battleships from the German Grand Fleet in Scapa Flow was being towed, 'upside down' to the breakers in Rosyth, and had two pilots on board, one a Forth pilot, the other a Navy pilot. At the time, the boarding point was at the Isle of May. All the way from there, until the tug was going into Mortimers Deep, there was an argument as to who should be doing the job, such that neither of them, was watching the tow. The tug was North of Inchcolm, the tow, was heading to the South of the island, being caught on the tide. The tow had to be slipped, and the upside down battleship drifted all the way through the Forth bridge, and stopped off Rosyth, where harbour tugs came out and brought her in.

Why tell you this little piece of history?

Next time you think that navigation would be safer if a ship had two pilots instead of one, just remember how much doubt that can cause. You will recall in Part 2, my comments at Rio Grande.

There used to be one particular terminal manager there who was notorious for being rude. He could get under anybody's skin. I can't tell you his name, but it is the singular of those crisps that come in green tubes, and are all the same shape. I don't think that even his wife liked him.

After 18 months as a pilot here, and having done my extra training trips to get my unlimited licence, I took into Braefoot West jetty the *Hekabe*, a gas tanker of some 53 000 cubic metres, roughly 30 000 tons. It was my first one on my own.

As we came alongside, the chief engineer, said, "is that ----------- down there?" The guy was a legend in gas circles.

"Sorry chief, I don't know, this is the first time I've been here." I had to be honest.

He gave me such a horrified look, and went white.

The captain smiled and said, "You are joking pilot ?"

When we were safely tied up, I let him know, that I wasn't. So extra training after 18 months, yes five trips to Hound Point, and five trips to Braefoot Bay, either jetty, then you are licensed for up to 120 000 deadweight tons. Bit of a jump, I know, so you can understand how the

Sea Empress went aground.

Then five trips alone to Hound Point, then you are un-limited. If it was ever to come to the Forth, you could take in the *Jahre Viking*, at 550 000 tons, with only five trips practice as experience. *Given that nothing ever changes on the Forth until there is an accident, then I would reckon it would be much the same today.*

Next port up-river from Braefoot Bay, is Inverkeithing, just tucked in a wee corner before the Forth Bridge. The town itself, just up the hill, is quite a pleasant wee place, but the port, or should I say, the mudflats, with the 1and a half jetties, dries out mostly at low water, and does tend to pong a bit.

For many years, it was a ship breakers' yard, the last major demolition job was the *Mauretania*, when I was still a wee boy.

As an aside, when I was up for masters in 1984, at Leith Nautical College, we practised how to swing a compass on a binnacle, that came from the *Mauretania*. It was only a few years later, when I met my old lecturer, that I found out that it came from the *previous Mauretania*, which was also broken up in Inverkeithing.

It is now a major vehicle and scrap fragmentation plant which exports, mostly to Spain. They do, however still use the original cranes.

Getting in and out can only be done at high water, but what you must not do, is go in too fast. There's plenty of mud to stop on, but that's not the point.

My first time in, alone, I took the advice of an ex-Leith pilot, of turning the ship round on an anchor, and going starboard side alongside, so it would be easier to get the ship out when sailing.

That was positively the first and last time that I ever asked him about anything, as I picked up just about every old wire in the place on the anchor. No wonder the ship stopped quickly. An ex-Fife pilot, laughed for ages, when I told him about it, but at least now, they, the wires, are all in a pile.

The last port on the Fife side (at the time), is Longannet Power Station, which is just slightly up-river from Grangemouth, but on the opposite side. There isn't much to it. You can only lie alongside for about 4 hours, but as it's only small tankers that go alongside occasionally, doesn't really merit being called a port.

There is another port further up-river, after the Kincardine Bridge, which used to be a swing bridge, but is now out of commission and is welded shut. It is however, still extremely busy with road traffic.

I mention this, as Forth Ports plc, will not want this little tale to be broadcast. You will understand why.

The port is at Alloa. It closed many years ago, and the buoyage in the river was removed. It could still be used by small craft, and the odd fisherman would go in from time to time.

In the early 90s, a consortium considered re-opening the port, for a type of ship known as 'sea-snakes'. These are mostly used in the Continent, and are effectively long flat sea-going barges. The wheelhouse, is on a telescopic post, which can be lowered for going under low bridges, and then raised again for normal navigation. Apart from off course, seeing where you are going. These would have been ideal for getting under Kincardine Bridge. Some of them can carry up to 3000 tonnes of cargo, usually with very little draft.

After an evaluation study was made, an enquiry was made to Forth Ports on costs for re-opening navigation to Alloa.

The first the pilots found out about this was a very hush hush memo, which came around, from the OM, asking that, 'if anyone was contacted by the consultants, on their views as to re-opening navigation, to politely decline, and refer the matter to him.' There were still a few pilots around who were still licensed for Alloa.

I got rather curious about this and made a few enquiries, as after all, if freight was going to be taken out on any scale, then that would be a lot less freight on the roads.

Forth Ports *never* had any intention of even considering re-opening navigation. They did after all, have a lot of spare cargo space in Grangemouth, but they did do a costing analysis, including putting in all the old buoys, re-surveying the channel etc. Took about 10 mins. Erring off course in their favour, came up with a figure which meant that any freight going out from Alloa would cost 32 times more than shipping it out from Grangemouth. The plan was shelved.

If buoyage was going to cost that much to put in, and maintain which was doubtful, then there is another way which navigation could be considered. It was already in use in many other places, and is so simple. Leading marks. You just bang in coloured posts, on land, usually orange, to show the line of the channel, and others to show the line of the channel for going out, where they cross is where the bend is. A kid could navigate like this. Restrict navigation to daylight, and away you go. If you want to be electronic, then a Microplot system, costing under £1000 and you don't even need the posts.

I was told to keep quiet about this. I wonder why?

We'll leave Grangemouth for the present, and the other ports, and go back down the river. Now here is a quirky little rule, pilotage into Leith is only compulsory, if the ship is carrying passengers. Pilots don't count, nearly, but no. The lock can handle ships up to 40 000 tons, but, if you use tugs, then the OM insists that you take a pilot.

Guess who is the exception to this rule? Correct. Me.

Oh it wasn't when I was a pilot, it was after I stopped piloting, and the ship was a gas tanker. But I'm saving the story for later, so that it is seen in the correct context. You'll love it. *TNT* didn't. He left his windows open.

The port of Leith itself, is the port for Edinburgh, and woe betide anyone, who suggests that Leith is only a part of Edinburgh. They are a tad touchy on this subject in Leith, which is a city in itself. The old port was expanded in the 1970s, by building a new breakwater, and then successfully building a huge lock in entirely the wrong place. It can take a great deal of skill bringing a ship in here, a fact recognized by the fact that there is a long lead in jetty to leeward, that ships can land on, and slide up, to enter the lock.

The same bent ruler as designed Kirkcaldy was used, as the line of the lock and the jetty are not the same. There is a shoulder, specially designed, just before the lock, where you can either damage your paintwork all the way down the side, or damage the shoulder and get a hefty insurance bill, or both.

Coming out can be rather hairy at times, as witnessed by the number of bits of fendering that are missing. Big chunks of it.

The best time to come in is 2 hours before high water till high water, and preferably with no wind, which is rare.

There used to be quite a few of the old fashioned type of docks, with specialist types of berths on some of them. They were inter-connected with narrow channels, with swing bridges. Names like, 'Imperial,' 'Albert,' 'Victoria' and so on. They were built as was Methil, of granite. Some now have been filled in and covered with monstrosities such as Ocean Village. I'm not against change, but in 40 to 50 years' time, they will look terrible, because nobody will look after them. Just look at Kirkcaldy Harbour, and that took less than 10 years.

In 1990 when I started here, there was a tremendous amount of traffic in concrete coated pipes, being shipped out to the North Sea. The barge was laying 2 miles a day, and never stopped, so, ships were moving constantly. Some didn't take pilots, but most did, just so they could find the right berth, or if they had a passenger or two. These oil rig supply boats have immense power. Most went in and out backwards, giving the master much better control, and with their transverse thrusters, just cocked a snook at the wind.

I first one I took out, was one of these monsters. 18 000 horse power on his twin screws, 16 000 horsepower on his thrusters, of which there were four. Everything controlled on four wee levers, with absolutely no 'feel'. Computerization has destroyed this aspect of ship handling. I can't remember its name, which is unusual for me. Bet Leith can!

It was getting on for low water, so I told the captain to take it easy, just lift her off the lock side gently, and ease her out.

Wow! he just tickled the controls, and she literally jumped sideways. However, the fenders are these floating wooden ones, about 3 feet across, and 30 feet long, which go up and down on the tide. They are kept in position, by ropes, which are attached at the top of the wall, pass through a hole in the fender, and have a weight on the end. Not for much longer though.

The wash from the thrusters got in behind them, and as the ship moved out of the lock, sucked all the fenders with her, as she is effectively going backwards. We never really paid much attention at the time, as we were busy watching where we are going, so the first we knew of this was an almighty scream from the harbour master on the VHF. Looking astern, that's over the bow, I was horrified to see that every fender was following us. The port was shut for 6 hours while they were gathered up, and replaced. But, all they had to do, was increase the weights on the end of the ropes. Did they? Not likely, and the same thing happened next day.

One of the funniest stories about pilots and Leith didn't happen to me, but to the ex-oil rig chap. I'll tell it here as I rather like it. He can be rather officious, in a pompous sort of way, so it was all somewhat fitting. A ship, which didn't normally take a pilot, came on at about 7 pm, just as the day shift were getting ready to go. On this particular night, they were all going to a function in town. The ship requested a pilot for Leith, and he fell 'in turn' for it, so a bit huffily, got in the pilot boat, and boarded. Going in the through the lock, and then going onto the berth, the master paid no attention to him. He enquired afterwards, why did he want a pilot, if he would not take his advice?

"Oh said the captain, I don't need a pilot to show me the way in, I need a pilot now to give me a lift to the railway station." He got his lift.

Here is another point that Forth Ports prefer people not to know. When there is any prolonged weather from the East, then as the swell builds up, it becomes impossible to open the outer lock gate. These are caisson gates, which are filled with water, so that they have negative buoyancy. If they were empty, they would float away, as happened with the *Melrose* in Le Havre (Part 1). As such, they are heavy, and slow to open.

The tug basin however is just inside the port, which is useful if you need a tug in a prolonged Easterly. You'll just have to wait. The obvious answer is to take them out, *before* the swell builds up, but hold on minute, logic to you and me, is not logic to them.

Taking this one step further. If it becomes necessary to instigate 'Operation Clearwater Forth,' for a pollution incident, who has all the anti-pollution gear? The tugs, and they are stuck in port. Just remember who wrote OCF, the Chief Harbour Master, *TNT*.

There are a few more stories to come, like moving a crane barge. Or trying to catch a fox! I kid you not.

But we now move to Granton, which is just next door. Granton, is a suburb of Edinburgh. Any place as rough as this needs to be attached to something. And it, is rough. It is also the home of the Forth Pilot station. Only very occasionally now does a ship come in.

The only one I piloted was owned by General Electric, and carried huge transformers that were built up the road. You didn't need to steer this ship in, it knew it's own way through the groove in the mud.

Remember the query about Athletes Foot, and the shower. Well that was the 'old' pilot station, and I mean *old*. The architect designed this place using Lego bricks, then built it out of driftwood. Why it didn't blow away, I'll never know. It would have in Orkney.

To one side, were the bedrooms, which were to give them their due, made up and 'cleaned' every day, except at the weekend, when they had to wait till Monday, so you didn't sleep after the first six were used up. The other side, was the 'kitchen', enough said, and the 'lounge?' Upstairs, was the 'control room'. This place was so rotten, that there were scrunched up bits of newspaper pushed into the window frames, to fill the holes where the wood had rotted away. And this was the headquarters of a pilot service pulling in nearly £2 million per year!

It was pulled down, well, it sort of fell, after being replaced by the current building, which for some queer reason, is circular (even the bent ruler is not bent this much),with a peaked roof, topped by a look-out post for the duty pilot. It looks like an enlarged chicken feeder.

Was it welcomed?

Not really, as the 'old place' had 'character'.

Now, to Hound Point Terminal.

When this place was first built, there was a lot of thought put into it, and unusually for a tanker terminal, does not look out of place. The best bit though, is where the tanks are situated ashore. You would never know they were there, unless of course you fly into the airport at Edinburgh.

There was an old coal 'bing', a tip of all the mine workings which was an ugly eyesore. This was scooped out, and expanded, covered in soil, then grassed. The tanks were built in the middle. Most people driving past are unaware that it is there.

Late in 1991, BP, the operators decided to build a second loading terminal, so had the area proposed, surveyed.

This was farcical, but the best was yet to come.

A barge was towed from Sweden, and taken into Granton. This was a jack-up barge which was going to be used to vibrate in, the new pilings for the jetty.

It was duly jacked up, and then the tops of the legs were chopped off, one at a time, and taken to the oil rig yard in Methil to be lengthened. These legs are some 2 metres in diameter and heavy.

I was talking to one of the managers about this one day, and mentioned that when it was brought back down to float again, that the extra weight so high up, may cause a stability problem on the barge.

"Oh, we've thought of that, and have done all the calculations. We are going to put concrete blocks on the deck to counteract the loss of stability."

I don't know who did the calculations, but he had very little idea about stability, as when it floated again, it had a 4 degree list to port, and was 1 metre down by the head. He couldn't look at me after that.

Now here was something I had never heard of before. Spudding in. Basically, it means, letting one leg go on freefall, until it hits the seabed, and goes into it until it stops. Then the rest of the barge is swung on this leg until it is in position, then the other legs are let go as well. Sounds a bit hairy to me.

The barge was towed into position, and the first leg was let go. Whoosh! Straight down, and straight through the bottom of the barge into a 60 metre hole that was missed on the survey.

Where the hell did that go?

Send for the divers, and after it was brought back up through the well, had the top chopped off once more, and sent to Methil, again for more lengthening.

I'm keeping out of the way for now, in case I get drawn into a stability calculation.

To the main port, Grangemouth. Where most of the pilots income is earned from.

In the early 70s, and just after I came to sea, a new lock was built in Grangemouth, the old lock was just too small. Well enough built, as it is now the LPG berth. For once, the designers, actually listened to the old seamen, before they sited the new lock. The prevailing wind, predominantly from the SW through to NW, funnels through the port, and somehow manages to blow almost all the time, up and down the length of the lock. You can call this wind, a poor man's tug. When the wind is from the East, it is a bit more tricky, but they built in a feature for that as well.

There is no water fed into the port system, even although the River Carron runs past to the west. All the water is pumped in from the river, or allowed to flood in during 'levels'. This is a strange sensation, and a bit eerie, when it happens.

The lock is sub-divided into a 'small' lock, a 'big' lock, and the 'whole' lock, by a pair of gates part of the way along. I go into this in detail, as here is where the rules are stretched, and sometimes, downright ignored.

A gas tanker, according to the rules, should have the lock all to itself, the bigger ones, need the whole lock, but the smaller one's can get away with the small lock.

Now, how do you get two gas tankers in at the same time, or even one gas tanker, and any other ship and still keep within the rules? This *is* done, and more frequently than you think. I complained about it, so Forth Ports cannot deny it. They probably will, but nobody trusts them anyway.

You shut the middle set of lock gates between the two ships, believing that you now have 'two' locks. Someone actually thinks this is clever. They don't always shut the gates.

This theory has been extended to the approach channel. According to the bye-laws, a gas tanker must have the channel to itself after passing the Hen and Chicken Buoy, until it is safely in the lock.

Seems sensible enough, other ports do it.

The Forth pilots have found a way round this.

After the H & C Buoy, slightly further West, there is to the North, A 'Secondary channel'. So if for example, a container ship is coming out, the gas tanker will go into the secondary channel, or if a gas tanker is coming out, then say a tanker, will go into the secondary channel.

Every single pilot on this river has on more than one occasion experienced what it is like to be on a ship, which has lost control of it's steering gear. The only thing that divides the two passing ships now, is a little steel buoy, which is about as much use as a man missing, in preventing a collision. It hasn't happened yet, although there have been a few close calls, but familiarity breeds contempt.

Since stopping being a pilot, I have consulted for Lloyds underwriters, and briefed marine lawyers. The latter would make mincemeat out of this 'bending of the rules'.

What do you do, if all three pilot boats break down at the same time?

You hire one of course, until you can get at least one of them fixed.

Where do you hire one from?

Now remember to think illogically.

Rosyth Dockyard, they're bound to have a boat!

They did, and duly obliged. End of problem? No? The start? Yes!

This is what actually happened the day before I started training, and I was in this tub at least three times.

The Forth is a fairly busy river shipping both in and out, petroleum products, some extremely nasty and highly volatile chemicals, lots of different types of LPG, crude oil, and so on.

In handling all of these, safety precautions are taken very seriously, by everyone that is, except the Forth Ports Authority, as it was at that time, now off course Forth Ports plc. Attitudes have not changed.

When a pilot boat goes alongside a ship, he goes to the leeward side, which incidentally would be where any leaking fumes or vapours from the ships tanks etc., would also be heading.

What do you think the heating system in this hired in old tub was?

A brazier type furnace in the middle of the cabin, venting through a chimney, without any sort of a flame screen. The door beside the ship was opened for the pilot. Horrified? I was.

Somehow though, after 3 years of dealing with Forth Ports and in the 10 years since I left, I'm not, because I know who hired it, and *he* is now the Chief Harbour Master. Here are another two incidents, that were 'hushed up'. The current chief harbour master knows only too well about both.

On the South side of the approach channel, there are a series of three Beacons, which at night, have red lights, which flash differently from each other.

Numbers 3 & 5, mark the edge of the channel, No 1, lies well south of the channel, and so doesn't really mark anything.

One of the ex-Leith pilots, and a very senior one at that, with over 20 years' experience in coming up the river, has now 'qualified' for all the ports, and now has to take ships down the river. Easy enough one would imagine, just reverse everything.

On this particularly very clear and calm night, he is on a loaded tanker, not a particularly big one, but still a tanker. A single hulled one at that. Fortunately this was also on a rising tide. After clearing the lock, he sets off down the channel, well to the south, as there was another ship waiting to come in, and promptly runs aground. Beside the beacon, which does not mark the edge of the channel.

The saving grace here, apart from the rising tide, was that the bottom, is soft mud.

The ship floated off on the tide, and carried on her way.

Now to me, the obvious thing would be, to move the No1 beacon to the edge of the channel, where it just might be of some practical use.

Did they move it? Of course not, they're waiting for someone to come along and knock it down, so they can get it moved on the ship's insurance. Just hope it's not a tanker which gets damaged.

It is in the same place to this day.

The second incident, that is kept well under wraps, concerns my old company, Geo Gibsons, a Leith pilot, a gas tanker called *Traquair*, and again going aground, but not on mud this time, something much harder.

At the time, it was in 1983, I was chief officer on the ship, and we were going up to Grangemouth to load. We were in regularly.

It was a filthy night, and we were going up slowly, waiting for the tide to rise sufficiently at the lock entrance, known as the 'sill'. I, at the time had just come from the engine room, where I was pumping out some ballast. For reasons best known to himself, the pilot let the ship drift out of the channel, and the ship went aground, between Crombie Jetty (this is a military jetty), and the Bo'ness buoy.

We knew she was aground, as she suddenly went 10 degrees over to port, and stopped.

Another hushed up fact, was that the captain, wasn't on the bridge at the time. He was watching TV.

The *Traquair* has a powerful engine for her size, so after a few seconds on full power, she slid over the bottom, and came upright again, only to go aground once more, by going back over to port. More power was fed in, and again, she slid off and came upright. This time she got back into the channel, and stayed there.

You will recall that I said pilots always blame someone else. He blamed me, the chief mate, and I'll never forget his words,

"we weren't aground captain, the ship took a list as the mate is pumping ballast."

What he didn't know, was that I was de-ballasting the after peak, to bring the stern up.

In dry-dock a few months later, it was plain for all to see, that this particular gas tanker had been aground, and it wasn't on mud either.

I could if I wanted to, even tell you the name of the pilot. His brother was a famous author.

But back to Grangemouth. After clearing the lock, a ship enters the tanker basin. There are seven jetties here, and are virtually busy all the time. Such is the advance planning for jetty use, that it only takes one ship running late, on her 'berth time' to upset everything. This happens from time to time.

There was one occasion in 1991, when someone chartered a tanker, belonging to 'The Peruvian Navy.' A right old bucket.

I won't go into details here, lets just say, that it took nearly a month, to get the scheduling back on track. She *was* that bad.

Again going through one of these old fashioned 'cuts' to enter Grange Dock, these are all the cargo berths, two container cranes, a heavy lift crane, and strangely enough, a tanker berth.

It is not actually that unusual to find a tanker berth in amongst cargo berths, but in this case, it is for discharging bitumen.

Felixstowe has a gas tanker berth in between two container terminals!

Further up, there is a swing bridge, and some other docks, which just aren't used anymore.

The Grange Dock turning area is quite large, but very poorly lit, mostly as the concentration of light from everything round about, puts it into shadow. Why mention this?

One lovely calm, but cold night, I piloted a ship up to Grangemouth, which was going to a lay-by berth, at No 8 Grange, a cargo berth. The ship was the *Shell Director*, a small and rather rough coastal tanker under the British flag, who was a frequent caller. Going to a lay-by was quite normal. Tankers could go there, gas tankers couldn't, even although they are a lot safer. Doesn't really say a lot for their safety procedures now does it.

When we cleared the lock, the boatman set off from his hut in a mooring boat in readiness. They have done this thousands of times and there was no reason to think that this was anything other than normal.

Unfortunately on this particular night, it was anything but.

The mooring boat disappeared through the cut on it's way to the berth, and ran over a large piece of plastic sheeting, floating in the water. (This piece of evidence came out later.)

It became entangled in the propeller, and stopped the engine.

Totally unaware of this, we came through the cut, and hit it, in fact we ran it over, and sunk it. The boatman was thrown in the water, and I can promise you, it's both dirty *and* cold.

The first indications that something was wrong, came from the fo'c'sle where someone had thrown a rope out which the man in the water caught, but couldn't hold on. The captain panicked.

I said,

"stop engine", then an urgent vhf call to the assistant harbour master, "man in water, Grange Dock in line entrance to No 8 berth, urgent assistance required."

Very fortunately indeed, other boatmen who were letting go a tanker, heard me on their radios, dropped everything, and replied, "we're on our way."

The man was rescued within 5 minutes, much longer and he would have been lost.

It does unfortunately still take an accident, for changes to be made to something that should have been foreseen. This does not say a lot about Forth Ports Safety Officer, who I also had a run-in with later on another matter.

First of all, none of the mooring boats had lights, none had as much as a lifebelt, and the man wasn't wearing a lifejacket. They do now.

It might surprise you, but I am no great lover of The Royal Navy, am even less impressed with the RFA, and have no time at all for the RNR. I'll back up my lack of respect for the RFA in Part 4.

My loss of respect for the RN, went back to my first trip as master, when I received a rather snotty letter from a RN captain, pointing out, that when we passed each other in the Pentland Firth, that I had failed to salute his vessel, by 'dipping the ensign'. Oh dearie me!

Since then, I have always dipped the ensign, and when I don't get a response, send a snotty letter back. Petty I know, but fun. It can be even more fun, when you pass a warship, and have someone hiding ready to drop the ensign, to suddenly see a matelot run like hell from the wheelhouse in response. If he trips, even better. One of the first 'ships' that I took into Leith, was an RN minesweeper, which was coming down from Rosyth, bound for dry dock.

One of the old wooden types, not the new plastic ones. There are two dry docks, but this one was going to the smaller of the two.

For some peculiar reason, I thought at the time, he had ordered two tugs, not little tugs you will understand, the biggest in the port. The one's used to berth the big gas tankers at Braefoot Bay. These tugs are bigger than the minesweeper.

So, armed with a radio, I jump aboard.

There were more people crammed into the wheelhouse, than some merchant ships have as crew.

"Good morning Captain, tell me, why have you ordered tugs?"

"Good morning pilot." This guy looked nervous.

"Well you see pilot, one of my propeller shafts is seized, and the other one rattles when we go astern." If this was allowed to happen on a merchant ship, someone would get the chop. The Royal Navy, have an almost unlimited budget, plenty of engineers, and even more spare time to fix it. However, the most important thing, is, why was it allowed to happen in the first place?

"Right then captain, we'll get the tugs on, and take you in 'dead ship.'

"Pilot, what size are the tugs wires?"

"They are 38 mm with Talaurit eyes."

"What's a Talaurit Pilot?"

Give me strength.

"The eye is not spliced in; it is made with a pressed collar."

It transpires that his cleats will only just take the diameter of the wire, but he was unsure if the bitts would take the load. Bit late for that now. He can get them put back in dry dock, if they come out.

While his crew were making the tugs fast, I explained the position to the tug masters. You could hear the visible groan.

"Tugs fast pilot."

"Okay tugs take her away, straight up to the top end of the lock, and port side alongside please, don't pull in opposite directions at the same time, or we'll all be swimming."

The forward tug took off like a rocket.

In the background, I kept heard this voice, growing in crescendo, calling, "**shoaling**, shoaling, SHOALING!"

"Pilot, we are shoaling, shouldn't you be doing something about it?"

"Captain, you are drawing 2 metres, the tugs are drawing 5 metres, and they live in this port, they are not going to go aground because their boss is watching from that window up there, so please, just relax." I must confess, the speed we went through the entrance was beginning to get me a little concerned, so as soon as we passed the middle gate with the after tug, I got him to put the brakes on. Wow! that was impressive, as she stopped dead alongside and in position.

There wasn't a sound from the wheelhouse. I later found out, that the 'captain', was normally an observer in a Sea King helicopter, getting his sea-time in. And they let these people go to sea?

"Pilot, my boss will be watching as we go into the dry dock, so if it's okay with you, I would like to take her in, as we have to do it by the book."

"Be my guest captain." This *had* to be worth seeing.

"If you could take us up to the dry dock entrance, and let the tug go, we'll take it from there."

When the gate opened, and at a more sedate pace, we went up to the dry dock entrance, and slipped the forward tug.

The next 15 minutes was like a silent movie with Buster Keaton.

A simple matter like throwing a heaving line, from each bow onto the dock side, a distance of no more than 20 feet is a simple matter, but to these guys, not.

The rope was in the dock, it was on a roof, then missed the dock, and fell in the water, one got round his radar scanner (how they managed that, I'll never know),one got onto the dock, both ends, as he forgot to hold onto the tail. It was embarrassing, even my Filipinos from the *Borthwick* could have done better.

Of course, the dockers didn't help much either with their 'suggestions'. It wouldn't be so bad, but it was flat calm.

"Captain, shall we do it my way?"

"Yes please pilot".

"Okay *Beamer*, (the after tug), reel in your wire until your stern is on his transom, give a big push straight up the dry dock, when you get to the sill, pay out your wire, and when I say stop, then stop paying out, and we'll be in position."

Two minutes later, we were in, and 5 minutes after that, we were finished.

About this time in 1990, a dredger appeared, and started dredging out a big hole, opposite Crombie Jetty, which is about halfway between Rosyth, and Grangemouth. To the South of the channel.

Three months later, it was finished, which will give you some idea as to how big the hole was. It cost £ 3 million.

There was an RFA ship, called the *Resource*. It was scrapped a few years later. I know, as I took the sister ship, *Regent*, to the breakers.

This hole, then had a mooring buoy put into the centre, and the *Resource* was attached to the buoy, where it swung for quite a few months.

It struck me at the time, that doing all this dredging, wasn't really going to last long, as a Forth Ports dredger, works constantly, keeping the entrance to Grangemouth clear, and his dumping ground was only about a mile or so further downriver from the *Resource*'s 'hole'. I must have been right, as about a year or so later, the *Resource* was back alongside at Crombie.

What does this say to you?

The pilot boarding point is according to the Admiralty Sailing Directions, is just North of No 5 buoy. Interesting. This has long since been a gripe of mine, as this is 3 miles inside the Eastern limit of the 'Compulsory Pilotage Area'.

How do you get there without a pilot? Technically, you can ask for your pilot at the Fairway Buoy, which is on the limit, but few ships do this.

This prompts a legal issue, which I took up with them in 1996, but off course, I was ignored. It is therefore possible for a fully loaded oil tanker, and a fully loaded gas tanker to have a collision in the compulsory pilotage area, with neither ship having a pilot on board.

Just hope this doesn't happen during an Easterly gale. Better still, just hope that it won't happen at all! But it might!

However, there is another pilot boarding and landing area, which you will not find on the chart (not the last time I looked anyway), nor will you find it in the Admiralty Sailing Directions.

It is even further inside the compulsory pilotage area, to the West and South of the East Stell Point, the northerly point of Inchkeith. This is used when the weather is Easterly, totally unofficially anyway, but it would be hard to explain away to a marine lawyer.

Up until the time that the Royal Navy moved out of Rosyth, there was, right in the middle of this unofficial area, an unlit buoy. This was known as the 'Nuclear Buoy.' This will give you some idea as how out of date some of the RNs ideas are.

The intention was that in the event of a nuclear strike on Rosyth, a destroyer or something similar, would set up an alternative command centre, moored to this buoy. The mind boggles.

This buoy caused more trouble than any other in the Forth, as it was constantly getting hit, usually at night. When it didn't get sunk, but floated away, there was a general understanding, that no-one would report it missing, as then it would take the Navy even longer to replace it.

There were at the time I was piloting, a lot of regular running ships plying between the refinery at Grangemouth, and the sea, plus a lot of container ships doing the same.

BP had 4 of these smallish tankers, one of which was the *BP Hunter*, which had as its relieving master a man who everyone knew as Frankie! I doubt if anyone knew what his surname was.

He could be a rather cantankerous individual, but as I found out, had absolute due cause to be this way.

I was warned before I even went to his ship, that he didn't like pilots. That he did all the ship handling himself, and that the pilot only ever did the transit on the river. Well, that's his prerogative as master.

The first time I met him, was to sail his ship from E2 berth in Grangemouth, to sea.

He was rather off-putting, that much was correct, as his first words were, "you're new here, so here is the drill, you keep quiet while I take the ship out, and when we're clear of the lock, you can do your bit then. Okay?"

"Fine by me captain."

I don't know why, but some people think that as you are new to piloting, or indeed, to anything really, that you don't know anything. I'd been master for 3 years before this, and could run circles round most of them, but I stayed 'schtum' for now.

This ship has a bow thruster, and this master had fallen in to the trap that most do. He went so slowly to get the full use of the thruster, that he lost control of his rudder. The efficiency of a thruster decreases as the ship increases speed through the water.

It took the proverbial age to get from the berth and into the lock.

"That's how I like to do it pilot, what do you think?"

This is obviously a leading question.

"For not hitting anything, ten out of ten, for ship handling skill, minus one."

Two can play at his game. He wasn't pleased.

The reason he didn't like pilots was fully justified in my opinion, as BP were trying to get their masters to go up for pilotage exemptions, which means learning all the bumff that pilots have to do, and going for the same exam. Just as he was awkward with the pilots, then they were awkward with him, and kept failing him. It wasn't that he didn't know his stuff, he did, and certainly a lot better than most of the pilots, but the pilots had decided that he was *never* going to pass. The pilots were determined to keep the number of exemptions as low as possible, as they thought that they were going to lose out financially. Some of them plied their trade when square rigged ships were the norm.

Frankie and I never really hit it off. Then BP sold their ships to Coe Metcalf & Co, of Liverpool, and then chartered them back. This company named their ships with Christian names and ending in M, such as Robert M, Susan M.

It was all supposed to be a big secret, before they were sold. Such a big secret in fact, that everyone knew about it.

I last met Frankie, in his role of union representative, as I came ashore, after docking the BP Battler, and I just couldn't resist it.

"I hear they are renaming the *BP Hunter*, Frank M."

If looks could kill. Of course the remark went round like wildfire, and the other pilots ribbed him constantly until the sale went through.

Another one of the unwritten rules involved the maximum length of ships that you could take into the lock at Grangemouth, at anything other than slack water. I made myself really 'popular' with this one.

For some weird reason, the maximum length, not tonnage, length of gas tanker (these are actually the safest ships in the world), that 'could' enter the lock at any time other, than slack water was 90 metres.

At the time, I didn't know this, so popped in a gas tanker at 110 metres. Perfectly safely, and with a strong ebb running.

A few of them 'hauled' me up on this, and told me to limit it to 90 metres in future. Why? Because that's how we do it here. "Okay you've done it this time, but if this carries on, then we'll have to do it too." Why not, they were supposed to be pilots, well supposed to be.

Now, there was more to this than meets the eye, as they had been delaying these ships of over 90 metres in the estuary, and then taking them up to, lock in, at slack water.

No pilot should have the right to delay a ship like this.

However, I wouldn't give way, pointing out, that the *Janne Wehr*, a regular container ship, was also 110 metres, and could come and go at any state of the tide, so why differentiate?

This has always been a gripe (another one I know) with me, that it should, to the pilot, make no difference whatsoever what the ship is carrying, as he is only there to advise on the navigation of that ship. We never did agree on maximum length.

Here is another one of these things that Forth Ports keep quiet about. Extra pilots.

I would imagine the same thing goes on today, especially as there are fewer pilots now than before.

When there are more ships to handle, than there are pilots on duty, an off-duty pilot can be called out, at the rate in 1992 of £42 per hour. This was paid directly to the pilot Gross, from Forth Ports, and in a lot of cases was not declared as income.

In 1990, a memo came round from the Operations Manager, stating that when it looked as if there was going to be a shortage of pilots, and an extra pilot or pilots were needed, then the ships should be delayed, rather than calling out an extra pilot. I wonder what some charterers would make of that, had it become public knowledge. Even more difficult explaining it even now.

Well then, back to Leith. Just inside the lock, on the port side, is the tug basin. Before it was built however, it had the remains of an old wooden wharf, which Forth Ports had been praying that someone would come in, and knock the rest of it down. Sadly, for them, we all missed. Some had a few go's, but to no avail.

They just had to get the crane barge out, to pull out all the old pilings. For some reason peculiar to themselves, they chose to do this in the coldest part of winter, when it was also windy. However, as it is just inside the lock, every time a ship is due, or to sail, it has to be moved, and for this, a pilot, and two tugs.

For all its size, it was the most awful thing to move. Whichever way you wanted it to go, it would go anywhere but. Of course, Forth Ports didn't help, by always sending two unevenly matched tugs. We always had the Inchcolm, and whatever else was handy, so one with 10 ton bollard pull, and one with 25 tons.

The skipper on the Inchcolm did not earn his nickname for nothing; Captain Bar Stool.

The only saving grace, was that as it was so bent anyway, a few more dents weren't going to be noticed, rather like the *Borthwick* really.

We had discussions amongst ourselves, what would be the best way to handle it, and we all came to the conclusion, that if it sunk, then that was for the best. To cap it all, whenever a pilot went near it, then it either snowed or rained, and there was no shelter.

We must have got something right, as shortly afterwards, the barge bit was scrapped, and the crane spent the next few years sitting on a wharf.

One day in Leith, I went to sail a survey ship, from the Imperial Dock. He was tucked right up in the corner. He was due to sail at midnight, but the captain apologized to say that his divers weren't back from the pub yet. Would I mind hanging on?

"No problem," as we could wait up to an hour, before rescheduling.

They poured themselves on board, just before 1 am, we let go, and set off for the lock. About halfway there, there was an almighty '*clunk*', and the ship stopped dead, before starting to go round in a circle. The engine was stopped, as the captain went to investigate.

"I must apologize pilot, but we will have to go back. The divers have dropped a probe, from the well."

"What? In their state?"

"This happens all the time."

I could tell by his resigned look that we had to go back. The ship eventually sailed 3 days later, with the same divers.

Sitting in the Lego box one day, I scanned the intended ship's list, to find that my old ship, the *Quentin,* was coming into Leith, to be laid up. Forth Ports excelled themselves here, as they would only let her come as far as the locks lead in jetty. Before she could go any further, she was to be tested, and given a gas-free certificate.

Within the pilots, there were two of us, who really knew what we were doing with gas. They had no-one, but then, 'they' are the experts. All they had to do was ask. Why am I so critical? Because, the ship for the last year had been carrying anhydrous ammonia, which is non-flammable. You could stick an incendiary bomb in and it still wouldn't burn. Of course it's 'flammable gas-free.'

The other thing about 'gas-free' certificates, is that although it says it is valid for 24 hours, it is in fact useless as soon as it is signed. It's a vagary of procedural law. It was nice to see the old ship again. And at least they had been looking after it. The theory put about was that it was costing the same to run, as it was earning, so they might as well lay it up, until a buyer came along. The truth of the matter, was that they couldn't get officers to work for the company. Surprise, surprise!

For me, one of the best things about going to all the ports, was the variety, never 2 days the same. For the old hands, this was a source of eternal moaning. One was forever moaning about something or other, and I, had to work with him.

One day, I took a small containership up to Grangemouth called the *Libra.* It was one of those nice warm days. When I was in the lock, and for some reason, we were starboard side to in the lock, which was not the norm.

When the outer gates started to close, one stopped, but the other carried on. Closer inspection revealed why.

"Granton pilots, *Libra.*"

"Aye, Doug," said Jack, the duty pilot.

"Better not send any more ships up the river mate, one of the lock gates has just fallen off! And I didn't hit it."

To the moaner, this was manna from heaven, and he was back on his pedestal right away, "I told them they didn't do enough maintenance, and now look what's happened. I told you I was right."

"Exactly how Gordon, do you do maintenance on a six-inch diameter anchor point, buried under 2 feet of reinforced concrete?"

It was very fortunate, that there were 'levels' that night, and we got the big boys out 'toot sweet'.

Now, 'levels' are fun. However they can be a bit hairy, depending upon which direction you are heading in.

High water at Grangemouth is at its maximum at 12 metres, which is coincidental with the height of the lock gates. On abnormally high spring tides, the height can go higher than this.

Before I go on, 'spring' tides occur twice per lunar month, that's roughly every 29 to 30 days. They occur one and a quarter days after a new moon, and the same after a full moon. After a half moon, they are referred to as 'neap' tides.

If you are heading into the lock, and it is above 12 metres, then the gates will open of their own accord, as the amount of water flowing in, just pushes them open.

What you have to remember, is that there is now a current through the lock, so although your speed coming into the entrance may be only 2 knots, 'over the ground,' as soon as you are in the current, your speed 'over the ground' may be as high as 5 or 6 knots.

This frightens some masters, who think 'they are going too fast', and will either stop, or reverse the engine. Big mistake, huge.

When you come out the other end, you are back again to 2 knots 'over the ground', and you will need this to manoeuvre in the harbour.

If however, you are trying to get out, when the water is coming in, then your 2 knots 'over the ground' will soon be zero knots anywhere, and you need to increase the power, to make any headway.

Another pilot was trying to take out a 20 000 tonner, and was on full power, just to stay where he was.

However, there is always an opposite to everything. For your higher than normal 'high tides', there are also lower than normal 'low tides'.

You must be careful here, as this can even affect some of the regular ships that usually can get out at any state of the tide. One particularly wild night, with winds gusting up to 100 knots, it was 2 days before Christmas, and it was a small German coaster, coming in with 600 tonnes of newsprint. I remember this, as the master and mate had their families with them, and were hoping to spend Christmas in port. They didn't.

The master was surprised that the pilots were still working. I didn't mind going out in the pilot boat, but it was a 'gey rough hurl' for the boys going back in.

We arrived at Grangemouth, dead on low water, and it was a particularly low tide. The inner lock gate looks particularly foreboding.

I explained to the captain, that we would 'flood up' in less than 5 minutes, so tell his boys to be ready to slip the ropes, the second the gates started to open, as we would be on the power that early. He gave me a strange look, as if to say, c'mon now.

It was like going up in a lift with a ship, we were up and away in under 5 minutes, which was just as well, as the wind was at its height at that stage.

We had to put an anchor out, and lie the ship back on it's cable, just to keep him alongside.

Now, here is an interesting subject, fog, or as the MCA likes to say, 'restricted visibility'.

Why should this be of interest? Because this rule is bent as much as any other, and at times, just plain broken. It hasn't changed one whit in 10 years. I know.

The minimum visibility at either Grangemouth, or the Bridges, or anywhere on the river is 0.5 miles.

Now who decides, when it is 0.5 miles or less? Anyone really, and you will be surprised just how often it is 0.51 miles.

I was on call one night, when I was asked if I would take a ship out of Inverkeithing to sea.

Well, it was a right pea-souper where I lived, so Inverkeithing could only be worse. "Oh", says the pilot at Granton, "the captain says he'll be happy to sail, if the pilot will."

That is not the point, if the visibility is less than 0.5 miles, then the river is closed. End of story. However, I had a little bit of a battle going on with Inverkeithing, through Forth Ports Operation Manager, regarding 'safe access' through the scrap yard, and safe access onto the ship. It really was and still is, a horrible place, if anything, worse. We were getting nowhere with the scrap yard owners, so, I said I would see what it was like when I got there.

I had absolutely no intention of sailing that ship.

High water was at 23 30, latest time to get away 00 30. The ship stayed.

I got back to Granton by car at about 2 in the morning.

One of the pilots said, "what are you doing here? You should be sailing out of Inverkeithing."

"Yes I know, I've been to Inverkeithing, and I spent the best part of 40 minutes walking around that damn scrap yard, getting filthy feet."

"And?" looking at me in a weird way.

"I couldn't find the damn ship."

Within a month, there were lights, and a path from the gate to the gangway. The ship sailed 24 hours later. There was an occasion, when it was borderline, and I got this tanker away from Grangemouth. This ship had the very latest ARPA radars, and they were good.

But who else should decide to come out and play that night? The Royal Navy, if in all things, a minesweeper.

I was listening to the conversation going on between the minesweeper and the signal station at Queensferry, and it was quite apparent, that all was not well.

Then he comes on channel 71, the port call up channel, with,

"I know where we are now, we are underneath the railway bridge, I can see it above me, so we'll just stay here until it clears."

So, he was lost eh?

I came on with, "hate to spoil your fun old chap (I took the piss whenever I could), but this is the outbound tanker. Which arch are you under, north or south?"

He didn't know. "Well, wherever you are, you better find somewhere else to play, as I will be going through the north arch in 15 minutes outwards for sea."

Ten minutes later, he came on with,

"I've found a berth, so we will tie up here."

What the hell did he find? He's only found the tanker terminal at Hound Point. Fortunately, there was no tanker alongside.

I heard that he was subsequently court-martialled. Personally, I would have thrown away the keys to the boat.

It need not only be fog though, I came through the bridges one night, and couldn't see Grangemouth. It's 9 miles away. By the time I was up to the Hen & Chicken Buoy, I still couldn't see it, so we anchored off the lock. The reason? Snow.

While we are on the subject of the Royal Navy, or as they are more commonly known to merchant seamen, 'The Grey Funnel Line', I might as well tell you a few other tales. These are all true, which I know you will find hard to believe.

There were two Dutch tankers, about 1600 tons, who were regular callers, and unusually for the Dutch, both had crews, with not only a sense of humour, but quite pleasant with it. They were the *Mare Altum* and the *Mare Eratum*.

On this particular day, I was taking the *Mare Eratum* up to Grangemouth. There was nothing else moving on the river, or so I thought.

After clearing the road bridge, what should be in the Rosyth Anchorage? *HMS London*, a guided missile destroyer, who, as we passed, finished heaving up his anchor, and set off outwards. Warships didn't take pilots, but this one certainly should have.

As we continued up-river, thinking no more about it, and carrying on my conversation with the captain, the VHF came alive with,

"Forth Navigation, this is warship London, just passing North of No 5 buoy."

The captain and I looked at each other, both of us thinking the same thing. How the hell did he get there so quickly? No 5 buoy is Northeast of Inchkeith Island, 10 miles downriver. We had only passed him 10 minutes ago, if that.

The mystery was soon solved.

"Warship London, this is Queensferry signal station. You are *not* north of No 5 buoy, you are in fact *south* of No 19 buoy."

Both of us burst out laughing.

It is very sad to think that there are people let loose on £300 million pound warships, who cannot navigate, or at the very least, look at a buoy, and read the number painted on it.

Is it any small wonder then, that the Royal Navy has not improved, and now spends it's time looking for submerged rocks that were found years ago, are on the chart, and makes sure they are still there, by running aground on them. I refer of course to the destroyer who got the one between Australia, and New Zealand in 2002.

I have a theory as to how the RN trains its bridge officers. At Dartmouth Naval College, 4 days are spent on bullshit, including how to speak like the 'yah' set, half a day spent learning how to drink Gin, and the rest of the day spent on seamanship, navigation being a 'Teach Yourself Navigation' manual read on the train. It's only a theory, mind.

But back to the *Mare Eratum*. I couldn't resist it, so on the VHF with,

"I didn't know the Grey Funnel Line employed Filipinos?"

Who should come on then, but *TNT* with,

"I demand to know who said that." This was one of his typical days, best described by the lion, singing to the hyenas in the film, The Lion King. 'Lights on, nobody home.' Who else could come out with that?

There was more to come though. Further up river,

"Forth Navigation, *Mare Eratum* passing Crombie Pier inwards, and just to make sure there is no doubt, it *really is* Crombie Pier."

There was a 'phone message left for me at Granton. 'The pilot is to contact the chief harbour master as soon as he is ashore.' As if that was going to bother me.

I did contact him, and I got,

"You will come to my office immediately and explain yourself."

My reply.

"When you can talk to me properly, as a Master Mariner, then call back. If you can't, then don't bother." And put the 'phone down. That was the last I heard of it.

To be fair though, not all Royal Navy officers are like *TNT*.

There was a period, when the Royal Navy had about 5 ships in Leith, for a recruitment/open weekend, which was received very well indeed. Typically, *TNT* was in his element, his own 'kind', not these rather rough 'merchant types.'

He made a complete fool of himself.

At the seaward end of the lock in Leith is 'The Pagoda'.

This is where Forth Navigation are situated on the top floor, the chief harbour master, and other time wasters are on the middle floor, and those that do all the work are on the ground floor. At the time, the lady who did the pilots bills had an office overlooking the lock on this floor as well. Her name was Edith, and she was a delightful person.

I went to sail a frigate, whose name I don't recall, but as I soon discovered, a frigate is much the same as a destroyer, only spelt differently, and has more 'sticky out bits on deck'.

The captain was a delightful gentleman, but he was looking as though he wanted to be out of the port, and back to some degree of normality. He was berthed just up from the lock, so it was just a case of letting his ropes go, and going straight into the lock, tying up starboard side alongside, abeam of 'the Pagoda'.

As we finished, and awaited the others coming out with him, the VHF came alive with,

"If you turn your eyes green 90, you will see a familiar face."

The accent we *all* recognized, as the captain rolled his eyes upwards.

This was far too good a chance to miss, so I replied with,

"Hello Edith."

I had to explain this to the Captain, who roared with laughter, and said,

"No 1, go and get the pilot a bottle of Gin."

Then,

"You obviously can't stand him either then. He's been bothering us all the time we've been here. I went shopping, just to get a rest."

One of *TNTs* best happened just after I left. What has he arranged to visit Leith? Nothing other than *HMS Ark Royal*! An aircraft carrier.

Two pilots are sent to Glasgow, to get the drawing of the waterline, to see if she will fit in the lock. Oh she fits all right, but the hull form from the bow to the stern is a curve. There is no flat side at all, which is going to be handy when she comes in contact with the fenders, as she will immediately start to twist.

What *TNT* forgot entirely about, is not if she fits at the waterline, but will the flight deck fit between the lamp posts?

Eh, no.

So coming in, and using Naval tugs, which are notoriously underpowered, down come the port side lamp posts. The starboard ones, I hear you ask. Oh they got them on the way back out.

On the other side of the lock wall was an impounded Russian coaster. One pilot says to the other, "wasn't it kind of him to put his floodlights on for us, as the lamps all fused." The captain of the *Ark Royal* was not amused.

Are other countries navies like ours? I'm afraid so.

There had been a big NATO exercise in the North Sea (no submerged rocks here, so it should be safe enough), and after the exercise, the various entities were coming in to either Rosyth or Leith.

I was coming down the river on the *BP Battler*, blethering away as usual with the captain. I'd had been on this tanker so many times, that it would have been quicker, and cheaper, if I had just signed on. There, at this time, was an interesting VHF conversation going on, on Channel 71, as opposed to Channel 72, the working channel.

It was between Forth Navigation Service, and a submarine of the Portuguese Navy, the *Albacore*. It went like this.

"Yes *Albacore*, Forth Navigation, can you give me your position please?"

"Ah, Forth Navigation, we are passing the Fairway Buoy, we go to pilot station, yes?

"*Albacore*, Forth Navigation, can you confirm your position, as I do not have you on radar."

"Yes, Forth Navigation, passing Fairway Buoy, eese red and white buoy with Fairway written on side, no?"

It was confirmed on another channel, that I was on turn for this one.

"*BP Battler*, Forth Navigation, Doug, can you see him?"

"Forth Navigation, *BP Battler*, frankly no, Hector, but let me try."

"*Albacore*, this is your pilot. Are you still submerged sir?"

"Yes sir, still submerged, you like us to surface now?"

"That would be rather helpful sir."

"See Hector, it's easy when you know how."

"Okay. That's one I owe you."

So, after leaving the *BP Battler*, having promised to tell them all about it next time back, I found out just how difficult it is to get on board a submarine.

Here is a useless piece of information for you, useful in a pub quiz perhaps, but don't lose any sleep over it.

Where is the rudder on a submarine? Answer, it is *before* the propeller. This may help with silent running when submerged, but when it comes to getting on board from a pilot boat, becomes a whole new ball game. Getting into port is even more difficult, as the cussed thing is nigh on impossible to steer at slow speed.

Fortunately the boys on the pilot boat knew what to do, so after bringing him into the lee of Inchkeith Island, we got him to go astern, and the pilot boat comes up bow to bow. We cannot go alongside, as the round of the hull, stops us getting close enough.

Then all the pilot has to do, is take his life in his hands, and jump, hoping that they haven't picked up any seaweed in the landing zone. (It was funnier later, when the small 25 man Norwegian subs came in. The pilot boat *does* come alongside, about 6 feet off, and then a plank is laid from the pilot boat through a hole in the conning tower. The pilot then crawls along this. If he is a big pilot, then too bad, as it was in this case.)

Having landed on the deck, entry to the top of the conning tower, is by a door on the starboard side, which of course swings out on a hinge facing forward, which you have to manoeuvre round.

The top of the conning tower, is about 3 feet square, which six of us are filling, but there is one man yet to come up the ladder. I was motioned towards the pilot chair. There was no way I was going on that. It was a disc of plywood attached to a bent rod, which fitted into a tube, the whole thing sticking out over the side.

I don't know if 'bugger off' translates into Portuguese, but it seemed to at the time.

Up top, there are no communications, so everything had to be shouted down the hatch. It's not a bad system really, at least it won't break down.

When we came out of the lee of Inchkeith, I knew why he had stayed submerged for so long. It gets wet up there.

To go into Rosyth, you, at this time needed a Navy 'pilot'.

Navy pilots, when they are not piloting, drive the Navy tugs. He boards by his own, very flash pilot boat, at No 19 Buoy, just down from the Forth Bridge.

After clearing the Oxcars, I called him by VHF, and he stunned me with,

"What side is your pilot ladder on *Albacore*?"

Off all the people, who should know how to get on and off submarines, you would think that at least the Navy should know. It struck me later, when driving home, just what a stupid question this was, as, when you come to think about it, where would you attach it to, and even more importantly, where would you keep it?

After the Navy pilot took over, I was invited down below. I was glad of that, as it was damn cold up there. You know all these stories you hear about, telling you what life is like in a submarine, and what it smells like. From experience, I can tell you that they are *all* true. Mind you, the glass of Port I was handed was heaven, as I am partial to the odd glass.

The Navy pilot, I knew was having a hard time berthing it, judging by the number of 'clangs' that echoed off the hull. Rather him than me.

We left together, me being very obliging by letting him go first. I was glad of that, as we were parked alongside another submarine, and he found the bit of seaweed. It was all I could do to stop laughing.

Another 'unwritten rule?' This one concerns the Forth Bridge, or rather, how you get under it. Oh come on, I hear you say, how can that be a problem. Well for some, it is.

By law, not bye-law, law, which goes back to the time the bridge was built in 1890, ships are not allowed to pass each other when going underneath the bridge. Fair enough, but there are 2 arches, North and South. The direct channel uses the North Arch.

Muggins here, was bringing a container ship up the river in a hurry one day, when Forth Navigation came on to advise that the first outbound ship was showing the same time at the bridge as ourselves, the second ship was 5 minutes behind it. Outward bound ships had right of way over inbound ships, which is sensible, as they are running with the current.

We are going to lose about 15 minutes by the time we slow down and speed up again, so I swung her out, and went through the South Arch, as the others took the North Arch. Now what could be wrong with that? Plenty, not for me, but for the others.

I was collared when I got back to the pilot station, with, "did you go through the South Arch?"

"Of course, why? what's wrong with that?"

"You don't go through the South arch if there is a ship alongside at Hound Point."

"Show me that in the rules, and I'll do it." He didn't of course, as I was by this time getting rather cheesed off with their dinosaur attitude. It was easy to see why *TNT* thought he could fit in here.

Of course, such an unwritten rule, could throw up surprises. This happened one Saturday, in the summer, when someone of relatively low intelligence decided to have a swimming race from North Queensferry to South Queensferry. They could not have picked a worse time or place. If they had swum from Aberdour to Kinghorn, then they would have covered the same distance, and kept out of the way of shipping. But they want to swim across the river, at its deepest and fastest 'cross current' place.

On this particular day, I was bringing in a gas tanker, the *Sunny Clipper*. This ship, when it was built, was originally a container ship, but the owners went bust before it was completed, and while it was still on the stocks, was converted into a gas tanker. It worked out well in the end, as there was one thing this ship had over other gas boats, it could really move. 16 plus knots, and that was harbour speed, at sea, properly trimmed, even faster.

Approaching the Forth Bridge, Forth Navigation came on the VHF, giving me an update on their progress. Now as often happens, it was a touch and go decision, as not all swimmers, swim at the same speed, so their numbers were stretched out.

Do I take the North Arch, and 'hurry' the stragglers along, or the South Arch, and hope the faster one's haven't got there yet?

I took the South Arch, and, there was a tanker alongside at Hound Point, so I am breaking an 'un-written' rule.

I'll break here and tell you a little story, which will explain why I didn't slow down.

In-bound one day, on the *Traquair*, as, we altered course, between the 'bridges', there appeared from South Queensferry, a windsurfer! He was going at a rate of knots, but, as usually happens, *wasn't* looking where he was going.

It soon became obvious, that both he, on his plastic board, and us, on our unforgiving steel gas tanker, were on a collision course.

When the whistle was blown, he looked under his sail, and most probably ---- himself. At the very last second, he adjusted his board, to come creaming down the port side, about 10 feet off. Then he hit the propeller wash, and ended up, 'tits up', minus his board.

When he got back to South Queensferry, the police were waiting for him, (after a VHF call from the pilot). He was subsequently fined £20 for, 'obstructing the safe passage of a vessel in a restricted waterway'.

So, back to the swimmers, why not slow down. Because ships have right of way. We try, when we are able to, accommodate others using the same area, but ships, have right of way. You also need your speed to alter course.

Another un-written rule? What is more important, getting ships in and out of port. Or a fox?

I do not wish to open an argument here, concerning blood sports, but a fox, is a pest, and should be controlled. It's 'natural environment' is not in the city, far less in the ports.

On this particular day, I was taking a bulk carrier into Leith, a ship of some 25 000 tons, and had two tugs on, one at each end. This was a slack water berthing, so I had a little time in hand, but not much.

The 'moaner' was taking in a small coaster, before the lock was reversed for us.

However, he stayed in the lock, and wouldn't move, because a young (baby) fox, was running up and down the fenders in the lock, and he was 'worried' that the ship's movement would cause it to 'fall' into the water. Oh dear. Oh dear.

Believe it or not, by VHF, he asked the linesmen, to go down onto the fenders, and 'catch' it. Have you ever tried to catch a fox?

There was one thing he had forgotten, these things have claws and very sharp teeth. In more places than you've got hands.

It was stalemate. Time for a decision. I must admit, that I do not suffer fools gladly.

"Gordon, get your bloody boat out of that lock, and fuck the fox."

Someone, actually went down on to the fenders, with a view to 'capturing it'. He failed. Did you know that foxes can swim? I didn't, but this one could, pretty decent effort as well seemingly as it disappeared into the port. I bet it still smelt though.

We made the tide, and I docked the ship.

When you are a pilot, you must expect the unexpected!

Not all ships are run in the same way, as I would run a ship. On a gas tanker, I can squeeze in more cargo than anybody, only because I know the gas trade better than anyone, and have so many tricks up my sleeve, that I now have a third arm.

So, how do you squeeze in 'more' cargo on a containership? Easy really, you go unstable. Is this a good idea? Frankly, no. But some people try it. Such was the case, not long after I started, that I went to pilot in this Polish container ship, which even approaching the pilot station, was 10 degrees over to port. If 10 degrees doesn't seem much, believe me, it's a lot, because 10 degrees one way, is also 10 degrees the other way, and the ship flops over according to how the rudder is put over, or if you catch a gust of wind.

Getting aboard, and up to the bridge, I said to the captain after setting the autopilot,

"You appear to be a little unstable captain, it's not for me to question, but have you got all your ballast in your double bottoms?"

"Oh yes Mr Pilot, it is all in. It is my crazy owner, he tell me to take this much."

This was a perfect example of a captain who was not strong enough to say *no*.

Nothing for it, we'll just have to manage, so wobbled our way up the river. A ship which is behaving like this will be extremely difficult, if not dangerous to run into the lock. There is another way, and this was a time for it. The ship will go alongside the lead-in jetty, and we will warp her into the lock. It takes longer, but it is safer. This is what we did.

This ship was so unstable, that she lay to port in the lock, but when she came ahead on the main engine, she flopped over to starboard, due to the centripetal effect of the propeller.

The intention was to discharge on the container berth, but the container cranes can only lift containers, when the ship is upright, or has a very small list. So we went to the heavy lift berth, to discharge enough containers, to get her stable.

Question. Which containers come off first, the ones on the high side, or the ones on the low side?

I'll bet you all said the high side. This is wrong, you take the low ones off first, which makes the list worse, then the high ones. Reason, if you take the high ones off first, then she will flop the other way, and be even more unstable. By taking off the low ones means you are putting the stability back in, before you take off the offending weight. Anyone who had ever worked on a ship carrying timber knows this all too well.

Shortly after this, I boarded a German container ship. The name I know, but prefer to forget about.

When I got to the bridge, I realized that this was going to be tricky, as she had on so many empty containers, that you just could not see where you were going. This ship had come all the way from Rotterdam, navigating by radar. Pointless really having a lookout, as all there was to look at, was the back of a container. How are we going to get this thing into Grangemouth? I did it this time, but swore I would never do it again. I am very strongly against having two pilots on a ship, but this was the one occasion that two, or even three would have been justified.

Going up the river, was the easy bit, I did it on radar, but for getting it into the lock, required a different approach. I stood on the highest container, halfway up the deck with a radio, and conned the ship from there. It was the only time I have handled a ship without being on the bridge. It worked out okay, but I often wonder what it looked like.

I seemed, for a spell, only to handle containerships, and this was the same as the day I went to Grangemouth to sail a ship by the name of *Paraguay Merchant*.

Needless to say, this ship traded to Paraguay, which you find by going up the River Plate, after passing Buenos Aires. It's a 'longish' way from here.

The ship was all ready to go, but the main engine wouldn't start, hence a delay, as the air bottles were recharged. This can be normal.

Although there appeared to be a full cargo on board, the ship was still going to call at Hamburg, for more.

I said to the captain, just out of curiosity,

"Tell me captain, what sort of cargo do you have? (I'd always wanted to know, just what was carried in a container.)

"Oh, he says, we have mixed cargo. We have 325 containers full of whisky, and we have one container with two tractors in it."

Mixed indeed! Did you know that you can get 2200 cases of whisky in a container. With it being Paraguay, I can assure you, that this is not the 'good stuff'.

The Forth Pilots, ignoring their 'un-written rules' have a great term of phrase. 'The Leveller'.

Just when you think that you have it all sussed, along comes the 'leveller', which is just a sharp reminder, that there is more to learn, just as every seaman totally respects the sea.

Anyone who is stupid enough to think otherwise is a fool, and that includes most WAFIs.

I first met the 'leveller' in Methil. Yes, that pilots training ground, with the very hard walls. We tested them that day, they were *hard*.

The ship was one of the Lys ships. This is a small Norwegian company, which has specialized ships, mostly trading between Scandinavia and the UK. A better day, you could not have planned, glorious sunshine, and virtually no wind. There was however a fair old swell, and we all know what that means. You do not fight the swell.

The ship had arrived the previous evening, and had anchored about a mile off the end of the breakwater. So, chuggidy chuggidy chug chug chug, off we go in the 'pilot' boat, and I jump aboard.

The captain and crew, were German, which was unusual in this company, and unfortunately, they were the 'Teutonic' type.

"Have you been here before captain?" I asked.

"No pilot, that is why I need a pilot."

So, I started to brief him about, how, to get into Methil, *stressing* the most important thing, apart from the swell, was *to take your time*. During this, the mate started to get the anchor up.

Then it all went wrong and never got any better.

Since his time of anchoring, a lobster fisherman has gone and laid a line of lobster pots, roughly along the line of the anchor cable, with the result that they both came up together, in a tangled mess. Only one thing for it. Cut them off. The winch had so little power, that when a pot came up, one of the crew had to go over the bow to cut that free. As time went on, the captain became more and more agitated. What about? Shore labour had been hired from 2 o'clock, and the ship was already late.

Eventually, the anchor came up, but it was now 2 o'clock, and the ship wasn't even in port yet.

"Okay captain, dead slow ahead." I should add that this ship was loaded with 2000 tons of cargo.

"No pilot, my ship is late, we must make up time." Then put the engine to full ahead. Now, bear in mind, we only have 1 mile to go, and full speed is the last thing we need, as speed built up, has to come off again. But little 'adolf' has lost it.

"Captain, pull the engine back to dead slow ahead please." He didn't, and then as the port entrance became visible, he panicked.

"Do we have to go in there pilot?"

"Yes, now stop the engine. Let her run."

"Is wrong, we keep on full ahead till she is steady, then I use bow thruster, no?" Most definitely, *no*.

By this time we are doing about 7 knots, and are rapidly running out of room.

"For goodness sake captain, stop the engine!"

Then the swell lifted her towards the port side. What does he do, after being told not to, he fights the swell, and just as the bow started to swing to starboard, the next swell lifts back to where he was a few moments ago, except by now, we are closer to the entrance.

"Okay captain, full bow thruster to port, dead slow ahead, and 'midships helm, until she points to the middle of the entrance."

Running dead slow, rather than stopped, allows some rudder control, plus puts pressure on the blades, which in turn, slows the ship.

"No pilot, is wrong, I go full astern."

The absolute worst thing he could do, as the transverse thrust is canceling out the effect of the bow thruster. The way he has on the ship, should never have been there in the first place.

"Okay captain, stand by for impact." All my fault of course.

Crunch, on the starboard bow. This wasn't a wee crunch mind you, this was a big *crunch*, more like Kerrruncchh... . But at least we were stopped. Not in the right place mind you, but stopped.

"Are you okay captain?" as he collapsed over the controls.

"My owner will kill me for this. This was the same as my last port, and now I have to tell him about this." He then started crying.

Saying something like, 'just wait till he sees my report,' was not the time, or place.

Now while we are trying to re-shape the entrance, all his dock labour are watching from the quayside. Being late already, could, to a logical brain, determine that turning the ship round in the harbour, to go starboard side alongside, could be left till sailing outwards. For now, just put her port side alongside, and get on with it. Logical? Oh no. Plain stupid to try to turn her round. Yes. (If you ever need a job captain, contact Forth Ports. You'll fit in well.)

He still wants her swung, so okay then with, as we come near the berth,

"Stop engine, full thruster to starboard."

He actually did it! Wow! He actually did it!

Only problem was, the thruster was damaged hitting the entrance, and as we got half way round, went on fire. They had to put the fire out. But off course, no-one is brave enough to go in with a fire extinguisher, so two of them squirted foam from the top.

"Captain, to get the fire out, pull the breakers on the electrical side, and shut the hatch and smother it. That way they are doing it will never work."

Ten minutes later it is out, or at the very least, wasn't smoking any more. That'll have to do for now.

To get her round the rest of the way, I said,

"Captain, have your men run a rope from forward to shore, and we can heave her round the rest of the way."

Eventually, we got alongside, and tied her up. Then the fireworks started.

"No pilot, I not sign your bill. You are f------ awful pilot. Look at the damage to my ship. Is your fault."

There is no point arguing, after all, if I sign the bill, it will get paid anyway, but I'm not like that, and I was most certainly not going to take the blame for this.

I sent in the Dept of Transport surveyor. That fixed him, as repairs had to be done in Methil, before he could sail. That took 3 days, which was 3 days after he could have sailed. Explain that one to your owner pal.

I did get a sneaky look at his 'report' later. Despite the fact that Methil had been there for years, it was in the 'wrong place'.

Why did it take 3 days to repair? Well first of all, they had to disentangle the anchor from the bow thruster cabling, and the cargo. The anchor had in fact ended up in the hold.

Damage to Methil? Are you kidding, this is granite!

A few weeks later, I had another Lys ship, the *Lyskill*, going up to Grangemouth with newsprint (that's paper on rolls to you and me). Coming out of the pilot boat, he had a very unsafe pilot ladder. There is not a lot you can do wrong with pilot ladders. Every port in the world uses pilot ladders approved by SOLAS (Safety of Life at Sea), and this is supposed to be strictly enforced. That is, at that time, by everyone other than Forth Ports.

After docking the ship, I reported the matter to the Safety Officer of Forth Ports, who paid the ship a visit.

The obvious thing to do, would have been to advise the ship to comply before sailing. Did he? No.

What he did was to advise the ship, to have it replaced before the ship came back. Stupid? Off course it is, as some unlucky pilot is going to have to use it to get off the ship. And, as you might have guessed, that was me.

I wrote to Forth Ports and told them exactly what I thought of their 'safety' officer, with a copy to the Department of Transport. Whenever

I had a problem like this again, I just sent in the DOT. Most of the rest of the pilots did as well.

They weren't best pleased, but I did not like their attitude to safety.

Mind you, the *Lyskill* were furlongs ahead of the *Ceri Povets*. This was a Russian ship, lying in the Grange Dock. According to her data, she was a, and get this one, 'live fish carrier'. That was what she was called officially.

In truth, she was a Russian Spy ship, converted to carry timber. Back cargo? Lada car spares. Anything they could get.

This must have been a murderous ship to navigate, as the chart room was two decks below the bridge.

Going down the river, after we cleared the bridges, I asked for a pilot ladder on the port side. I saw the bulwark ladder going out, and thought no more about it. The captain asked me if I would take the ship out to the Fairway Buoy. No problem captain, that's all part of the service. His next question stunned me, and I thought I'd heard them all.

"Mr Pilot, what is the course for Rostock?"

In a one'er? Apparently, so I countered with,

"Off the top of my head, I would say, about 060 to 'The Kattegat'.

"Is not correct, from Fairway buoy, course is 090 degrees."

"If you go 090 from the Fairway Buoy, captain, you'll be aground at North Berwick."

"Oh no, Mr Pilot, come to chart room please." The pilot ladder was not yet out, so they were reminded once again. The chart room. One chart for the whole of the North Sea, and about 20 years out of date. In the middle, the Ekofisk field. The plan was to head out from the Forth to Ekofisk, then alter for the Kattegat. Why Ekofisk? Because it had a huge flare on it, and by this, that was their only way of navigating. The sooner this thing is away, the better. But I've not got off it yet.

"Captain, what about the pilot ladder?"

"I am sorry Mr Pilot, but we do not have a pilot ladder." We had to borrow one from another outbound ship, transfer it in the pilot boat, rig it, then take it back. That ship never came back. Was he missed, no!

The saga of the chart was not however confined to Russians. There was a small Norwegian coaster that came into Methil from time to time. This thing had dents in the dents. The captain and mate were Norwegian, and both were as daft as a brush. They'd been sailing together for years. They thought, that they had a chart somewhere, but weren't quite sure where. Strangely, they never got lost, and if they said they would be at 'x' time, then they were there at 'x' time.

If this sounds irresponsible, then consider that to this day, there are cargo dhows trading around the Persian Gulf, Pakistan, Oman etc, that navigate by the taste of the sea, which bird flies past, where the moon is and so on. They don't get lost. One day, I am going to do a trip with them, just to see how they do it. But there is more to it than that, as I've already been on board one, in port mind, and the food they prepare is out of this world. Then I'll write about it, and explain how it is done. It must be clever.

Then there was the *Geroro*. This was a ship that even its own crew avoided. Whoever thought they could get away with this was the eternal optimist. Can you imagine, having Serbian officers, and Croatian crew, topped with a German master. It would be a full-time battle keeping them away from each other's throats.

Could be possible, were it not for the fact that the ship was fucked. Twin screw, forward bridge, cargo capacity 2500 tonnes if you could find anyone daft enough to put cargo in it. But some did.

She was into Leith a few times, and pilots avoided it like the plague, but when I came across her, it was in Grangemouth, and that's 22 miles from the sea, 18, if I could get away with it. To cap it all this day, he had ordered a tug. One tug, unless you are in a river, is about as much use as an ashtray on a motorbike. Where do you put it? Please, if you read this, order tugs by even numbers only. On the *Geroro*, aft, the back end. Why? Because at the other end, he has one of these funny wee signs that says 'bow thruster'.

The first thing I find, is that the bow thruster doesn't work, only by this stage the stern is away from the wall, and the bow, 'ain't going anywhere.'

Change of plan!

"Okay captain, we'll haul the stern up towards the cargo berths, then come ahead on the rudder and push the bow round to port." The grunt was, I reckoned, a nod of assent, or whatever they call it in Serbia. The actual captain was away for his tea. He knew something I didn't obviously. This was the mate.

Next problem, was getting the ship to go ahead, or in fact, to move at all. The weight of the tugs wire was enough to stop the ship, far less using any power.

I thought that if I balanced the weight of the tug, against the ship, then I could steer. Nice plan, if both rudders actually work, but one had a mind of its own, which probably explained the twisty wake, as we went through the tanker berths towards the lock.

"What side do you want in the lock Doug?" asked the assistant harbour master.

"Whichever one she hits first will do!"

So, get rid of the tug, flood the lock down, get ready to sail out and wishing I was in Methil, we sail for the sea.

Normal pilotage is about 2 hours, at about 13–15 knots. On the *Geroro*, however, it is a marathon 4 hours, and *that* was with the tide.

"Do me a favour captain," as I left, "don't come back."

The longest it ever took me to get to Grangemouth was on a ship called the *Hoo Plover*. These ships have things called 'Aquamasters', which are really just a glorified outboards. On this particular morning, one had broken down, so he is down to one. To cap it all, the ship is loaded, with about 2000 tons of salted grit. The local councils had run out, so if you feel grateful for not having skidded on the roads, just remember the effort it took getting it to you.

Was it slow? I could swim faster.

I boarded at 3:45 in the morning. Passing The Beamer at 8:30, some of the day shift pilots outwards, meant that they were going to be finished before I even got to Grangemouth. There is nothing more boring, than watching the wake you created going past you faster than you are. We eventually got to the lock at 11 30, but had to 'wait' for the ship coming outwards. Was this hard? Not half as difficult as explaining to my wife afterwards why I was so late getting home. She thought I was in the pub.

Next day, however, after the unit was repaired, the ship set off down river and in ballast. Did he go faster? No chance, as the captain decided to leave his 'running in' time, until after the pilot had left. Sorry Dan, but it was a long slow slog back down the river.

Has anyone hit 'The Beamer'?

Answer: Yes. Next question, who? Only the most experienced pilot on the river, and an ex Grangemouth one at that. So how? The old reason, familiarity breeds contempt.

'The Beamer' is a small island, just inside the line of the Forth Road Bridge. Rocky? This stuff is granite, the hard stuff.

A useless piece of information. Where is the deepest part of the Forth?

Underneath the North Arch of the Forth Bridge, according to the chart, it is 86 metres, but with tide on top, about 100 metres.

What did he hit 'The Beamer' with? What do you think, a tanker of course. Who 'covered it all up'? none other than Forth Ports. But why did he hit it? as he has only been down this particular bit of the river about 10 000 times. Because he has decided to change the rules.

Why? Goodness only knows to this day, but this man's logic was to come unstuck later. It wouldn't be so bad, if it was only him, but this became infectious.

A few days later I brought in the *Yolanda*. This was a regular running containership, and will feature later. The crew were Dutch, and very easy to get on with. The master decided that he would do his own ship handling, and between them he, and the chief engineer, did so. They were good at it too.

On this day, we showed the same 'bridge time' as the outward bound ship, which was an Italian gas tanker.

Normally, this ship has priority, so I slow the *Yolanda* down. What does the pilot on the gas tanker do? He slows down as well. Why?

I've tried for 10 years to get an answer, and am still no nearer to solving it. But then again, he went to a clinic to 'dry out' later on.

The net result, was that I had to squeeze the *Yolanda* between

'The Beamer,' and the gas tanker. Close? How does 10 feet sound? In Grangemouth, this old clapped out chemical tanker called the *Stolt Hacienda* was lying alongside No 5 berth, and getting ready to sail. The captain was British, and one of those who like to think they are engineers. The chief mate had just joined that day When the main engine started, I was out on the port bridge wing, and said as the captain appeared,

"It sounds as though you've got a few sticking valves on your engine captain."

"Aye pilot, you're right. I'll go and fix it. Back in 10 minutes."

Suddenly, a few minutes later, there was a colossal roar, flames shot out of the funnel to about 40 feet, and this was followed by a huge 'clump' of heavy black smoke, which initially went up, before slowly drifting away towards this other lovely clean white tanker. Then the engine settled down to a steady rumble.

The new mate looked at me, horrified. "What do he do pilot?"

"I think he fired a cylinder. I've seen this done before."

"Any spare seats in the pilot boat? I think I'll come with you."

Just then the captain re-appeared, looking distinctly like a panda.

"Chief hates me doing that, but it works every time."

What he did was to pull the fuel rack back, then drop in a full ahead burst to one cylinder. The pressure on the crosshead goes up by a factor of ten, and you can actually bend the crankshaft, but it sends a shock wave through the scavenge space, which dislodges all the soot. It is dangerous to do though.

As a small aside, here's one you'll like, as I got my own back on *TNT*, 2 years after I left.

I was working for Bergesen of Oslo at the time, but had had an accident and dislocated my left elbow. Actually I fell off my bike when I was showing off to my daughter, as we cycled through the woods. Nothing is more painful, as I also ended up upside-down in a Bramble bush, the very spiky type, and had to be hauled out by the Police and two Ambulance men.

Vships Norway came on the 'phone with, "Doug, are you busy on Friday?"

"No, but I'm off injured just now, with my arm strapped up."

"Is it painful?"

"No, just awkward, why?"

"Could you go through to Leith, and take the *Norgas Pilot* down to the dry dock in Newcastle? We don't have a captain available."

She had been laid up beside the *Quentin* for the last 2 years, but had a skeleton crew maintaining her.

"I suppose so, but I work for Bergesen just now."

"Oh," he says. "We'll just forget to tell them."

I drove through, met the superintendent, got her certificated for a 'coastal' passage, and set off next morning at 4am.

Do you think I took a pilot? You must be kidding, as you'll find out why later.

I knew the agent from Gibsons, so asked him to book me two tugs, but *no* pilot. Absolutely, most definitely, *no pilot*!

"Oh says the OM, if he takes tugs, we like him to take a pilot."

"It's Captain Harvey on board!"

"Oh. Better not argue then."

Now the chief harbour master had left his office window open on 'The Pagoda' overnight. Oh goody!

"Chief," I knew him from before, "do we have any ACC 9?"

"Yeah, about 50 litres. Do you want to clean the blower?"

This is a chemical injected into the turbocharger on the exhaust side, to keep the blades clean, and in balance. It's done about once a month, but as she had been laid up, we'll do it as soon as possible. Nowadays, with environmental concerns, it's not used any more. Believe it or not, the ecological equivalent is 'ground up Walnut shells!' They work a treat too.

"Okay, fill the tank, and when I come up to full ahead, give it a full charge." Timed off course to be just before we passed *TNT's* office window as we came out of the lock.

Perfect, got the lot, bang on.

It comes out the funnel as a very sticky, smelly black goo, which is murder to come off anything it comes into contact with. About the only thing that will dissolve it, is a mixture of sulphuric acid and methanol. If you try to wash it off with water, it only makes it worse.

Guess what Forth Ports tried to use? Remember now, they aren't very bright.

A change of subject for a wee while then. Getting ships in and out is a fairly hazardous occupation on the Forth, but not half as hazardous as getting to them in the first place! Well for sailing them, or leaving after they are docked. Grangemouth isn't too bad, in fact, the only tricky one is really Leith, the home of yes, good old Forth Ports, who can make even the simplest matter, difficult, while thinking it is 'efficient'. It usually ends up unsafe.

In 1991, before the place was tidied up, we all used to get a taxi from Granton, as our own cars were taking a terrible pounding. The Taxi firm? City cabs. The black one's. Why? Because Forth Ports paid, and they were the cheapest.

They also have the hardest springs. When you got in, you didn't sit on the seats, no, you sat on the floor. Why? Because as soon as you go through the port gates, that was where you were going to end up, so you might as well start off there.

What could be simpler than driving through a gate? Building a security post off course, with a barrier. Ah, but, security is important! Anywhere other than Leith it might have been. Plus, do you have any idea just how much traffic goes into and out of a port each day? Masses.

To speed up pilots getting in and out, plus various other layabouts, a system off coloured discs was organized, set into a plastic licence holder, the 10 pence variety. Pilots were yellow. We even got instructions on how to put them on from the OM! That must have taken him a whole day at least, but what he forgot to tell us, was where to stick them. I could think of a few choice places. Mostly rude.

The intended place was the top right-hand corner of the windscreen, but why make it easy for him? We had them anywhere but the most favoured place was the rear near-side window in the top corner, so the security guard had to come out of his hut to check it. Every time! Then we latched on to changing the place regularly, so he had to search for them. Childish? Of course, but fun too. Even more fun though when we started to make our own in different colours.

Then they built this enormous security gate beside the small dry dock, and you had to sign in and out. How do you make that complicated for them?

Easy, you don't sign in, in the first place. All you had to do, was to drive around the back of the Albert Dock, cross the swing bridge, and come in from the other side, so your 'coming in', is their 'going out'. It took them ages to work out how it was done.

How do you upset their office staff by rattling the windows when they least expect it?

It is situated beside the Albert Cut, and the signal for coming in was four short blasts on the ships whistle. But if you wait until the very last minute, and the captain has the air pressure up high enough, then it was even possible to shatter the outside pane on the double glazing as well. Even Granton didn't escape. Security was beefed up by putting on a chain with a padlock on the huge steel gates, which was a real pain every time we went in and out. Of course, every pilot had to have a key. They gave up on this idea, when we kept losing our keys, and after they ran out of chain, after getting through 150 feet of it. Then someone pinched the gates. Remember, Granton is a bit rough.

It really is quite sad that master mariners get up to these things, even at 55 years old.

What is the difference between a degree and a Master Mariners' Certificate of Competency? A Masters 'ticket'.

After 3 years at university, you can obtain a degree, which is yours for life. More advanced ones take longer though, such as medicine.

When I was at Aberdeen University studying Mathematics, others were doing things like 'Social Anthropology', History of Art', 'Theoretical Astronomy', and the practically unbeatable one, 'Theory of Social Work in the 50s and 60s'.

It takes a total of 12 years to obtain 'a ticket'. Varying between sea time and college courses, plus thousands of pounds, invariably of your own money. Anything up to £25 000 by 1984.

Plus. It can be taken away from you, either temporarily, or *permanently*. By the Department of Transport as it was then, or the MCA Maritime and Coastguard Agency as it is now. Most masters carry triple or quadruple certification. British, backed up by Liberian and Panamanian, or in my case, also Norwegian. Very very rarely nowadays is British actually used first.

Why do we call *Snow White, Snow White*?

This was my old superintendent from Gibsons who caused a lot of the trouble when he joined Forth Ports plc as superintendent on pilot boats and tugs.

Gas tankers he couldn't do, too difficult, but he would be okay on pedaloes though. With the wind behind helps.

He came by the name before Gibsons, when he was a 'plumber' in Christian Salvesens. He could go into the engine room in an immaculate white boiler suit, 'work' all day, and come out spotless. The term 'plumber' on board a ship is a derogatory term for a lousy engineer. And he is lousy. You can tell lazy engineers. The only bit that gets dirty on a boilersuit is the backside.

From 1981 to 1988, he only looked after one ship, after building it. The *Traquair*, referred to before.

After it was built, I spent the next 4 years re-building it.

Being done on the cheap, it was built in two shipyards, a proper one, Fergusons on the Clyde, and a pretend one, Ailsa's in Troon. Built in two halves, The stern and No 3 cargo tank on the Clyde, the bow and Nos 1 and 2 cargo tanks in Troon, then brought together in dry dock, and welded together on one side only.

How do you do that? Easy, when you know *Snow White*. It matched on the port side, but was 4 inches out on the starboard side, and had to be rebuilt over eight sets of frames. You can actually see the bend. I bet working out the Gross Tonnage was hard. Well, harder than usual.

One of a superintendent's biggest headaches when building a ship, is signing off the plans and drawings. If a mistake is made, it costs a fortune to put right, sometimes, you just have to start again.

Snow White is an expert at cock-ups.

Did you know, that he can get oil to flow up-hill, all by itself?

The generators lube oil header tank, ended up on the deck below the generators.

The fans feeding air into the engine room weren't big enough, so the purifier flat was superheated. 10 minutes in there was your limit.

A chief got him and *Old Baldy* a beauty in Grangemouth, one summer's day, as neither was paying any attention to the problem. They were taken down, and as soon as they were in, the chief legged it to the other side, and slammed both doors, sealing them inside for over an hour. Best way of sweating out at least a stone. Bigger fans went in the next dry dock.

The emergency diesel generator room access was a challenge in a new sport, known as vertical pot-holing.

Boy oh boy, could this ship hit things. The only one I know that could possibly have taken on Methil. More stories in my next book.

Snow White is also *the biggest two-faced liar in the world*. Even *Carrot Top* couldn't stand him. They shared an office too.

I know he knows more about Captain O'Shea's death than he lets on about. He was, Captain O'Shea, my friend.

We'll hear more of him later though. Oh, *yes we will*! So, back to *TNT*.

One of his 'circulars' to pilots regarded the *RFA Resource* lying alongside at Crombie Jetty, and 'due to the effects of interaction,' ships passing Crombie were instructed to slow down. Fair enough. But *TNT* being *TNT*, just couldn't leave it at that. Idiot. We were informed that this ship had up to 5000 tonnes of ammunition in her.

Question. Just why is a ship in peacetime, carrying 5000 tonnes of ammunition, when it is berthed alongside one of the biggest underground arsenals in the UK? There are tens of thousands of tons of the stuff in there, so why keep some in a ship. Especially as it is beside a busy tanker waterway. That seemed to be asking for trouble. They could off course put her back in her swinging area, after scooping out the hole, had it not filled up again. Or put her alongside the old

Crombie jetty, inside the new one, or alongside in Rosyth, or indeed, take out the ammunition, and put it back in storage. I wrote to him and asked why? I never received a reply, but I did find out why.

After I stopped piloting, I took the *RFA Regent* (the sister ship) to the scrap yard. Both ships are nearly unstable when empty. I did a damage stability calculation for the *RFA Regent*, if one compartment was damaged below the waterline, and allowing for 5000 tonnes as bottom weight, to see what would have happened. She would, most probably have capsized.

Oh, I hear you say, even a ramming collision would not hole her. Ah, but I know something you don't. The *Quentin*, which had in the past been trading in and out of Grangemouth, and was now laid up in Leith, has a secret weapon. The bulbous bow. So. other ships have them, what makes her so special? Because it contains 50 tonnes of concrete, and the forward end is in line with the flare of the bow. It is effectively, a battering ram, and in its life has actually done quite a lot of damage.

Some of the chemical tankers passing by, are carrying some of the most dangerous chemicals known, and in the event of a steering gear failure, could hazard their own safety, by hitting her.

The absolute worst one, is a noxious substance known as acrylonitrile. This stuff is carried alone in one stainless steel tank surrounded by eight other empty tanks, and under nitrogen. If it mixes with sea water, it produces chlorine gas, on an expansion factor of 600 to 1. At the time, it was imported into Grangemouth twice a month, in 500 ton parcels. *TNT* knew about this, because I told him.

'Noxious' does not relate to smell, as ammonia is very 'noxious', but is not regarded as a noxious substance. It just means, bad!

So what is interaction?

This is an effect which can affect how two ships handle when passing close to one another, usually when going in opposite directions, or when one is stopped, and another sails past.

It was used to best effect by the pilots in the Manchester Ship Canal, which is quite narrow. Two ships head straight for one another, and at the last instance, both turn to starboard, using the pressure between them initially to keep the bows apart, and then the interaction to pull their respective bows towards each other's stern, and then the pressure again, to keep their sterns apart. It sounds hairy, but believe me, it works a treat. The Ship Canal pilots incidentally, took their own helmsmen with them. These guys were pilots in training.

Like all these things though, the further apart you are, the less the effect. It disappears entirely, at anything over one cable for ships running at anything up to 16 knots. Most ships passing the *Resource* were more than a cable off, so the effect is negated. The size of the passing ship is also a constraint, as small ships (most of the ships trading in and out) have very little effect, unless they are very close, say, within 50 feet.

How it affects a ship lying alongside, is that it causes the ship to surge, either forward or aft. It can be negated entirely, by keeping the 'springs' tight. From my knowledge of the *Regent*, the *Resource* used 8 inch polypropylene ropes, with a breaking strain of 46 tonnes. Two springs out each end, and properly tended negates any tendency to surge.

TNT had read about interaction in a comic, but you could explain this all day to him, knowing that bugger all was being taken in.

How about *TNT* then? Obviously, he had to do something to gain this stage of notoriety.

Forth Ports plc, is supposed to be the 'Competent Harbour Authority,' for the River Forth in Scotland, also known as the CHA.

However, your, mine, and almost everyone else's definition of 'competent', is nothing at all like Forth Ports'.

The *Chambers 21st Century Dictionary* defines competent as "adj/1 efficient. 2 having sufficient skill or training to do something. 3 legally capable."

That rules out Forth Ports plc then.

Somewhere in the senior management, there exists someone who appointed *TNT* as chief harbour master. He must have been asleep that day. This company is supposed to be charged with the safe navigation of shipping on the river and estuary. If so, how did they get him?

His first claim to fame, was by upsetting every single pilot on the river, by sending them a letter, which although fully typed, was addressed in a scrawl, in my case, 'Dear Douglas', and signed with, 'Sincerely Tony'.

None of us had even met him, so this familiarity went down like a lead balloon. I regard this familiarity as rather insulting. I am not alone.

However, he claimed to possess a Master Mariner's Certificate of Competency, so was fully familiar with the difficulties of our job.

How did a Royal Navy Officer get a Master's Certificate?

There was a period, when RN Officers could apply to the Dept. of Transport for a Masters, if they met certain criteria, such as length of service, rank and so on. In effect, they gave them away. The idea was that after leaving the services, they could be absorbed into, what at that time, was a fairly large British Merchant Navy.

Very few were absorbed, as they knew bugger all, of practical use.

By claiming to be on a par, with those of us who worked for them, immediately distanced him. Try explaining anything to him though.

It got worse, he was 'sure that with our cooperation, we would all set about improving the Forth into one of the best in the country.'

Who said there was anything wrong with it in the first place?

Not an auspicious start. But then he excelled himself. Dumb? Yes.

He came on the VHF one day just after starting with, "I would like the pilot who just brought that ship into the lock at Leith to come to my office. I would like to discuss how you handled that ship."

He had only gone and picked on one of the most experienced and competent pilots, who had been coming into Leith for over 20 years. This brought new meaning to the term 'gobsmacked'.

Realising that he has not got off to a 'good start', he organized a wine and cheese party, so that he, Forth Ports staff and the pilots could meet informally.

How many pilots do you think turned up? Right. None.

But then, he went and put both feet well and truly in it, from then on, there was no looking back. With a ship called the *Donoarainia*. A Greek tanker, of 28 000 tonnes. Where? Grangemouth!

How to 'prang' a ship, 'big style'.

It was one of these lovely spring days, where nothing could go wrong. Well, nothing 'should' go wrong, but did!

It is one of these vagaries, but handling 'big' ships, is actually a whole lot easier, than handling 'small' ships. Getting them into locks, where clearance may only be 10 cms per side, is very straightforward, as long as you remember the Golden Rule, *take your time*!

I ran a 30 000 ton fully loaded gas tanker through the Panama Canal with 15 cms clearance on each side 2 years ago. Simple.

They didn't on this day. The tanker caught the port side gate, and opened up No 1 port cargo tank.

With a bit of quick thinking, the ship was popped into the lock, the outer gates closed, the chief mate on the ship pumped some oil from No 1 port, dropping the head of the tank to below the split in the hull, and the situation was saved. The oil went into other tanks in the ship.

How much was spilt? About 3 tonnes. Where? On the floating wooden fenders. Serious? No. So why *TNT*? Because this is his big 'chance,' to put Operation Clearwater Forth into action. At the time, he was in his office in 'The Pagoda.'

Heavy fuel oil is carried heated, as soon as it hits the water it turns into something close on asphalt. Even the amount of 'oily sheen,' is negligible.

We first heard of this by VHF at Granton, at about the same time as *TNT*, who arranged a 'police' car to Grangemouth. Gosh these guys can drive! I know, as I followed. But the 'fun' was yet to come.

It takes 1 hour to drive from Leith to Grangemouth. That's on a good day. The 'Police' can do it in 30 minutes, but then, they do have the advantage of blue flashing lights. Well, 30 minutes is long enough with *TNT* in your car, prattling on as usual.

So, how do you beat 'The Police?' You don't, as simple as that. But copy them? Of course, but this is for 'bored' pilots, and only after eating a box of 'Quality Street.' Why? because the 'purple and blue wrappers' come in dead handy.

Pilots have powerful strobe lights in a pocket on their lifejackets, which if set off at night, with a blue and purple wrapper covering the lens, looks to someone in front, looking in a mirror, as though The Police are behind them. Only at night though, and make sure first that it isn't a Police car in front.

Operation Clearwater Forth, which he, *TNT* wrote, was such an important document, that nobody read it.

The Harbour Master at Grangemouth and his team, couldn't even find it, and were all on their knees in filing cabinets searching for it, when with perfect timing, found it, as he walked in the door. One of them shouting, "here it is. Aw no, someone has had his chips on it. With tomato ketchup!"

I lifted a copy of the up-dated version off the Internet a few days ago. Now I can read legal documents, but this has me beat. All I can deduce is that nobody is responsible for anything. To help you out though, there is a line drawing on the last page to make it clearer. I think it was drawn by a Starling after being chased over an ink pad.

By the time *TNT* has arrived, so have the Fire Brigade. I have a lot of time for these guys. They have *none* for *TNT*.

The lock side is a hard hat area, but *TNT* ignores this, goes up to the Fire Officer and says, "Right, I'll take over now."

The Fireman could have been my twin, and doesn't suffer fools at *all*, said,

"You can f--- off now, you have no safety helmet!"

With his tail between his legs, *TNT* is sent off to get one.

Being a bit slow on the uptake, *TNT* is back a few minutes later, ready to take over again. Now I should add, that he is wearing a blue pinstripe suit, and has a pair of binoculars round his neck.

I wrote to him in 1996, when I was in a bit of a devilish mood, and asked him why he needed binoculars?

A 28 000 ton tanker, which is 550 feet long, is towering 30 feet above you, and a further 80 feet to the top of the bridge, that you are standing 8 feet away from, is not exactly something that you are going to miss. Even in fog at night if you are short sighted.

I asked if he was going to conduct a minute inspection of the paint thickness, looking for irregularities.

Oh, I got a reply. He banned me from entering the River Forth on *any* ship. I may have touched a nerve here.

Off course, this prompted another letter. Under what rule or law was he going to stop a British subject from entering his own country?

And, if I did come in on a ship, what was he going to do about it, set up a road block perhaps?

We are still not on speaking terms, which I must admit, I find a little strange.

It may be that he found out, that I sneaked in and out one day without telling him, or it may be that he still hasn't got his office clean yet. That must be it. It couldn't have been anything I said, as I have a long history of being *very* diplomatic. (?)

So, back to the lock, there was more to come! It gets better and better.

Having upset the Fire Brigade, he now has a go at the Police!

"Right Officer, go aboard and arrest the Captain."

"What for?" he asked.

"Oh... you think of something."

How about, "he's got a hole in the hull? And it's been leaking oil?"

The Officer, who has not a clue about ships, and why should he after all, decided that he should start off by writing down the ship's name in his wee book. They *all* have these.

Greek ships are different from any other European ships. The name and port of registry are written on the stern in Greek! And why not, they are Greek after all.

So PC Plod starts copying it down in Greek!

"He said to one of the lock men, "how do you guys know how to pronounce the names of these ships?"

"Oh," he laughed, "we just read it off the board on the bridge wing, where it is in English."

Next problem, how is he going to get aboard.

TNT decided to help. Now remember, he is super duper clever and trained by the Royal Navy, a former Queen's Harbour Master no less! With a 'Master Mariner's Certificate of Competency!' Chief Harbour Master for Forth Ports plc, an important man! "Captain, lower a gangway, I'm sending the Police aboard to arrest you."

Yeah! Well done *TNT*, that's bound to work. Show him who's in charge here! Exert your authority, after all, no one else is paying any attention to you, so you might just manage to get your score up to? 1.

Back came the reply from the Greek captain. Absolutely Ace.

"If you want to send the Police aboard to arrest me, then you can get your own f------ gangway."

"Eh *TNT*? Have you ever considered another line of work, such as knitting?

Score: Ship 1, *TNT*? Nil. (At least it's not minus).

There was no holding him now though. If you are going to foul up, you might as well do it properly.

"How dare you move this ship without my permission, as it started to move out of the lock towards its' berth. Stop it immediately!"

Now here is a really hard question. Did the ship stop?

If you need an answer to this, then I think we need to have a talk.

But as the ship moved out, what should arrive outside the lock, but two tugs, from Leith. No risk of running them aground though, they had been given their training, and it was daylight.

What were they there for? In case there was any pollution. The only thing was, that with the delay to the ship in the lock, the tide was now on the ebb, and if there had been any oil in the river, then it would have been 3 miles downriver by now.

Not that that would have made any difference though, as good old *TNT* has only gone and sent the two tugs 'without' any pollution gear, and left the two that had, in Leith.

After the ship was tied up, was there an investigation into the cause? Of course not, this is Forth Ports plc. And *TNT* was there remember.

But I'll let you into a few secrets. I used to like this pilot, until he s--- all over me, just like most of the rest of them. He has retired now, so it's not going to make any difference.

The clearance in the lock may only have been 10 cms, but this is between the ship and the fenders. The fenders are a metre wide, so this ship is at least 1.1 metres away from the lock wall.

The lock gate is recessed into the wall, when it is swung open, so for a ship to hit it, means that the ship is at least 1.1 metres out of position from the centerline of the lock. When you consider that there is a tug on the bow, one wonders how he could be this far out. To open up a tank, the ship had to be swinging *in*, when it should have been swinging *out*, or back to the centreline at least.

It is actually very easy to understand how it happened.

This man was an ex-Fife pilot, so his experience of getting in and out of Grangemouth was very limited. But this throws up another quirk.

A new pilot is limited to 3500 tons gross for 18 months, but the ex-Fife and ex-Leith pilots weren't. After five trips in, they were unlimited. And you wonder why there were so many accidents?

A few months after I left the Forth Pilots, he was in a clinic 'drying out'. This was not a new problem either. For him, or some others.

I got the rest of this story from a very disgruntled Forth Ports employee about 3 years later, who just needed a good moan.

The ship's insurance, paid for a new set of fenders. These are made from oak and are not cheap. But the old ones, splashed in heavy oil become the property of the underwriters, just as a smashed car would be, if you got a new one after an accident.

Arrangements were made for their disposal, by burning them.

Were they? Oh no, they were carefully stored away in a shed, where they were dismantled, run through a saw to remove the oil soaked wood, rebuilt, and slowly returned to service, after other ship's insurance companies were billed after incurring damage. Call this clever if you like, but most people call it fraud. Note, that I did not mention who benefited though.

A change of direction again? I think so, just to keep your interest, so we'll tell a few stories about ships with odd problems or cargoes, before I tell you about the gas tanker that ripped its' bottom out, and then the Forth Ports Authority's (as it was at this time, but with the same incompetents) atmospheric pollution all over Edinburgh and Leith. This one will amaze you, as the pollutant was a carcinogenic gas!

One of the first ships I took up to Grangemouth, was a German coaster, 499 Gross runs in my mind. There were a lot of these.

We were waiting off the lock, at dusk, and as the light was dimming, I asked the captain to turn up the light on the Rudder Angle Indicator. I was steering at the time.

As soon as he did so, the bulb blew.

"No problem captain, we can just put a torch in front of it, until we are in the lock."

"No pilot, this is German ship, we fix it."

This I had to see, as he had hands like an ape's.

Armed with a screwdriver about 40 cms long, he climbed up onto the bridge console, so I had to steer from one side. First of all his knee landed on the whistle button, which of course jammed on. After finding the master switch, he had another go, and this time, removed the front panel.

"See mr pilot, here is the problem, the bulb is broken."

I'll not pass comment I think, being of the, diplomatic type.

But then, as he started to climb down again, the wiring on the front panel touched the main part of the box, and there was an almighty blue flash, he got an electric shock, and then fell off.

At that stage, the green lights for the lock being ready came on, but the Rudder Angle Indicator isn't working at all now.

I actually got the ship in by 'guessing' where the rudder was in relation as to how she was swinging.

It was fixed in the lock, and we had a good laugh about it afterwards. He was *so* embarrassed.

German masters are either 'Teutonic and arrogant,' or very pleasureable. It depends which part of Germany they come from. The best are from the North.

I again, brought in a German ship, and as we came up the river, said to the captain,

"You know, for a ship that is fully loaded, you seem to be awful high in the water."

"Oh yes pilot, see if you can guess what our cargo is. I'll give you a clue, it is very light and is used in sport."

Thinking that a ridiculous answer was called for here, I countered with, "ping pong balls?"

He laughed and said, "you are not that far away," as the mind conjured up an image of a shipload of loose ping pong balls.

"Actually, it is two 'all-weather' playing fields."

This was the soft springy rubber stuff, which was being delivered in bulk. One day, I sailed a Russian tanker from Grangemouth, and the captain asked if we could wait in the lock for about an hour or so. This was a bit unusual, but I cleared it with the lock, then asked why?

"We have cargo to load."

This gets better and better.

He explained. They had bought up a lot of old Ladas, to take back to Russia, and were all waiting in the car park at the lock. So, starboard side alongside this time, and they were craned aboard. There were 12 of them.

But it got better still!

"Where are you going to stow them captain?"

What a stupid question.

"Oh, first of all, we fill the tanks with petrol, then they will come down to the stern."

But the petrol is in No 1 tank, so they were driven up the deck to No 1, driven mind, not pushed, filled up from the cargo, and then driven back down the deck to the poop. All, as we went down the river. It was like something out of Wacky Races.

And mind, this is a *tanker*. (Dick Dastardly was in The Pagoda).

Russian ships at this time had one lovely feature. Although they didn't have much, they always provided you with a little glass mug, in a silver holder, hot water, tea or coffee, and a tray of either cheese, or salami or whatever. Some could be a bit chewy mind.

Sometimes it was brought up by the 'stewardess'.

Boy, oh boy could some of them look rough.

The worst ships for getting something to eat on, were usually Norwegian, which I always found hard to understand. It was not uncommon for the captain to be relieved for a meal, and the pilot was left to go without.

When this happened, I billed the ship for an hour's overtime.

The sky blackened about this time, I knew it was too good to last. What should arrive back on the river to trade between Teesport and Grangemouth? The *Borthwick*. Only now, she is no longer owned by Gibsons. They found some company more stupid than themselves to actually buy it. For years, they couldn't even give it away.

Who bought it? Vlasov, or otherwise known as VShips Cyprus.

Both the captain and chief engineer had been in VShips Norway when I was there, and the chief and I sailed together on the Norgas Challenger. It was nice to see him again, and to see that he was going to have the same trouble on the bridge as Gibsons chiefs. He was *big*, (fat). The bridge front is so narrow, that if two fat people want to pass, then one has to go round the chartroom to get to the other side.

The captain I decline to talk about, as I'd heard about him, and later, it all turned out to be true. He was a fairy.

The first time I took her out of Grangemouth, involved putting a few ghosts to bed, but I was not going to let Forth Ports see that I was 'scared' of her.

I still wish that I had let her sink though, when I had the chance. She was still, shall we say, rough, only now, she had Indian Crew and was destined to get even worse, especially with winter coming.

Here is a good one. Forth Ports were involved in setting this up.

Do you remember when the QE2 came to anchor off Anstruther for the Millenium Open Championship at St. Andrews?

Was it a success? You must be joking, as when the passengers wanted to go ashore, with the intention of bussing it up to St Andrews, or for coming back after a day's play, for a bit of dinner and so on, *just* happened to coincide with the time that there was no water in the harbour at Anstruther. Low water!

A useless piece of information, not related to the River Forth, but concerns the *QE2*.

The pilots and VTS operators in the Solent going up to Southampton, are not allowed to call the *QE2*, the *QE2*. Tony would love this bit of bullshit. They are in big trouble if they slip up. It has to be transmitted as *Queen Elizabeth 2*. I think the Queen would have a little chuckle at this.

But back to the Forth. On the subject of passengers, this must be the easiest type of cargo to load and discharge imaginable. They just walk on and off, themselves. Even the ship often has the gangway.

In 1992, Forth Ports were paid £2.50 for every passenger who came ashore. Even if they forgot their 'brolly, and went back for it, that was another £2.50.

The only expense incurred was getting someone to keep count. They often had to employ a student for this, as the numbers frequently went passed 99, and not many Forth Ports employees knew what came next. (Actually it's 100, 101, 102... .)

There was one very unfortunate passenger ship in the early 90s, which came and anchored off Leith. For once, it wasn't Forth Ports fault, but they still made a <u>lot</u> of money out of this.

The ship was the *Akdeniz*, Turkish flag, but chartered to a German Company, so most of the passengers were German.

On the first day, they came ashore for a coach tour, which went to Edinburgh, Perth, Crieff, the Trossachs, into the Highlands, and back to Edinburgh. On the second day, they came ashore for another coach tour, which went to Edinburgh, Perth, Crieff, the Trossachs, into the Highlands, and back to Edinburgh.

On the third day, the went for a different coach tour, which went into Edinburgh, the Highlands, the Trossachs, Crieff, Perth, and back to Edinburgh.

On the fourth day, they all went home.

Then the ship came into Leith for 2 weeks. Why? The Dept of Transport detained her for safety defects. She eventually left, temporarily re-certificated for one voyage as a cargo ship to Bremerhaven for dry docking.

She was only meant to be in the Forth for 12 hours.

Now to Forth Ports foray into the world of gas tanker operation. Now remember the definition of the word 'competent'. Having sufficient skill or training to do something.

First of all, you need a rock, a buoy with no light on it, marking the rock, a gas tanker mind, preferably loaded, which this one just happened to be, the River Forth, and lots of darkness, lots and lots off it. Oh, and the Forth Ports Authority. It was in 1985.

The ship was a small single hulled, pressurized ship from the Tholstrup fleet. Danish. Not a bad little company either.

She was anchored in Musselburgh Bay, which was where a lot of small ships used to anchor. Used to anchor, I said.

She had a full cargo of 1,3 Butadiene, (uninhibited, which makes a big difference with this stuff).

The captain ups anchor, and sets off to get his pilot for Grangemouth, at the unofficial pilot station (another one) just off Granton. That was the plan.

Unfortunately, the rock got in the way, and ripped the bottom clean out of the ship, leaving it hard aground.

Please don't think that I'm being flippant with this story, it's just that I know the whole story, which just gets better and better, but at this stage is pretty serious. I agree.

Enter the Forth Ports Authority.

This is what happens when people who have not the first clue about what to do next, start telling others what to do, using the law or their position to back them up.

An exclusion zone is set up. 5 miles all around, extending up to 10 000 feet (vertically). So all the aeroplanes have to make detours.

Then a pilot had to stay on board. Goodness knows why, as he isn't going anywhere. He's hard aground remember.

Then another ship has to come alongside and off-load the cargo, with another pilot. And the harbour master! People are now starting to get in the way, of a cargo transfer operation, which on a pressurized gas tanker, is so easy, a kid could do it. Put a pipe between two ships, open the valves, and stand back, until it is empty. But the Port Authority wants checklists. The ship will not float off, no danger of that with all these extra people, and all this paper.

So, cargo taken off, second ship away. Now they want to tank clean her, before hauling her off, and take her into Leith drydock. See how they make money out of anything.

Now, I'll get technical. Butadiene is one of the most toxic, carcinogenic poisonous types of gas carried at sea.

The TLV (used at that time) was 5 parts per million. The TLV is the maximum amount of gas that may fill a space in air, that a human was allowed to work within for any 8 hour period in 24 hours. It is now called the TWA (time weighted average) and is 0.5 ppm.

Tank cleaning is done by going through an inert atmosphere, before flushing with air. Not inert gas, as the CO2 reacts with the Butadiene and forms peroxides. Usually with nitrogen.

But Forth Ports Authority, have a quick way of doing it, and I know where they got this from, but I'm not telling you.

The procedure is fully approved by the harbour master, and is really very simple, just like him. I know who he was too.

You take the lid off the tank, and then fill it with water. The water displaces the gas, which goes into the atmosphere. You can't see where it goes, as it's invisible, but it's a fair old bet that it drifted over Edinburgh, or Fife or wherever. Never mind that it's carcinogenic.

Then, you put in a submersible pump, and pump out the water.

Good eh? That's a new one for the gas instruction manuals.

Now the hard bit. Getting her off the rock and into the drydock.

Put on three big tugs and pull like fuck. Forth Ports tugs of course.

They got her into the dry dock, where the damage was assessed.

The rest of the story doesn't concern The Forth Ports Authority, apart from a shocker, but it's so good, that I'll tell it anyway.

Three tenders are submitted for the repair.

No 1, in Hamburg, £2 million, plus 3 months.

No 2, in Rotterdam, £2.2 million, plus 3 to 4 months.

No 3, in Sunderland, (where Gibsons go), £ 350 000, and 30 days.

It was awarded to Sunderland, but first they have to get it there, so build a cement box, to keep her afloat and stable.

On ships, everyone is an expert with cement boxes as they invariably hold most ships together at some point, or in some cases, all the time. Even the RFA.

So, off she goes under tow, and straight into dry dock, where it was agreed that this wasn't just a cement box, *this was a huge cement box*!

Normally they are removed by jack hammers. They wouldn't even look at it, this called for another approach.

Dynamite!

Even with this, it took 14 days to get it out. It weighed over 200 tonnes, and was reinforced with, wait for it, railway lines.

Who do you think just happened to have a supply of old railway lines? You should know by now.

Now to finish the story, the ship was away in 30 days, fully repaired, and every other Tholstrup gas tanker went to that repair yard from then on. That is how to get repeat business.

Now what would be the obvious answer to prevent a repeat of this?

Yes, of course, put a light on the buoy.

Guess what, to this day it doesn't have one.

But there is another thing put in place.

If a ship anchors in Musselburgh Bay now, then the pilot has to board the ship there. Even although it is well outside the compulsory pilotage area.

Let's just hope the pilot can see the unlit buoy in the dark, but I doubt it. Mind you, radars are a tad better now.

Remember my reference to a shocker. Three people who work for Forth Ports plc know about this, and are determined to keep it covered up, and after their hefty fine, even more so. But the next time they come up against the courts, they will have a hard job explaining this, as it concerns the safety of their employees, or rather their contempt for their employees. Nothing other than Utter Contempt! Remember… Competent?...?...?

With no bottom in this little gas tanker, the cargo tank is exposed for all to see. Cargo tanks from the beginning have been insulated, and as in all things, insulation has been developed over the years, but with this ship, was rather primitive.

What did Forth Ports find it had in its insulation?

Blue asbestos.

What did they do about it?

Absolutely nothing.

Even in 1985, the dangers were recognized, far less nowadays.

If you think I'm making this up, then I know of a fourth person who knows of this, who has no connection to Forth Ports plc, or ever has had, and can also tell you how the shipyard got round the problem, without invoking the necessary legislation.

Now, what else has run aground about here? We'll get back to Tony soon, I promise.

To the South of Inchkeith Island, is the 'Herwit Rock'.

At extremely low, low water, it just breaks the surface.

During the Second World War, a steam trawler ran aground on it, so well, that she couldn't get off. She was abandoned.

This actually paid off quite well, as now, everyone knew where the rock was.

Later, along came the Forth Ports Authority, who decided that the rock should be marked with a green buoy. Not as daft as you might think, as the trawler is now breaking up, and there was not that much left.

Put the buoy beside the rock perhaps? Oh no, much too easy, let's put it 1.5 cables (0.15 of a mile) south of the rock.

For years, the Fishery Protection ships ran in and out of Leith, and there became a standard procedure that there was enough water for them to pass *north* of the buoy, and *south* of the rock. For many years, this is what they did. Until one day!

The ship was the *Switha*, and as it transpired was on her last few trips before going off somewhere else. As per normal, the master came north of the buoy, but unfortunately, just a wee bit too much north, and went hard up on The Herwit.

By this stage, all that was left of the trawler, was her boiler. But not to worry, there is now a new radar target.

However, *TNT*'s pals, the RN decided to 'help', in getting her off.

She was too far up to be pulled off, so they filled her with 2 tons of high explosive, with a view to 'blowing her' off.

Good plan eh?

Now bear in mind, that this was a 'Fishery *protection* vessel.'

Everything was cleared for miles around, and the charge set off. In 15 seconds flat, there was not a single fish left alive in the Forth.

The *Switha* never even moved.

To explain themselves, this was a 'controlled' explosion to release the remaining fuel from the ships tanks. How much high explosive would you need for a VLCC then?

In Scandinavian countries, where they care for the environment, the owners would have been ordered to remove the wreck, and to give the Fishery boys their due, they did make the effort, by selling the wreck to a local 'salvage' firm. The only real thing of value was the propeller, which was phosphor bronze, and that alone would have paid for the salvage costs. However.

The night before salvage was due to start, some locals nipped out under cover of darkness, and pinched it.

She, over the next few years started to break up, and the last time I looked, there was not a lot left.

If you are interested, next time there are ultra low tides, take a pair of binoculars, and have a look. You can even see the old trawler's boiler.

Haven't got any binoculars? 'Phone me, and I'll give you *TNT's* number, as he has a spare pair, unless of course the *Donoarania* is back.

Here is a wee story which illustrates the difficulty in getting pilots to change. The older they get, the worse they get. Most are brain dead by 45, or 5 years after starting, 4 if they're a teuchter.

A rather elderly pilot (at least 55) from many years ago was taking a ship up to Grangemouth one day, and required some details from the master.

"Captain, what is the ship's length?"

"100 metres pilot."

Oh, groaned the pilot, metres, so starts to work it out in feet, eventually getting to 328 feet 2 inches.

"What is your beam?"

"15 metres."

Another groan, but came up with 49 feet.

"What is your draft?"

"5 metres."

This was getting too much, three calculations in 20 minutes.

"16 feet 3 inches give or take a foot or so."

The passage continues upriver, and when the ship clears the bridges, the captain asks, "how far is it to the lock pilot?"

With a wee glint in his eye, "it'll be another 3 leagues captain."

You've waited long enough, let's get back to *TNT*, and I won't change the subject now, until after the Forth Ports Kangaroo Court was destroyed. That's right, their Kangaroo Court, convened to get *TNT* out of a colossal jam, and all of his own making. Now you will see just how thick they all are, but remember, *TNT* is in a league of his own by now. Nobody has joined this league since either.

When the abbreviation CHA comes along for Competent Harbour Authority, read it as IHA, Incompetent Harbour Authority. You'll soon realize why, believe me.

One day, we all arrived at Granton to start work, and there was a new notice on the notice board, to which we all replied after reading it, "how are we supposed to do that?"

It was a directive from the Queen's Harbour Master in Rosyth, advising that Rule 10 of the Dockyard Port of Rosyth, had been amended to: "ships transiting the area up-river from the bridges shall not exceed a speed of more than 10 knots *over* the ground." It used to be "10 knots through the water." Rule 10 came from the turn of the century, the 20th century that is, about 1901, and was introduced when Royal Navy warships used to burn coal.

It's intention was to reduce the wake of passing ships, when colliers were alongside 'coaling.'

After oil was introduced, the rule slipped into oblivion, and was forgotten about by everyone, everyone except of course, *TNT*.

So, why was *TNT* involved as chief harbour master, if this came from the Queen's Harbour Master in the Navy Base?

Well, this Russian tanker had been coming down from Grangemouth, a ship of about 14 000 tons, and after passing the unstable *Resource*, had a steering gear failure. It happens. By the time the ship was stopped, a channel mark was destroyed, and the ship had its' anchor round the Forties/Grangemouth oil pipeline, despite that this is an 'anchoring prohibited' area.

TNT, after engaging overdrive in the brain, decided *all by himself*, that the cause of the accident, was 'excessive speed'.

So, in his special capacity of Forth Ports Chief Harbour Master, went to see his 'wee pal' in Rosyth, and pull a bit of 'rank' on him. Highly improper, but what's that to our *TNT*?

The Queen's Harbour Master has the rank of Commander, which is what our *TNT* had when he was there as well. But, when you retire from the Navy, the day you retire, you are automatically promoted one rank, so that you can get a bigger pension.

So, 'The Captain,' asks, 'The Commander,' to promulgate a revised version of Rule 10, changing 'through the water,' to 'over the ground.' *But*, keep it quiet, until it is passed into law. We don't want the pilots finding out. (The only people who use the word promulgate are the Royal Navy, they just seem to love it.)

What is the problem then?

Going up-river it isn't always so bad, but can still be a problem.

Coming down river? You try this simple calculation, and see if you can get the same answer as *TNT*, who got 10 knots. Ships minimum dead slow ahead speed, continuous running, 7 knots. Speed of current on a spring ebb, 6 knots. Windage effect of 30 knot wind (yearly average), 2 knots. Now, add it all together, $7 + 6 + 2 = 15$. So how did *TNT* get 10?

The minimum speed the ship can make 'over the ground' is therefore 15 knots, but to comply with the new *law*, and it is now *law*, we cannot do more than 10 knots.

Now this is a worst case scenario, but even on flood tides, getting the slowest container ships down to 10 knots, meant that the ship was being put in danger, it was uncontrollable.

However, there is more, which has been equally well thought out by *TNT*. The revised Rule 10 is going to be 'policed', by the Forth Navigation Service Radar Coverage, to ensure that all ships comply!

It gets even better. *TNT* now on full speed, has also decided that from the bridges to clear of Inchkeith, the speed of a vessel will be restricted to 12 knots.

This immediately throws up a legal problem, and that is just for the last part. The limit of the Port of Rosyth is not North of Inchkeith, but further up-river, at The Oxcars, and Rule 10 only applies within the Dockyard Port Limits. To *TNT*, far too hard a problem, he is already away cocking up something else.

Now you see where his name came from: Ten (K)not Tony, sounds more plausible than Twelve (K)not Tony, so from now on, I'll just call him Tony (a dear friend, really. Believe that and you'll believe anything.) So, what do we all do first, we are invited to write to the harbour master and place our concerns over this matter. I did, as I could see the dangers in this right away. Many pilots didn't write, but they were the ones who shout the loudest, but when it comes to action, do the least. That covers most of the Forth Pilots, even to this day.

The most important part of my letter, was that I told him straight, that "under absolutely no circumstances whatsoever, would I, as pilot, advise a master to place his ship in danger, just to comply with a stupid rule."

That was my position then, that is my position to this day.

It was at this point that Tony singled me out for, 'special attention'. He picked on totally the wrong pilot. But then, he would.

In that it was in force immediately, meant that it wasn't applied immediately, but after 14 days, so everyone could be advised. During this period, there was a meeting between the Queen's HM, the senior pilots, and off course, Tony, where it was put to the QHM that it was un-workable, and dangerous. He listened to both sides, then said, "well it looks like I've been made a fool of here, so we should change it back."

Tony then jumped in with, "oh no, it'll be all right, you'll see."

When I heard this, the penny dropped. There was an ulterior motive at play here.

I'll put this bit in here, but it only comes into play later.

The 'ulterior motive' came from a topic being discussed by the UKPA (United Kingdom Pilots Association), concerning the 'control' of shipping in the Dover Strait. For legal reasons alone, it would never work. It is also totally impractical.

The concept was to introduce a system for shipping similar to that of Air Traffic Control. This will not work for ships.

ATC works in a three-dimensional field, where aircraft of different speeds, fly at different heights, and can be separated then on one level plane, distance apart, between each other fore and aft.

Ships however only work on a two-dimensional field, so different speeds have to be built in here as well. It is frankly impossible to do.

The other difficulty is legal, who is in command, the ship, or the operator ashore?

ATC will tell an aircraft if it is out of position, and this will be corrected.

But what would happen if a ship refused to comply with 'an instruction' from say a VTS service, after all, the ship may have a perfectly good reason for being where it is, and a radar ashore cannot see in a three-dimensional field, whereas, a ship can, by running its echo sounder. Plus, not everything shows up on radar, such as yachts.

In ATC, they are only dealing in one medium, air including wind. The sea however is a completely different matter. A ship of 1500 tons could be making 5 knots through the water, but getting pushed back by the weather at 5 knots, so is effectively hove-to, while a ship beside it of 50 000 tons could be running along at 5 knots, and only losing 2 knots to the weather, so is still making 3 knots. (There is a system for ships at sea, known as 'weather routing', where the met office will give the best route for a ship to avoid the worst of the weather. Now the met office are only interested in weather, so if their 'route' goes over the top of an island, that is not their problem. That is for the ship to identify and avoid.)

The proposal is far too complex, and would need more people ashore than on the ships. It is just not practical.

Then there is the problem of Third World countries' crews. Some of them are still employing deep sea pilots.

Without having thought this through, Tony is going to introduce it onto the Forth. He was actually quoted in the Press later on this very subject. I'll explain about that later. After 14 days, it comes in to effect.

10 minutes it lasted before the first ship was called up,

"Bill, your speed is showing at 14 knots."

"Okay then, I'll haul her back a bit."

Immediately, a legal question. Just who is doing what here?

The pilot is advising the master, but VTS is advising the pilot, who in turn is slowing the ship down to comply with VTS. So, why does VTS just not advise the master, and do away with the pilot?

You could go round in circles indefinitely here. The one thing that causes more accidents than any other is when there is 'doubt' on the bridge of a ship. Now there are three players, instead of two. *More* doubt.

But let's try and keep it simple.

One afternoon, I came down from Grangemouth on a small British tanker, the 'Astraman.' There was nothing else moving.

FNS (Forth Navigation Service) called up on the VHF.

"*Astraman*, FNS, do you know what speed you are doing?"

I replied, "about 10 knots."

"You are showing on radar, a speed of 14.6 knots."

Now the *Astraman* would be lucky if it got to 10 knots 'through the water' going downhill with the wind behind.

She is an old clapped out ship, with two engines geared onto one propeller shaft. One thing she does best is vibrate. On the starboard side of the wheelhouse, was a Decca Arkas radar, which had a brush wedged in-between the front end, with the handle squeezed up against the deck head panel. Its purpose was two-fold. It stopped the deck head panel from rattling, and it stopped the radar display from shaking.

"Okay FNS, I'll haul her back a bit." Which we did.

He was back on a few minutes later with,

"*Astraman*, you are still showing 14.6 knots."

The feeling that came across here was that 'you will slow down as I told you to do'.

"Okay, we'll haul her back a bit more."

A few minutes later, "*Astraman*, FNS, your speed is now 14.8 knots."

I ignored him, as we are now coming to the bridges, and to slow her down any more would mean we did not have enough speed to get her to turn fast enough in safety.

Why she 'speeded up' was because the surface water increases in speed, as the river narrows. All the water over a vast area above the bridges, is now trying to squeeze into a small area, on the outgoing tide.

His remark also brings up the most important point of all.

What is more important, the ship's speed, or the safety of navigation for the whole ship? In effect, the safety of the ship?

You can imagine the letter to your owners,

Dear Sir,

It is with regret that I have to advise you that on 14th May 1992, the *MV Tony* was lost on the rocks known as 'The Beamer'. Unfortunately, the ship's cargo, 5 million tins of 'Spaghetti Bolognese' and 2 million tins of Soup (various varieties), was also lost. It was last seen drifting ashore, where a vast team of volunteers were gathering them up, probably with a view to handing them in to their local Police station, they being the honest citizens of Fife.

However sir, it is not all bad news, you will be delighted to know, that at the time of the unfortunate grounding of my vessel, we were in fact fully complying with Rule 10 of the Dockyard Port of Rosyth.

We were at the time, having trouble steering the vessel.

Yours faithfully
Dumbo the Elephant.

When I got ashore, the rest of the pilots agreed with me that this was the stupidest thing ever tried. I was still fuming at the VHF tongue lashing that FNS gave me on the way to Inchkeith.

There were other incidents, but I'll stay with this one for now, as this is where Tony and I started to fight. The difference between us was that while I kept it totally *legal*, he as Forth Ports Chief Harbour Master broke every rule in the book, plus a few he made up.

Tony swung into action. He actually wrote a letter to the QHM, advising him, that he was reporting the *Astraman* as being in breach of Rule 10 etc, with a speed of 14.8 knots. He sent me a copy.

Now, and at this point, I feel sorry for the QHM, as he doesn't want this in the first place, he doesn't have a clue what to do next, as not a single procedure is in place, for anything. So he writes to me, me mind, not the master of the ship as he should have done.

I wrote back, just to inform him, that he should really have written to the master, and that as he had not got any procedures in place, neither had Forth Ports, and if this was to be a disciplinary matter, then there were no disciplinary proceedings in place at Forth Ports either.

None of them had thought of anything.

Tony is however, unfazed, and then writes to the vessels owners, asking for an explanation.

He got one from the ship's master, who was one of these 'weak' masters, who'll say anything, just to make it go away. Life ain't like that pal.

The sum total of the master's excuse was that "the pilot had not informed him that there was a speed restriction in place."

If you ever read this captain, remember, the buck stops with you.

It also prompts the question, did his in-bound pilot inform him that a speed restriction was in place?

Also, ignorance of the law is no excuse.

Tony also wrote to me, so I sought legal advice from the pilots' Legal team in London, who said I should send in a Statement of Facts. Which I did, a *very* simple Statement of Facts, about six lines in all.

Not getting anywhere fast, he decides to exert more pressure, not on the master mind, but the pilot.

He gets the ship's superintendent to write to the pilot, asking to be informed as to what was discussed between the master and the pilot of the *Astraman*.

I can assure the non-marine readers at this point, that the word 'incredulous', is being used by the marine reader.

So how did he get the superintendent to do this?

This, you will find hard to believe.

The superintendent was known as Captain 5 Days. When he was offered the job in Rowbotham Tankships, a division of P & O no less, he had no experience as master, and as the company want his business card to include the word 'Captain', put him on a small tanker for 5 days, while it lay at anchor. You cannot do much damage at anchor. The other problem, was that although they want him as marine superintendent, his tanker experience is a bit rusty.

But where was he working before he got this job? He was an operator at Forth Navigation Service. One floor up from our friend Tony. Ideal experience for a marine superintendent? Of a tanker fleet?

Under the old boys' club syndrome, Tony 'leaned' on him, for 'a favour'.

I'm not supposed to know all this you understand, but I was also a marine investigator after I stopped piloting, and it's amazing what people will tell you. Especially from within P & O.

So, Captain 5 Days' letter arrives, and I very promptly answer it, after 2 weeks.

In the meantime, another letter arrives from the OM.

This one says, to forward a copy of my response to him.

Question, how does he know about my letter from 5 Days?

In response to him, I sent back the one word letter.

Dear Sir,

No.

Yours faithfully.

That sound clear to you, does to me, but not somehow, to the OM. So promptly answering 5 days' letter, it went like this,

Dear Sir,

Following your letter blah blah blah etc, the topic discussed between the pilot and master, while the vessel was being piloted between Grangemouth and the Sea was the selection and price of pianos.

Yours faithfully.

We did actually do this, as he was thinking of buying a piano, and I had just bought one for my daughter.

I didn't get any more letters from 5 Days, given up no doubt, after he saw the signature, as he from his days at FNS, knew it was not wise to argue.

Then everything went quiet, nobody got caught, not even me.

At a pilots' meeting, we had these bun fights occasionally, I kept them all informed as to what was going on, and they all agreed that I would handle my situation myself. It is important to mention this here, as it was denied later by that cowardly pilot from Dollar that I was fighting a 'one man war' with Forth Ports. Liar, but typical of him.

Pilots bun fights were a constant source of amusement, as they would spend hours discussing totally irrelevant rubbish, convincing themselves how good they were.

One such discussion was how to escort tankers down from Hound Point. Someone actually, did actually suggest putting the tug on a wire, on the bow, and have the tug running 40 feet in front of the tanker. Now that is scary.

The only useful thing *ever* achieved, was going for a beer afterwards. Pilots have 6 weeks straight holiday in the summer, apart from the rest of the time, only working 2 weeks out of 5. To do this, shifts are stepped up to week on, week off. Gosh it's tough!

Just as I came on holiday, the 'phone rang, it was Sanko Kisen in Rotterdam. I knew them from before.

"Captain Harvey, are you busy for the next 3 weeks?"

"No, why?"

"We've got a difficult cargo to load in Philadelphia, and need a specialist master."

"Call me back in an hour, I'll discuss this with my wife first."

The up-shot, was that I went to Philadelphia and loaded this difficult cargo, but that's another story for another book.

After Philadelphia, and a family holiday, it was back to work. First day at Granton, in the 'chicken feeder', our 'new' pilot station, and it was going to be a busy day.

"Doug, the Sunny Clipper has a Hen and Chicken time of 1100, can you get the containership up the river in a hurry and get her in before that?" asked the duty pilot.

"No problem, speed restriction?"

"Forth Ports have cleared this rule."

Fine by me, so I jump on board this biggish container ship at about 08 30, and it's going to be tight getting her in before the gas boat, who boarded just after me.

I explained the situation to the captain, we got the handle down, and went up river at over 18 knots. Not a thing was said.

Everything worked out perfectly.

It was rather a satisfying start, didn't last long though.

After docking the containership, I went to sail a fairly big cargo ship, of about 8500 tonnes, her name was something Forest, anyway, it doesn't matter now.

So after clearing the lock, we set off down river.

After passing the The Dhu Craig Buoy just off Rosyth, FNS came on with, "xxxxxxx Forest, your speed is 15.4 knots, you are instructed to slow down to no more than 10 knots over the ground."

That one simple statement totally destroyed the safety of navigation on the River Forth in Scotland.

The Air Traffic Control system, was now in operation. Responsibility had been taken from the master, and was now in the hands of FNS.

The word used was 'instructed' mind, not 'requested'.

I was having none of this, and you should have heard the captain, who went a similar colour in the face as Paranoid Pete in Gibsons. (That's also a story for another book.) Purple by the way.

"I will remind FNS, that the vessel will proceed at a speed conversant with the safety of navigation." I said in reply.

We were almost at The Beamer, so kept on going, as to slow down now, when we need to turn between the bridges, is utter madness. Anyway, the turn will take off some speed.

Remember, on the *Norgas Challenger*, when I lost my main engine, it was having the speed on that allowed me to anchor safely.

It took me a long time to settle down after I got ashore. The other pilots couldn't believe what had happened. Nobody could.

It was acceptable to take a ship up-river at 18 knots, as Forth Ports needed her in, in a hurry, and ignore the rule, but when there is nothing for them to gain, you cannot ignore the rule.

No-one can operate like this, there could only be one thing for it.

The Chief Harbour Master is having a witch hut.

Or Forth Ports plc are.

And so it proved to be.

The final straw for me, when I just blew my top, happened on a Friday afternoon. There were two containerships to sail, and two gas tankers. (Small ones, but still gas tankers.)

I had the first containership, the *Yolanda*. One of our regular Dutch running ships.

The two gas tankers went first, and the old adage of shutting the middle gates to make two locks should have been used. It wasn't, they were left open. The whole river is now a mess, with rules being broken right, left and centre, nobody *at all* caring about anything. If this is not sorted out soon, there is going to be a colossal accident.

There very nearly was, and on the same day. With a gas tanker! After clearing the lock on the *Yolanda*, we set off down the river, the second container ship running about 15 minutes behind me.

Between Crombie and Rosyth, FNS came on with,

"*Yolanda*, you are showing a speed of 11.5 knots."

"For your information FNS, and make sure you get this on the tape, the ship ahead of me, is going away from me, the ship astern is catching me up, and you have called <u>neither</u> of them. The *Yolanda* is now increasing to full speed, and fuck your rule 10. I will be forwarding an official complaint to the Dept of Transport when I get ashore. Now, do not call this ship again. By the way, the master is in full agreement with me."

I remember the words to this day, mind you, a semi-photographic memory helps a bit.

The master threw all the power on, and we went flat out. He told me,

"It is about time someone got this sorted out. Good luck pilot."

I think we hit 17 knots, but FNS did not call back.

Now, Tony, when you read this, I do <u>know</u> that you were in FNS at the time, and the big grin on your face was noted. I am not the only one who detests you. I can't think of someone who likes you either.

I was so angry driving home, that I had to stop, I was shaking so much.

I received the letter from the CHM, which I returned almost immediately. It would have made *absolutely* no difference whatsoever, whether it had been a polite letter, or the full blast of both barrels which he got, as my days as a pilot were numbered anyway.

My final paragraph to him was the most insulting of all,

"If you wish to make a serious contribution to maritime safety, then can I suggest that you take up a career as a pig farmer."

I had just been informed that *Snow White*, was joining Forth Ports.

I'll take the opportunity here to 'apologize' to Tony with the reference to pigs. I have since found out how difficult they are to keep, so please, change pigs into goats.

A few days later, I was in Leith to sail the *Venta*. This was a very underpowered Polish cargo ship, and very light, she was really like trying to control a sail. This would be fun in the lock, as it was a windy day, and the wind was straight across the lock.

Going into the lock was tricky but I 'crabbed' her in, and then slid her up to the far end, beside The Pagoda.

They were all watching of course. Getting her out without a tug was going to be nigh on impossible, unless I could get the bow up into the wind. Fortunately, the tug, *Inchcolm*, was waiting outside, so if I was stuck, he could help.

Coming out of the lock the wind caught her, and she just did not have enough power, and came alongside the lead in jetty about 50 metres from the lock.

"Inchcolm, could you drop your stern in between the fenders and the bow and push the head up into the wind?"

"No problem Doug," and less than 5 minutes later, we were away.

3 days later, I received a letter from the OM, stating that he would be having an investigation into the *Venta*, as "sailing from the lock was not achieved in a conventional manner."

The witch hunt was definitely on, as this pillock has never handled a ship in his life. Remember what I said in Part 1 about those ashore being 'super expert' in ship handling.

In any aspect of ship handling, try and define 'conventional'.

With this idiot, try and define him as 'conventional'.

Friday. "Recorded delivery letter for you sir, sign here please".

1) I was suspended as a pilot with the following 'charges': When asked to give specific information regarding the *MV Borthwick*, Captain Harvey deliberately misled the CHA as to his conduct on board this ship. Forth Ports were now in possession of certain information which shows his un-suitability as a pilot.

2) When asked by the Managers of Forth Ports for information, regarding ships piloted, he replied in an undignified and personally abusive manner.

What Forth Ports did not know at this stage, was that I had been briefing a solicitor for nearly 3 months.

I also received a letter from the 'Golden Lion Pilots,' informing me effectively that they were distancing themselves from my letter.

Typical, a shower of gutless wimps. I found out later why they did this. Here is why.

The OM, Forth Ports bully boy, called the senior pilots team to a meeting, and apart from passing my letter on, (without my consent) informed them as to what they perceived the 'truth' about the *Borthwick* to be. He knew this would 'swing' the opinion in Forth Ports favour, so I was left isolated.

Now having pre-guessed almost every stage so far, I did not think that merely walking away, was the solution. It wasn't.

Remember Rule No 1. Forth Ports plc cannot be trusted.

I cannot state this often enough. Even today.

At the time, I did not know of this next bit, I only found out much later.

Forth Ports plc were embarking on the most vicious, evil, vile, vitriolic thing I have ever heard of, and this came from the very top, and right through this rotten company.

They were, apart from revoking my pilot's license, attempting to have my Master Mariner's Certificate of Competency cancelled, with the allegation 'abnegation of command of a gas carrier at sea'.

In English, this means that the master voluntarily gave up command of the ship to another officer. *That did not happen!*

I didn't know this accusation was being made at the time, but I elected to fight. I also didn't know that they had pre-warned the Dept. of Transport.

Just what has this to do with a harbour authority?

First thing, full disclosure of everything to my solicitor, and we agreed that we would also appoint a QC. If necessary, we would also appoint a marine lawyer. I was paying for all of this. Forth Ports did not expect this, as no-one is supporting me, so reluctantly, had to swing their Kangaroo court into action. In this case, their Kangaroos had already decided on the outcome, and as to being impartial until hearing all the evidence, they showed about as much impartiality as they cared for about safety. It is agreed by my legal team and myself, that anyone who gets in the way, will be 'flattened', legally, and if necessary, morally as well.

(When you embark on a course such as this, then there is no going back, and although I could win, I was most certainly not going back to piloting.)

The first discussion between my solicitor and Forth Ports, revealed that it was really the *Borthwick*, that they were interested in. I still do not know where it gives the CHA a right to investigate the affairs of another company. Even to this day, I do not understand.

Now *Snow White*, we know is a liar, and will say anything if it is to his advantage, and to hell with everyone else. What Forth Ports said to him was, we believe that this -------------------------------- happened on the *Borthwick*. *You will agree off course*. He did. Total pack of lies. (If he didn't, he would be looking for another job, and that *was* put to him). Who by? the OM. (I was told about this some 4 years later).

Snow White, in order to protect himself, furnished other 'witnesses', who were *Ratters*,(Tees pilot, and my chief officer on the *Borthwick*), and *Gonzales*, Chairman of Denholm Ship Management in Glasgow. Forth Ports couldn't believe their luck with him on board. Unigas International were waiting in the wings.

Geo Gibsons (now under totally new owners) do not want to get involved, even although there were still some people in the company, when I was there. Unfortunately for them, they did become involved, and were absolutely furious when they found out.

One of their masters, known before as *The Poison Dwarf*, decided to chance his luck, and approached Forth Ports with an offer.

If he could have a pilot's job, then he would also tell them what happened, as a witness. He was snapped up. *But*, he also thought it was an open and shut case, plus, he was nowhere near the *Borthwick* at the time. So much for the 'selection process'.

He was hauled up before the full board in Gibsons and asked to explain.

"Oh, I just told them what was common knowledge."

It was then that he found out that he was going to cross examined by a top QC. Had he checked his facts? No. He was a very worried man who left that meeting. Plus, he had implicated his company. *The Poison Dwarf*, was my chief officer on the *Quentin*, and I also knew a thing or two about him, that he would prefer was not made public. The dangerous things *he* got up to in Gibsons.

Where Forth Ports went wrong was that they started off with the conclusion (theirs) and then started fitting the evidence to suit, believing that no-one would challenge them, after all, their 'witnesses' would certainly make the case for them.

They would then investigate their own allegations.

They *honestly* believed they were *above the law*, and could get 'away with it' due to their status as a Competent Harbour Authority.

They also thought that they had better lawyers.

Then off course, if they had to back down on Charge No 1, then they could fall back on No 2.

And. To think that all this was to save the 'face' of the most idiotic man they employed, who, despite being told *not* to do something, still went ahead and did it.

The man who totally compromised the safety of shipping on the River Forth, no matter what the consequences may be. A gutless man who could not admit to making a mistake, someone buoyed up by his own ego, and although now ex-Royal Navy, still thought that his rank commanded respect. People earn respect Tony, by their actions, it is not automatically granted because you have a posh voice, or consider yourself 'someone'.

Ex-services personnel are in most case regarded as officers and gentlemen. I recently heard a most apt definition of this.

Q. What is the difference between an officer and a gentleman?

A. A gentleman gets out of the bath to have a pee.

All I can say of you Tony is that you were once an officer.

Forth Ports plc needed a scapegoat. (Only this one kicks and bites.)

Some pilots told me, that I should not have sent that letter. It would have made no difference whatsoever, they were always going to try and use the *Borthwick* against me anyway.

The first thing my solicitor asked was, "did you get a reference from Gibsons/Denholms when you went to join VShips?"

"Yes, it was provided by a Mr A. ------- of Gibsons."

Who just happens to be *Snow White*.

A fax was sent to Forth Ports, asking for him to confirm this.

He denied it, so we set out to prove it.

The personnel manager of VShips UK who took the reference, had since retired, so we had to track him down.

It took a bit of effort, but I tracked him down in Gozo, next to Malta, but he wasn't on the 'phone.

At my behest, my solicitor appointed a private investigator from Birmingham, to fly out to Malta, then Gozo, and trace him. He found him, and he was happy to sign a document to the effect that he had received a favourable reference. From a Mr A -------, of Geo. Gibsons. *Snow White* was lying, and it's now proven.

Round 1 to us.

After giving my solicitor my affidavit, I set off trying to find the rest of my officers from 3 years ago. This was hard.

I tracked down my chief engineer to a shipyard in Belfast, and contacted him, asking him only if he would agree to my solicitor taking a statement from him. He would.

My solicitor went to Belfast and took his statement, before writing it up into an affidavit, which he happily signed.

Round 2 to us.

My second engineer proved to be harder to find, but I found him. In Thailand, where he lives with wife and family.

By a stroke of luck though, he was coming into Edinburgh next day, as stand-by engineer on of all things, the *Quentin*. This was fortunate, as I could show my solicitor round a ship at the same time and he could take a statement afterwards. Round 3 to us.

Now my chief officer had been contacted by my solicitors, but had not responded.

Now we knew why, he was a witness for Forth Ports. *Ah*! Now this is starting to make some sense, what has he gone and said?

He claimed to have, "taken over the command of the *Borthwick* at sea, brought the ship home and docked it in the Tees."

Furthermore, he has secured his initial job as assistant harbour master in Teesport, plus his now pilots job on the same claim.

But we have three affidavits that say differently.

So, we'll let him stew for now.

Now, my second mate, and third engineer, where were they?

Oh, I found them. They were sailing together on the same ship. The *Teviot*, Gibsons latest gas tanker, which was running between Antwerp and Braefoot Bay.

So my solicitor goes to Braefoot to see them. He didn't even get through the gate, as Gibsons senior managers were on board, and gave the statement, "The second mate and third engineer do not wish to become involved in this matter. Gibsons Senior Management endorse this decision." Fair enough, if this goes to court, we'll use that in evidence. Round 4 to us.

Now, it is time to start punching holes in *Ratters'* statement.

If he 'docked' the ship, he would have signed the pilots' bill.

I drove down to Teesport, and saw my old mate there, who agreed to go back through all the bills for the 9th March 1989, until he found the one for the *Borthwick*.

Bingo! Here it is, with my signature on it. It was photocopied, and then endorsed by a notary public. That will stand up in court.

We did find a few more holes, but he can explain them, if he can. Now for Unigas.

When we sailed from Stanlow, on that final voyage, there was a difference of some 40 tonnes of cargo between the ships figures and the shore, the ship being higher. I didn't note protest, as I knew there was an error in the calibration tables. But how to prove this difference?

I drove down to Liverpool, and went see the agents, who still had a file, and as they weren't Unigas agents any longer, were happy to let me have copies of the cargo calculations, plus various letters.

This we keep in reserve.

Question? Why does *Gonzales* want to attend a Forth Ports Kangaroo Court, when he is chairman of a large ship management company with worldwide contracts, and when he knows he is going to be cross examined by a top QC? This puzzled us. Was he given some sort of assurance perhaps?

I decided to take a long shot, just wondering, if ?

I drove down to Cardiff, to the offices of The Registrar General for Shipping and Seamen. In there, I found what I rather suspected, as I traced the original Official Log Book and Crew Agreement for the *Borthwick*, under the Isle of Man flag.

To cover up his earlier mistakes, he has falsified them!

If we take his signature as being true, and accurate, then I left the ship in Stanlow on the 26th of February 1989, and never went to Lisbon, or indeed Tees. Then all the things he claimed happened, never did happen, so he is a proven liar.

If on the other hand, we accept that I did go to Lisbon, which I did, then he is guilty of fraud.

Got yourself in a bit of jam I'd say Bob, never mind Forth Ports, who are relying on you as a witness.

I had the records sent up to the Dept of Transport Office in Glasgow, just in case my QC, decided to take matters up officially. Well, two can play at this game.

At the start of all this, Forth Ports gave us three dates to choose from, for their Kangaroo Court, of which we took the last.

As we still had not gathered in all the evidence, we asked for an extension.

"Why they asked, it's a fairly straightforward matter?"

"Oh, it's just that our expert witness, who is coming up from London will not have sufficient time to be briefed."

"What do you need an expert witness for?" They were mortified.

We didn't tell them, as at that stage, it was none of their affair, but now, in Leith, the alarm bells were ringing, *big* style.

The Kangaroo Court was due to sit at the end of November. This was 3 months since it started, and the strain was terrible, as I did not know if I was going to keep my Master's Certificate of Competency, but I was not going down without a fight. Especially for an arsehole like *Ten Knot Tony*. The Chief Harbour Master.

On the Tuesday, my solicitor received a fax from Forth Ports, which after decoding from the legal jargon, went like this.

"Our witnesses have heard that Captain Harvey will take legal action against anyone who speaks against him. We would be obliged if you would agree to immunity for our witnesses at the forthcoming hearing."

Our reply, after consulting with my QC.

"If your witnesses are telling the truth, *and nothing but the truth*, then they have nothing to fear."

To a man, they all ran away!

This left Forth Ports with an allegation that they could not substantiate. The case collapsed.

They did however still want me off their river. See what I mean about it all being concluded from the start. All that had to be agreed was what it would cost them for my resignation. They would not entertain damages, even although they had tried to destroy, not only me personally, but my qualifications as well, thus denying me any possibility of returning to sea, and earning a living to support my family.

Before this could start though, Forth Ports had to be fully briefed on the missing evidence. After all, it was *they* who wanted to know *all* about the *Borthwick*, so they were going to be told *all* about the *Borthwick*.

My solicitor sat down with their directors, not you will notice, the OM, or shall I say the Forth Ports' bully boy, and gave it to them straight.

All the damage, which their new superintendent had been responsible for, *but not attended to* on the *Borthwick*, thus leaving the ship in an un-seaworthy condition. All about the 5th rate crew supplied. All about Denholms. Every sordid little detail.

When he got to the bit about the tank calibrations fraud, which had been covered up, their heads seemingly went down, as they wrote and listened, muttering, "we'd rather not be hearing this."

Well, if you go poking around in another company's affairs, then you are liable to get your fingers well and truly burnt.

You have now got yourselves implicated in fraud.

Now you know why I refused to have anything to do with it. I got 2 months' pay, £6000 in return for my resignation as a pilot.

I had absolutely no intention of working with such a gutless shower of pilots again. They prefer to believe lies, rather than one of their own colleagues. How you can look at yourselves in the mirror?

I also received a promise from Forth Ports plc that, "if anyone asked, they would say that the allegations levelled against Captain Harvey have been fully investigated, and have been found to be entirely without foundation."

This must rank as one of the most useless pieces of English ever uttered, as the only people levelling allegations were they themselves, after they made them up, and then 'investigated' nothing.

However, it was a comment made by one of their directors, that was the saddest thing I have ever heard.

"It is very fortunate for Forth Ports, that the Forth Pilots have chosen not to support Captain Harvey, as, if they had, then they would have been in a position to dictate their terms and conditions for years to come. They will never get as good a chance as this again. You have all done very well."

Complimentary? No, because the independence of the pilotage on the River Forth was destroyed from then on. It can only get worse, and has. The safety of navigation has suffered. Very seriously indeed.

Rule 10, although still theoretically valid, was never used again. Responsibility for navigation and for the ship returned to its rightful place. To the bridge of the ship with the master.

The chief harbour master is off the hook.

I was their scapegoat. This was the third time.

But it doesn't end there!

I swore it would never happen again, but it did, only this time the costs ran into many millions of dollars. All in all, in excess of $10 million. That doesn't include the $50 million the company were fined for one of their other ships at the same time. The sad tale is in Part 7.

Safety of shipping on the River Forth has been restored, and *I take the credit that many accidents have been avoided*. Not those charged with the safety of shipping, Forth Ports plc, who as you have read and are about to see are no closer to achieving this in 2004 as they were in 1992, after f...ing it all up.

What did it cost for me to clear my name? Financially £25 000, less £6 000 to resign, over £20 thousand, with expenses.

But that is nothing compared to how it affected my family. My children suffered, my marriage suffered, and eventually broke down because of it, and then I had a nervous breakdown.

This book has been many years in the planning, and it is only now, 10 years on, that I am able to do it.

It was my intention to keep this until I retired, but it has been brought forward, as this is the only way that I can get Forth Ports to listen to me. Writing them a letter is a waste of time, as they will ignore it. Remember, they were warned by me about the *Havkong* blowing off the jetty at Braefoot Bay. They 'lost' that one. Why? Because, as I said, I live here, and I have noticed something on the River Forth which if not addressed very soon, could have a serious environmental impact on this area. This is within the compulsory pilotage area, and happens most days.

The new Chief Harbour Master is the old Operations Manager, and he should have fixed this by now, only this man is as much out of his depth as his predecessor. Remember what I said about people who call themselves captain?

They, Forth Ports, have recently been fined heavily, one of their failings was lack of 'risk assessment'.

The reader should be aware by now, that not only am I a highly experienced master mariner, a former pilot in this area, and a marine investigator, but not much gets past me. What I have spotted is not something that the average non-marine individual would even be aware of.

Forth Ports plc should be though, especially the Chief Harbour Master and the rest of his little cohort. Then again, the Chief Harbour Master should be able to draw upon all his bridge experience where he should know that when something goes wrong, it goes wrong very fast indeed. His 'bridge experience? Highly questionable indeed.

I'll set you off in the right direction. Look at the outbound loaded tankers from Hound Point. You have the escort tugs in the wrong place. If a tanker loses its steering gear, for any of several reasons, then you may not be able to stop it grounding.

You have in the past repeatedly failed to heed my warnings, using me as a scapegoat once, and banning me from the river when I showed up your failings in maintaining your own safety procedures.

Let it not be forgotten Forth Ports. No matter what your company may digress into, or how successful you may be, your primary responsibility is to provide an infrastructure on the River Forth that the shipping that uses it, can do so safely, and that the coastline surrounding it is safeguarded from accidents and pollution. At the present time, you are not doing so.

Again!

I trust you will remember the meaning of 'competent'.

Now that 'Tony' is off the hook, you would expect him to have learnt something from all this. Well, not if you're Tony I suppose.

The Tall Ships were coming into Leith, although on that day, it was foggy. These are not the easiest things to handle, and as usual, they all arrive at the same time. It was actually reported in the newspapers, that Tony had come out with, "we bring them in one at a time, and leave the others circling outside, similar to stacking aircraft by air traffic control." Oh well, I suppose using the adjective 'similar' is at least a start.

What did Tony do, the day after the case ended?

He only went through to Glasgow to give a lecture.

His subject:

Safety of Navigation in a Busy Tanker Waterway!

I kid you not. It takes some believing though eh? But it's true.

What did Forth Ports plc do with all this information about the *Borthwick*? After all, it is trading in their river to their biggest client BP, who they, Forth Ports plc know are being defrauded?

They do what Forth Ports always do. Nothing, cover it up, sweep it under the carpet, and hope it will all go away.

It did, see Part 5, but.

Sorry to disappoint you boys. It just came back. I just cannot wait to hear how they are going to talk their way out of this. I'm willing to bet as well, despite not being a gambling man, that you the reader can't wait either!

Finally, there was a twist to all of this.

After taking December off, I went job hunting again, then received a call in early January. It was from VShips Cyprus.

"Good morning, is that Captain Harvey?"

"It certainly is Rod, what can I do for you?" I already knew him.

"Doug, are you busy on Friday?"

"No, why?"

"Could you go through to Grangemouth and take command of the *Borthwick* for the day?"

This just has to be interesting, especially Grangemouth.

"I would think so, but why, just for the day?"

"The ship is up for Safety Radio Survey, and needs two radio certificates, but the captain hasn't got one, so we could use yours."

How the captain got a masters ticket without a radio certificate would be an interesting tale.

"Okay, I'll be there for 08 30 on Friday."

I drove through, 'took over', gave the captain my car keys and he nipped off to Stirling for the day. Now all I have to do, apart from the survey, is make sure I get myself noticed, preferably by a pilot, as master of the *Borthwick*. Gossip goes around this place faster than in Orkney, and that's saying something.

Ah! That sounds like a mooring boat, so nipped up to the bridge wing, and gave the pilot in it a wee wave, as he went past. Perfect, only the biggest mouth in the place. I'll give it half an hour.

I was wrong, 20 minutes before the 'phone rang.

The survey was completed, I 'handed back over' to the captain, and went home with a days pay in my pocket, having had a super lunch, and stirred things up a bit.

I often wonder how long it took them to work out what was going on. I bet Forth Ports were cringing.

There was also the question of my pension fund. Remember at the start, how it was handled illegally. Well even this had a twist in its tail.

I had a 'phone call from the pilot who represented the PNPF, a Forth pilot, and a silly little man at that.

"It is about your pension fund. If you want to take it out, then you have to do so within three months, if not, then it will have to stay there until you retire."

You would think that after having just taken on Forth Ports, and beaten them, that it would be getting through some skulls, that I am not going to be bullied. Plus, that I just happen to know what I am doing.

"Alec, it's my money, and mine alone. I will decide what to do about it and nobody else, particularly a low life such as yourself."

So, why is 3 months the operative period?

I wrote to the PNPF and asked for a transfer value. It came to £11 600. So, I'll wait 4 months, and see what it is then.

I transferred out after 4 months, £16 500.

They were consolidating funds, and increasing existing funds accordingly. If I had listened to him, I would lose, and he would gain.

Tough old boy, you should not have warned me.

In 1996, I attended a CDI Inspectors course at the College of Advanced Maritime Studies in Edinburgh, and during this course came up with an idea that could effectively 'kill two birds with one stone' so to speak.

I could attend to every ship's worst navigational nightmare, passage planning in pilotage waters, and at the same time, correct all the errors in Forth Ports channels to Grangemouth.

For example, in Teesport, a ship needs permission from the VTS to enter the channel. In the Forth it doesn't. There are lots of little things like this.

Believe it or not, I swallowed my pride and put this idea to Forth Ports, who agreed to listen. The upshot was that they listened to me, but 'for legal reasons' would not proceed with my ideas/proposals.

Oh well, at least I tried. Oh, by the way, the same errors exist to this day. They might listen yet though. Or be forced to.

You will know the old saying, don't get angry get even. Well, this is how I sorted out my two former chief officers, *Ratters* and *The Poison Dwarf*. They won't cross me again in a hurry.

Four years after this, I took command of a gas tanker known as the *Balder Phoenix*. It was a horrible thing. More about it in Part 5.

We were loading in the UK for Portugal, my usual old haunts in and around Lisbon.

Going into the Tees one day, I asked the pilot if *Ratters* was still an assistant harbour master here. Oh no, he said, he's now a pilot.

I nearly fell off my chair. That is one low life who will never be on board, while I am in command. Can you imagine what would happen? When it was time to sail, I got on the VHF and asked for a pilot, then added, "and can you tell me his name please?" This is highly unusual. "Why?" they asked.

"Because if it is *Ratters*, I don't want him."

Every ship in the Tees is listening in, and they are all asking the same thing. What is wrong with *Ratters*? (Or, what is right?)

Next time back in the Tees, same question on the VHF. Even more captains wondering the same thing.

Who comes to pay a visit? The Chief Harbour Master for the Tees.

And get this, starts laying down the law.

"Captain, we do not operate a choice pilot service here, if *Ratters* comes on turn for this ship, then you will just have to take him."

"Better tell him to bring a parachute then."

"Why?"

"Because as soon as I get my hands on him, he'll be flying over the bridge wing, and I don't care what's underneath. That man is not coming on board this or any other ship I command. Finish!"

"Well, the only thing I can suggest, is that we delay your ship, until a pilot becomes available."

"Fine, I'll accept the delay, as long as you explain why to the berth operators. I'll make up the time lost on passage."

We left it at that for the present, but he was most concerned.

The next one to have a go, was the senior pilot. I knew him from old.

"We know what he has done (Do you? I'll bet you don't), so, if you could just give us a call before you get in, we'll arrange for another pilot to be on turn for you, as long as you don't embarrass us on the VHF. About 30 captains have asked us why you won't take him."

That is the agreement that I have to this day. I am the only master who has a 'choice' pilot in the Tees. So you see, *Ratters* (Tees Pilot), when you start lying, you have to keep on lying, and it only gets worse and worse. Then you can't remember all of your lies. See you some day, old boy.

Try telling the truth too, it helps, and is much better. If you know what 'truth' means. Oh, and I'm sending a free copy of this book to most of my friends in the Tees.

Now *The Poison Dwarf* was different. This cost me 20p.

My solicitor (who became a close friend) and I were having lunch one day, while we hatched this plan, and executed it in the afternoon.

He 'phoned Gibsons and asked for the managing director, who he got, then asked him if *The Poison Dwarf* was at home. We actually already knew, because we had checked.

Oh, did the brown stuff hit the fan!

He was called up at home, and told to 'get it sorted'.

It was a very nervous chappie who came on asking for Mr _____."

His secretary was all primed up.

"I'm sorry he's in court just now, can I take a message?"

"It's just that I'm going on holiday at 2 pm, and I need to speak to him urgently. I could delay going on holiday till 4 pm."

"If you could call back just before 4 then."

We were in the same office listening to this.

He called back at 3.55, with "Is Mr _____, back yet? It is very urgent."

I'll bet it is.

"Sorry, no, he's been delayed, but I'll have him call you as soon as he comes in."

247

He called back at 4.30 with "I've had to re-schedule my flights, but I have to know now when I can speak to him."

His other ear was red hot from Gibsons, wanting to know if it was sorted yet. Remember it's a Friday afternoon. POETS day!

"I'm sorry he's not here, but I managed to get him on his mobile, and he has asked me to pass on a message to you."

"Yes, I'm listening."

"He says. Go off and enjoy your holiday, and he'll have a nice big fat writ waiting for you for when you get back."

Now go and explain *that* to Gibsons, you moron.

Publishing this book will be adequate for *Gonzales*, who has now retired, but has so many enemies in the shipping industry, that they will do it for me. Oh, and Bob, try and remember to thank me for saving you money. You won't need as many Christmas cards now.

Snow White? Wait till you read my next book! But how about one or two things that weren't in his CV (curriculum vitae).

How about the time he deceived none other than the Norwegian Government, about a certain gas tanker he was temporarily covering while *Carrot Top* was on holiday? The ship? You have to ask? The *Borthwick* of course! Let's see if he can explain it before you buy my next book, or if he can explain why he was partly responsible for pumping over 20 000 litres of hydraulic oil into the sea.

Question?

How did Forth Ports train the pilots for Rosyth, when there was no-one to train them?

I don't know.

But knowing them, they would just add on 'Rosyth' to all the pilots' licences, and hope no one asked awkward questions. Sorry to disappoint you Forth Ports, but this guy just asked, because if untrained pilots 'trained' the masters on the Superfast Ferries, then you might find yourself in yet another home made, 'bit of a pickle'.

Remember when the *Sea Empress* ran aground in Milford Haven. Well, she loaded at Hound Point.

The MCA wanted to interview the pilot who sailed her out. Was he cooperative? Come on now, these are pilots we're talking about.

No. He disappeared off to his croft in the Western Islands for 2 weeks, where there is no 'phone.

And finally. If you live locally, and use the Forth Road Bridge, then the next time you pay your toll (80p), ask yourself what it is for.

The bridge was paid for long ago, so to use up some of the money, the Bridge Authorities built 'guard' buffers around the base of the towers, to prevent damage, should a ship hit them.

Sensible?

Well the only people who have ever hit the bridge were the Royal Navy, and they didn't build the guard buffers until *after* the navy had left Rosyth. Work that one out.

I'll ask this question here as no-one seems to have noticed this as well. If you keep having traffic jams at the tolls every night, but not in the morning when there are no tolls, why not do away with the tolls (the bridge is paid for anyway) and avoid the jams. Think positively, no road rage or frustration as well.

But I'm just a seaman, what do I know?

Comment:

I said at the start that the standard of pilotage is declining. How can this be reversed?

Within virtually every CHA in this country, the ports have the pilots 'under their thumb'. This is not a good way to do anything, as it suppresses the talent available. Most pilots will not say anything for fear of their jobs, so standards will continue to fall. The Humber scenario is a perfect example of this.

For those of you who do not know what this was, Associated British Ports (ABP), decided that pilots were being paid too much, so offered them all new contracts. The upshot was a reduction of pay by about 25%. The pilots understandably were a wee bit upset about this, and went on strike. ABP then sacked the lot of them, about 160 pilots. Only six accepted the new deal, thus labelling themselves with that disgusting term 'scabs'.

This therefore meant that ABP had to get new pilots, and 'train' them. If you had two legs, could see where to get your bill signed, and were fit enough to climb on board a ship, then you could get a pilot's job, on an extremely busy river where experience is not something gained overnight. There were quite a few accidents, and rather a lot of concrete reshaped.

But there was something else, which I only found out by chance. The person responsible for all this in ABP, was none other than the Pilots' own Representative for the Pilots' Union, now working for ABP. He must have been given an awful lot to turn on his former friends and colleagues like this.

Not only have standards fallen on The River Forth, but you can now include The River Humber as well. There are others.

It is perhaps time to consider bringing all pilots under one roof so to speak, in a centrally controlled body, which *also* has the responsibility for recruiting and training. CHAs then having contracts with this body to supply them with pilots.

It has been demonstrated by all CHAs around the UK that previous command experience is not required, and similarly, ship handling experience is not required. To this end then, recruitment to pilotage need not be limited to the merchant navy. A central training school, teaching the basics, before 'in house' training on a river *before* qualification as a pilot, could attract competent individuals who show a satisfactory educational standard. A pilot only requires about 5% of the knowledge that a ships' master needs, and the pre-requisite of a Class 1 Certificate thus superfluous.

Women as well as men could do this job, and with its shift patterns should be ideal for a job-share basis.

The other major benefit, is that standards around the coast can be raised overnight. The pilots 'police' the port authorities rules and regulations, reporting back any infringements to be sorted out by people with 'clout', thus preventing accidents *before* they occur, without pilots being suppressed by the so-called Competent Harbour Authorities.

Another matter which must be opened up, is accident or incident reporting. At the present time, after a report is submitted, it only goes as far as the CHA. It then requires the pilots permission to be released to a third party. Shell in the case when we sank the mooring boat, required my permission.

Sending it back to a central body, would mean correlation of information, which could be shared for training purposes, or improvements in an area under pilotage. It could also be released to the press, thus shocking some individuals into getting their act together. Such as Chief Harbour Masters.

Improve the standards of CHAs?

Here is something very few people know about, and certainly Associated British Ports who run Southampton, and thus Southampton VTS (Vessel Traffic Service) will have apoplexy over.

Am I the only master who has averted a near collision in The Solent, just off the Nab Tower, between a passenger ferry and a guided missile destroyer, of the Royal Navy no less? Actually *HMS Edinburgh*. I sincerely hope so.

How did this come about?

Because Southampton VTS gave out false information regarding shipping movements, which led to utter confusion. The destroyer was the main culprit. He was showing lights which unless you were fully switched on and knew what they really meant, showed that the direction he appeared to be going in, was in fact the reverse of what he was. It is better to say nothing, than contribute to yet another f..k-up. What we do not want or need is another *Herald of Free Enterprise* incident, but unless a lot of people start getting their act together, is exactly what we are going to have.

If this book rattles Forth Ports plc and most of the others, then it will only be for the good, as I for one do not really want to see yet another tanker going aground, which is unfortunately in 2004 even more likely.

To plagiarize is to copy another's work while calling it your own, but in this final part, you have my permission to do just that.

Write to the Chief Harbour Master at Forth Ports plc and ask him this question. (Address is on the Internet.)

"How was it possible in 1992 for a loaded ship to legally navigate through 8+ miles of compulsory pilotage area *without* a Forth Ports Authorized pilot on board, to pass beneath both bridges, and close on some rocks, before heading off to sea, and in 2004 is now illegal and *without* Forth Ports plc having changed anything at all? The ship was neither a Navy ship, or an RFA ship, but a foreign flag ship whose master and crew were non-British nationals. No-one on board had a pilotage exemption."

If the Chief Harbour Master cannot answer this, then he is truly out of his depth, and that is a disgrace. But if he can, then why did he allow it in the first place?

Send a stamp addressed envelope to guarantee a reply, but be warned, you are unlikely to get the correct answer.

Finally, to end this part on a happier note, see if you agree with me on this. According to Forth Ports Bye-laws, "in Grangemouth, a railway locomotive 'has right of way' on the roads within the port area."

1) I may be a bit thick here, but there are two things that come to mind. I always thought railway locomotives ran on rails, not roads, and...

2) Who is stupid enough to argue with a 100 ton railway locomotive and with limited steering potential with a car...?

In Part 5 of this book, I will introduce you to the world of International Marine Fraud, or to put it another way, how big gas tankers can steal cargo, by making it disappear, then re-appear, and the practically unbeatable, how to change propane into butane, then back to propane, without actually doing anything to it. When you have mastered that, we'll extend it to ships fuel. Just to keep it interesting, I'll intersperse this with the wonderful world of ship delivery.

This is *all* true.

PART 4

Ship delivery. The only way you can describe this is *Fun*, with a capital F.

It does take a great deal of skill, however, and you really have to know what you are doing.

My first 'delivery' was a small double-ended ferry for Shetland Islands Council, built at Fergusons on the Clyde, and named *Leirna*. This yard know how to build ships, but if you are ever going to build another one of these, could we please have a rudder, and a huge skeg? The only time this ferry went in a straight line was down the slipway.

This 'ferry' was totally over-engineered, at a cost of £2.8 million, designed to run from Lerwick to Bressay, a distance of 0.5 miles. It could carry 250 passengers or 28 cars, all to an island with a population of 500, who, if they could get away with it, left their cars on Bressay, and walked on board, because then the passage was free. It berthed beside the shops in Lerwick at the other side.

What made it difficult to steer? Only a Voight Schneider Drive at each end, and lying 10 degrees off the vertical.

This type of propulsion can be likened to helicopter, but on the vertical, and under water. They are very popular on tugs who need a greater power to weight ratio than ships.

The problem was that the wash from the forward unit upset the flow into the after one, until we realized that it worked better when offset by about 10 degrees. The ferry is then effectively going sideways and ahead at the same time. A slant really.

Going down the Clyde was like an S. If the head swung off, it was actually quicker to round in a circle, than it was to steady her up. It didn't half look odd.

No pilot of course, as she was under the minimum length, and although as she was double ended, there was in fact a right way and wrong way for her to head. Of course, she is the wrong way round lying alongside the building berth, so after getting her safely under way, we have to turn in the river. Gosh, this was trickier than it looked, as she took a full circle, so a more gentle approach was called for, as we kept on going round, to this time, face the right way. We excused it as a demonstration of my ship handling skill!

I've been steering ships for many years, so was rather embarrassed to be swinging all over the place, until one of the shipyard engineers (there were two of them who came with us) said, "I must say Captain, but you are steering remarkably well for someone who hasn't handled one of these before."

We had a magnetic compass and an un-stabilized radar, but both started spinning as soon as we left the berth, and only stopped when we arrived in Lerwick. Navigation is going to have to be the old way.

The route chosen is known as 'the inside passage'. It is only really suitable for small ships, say up to about the size of the *Borthwick*, which incidentally, when I was second mate did actually do. The captain was a braver man than me, as I don't trust that ships steering gear. But then *Fergus* hit everything anyway.

There are in fact two ways after clearing the Mull of Kintyre, either up through the Sound of Islay, or for the really brave, or foolish, through the Gulf of Corryvreckan. I have been through on a gas tanker, which *was* the *Borthwick*. The only time you can seriously attempt this passage, is at slack water, which it was fortunately.

Gavin Maxwell, author of *Ring of Bright Water* fame, had reputedly tried to attempt this in an MTB, and the tide just spun him round and 'spat' him back out again.

It is also known as The Giant Whirlpool, and can be heard in Oban during Spring tides. It's an awesome sight.

But first of all, we have to round the Mull of Kintyre, as typically, had to be done at night. We had by this time learnt to keep the land off to one side, but after leaving the Firth, realized that we had now, 'run out of lighthouses'. So from here we'll navigate by the stars, which was indeed fortunate, as there was one in the direction we wanted to go. Then it was back to lighthouses.

We passed the distillery on Islay at 6 in the morning. We were still passing it at 10 o'clock, the tide having turned against us. Our 9 knots was just sufficient for us to make headway. Of course the opposite when it turned with us, then you knew you were moving.

It really is beautiful scenery around here, which we enjoyed as we steamed up through The Sound of Mull, passing that quaint village of Tobermory. I had actually been up through when I had command of the *Borthwick*, and anchored in Tobermory Bay. Just to overhaul a unit on the main engine. The harbour master was glad when we left. Or was it relieved?

You have to take these chances when you get the opportunity, as disabling the main engine is strictly forbidden during cargo operations. Nobody of course will tell you when you have got to, as long as it isn't in 'their' port. Even at anchor in The Forth, if the Port Authority find out, they will insist on a tug standing by.

But this doesn't affect us on the *Leirna* as she is brand new.

The hardest part of steaming up the inside route, is passing through Kylerea, which to compound the problem for us, that it was now dark as well. Not even a moon. Plus there is a bend halfway though. Fortunately, there was a fishing boat just ahead of us, and we just followed it. Thanks matey!

The weather at this time certainly favoured us, as apart from coming round the Mull of Kintyre, when it got decidedly bouncy, much to the consternation of Ferguson's engineers, who were sea sick, was almost flat calm.

Accommodation was ropey to say the least. I had my sleeping bag in the ticket office. The others just had to do with the passenger cabin. There were no niceties, such as mattresses.

One of the crew was the cook for all of us, and it was amazing what he could prepare. First night out, it was mince, breakfast next day was mince. Lunch? Yep you guessed it, mince, so I asked him why we were living on mince.

"Because I like mince." Nothing like stating the obvious is there.

I'll try a different tack now, so,

"Did you not get anything other than mince, when you disappeared to the supermarket with CQ."

"Aye, ah got a chook." Chicken to you and me.

"When are we getting that?"

"When we run out of mince."

Roll on that day! We weren't going hungry anyway. There was also a plentiful supply of biscuits.

The one thing that may prevent ships bigger than this from going through the 'inside passage', is that someone has gone and built a bridge just outside Kyle of Lochalsh to Skye. Judging by the protests about the toll incurred might suggest that the ferry would have been a better option. But then again, it stops tankers (oil and gas) from going aground and polluting the place.

So we enter The Minch. Hoping that the fair weather holds. In this part of the world, it can be vicious, and there are few places in which smaller ships can get shelter. I've seen it in its foulest mood, and it is not pleasant.

I elected to pass to the east of Orkney, just in case the weather did break, as opposed to the west. Just a few days after we passed was when the tanker *Braer* was lost.

This meant taking on the Pentland Firth, but I know how this place works remember. Plus, I could have a blether with my pals Charlie and Alan by VHF, in Scapa Flow. I hadn't seen them for a good few years, so it would be nice to get up to date on the local gossip. *And* there is always plenty of that!

But first of all, we have to round Cape Wrath, which brought on its own excitement, when Percy, the mate, and also a Tay pilot said, "what was that bang just now?"

It's only an RAF bombing range, and our passage just managed to coincide with the arrival of four Tornado jets. Just to the east of the Cape, is a rock, standing on its own, which has been well and truly bombed, and there are a few more coming on this day. Well, they have got to practise somewhere, and this is fairly un-populated. Even the light house is un-manned now. You learn something every day, when you sail with me.

Now for the Pentland Firth. The tide will be in our favour, so we should get a good push going through. In fact, as I came past the Lother Rock, on the southern tip of South Ronaldsay, I was steaming North, and going East!

Charlie asked me what the *Leirna* was like to handle? I had to say, "it's like trying to steer a 40 foot container, with an outboard." He knew what I meant.

With the weather now holding, and actually now down to a glassy calm, which is always suspicious around Orkney, we set off on the second last leg, to Fair Isle, you know, from shipping forecasts? I never appreciated just how isolated it is.

Amazingly, we are actually going to arrive at a sensible hour, just after 8 in the morning, and we did have a welcoming party, in the form of the pilot boat.

The ferry that the *Leirna* is replacing is still on the berth, so we tied up on the other side.

CQ, my boss, asked if "I would stay another day, and do a link span trial?"

"Sure, no problem," wondering just what a link span trial actually was.

All it is, is a test to make sure their new ferry actually 'fits' the terminal.

Bit late to find out now, I thought.

So, the paperwork is completed. I like this company, only one signature required. Then a hotel for the night. But there was one other thing for the crew to do, get a shower. Oh, did they pong?

Then it was homeward bound.

I actually delivered this 'ship' when I was fighting Forth Ports, and it was my wife's idea to go, as seemingly, I was like a bear with a sore head, with nothing to do, but sit around the house all day. It was very therapeutic. So, thank you Muriel.

Plus, it got my 'foot in the door', with this company, if I ever needed a job. Actually, I've delivered eight ships over the years.

Thursday 15th January 1993, Devonport, and wet. Lying in the Naval Base, the *RFA Regent*, a grand old lady of the sea, but as comes to all ships, time to retire. My job was to take her to the breakers in India, a final voyage of some 6000 miles.

It is always a sad time when the life of a ship is nearly over, especially one which has performed magnificently for her country over a period of 25 years, been involved in various conflicts around the world, has been a fine home to many British seamen, and was and still is a fine tribute to the men who built her.

On the surface, she looked fine, on the surface that is. Underneath was a different story. Remember, she had been run by the Royal Navy, or at least the RFA, so it will come as no surprise to the educated that she was in fact un-seaworthy.

Ship delivery is not as exacting as running a ship full time, but it is certainly as demanding. For ships bound for the scrapyard, there are no particular niceties. Spare parts for example are the absolute minimum required, and some of the more traditional shipboard practices do not really exist, you just have to make do with what you have, or what you can make, re-design, or just generally bodge together. Safety equipment or navigational equipment is never compromised, however.

An ability for a master to think on the spot is a great advantage, as is the ability to keep a straight face when you are trying to convince some foreigner of some obscure reason or varying point of view just to keep operating. Sometimes he may not even be a foreigner. A massive knowledge of International Maritime Law and Regulations is a distinct advantage. Making it up as you go along helps as well, maybe even more so.

My crew for the voyage were all hand picked, although whose hand it was, would have been hard to say. Rough, took on new meaning, 'pirates' would better describe them. For those of us old enough to remember the old 'pool' system, this lot roughly comprised a mixture of Liverpool, Leith, and Grimsby, with a few DBSs thrown in just to make it interesting, plus an Irish/American who had also been a lumberjack (probably last time he washed as well.) In the main, everyone at least spoke English, at least I think that was the language used by the third engineer, as he never seemed to be able to get past one syllable. Cantankerous old s--.

The Royal Navy looked at my shower of pirates, and said, "we operate this ship with 250, even on lay-by, it has 40, and you are going to try to take it to India with just 14, who for good measure have never actually seen the ship before?"

Seemed reasonable enough to me. Not quite true actually, one of the crew had sailed on the Regent as a quartermaster about 20 years before, so we could at least find the bridge, and the engineers puzzled out that the engine room must be underneath the funnel.

We all had a good look round, and then went to bed, because Friday was when we had to re-name her and begin to re- certificate her, with an intention of sailing on the Monday morning. If this sounds irresponsible, remember, we are all seasoned professionals.

This ship was sold, under one of three types of contracts:

    1) On an as is where is basis.

    2) On a minimum SOLAS basis.

3) Totally stripped bare.

1) Roughly speaking, you take off the regular crew, and put on your own, after re-certificating to any flag you like. At this stage of the game, anything is better than keeping her under the British flag, which has been the most abused 'flag of convenience' of them all.

2) Stripped of all equipment, except fire fighting equipment, safety appliances, and so forth. However, anyone who knows anything about ships, will know that given this option, the Royal Navy will dump on every dud piece of equipment from stores that they can find.

3) As it says, nothing left. Not quite true, as you read on, as there are so many compartments on this ship that they have missed a few.

She was bought under option 3, for the grand price of £2 100 000. That in anyone's language, is a lot of scrap.

What do the Indians do with it? Cut it up into 2 metre lengths, and send it to the rolling mill, to make concrete reinforcing rods. What they cannot cut up, is melted down. They got through 22 million tons in the year 2000. That's a lot of ships.

Ah! but Friday, the start of 6 days of problems, where we were ably assisted with the degree of competency that only the Royal Navy can provide, not forgetting of course, the Royal Fleet Auxiliary, who, to give them their due were marginally better, although, not much.

The *RFA Regent* had to be re-named for the passage. Normally on a 'scrapper', the name would be changed into *Reg* or say *Gent*, just by painting out the appropriate letters. Did the new owner want this? Oh no, he was re-naming her *Shahzadelal*, in honour of his father. A magnanimous gesture no doubt, but for us, a nightmare. Why?

First of all you have to paint out the old name. Easy enough, a paint roller on a pole, lean over each bow and the stern, and obliterate it. Leave it for 2 hours to let it dry, and then paint on the new name.

Ah, but, how do you do that when you have no means of getting over the bow to paint it on? There was not a single usable rope, apart from the mooring ropes on board, so Plan B came into effect.

One of my crew, who was it later proved to be, a rather resourceful chap, had acquired on one of his forays, a length of sackcloth, a tin of paint and a brush, and came up with the concept of painting the new name on this, then tying it to the rails. Mmm, if we can get away with this, then fine, so off you go.

When he tied it over the stern, he did in fact manage to get it upside-down, which from the shore, looked stupid, but not half as stupid as the port of registry, painted on underneath it. Remember the problem with the rigging, well back it came. The solution was to hand.

Sellotape a can of spray paint (black of course) to a brush handle, jam open the nozzle, and write it freehand while leaning over the stern. Now, I will remind you that, it is January, and it is not a calm day, in fact, it is decidedly draughty, as in about force 6. The net result was that the port of registry *Kingstown*, was actually painted on the stern… , in a sort of shorthand, it may even have been Swahili, but it did the job, so long as no one actually looked at it.

She is now re-named, all we have to do is steer the surveyor away from the stern.

When the ship was the *Regent*, which was until 12 00 on the Friday, when she became the *Shahzadelal* she was classed as a British ship, fully certificated in all respects, complied with Lloyds, and had been surveyed by the same surveyor for the last 5 plus years. To all intents and purposes, she was *seaworthy*. At 1200 plus 1 second, when she became the *Shahzadelal*, under the St Vincent & Grenadines Flag (some would say, a 'flag of convenience',) she instantly became *unseaworthy*. But, and this is the cruncher, it was the *same* surveyor from Lloyds who was appointed by the StVincent & Grenadines Flag State, who was to re-certificate her, as who had surveyed her for the last 5-plus years.

What was wrong? and much more importantly, for taxpayers, why? Talk about opening up a can of worms!

The *Regent/Shahzadelal* is a steam ship. In order to start her up from cold, the first thing is to start up the FD fans (FD stands for Forced Draught).

These fans are used to sweep out the combustion space in the boilers, before putting in the fires, and then supplying the air(oxygen), in order to keep them running. When the boilers are up to pressure, then the steam cycle keeps everything going.

The electrical load on this ship requires a diesel generator of 330 KVA, just to drive the fans. The Diesel engine on the *Shahzadelal*, was a V12 Paxman, located 'midships, just forward of the emergency second bridge, in its own compartment.

It didn't work. Oh, it ran, after a fashion, and I do not profess to be an engineer, but when it was run up, I immediately ordered it to be shut down, before it blew up. I had seen this before with medium speed diesels, and now, standing beside it, did not really fancy seeing yet another explosion.

The V12 arrangement was in four blocks of three pistons, so we took the head assembly off one block. In one piston, there was daylight down the side of the piston, on the second, the valves had long since seized, and in the third, the piston had a hole in it. The reason for this? Neglect. But why was it neglected? Arrogance? Too much bullshit, not enough effort, and far too much time spent in the NAAFI bar down aft.

What made it worse, was that the surveyor knew about this, but had done nothing about it.

An engine does not get into this condition overnight. This has been going on for many years, so the RFA have been running a ship which is 'technically' un-seaworthy. It makes you wonder what their other ships are like. Having seen some operated by the Royal Navy, I could well guess.

We, off course had no spares, and as we have to get the ship away, now have to set about finding an Emergency Diesel, PLUS an alternator, which will deliver 330 KVA.

Now, do you think that the Royal Navy helped us? In a word ... *no*!.

A more obstreperous bunch would be harder to find, but they took on the wrong guy!

My company were Wijsmuller Bros, a major salvage company, who put all their resources to bear in tracking down a composite unit of a generator pack, and found one in Birmingham, paid for it, then discovered that it was the wrong phasing. Hopeless try.

Un-beknown to us, the Royal Navy had one all the time, less than 1 mile up the road, but that came out later.

Now while this is all going on, we are still re-certificating in other departments, only now, we are joined by the salvage surveyor, who wants to look inside the ballast tanks.

The sister ship to the *Regent* was the *Resource*.

I could never understand why, it was necessary for the RN/RFA to keep 5000 tonnes of ammunition in the *Resource* in peacetime while she was lying alongside the arsenal in the River Forth (Refer to Part 3 on pilotage). I found out in Devonport, both ships' are unstable. Wonderful, now I have to take an unstable ship all the way to India.

The Salvage Surveyor, however, wanted to inspect the ballast tanks. Which ones? We so innocently asked, hoping like heck, he did not want them all.

"We'll start with the fore peak tank then", okay, so the mate took the lid off, after a fight, suggesting that it was more than 5 years since that was off.

"But it's full of water!"

"Well, what do you expect on a fully ballasted ship?"

"How am I going to inspect that?"

Silly question really, as we suggested diving gear.

"You're not taking me seriously"!

"Oh yes we are, its' just that we have an awful lot to do, it is now the weekend, and I'm trying to get away by Monday.

"I'll see you on deck then, and we can discuss this", and with that he disappeared into the gloom.

"You know mate", I said, after a few minutes, "I thought the deck access was the other way".

"Yep", he's gone off towards the holds.

"Well, go find him then".

Nah.

"He'll be really cheesed off by the time he gets on deck, so won't want to come back down here, let him wander. Then he can sign us off, and that's one more surveyor out of the way. It worked. He wasn't overly pleased, as in, not at all.

My crew are at this stage getting on with storing, and doing rather well.

At this point the *Regent*'s master showed up, 'to give us a hand'. It took approximately 2 minutes on the bridge, for me to realize that he was a singing and dancing captain. Clueless. He did not know how to engage the autopilot, stating "Oh, the second mate will show you how to do that," and he did not know if the propeller was left or right handed, In short, a waste of space.

He actually became quite angry with me, stating that he had arranged for some of the crew to stay behind and assist us!

As if we needed it, so, I had a go at him.

"Your bosun, who stayed behind was asked to help us in running out a lifeboat. He did not know how to do it, so that doesn't say much for one of your crew does it. Or your safety procedures, yours."

"Your emergency generator is a disgrace, and your ship is un seaworthy. Try explaining your incompetence here."

"The engineers are actually way behind the standard of mine, who work in the real navy, the merchant one, not this hybrid."

"The two ABs who stayed back, have spent all of their time in the pub, and to cap it all, you are here now, and know about as much as the bosun. Now disappear back to your party, and stop wasting our time. We've better things to do."

He was a bit miffed, and I rather got the impression that he was related to Ten Knot Tony.

The Lloyds surveyor, having been found out about his previous inadequacies, has now decided to play it by the rules.

All of our new safety equipment complies with the rules except for two items, which we do not have: A Ship's Bell. A Ship's Gong.

Both are a requirement under the 1972 Collision Regulations.

For the un-initiated, they are required for fog, but nobody ever uses them, due to the stupidity of the requirement.

Can you imagine, for example, standing on a 450 000 tonner at anchor, in fog, ringing a bell forward, then a gong aft 350 metres away, to warn a ship approaching that you are at anchor. Plus you are in radio contact fore and aft, so that you can follow each other. Ludicrous. However, it is in the rules so we must comply. But, costs are tight, so we must find a way round this rule. The solution came out of the blue.

CQ, my boss had been a cadet in Plymouth, so fancied going off to the pubs that night, to find his old watering holes. Only one problem, Plymouth had changed more than just a wee bit in the intervening 25 years. So we all got lost. And, as seamen do, ended up way out of position in a pub, which just happened to have '*a bell*'.

I just arranged with the barman to borrow it for a day. After all, we only have to show it to the surveyor, to show that we have one, it doesn't actually have to sail with us, although he thinks it has, but then he didn't fix the engine. The *gong*, that is another matter.

Now where are we going to get a gong without actually buying one? Easy.

By now, full of beer, and being somewhat gregarious in finding our way back to the dockyard gate, led us down a street full of guest houses.

Now while we were staying on board, my boss wasn't, he was in a hotel ashore. Not after that night, he was now booked into a guest house, somewhat confusedly, with no luggage. Why? They had a Dinner Gong! A lovely polished brass affair, hanging in a stand. We just… sort of borrowed it, when he was signing in. However, the night was not yet over.

Have you ever tried to get anything out of a naval base? I have never tried, being far too honest. But have you ever tried to get something in? Now that *is hard*. For example, how do you hide a *bell*? How do you hide a *gong*? To this day, I do not remember exactly what excuse I used, but with RN security, the triple B perhaps? Bullshit Baffles Brains!

At 10 00, however, I had to explain it, when Port Security came down.

Yet another officious tedious individual with not enough to do.

Do you know, that this *security* wally wanted us to remain on board until we sailed, and would not allow a British Subject access to his own country. The only way I could get ashore was to tender my passport to security going into and out of the dockyard. A British passport holder to show his passport in his own country. Fat chance. Did you know that a Panamanian Masters' Certificate, is also Red, has a photograph, and looks like a passport? Obviously, security didn't, because for the next 3 days that is how I got in and out. Security was so lax, that my crew went in and out on my certification, just for the heck of it. But then, light fingers were at work as well. Especially the barrel, and the flags.

Now all the time that this was going on, my engineers, having found the engine room, had set about testing the turbines and associated equipment.

At the time, I thought that they were being overly cautious, shutting down each night after a day of testing, so proceeded to stress that we had to be up and running on the Monday. The Diesel Alternator was due that night.

Monday came and went, we are now certificated to go, except for the Diesel Alternator, which is still in Birmingham, although, later in the day, it became apparent that it was of no use.

In the meantime, the Royal Navy start to press us for the berth, as they had a destroyer due for the Tuesday.

On Tuesday night, all is ready to go, apart from having a Diesel pack, which surprise, surprise, the RN had all the time. Wednesday.

Who should decide to pay us a visit? just as the Diesel pack was being delivered. The Queen's Harbour Master. With two matelots in tow. Now, I have just spent £20 000 in legal fees clearing my name from a bunch of dimwitted idiots in the River Forth, one of whom was an ex-Queen's Harbour Master, and I am in no mood to take any more nonsense from Queen's Harbour Masters. Bearing in mind that I have just climbed out of the lower holds, and being somewhat dirty, I do not expect to be addressed, whilst still catching my breath with.

"Are you the Captain?"

Breathlessly. "Yes."

"I have been calling you on the VHF for the last 2 hours and you have not answered, why?" This in one of those accents that immediately annoys, you know, the high and mighty type.

"Because for the last 2 hours, you have been calling the *Regent*, which ceased to exist last Friday, this ship is now the *Shahzadelal*. Under the VHF regulations, I cannot take traffic for another ship, of which you should be fully aware." That stopped him, but only for a few seconds, so he had another go.

"That is beside the point, I have ordered a pilot and three tugs to take this ship off the berth, and take her out to the sea buoy where you can finish your preparations at 3 pm today. I need this berth for a destroyer."

"Really!"

"Now let me tell you something. It is your fault that we are still here, due to your neglect of this ship and there's plenty of it. If you insist that I sail, then I will proceed with this; the first thing I will do will be to declare Port of Refuge. By law, you must give me a berth, and as we are alongside, this will do nicely; secondly, I will send a telex to Lloyds informing them of the actual condition of this ship, then I will send a telex to the Admiralty accusing you of an act of piracy, which is still punishable in the RN by hanging from the yardarm, there are two up there, port or starboard, take your pick." That took him back a bit. "Um," was the answer, "when will you be ready to sail?" 10 30 tomorrow morning. I'll fix it then, and with that he escaped, with two grinning matelots in tow. I would have loved to have been a fly on the wall that night.

It would have been nice if the chief engineer, had told me he had put a huge electrical surge through the ship when he started up, rather than us having to find that he had blown the autopilot clean off the bulkhead. That also rather explained the funny burning smell. So now, on top of everything else, we have to hand steer this unstable ship all the way to India.

I have worked on some odd ships in my time at sea, but never have I seen a master's cabin quite like this one. There was a fireplace, complete with an electric fire, but funnily enough, no chimney. There was a doorbell at the entrance, it went ... bing-bong. Then there was the bedroom, with a bed so big, it would have done a rock star proud. Even with double sheets, they still did not get to the edge of the mattress.

Ah! but the bathroom was the best bit. You could have had a dance in here. The four-legged Victorian enamel bath most probably now graces some rich Indian's home, and no doubt, immensely proud of it.

My crew, well the other 13 pirates, had their choice of cabins, and ended up in all sorts of places, but the best remark came from the lumberjack, "you know, Cap, there are so many toilets on this ship, that I could use a different one every day, and wouldn't need to flush it." Wanna bet mate!

Just before we sailed on the Wednesday, the lumberjack came up and said "do you think these will be any use," holding three flags on poles on stands?

"Where did you get these?" I asked horrified, as I knew what they were for.

"Oh, they were flapping about on the dock."

"Well put them back quick, these are for the destroyer captain, who'll use them to position his ship when he comes alongside." If you ever read this Captain, you'll know why your ship ended up the opposite way round, from the RN's intention. Oops.

For sailing, I got 2 pilots, or rather one pilot and one Navy 'pilot', and three tugs. Two tugs would have been enough, the third was just a nuisance, but in Navy parlance, the third tug is known as a 'dog', a term that perhaps should have been given to the Navy pilot. I also had a port pilot.

This really annoys me when ports do this. They draw a line on a chart 1 mile to the south of the limit of the Navy base, and then insist that ships have a pilot, to cross that 1 mile, along with a hefty bill. They don't do anything. However, he left with my boss, CQ, who had found a safety helmet shaped into a helicopter in a cupboard, and chose to wear it going down the pilot ladder.

A pity they hadn't used their time more usefully, by repairing the emergency diesel perhaps.

CQ told me afterwards, that he had to go and see the QHM, and the conversation went like this.

QHM. "Your captain is a bit tough is he not?"

CQ. "My captain is a highly experienced master and pilot, and I have every faith in him to deliver that ship to India."

QHM. "Oh I don't doubt that for a second, but would he really have sent those telexes, if I had put the ship on the buoy?"

CQ. "You would never have gotten the ship off the berth. You should see what he can do with anchors. And yes he would have sent those telexes, they were already written, and in the memory bank of his Inmarsat 'C'."

QHM. "Give him my regards when you next see him then."

Oh, was it good to get away to sea, but as soon as we got onto sea revolutions, our GPS navigator packed in.

"We'll have to go back", said the mate.

Not likely, not after we have just escaped!

"But how are we going to navigate?" Easy really, unorthodox certainly, but it works. Still had a sextant anyway, if any of us can still remember how to calculate a sight.

"What we will do, is steam on a course of 180 degrees from Devonport, until we meet all the other ships bound for Ushant, hunt around for one going at about the same speed, and then follow him. We'll get a radar fix at Ushant, and there is still a Consol station about here somewhere. If there are no ships, then after we round Ushant we'll head south west until we pick up Finisterre."

He gave me a strange look, but then, before GPS or Decca, that was how you would navigate. I have in fact been all the way across the Atlantic without getting a fix at all, everything done by dead reckoning.

If the GPS doesn't work by the time we get to Gibraltar, then we'll call in and get a new one, okay?

The weather for January was exceptionally fine, which was just as well, as there is nothing more boring than hand steering, but hand steering in heavy weather is worse.

When we passed the Straits of Gibraltar, Lloyds signal station called us up, and do you know what the cheeky so-and-so said, "Is that the old *Regent*? Well, I've lost my sweepstake, I didn't think you would get it this far."

So the Navy are running a sweep are they, that is worse than a red rag to a bull to us lot. We are going to get this ship to India, even if we have to row it the rest of the way.

The leg of the voyage from the Straits of Gibraltar to Port Said is just a case of running around the North Coast of Africa. There isn't much to see, apart from other ships, so a few diversions were needed to maintain interest.

One of these was getting the swimming pool ready for the Red Sea, where it is always hot, and the Indian Ocean, which at this time of year is in the North East Monsoon.

One afternoon, all available hands to, and get the covers off the swimming pool. Gosh they were heavy, and the lifting lugs had long since broken off. But we are nothing, if not resourceful, and after a fight, four of them are off. However two of them fell in. They were even harder getting out, but brute force and rather a lot of ignorance paid off yet again.

The pool was filthy.

After a good scrub out, and a pair of fire hoses to fill it, it did in fact look usable. The lumberjack, who was not overly well qualified in the common sense department, decided to be the first to try it, and jumped straight in. Remember it is still January, and although it is the Med, it is still, *cold*. Approximately 1 second after he submerged, he was back out, just as you see penguins jump out in the Antarctic, only he was now blue. Idiot.

"Right then, who fancies a barbecue?" Now, I was brought up on oil and gas tankers, so had left it to the others in the know. Did they?

In a word, no. A barrel had been acquired in Devonport, but it was not quite empty. After draining off what looked like aviation fuel, it was split length ways, in a rather haphazard way. With an angle grinder. This brought back memories of *Blunderman*. The cook then set it up on a rather rough looking stand, and lined the half barrel with a few firebricks, on the poop deck, in case it had to be chucked over the side.

"Did you clean out the barrel cookie?"

Obviously not, for as soon as a match was offered to the paper and wood, there was a definite 'whoosh!' No eyebrows left, but it was burning away nicely.

The first of a few barbecues was held that night, as we huddled in duffel coats, choking on smoke, and trying to convince ourselves that this was a lot of fun.

But, the Suez Canal is fast approaching, or as it is known nowadays, "The Marlboro Canal." I have yet to meet anyone who actually likes going there. It is a terrible place, and will never improve unless you have a spare nuclear warhead. Then there will be a long queue of shipmasters waiting to detonate it.

There is one thing to do first though. We need to make a pilot chair, or face a fine of $1000, cash, which we don't have. It is sad really, as the fee for this ship to make one transit is $ 100 000. Plus about 50 cartons of Marlboro, which of course we do not have. This is going to be a right bundle of laughs.

"Right then boys, we are spending the afternoon building a pilot chair." All it is really, is a chair on high legs. Great if you have a chair to start with. All we had were a few sofas in the 'midships officers' saloon, two decks down.

I soon found out why they were left on board. It took four of us, just to pick one up.

"Are you sure about this captain?" said one of the crew, as we were halfway out the door.

"Too late for that now, come on, keep pushing." It was a hell of a struggle getting it out, plus decidedly dangerous getting it to the port bridge wing, but we made it. The language was, shall we say, choice.

"He capn," said an AB, pointing at the doors, "these effing doors are smaller than that last effing door."

"Oh quit griping, it'll go in if you give a big shove." It went in, took a bit of stopping, but was in, minus the legs.

"Okay cap," breathlessly, "what now?"

"Obvious boys, it needs some legs. Nip down to the back end No 3 hold, and bring up about 12 of the pallets lying in the corner.

Gosh, were they heavy. Oak I think.

"Right, now nail them all together in two piles, and we'll tie the sofa on top."

Oh, did it look rough, but we did now the biggest pilot chair in the world. It could seat six or more in a line, providing everyone moved at the same time.

If you arrive by 18 00 local time at night, then you should get through the canal that night. There is, however, a tug/launch that patrols the anchorages north of Port Said, making sure you don't 'flog it'. Actually, it makes little difference when you arrive, even up to 22 00, providing you have enough Marlboro. Before 18 00, five cartons, after, anything up to 50. With most ships costing thousands per day, it is cheaper just to hand over the Marlboro, than lose a day. *And* the Egyptians know this. The 'canal' Egyptians are totally different to the rest of this country's populace.

We arrived at 15 00, and looked forward to a few hours rest, as transiting the Suez Canal is immensely tiring. No sooner is the anchor down though, then we get a call to bring us into the buoys in Port Said, for, 'clearance'.

The Suez Canal is meant to be a 'Freeport', so minimum paperwork. That is 'minimum' being only one piece of paper less than as much as they can get away with.

There was at the time a racket going on, which you had to be wary of.

Everything which is 'official' has to be signed and stamped with the 'ship's stamp'. Actually, in some ports, the 'ship's stamp' is the most important thing on board. Lisbon is a perfect example.

In the general mêlée, a few extra people were offering up bits of paper in Arabic for signing, and 'ship's stamp,' then presenting them to the agent 2 days later for payment for what was a non-existent service.

You have to be careful.

How many doctors do you know who smoke?

None I'll bet, but in the Suez Canal, they all do, judging by the amount of Marlboro they get through.

It was many years later that I found out what they do with it all, and why, but I'll leave that to the story about delivering a tug from Hong Kong to the UK. Grimsby to be precise.

Going onto buoys with a motorship isn't really a problem, but with a steam ship, with a skeleton crew, is tricky. So up anchor and in we go.

You will find that in almost every port in the world, where it says on the chart is where the pilot boards, is nowhere near where he actually boards. The Suez Canal is no exception. On this particular night (it gets dark quickly), we were following in a Russian trawler also on a delivery voyage, only he is not well organized, and has put his pilot ladder over beside an overboard discharge. The pilot refuses to board, and a multi-lingual argument breaks out on the VHF, most of which consisted of the word f---. Unfortunately, I am starting to run out of sea room, when the trawler turns around in the channel, and comes out again, heading for the same bit of water as us, plus the first of the third-generation containerships outbound, doing close on 30 knots.

Only one thing for it, double ring full astern to stop dead, then full power ahead swinging round the trawler/pilot boat and into the canal. Whew! Missed, but only just. Even although we are going for scrap, the other ship isn't and a collision is enough to ruin your whole day. Plus, it helps if you have a photocopier, which we didn't.

Just before we got to the buoys, my crew were up to their tricks again, and had switched on every cabin light down the entire length of the ship, plus every one aft. Why? Well, it looked like a navy ship, and navy ships have big crews, so every bumboat man is coming on board to set up shop. About 60 of them.

Going on to the buoys, we were given a tug, which for its 'pay' gave us a nudge or two. During tying up, it started to snow! In Port Said in Egypt?

What else can go wrong? Anything, and did.

Your mooring ropes go out as slips, that is, the rope is run out from the ship, through an eye on the buoy, and then passed back up to the ship. One mooring rope is now doubled, so it is heaved up tight. For letting go, you just throw the eye in the water, and heave in the lot, simple. However.

The mooring men have developed a rather nasty trick.

One stern line goes out singly and onto a hook. Why? Well it's supposed to be a carton of Marlboro each for tying your ship up, and another for letting your one rope go. Fat chance with me here, as we haven't got any Marlboro.

They don't actually say. "Can I have a carton of Marlboro please captain?"

What they say is, "do you have a present for me captain?"

Of course, with my literal sense of righteousness, I take them at their word (because I don't have any Marlboro. CQ was a bit tight on the budget see. Okay for him, but it leaves me with the problem.)

Coming off the bridge, I am met by a host of Egyptians, all wanting to be first.

You will recall earlier, the difficulties with 'gross tonnage'. Well in the Suez Canal, they have gone one step further, and have a 'Suez Canal Tonnage'.

For this, a ship has a Suez Canal Tonnage Certificate. (There is even a Panama Canal Tonnage. I'll come to that in due course.)

Now, if calculating Gross Tonnage was difficult, calculating Suez Canal tonnage is easy. You just multiply the Gross Tonnage by the Variable Constant then divide by the number of people on board, add in the weight of 1000 chickens, and multiply by the first number that comes into your head, making sure that the figure you finally arrive at is about 8% more than the original Gross Tonnage. The most important bit however, is to make sure you declare it to two decimal places. If it isn't to two decimal places, then they think that you are cheating.

Then put it all down on an orange sheet of paper, and hand it over with a carton of Marlboro. (Which we haven't got.)

On this voyage, the certificate wasn't available in Devonport, so it was sent by courier to Port Said, and as soon as it came out of the envelope, went straight back ashore with the 'surveyor', who was a bit mystified with his 'present'.

So, tied up to buoys, all the paperwork done, we can at last look forward to a few hours rest.

Oh yes! Their 'presents'. Well, they all got the same thing, a helicopter rotor blade bolt.

They all gave me the same puzzled look, as if to say, 'this isn't Marlboro', but then, beggars can't be choosers. (We found dozens of these in a box down aft.)

"But captain, for our 'present' we mean Marlboro." They all chorused.

"Oh no, you asked for a present, so I gave you a present." There was an awful lot of mumbling, and it wasn't happy mumbling either.

Back to the bumboat men. We now have about 60 shops set up, roughly just over four each, and all with the same junk.

How many people in the UK need a camel saddle? I once watched an AB bartering for hours driving the price down from £20 to £15 for one of these. When we were back at sea, I asked him if he had looked underneath it.

"No, but why?"

Go and have a look.

It said, 'Made in Birmingham.' Cost in the UK, about £12.

The rest of their junk is all the same. Tin plates with pictures of pyramids and so on. They stamp them out in small batches of 10 million at a time. Occasionally, they have socks for sale.

Then we have to accommodate all those who ride along with you. First of all the 'mooring boat men'.

Their boat is hanging underneath one of our derricks, and tied off to the rails. We need this if we are to tie up anywhere in the Canal, for example, if fog rolls in. I've never seen it done.

The Suez Canal is not just one canal, there are all sorts of secondary canals, and lay-bys, plus of course, the Bitter Lakes in the middle.

They were put up in the hospital, which on the old *Regent* is massive, certainly a Four Eight-some Reel place. I do not know which one of my crew told them that the instrument sterilizer was a tea maker, but it kept them amused, and prevented them from stealing anything. Not that there was much to steal anyway.

Actually, they can be dead handy when you *do* want something 'stolen'. Some years before, I worked on a gas tanker, and had done an oil change on the LPG compressors. The problem was getting rid of the old oil. Can't just throw it over the side, so I poured it into the waste oil tank for the incinerator, completely forgetting that it holds a lot of LPG in solution. Boom! And the top 20 feet of the funnel disappeared over the side. From then on, it went into drums, and allowed to be 'stolen'.

The other who rides along with you, is the 'electrician'. It takes years of training to be able to do this properly. How to switch on the Suez Canal Searchlight.

How to switch it off again. But as he is a 'professional', he has to have 'officer' status, so gets a cabin. We however didn't have enough sheets etc, so he ended up with a survival bag, which although it is lovely to sleep in, also glows in the dark, making it tricky to get to sleep. But these guys have plenty of practice in this department.

You will also notice, that whatever company you work in, lunch and dinner going through the Canal is always the same. Roast Pork or Pork

Chops and so on. Why, because Moslems won't eat pork, so get a load of sandwiches instead.

If they were more pleasant in their approach and behaviour, then they would be treated much better, but they are so arrogant and filthy, plus they leave a terrible mess behind, and they get treated accordingly.

My chief engineer was walking around with a huge grin on his face, I felt inclined to ask why.

"Oh, he said, an Arab came into my cabin, and insisted on buying my electric fire. Gave me $40 for it and left happy."

"So what's so funny then?"

"Oh, it's 440 volts, and won't work ashore."

Now I know enough, after many years at sea, to know, that an English Chief, who was also Yorkshire, and lived in Sheffield, *never* just happened to have an Arab walk into his cabin to buy a fire! It took me to find his cabin, and I was sailing with him.

My second mate, who apart from being first trip second mate, was quite good, but worried a bit too much. He looked concerned.

"What's wrong Bill? You look worried."

"It's the stern line captain, it's not out as a slip."

"Oh don't worry about that, we'll just cut it. It is 8 inch polyprop and they break at 46 tons, so we'll assume it will take 40. When I come ahead on the engine, you stand by with a sharpened fire axe, and when it starts to sing and twang, chop it.

The recoil will take it clear of the propeller and Bob's your uncle. We'll put on a preventer to hold the loose end on board."

He gave me that, 'I'm not too sure about this' look.

Like all things that happen at sea, it is usually the middle of the night when we set off southwards, in our case, at 1 in the morning. True to form, the boat men don't show up, pity really, as I had loads of helicopter bolts to get rid of yet.

"Right second mate, chop it when it starts to twang, but not before." As I came ahead on the engine, the stern line is holding us back, but the load is coming on nicely. I can't see this mind, but I'm in radio contact, and was given a running commentary by the AB who was hiding round the corner.

Now to give the second mate his due, this was the first time he had to actually do this, but left it just a touch too late, milliseconds really. Only one blow with the axe was required, as it went with a tremendous BANG, and flew away at a heck of a speed, going in a big arc, before falling over the roof of a parked taxi, the rest demolishing the glass door of a shop. It went from closed to open, at 1 in the morning. Bit short of customers though. Time to look the other way.

If it sounds exciting going through the Canal, believe me, it's not.

It is about as exciting as watching paint dry, and I'd rather watch the paint. The only excitement, is anchoring in the Bitter Lakes, waiting for the northbound ships to clear. At least you get a break.

The first pilot didn't want a helicopter bolt, so he got a fire brick instead. The second pilot got an old fan, which didn't work, but he seemed happy enough. We all had bacon butties on the bridge, extolling the virtues amongst ourselves as to whether smoked bacon is better than un-smoked. The pilots annoy us, so we annoy them.

I had a cook once many years before, who asked me if he could go for a swim in the lakes, as we lay at anchor. No problem, so in he jumped. 1 minute later, he was out again. Problem? Now he knows why they are called the Bitter Lakes. They are damn cold.

The last stretch to the sea, is the longest of them all, not in distance mind, but because you are thoroughly fed up by this time. The pilot this time asked for his present, so I offered him a lifeboat, well, we were going to scrap, and if one was missing, could always say that it fell off on passage. He refused, so went away with a rotor blade bolt instead. The very last pilot didn't even bother to ask. This would of course not work with any ship, if we were coming back, we would never get away with it, so it would have to be Marlboro, but I had some fun with that as well on the tug from Hong Kong.

Definition of the Suez Canal, as appreciated by all seamen of any nationality: Port Suez is the arsehole of the world, and Port Said is 86 miles up it! Clear at last 4 in the afternoon, put her back to economical revs, and off we go for India, only 3000 miles to go. The stability problem, that was shared with the *Resource* was always in the back of our mind. We had to be stable for beaching, and had also been told to arrive on the beach with no fuel, and no food, the latter for some reason, I never did fathom.

As each fuel tank empties, they are in the double bottoms, it had to be filled with water for ballast. You have to be careful here, as, as soon as you fill the tank, then there is no going back to look for that last wee bit of fuel. The only way to fill it, is by fire hose, down the sounding pipe, and it takes an age.

You know in the movies, they say, "open the sea cocks and we'll scuttle her." I've been at sea for 30 years, sailed on over 60 ships, and never once have I managed to find a sea cock.

Everything is going well though, we are on schedule, fuel is spot on target, allowing for 24 hours at anchor before beaching, which if we keep to schedule, will coincide with the highest tide of the month. This ship burns 25 tons of fuel per day, at anchor, that is for going nowhere. 30 tons a day on passage, and we were nursing her along at between 9 and 10 knots. Pure clean Gas Oil too.

A spot of relaxation, another barbecue, actually we had a few of these, as the Red Sea is always hot, and no matter what you do, you cannot find a breeze to cool down. The accommodation gets to be like an oven.

Practical jokes always pass the time, as long as no-one gets hurt. Plus, I am the worst for setting them up, so, on the Notice Board. 'Cabin Inspection at 10 o'clock tomorrow morning.' Who ever heard of a cabin inspection on a ship 10 days away from a scrap yard? My crew obviously, as they all went off and cleaned and tidied up their cabins. All of them, even the chief, who I thought would know better. Next lunchtime, they all asked, "well, how was it, the inspection?" "Ocht, I didn't bother, it was too hot." Then they all twigged. Grr.

You can always tell when some people get bored, they think of home, and that brings them round to the subject of how they are getting home. Still a week out mind, and they all start badgering me. The Chief was elected 'shop steward'.

"Are you going to send a telex to CQ requesting details of our travelling arrangements?"

"Oh no, Colin will send them when he's ready." Mutter, mutter, mutter. "Okay, I'll send a telex to CQ."

I have absolutely no intention of sending a telex on this subject, as even CQ doesn't know the dates for beaching, far less getting out, and back to Bombay, so it is time for the 'fake' telex. I've used this a few times on other ships, usually when someone is trying to get out of working by always going to the doctor, when there is nothing wrong with them. I've got other tricks as well.

Making the fake telex is easy, you type it up on the screen, as though it has come in, then put it into the memory, and then pull it out to the printer, when there is someone else there, but is not paying any attention to what you are doing. Time it right and it works a treat. As it did on this day, as Donald, our 'Radio Officer,' said, "Captain, there's a message coming in."

So there was… . What a coincidence!

"It's our travel arrangements." I had made up the most awkward way of getting home from India that I could think of, it went like this,

"After beaching Bavnagar, overland bus to Kandla, then train to Delhi, but as train can often be 12 hours late, flights only on reservation yet and not confirmed, but will be Delhi to Tehran, then Moscow with Aeroflot, onwards after transfer to St. Petersburg, then Paris and London. Regards." Now if I had seen that, I would have smelt a rat straight away.

They didn't and it gave them 3 days moaning, about how only Wijsmullers could find the cheapest route. The best was that the Irish American, only had his American passport with him, and he *was* worried about going through Tehran. Finally the penny dropped, when the real telex came in, only the R/O got there before me. It was Bombay to London direct.

Sitting down aft one afternoon, we were discussing just how many compartments there were on this ship. Yeah, we were pretty bored by now, but there was one compartment, that none of us could find the door to, and it was up beside the funnel.

Finally, the electrician worked it out. You got into it, by climbing up a ladder from the top of the engine room. So, armed with a few torches, we set off for a look. After getting very hot, and very dirty, we got the door open. What a waste of time, it was full of bricks. It was the boiler fire brick store.

But with India now approaching, it is time to start on the paperwork, and believe me, there is lots of it. You even have to declare on a separate sheet for each person, all of your belongings, even down to counting how many socks you have. And you need six copies for each person. Plus, there was only one typewriter, so I ended up with the job. Then a separate declaration for money and gold, again six of each, then a load of declarations for what you *do not* have. Such as no guns or firearms, no explosives (I'll come back to this one), no bonded goods (already used up), anything you can think of really, and yes six copies of each.

Later on you'll hear about the *Quan*. This was when I had to clear in 45 ships, but I had a photocopier. Albeit, in Russian.

Do ships carry explosives? Yes they all do. The distress flares and line throwing rockets are classed as explosives. Before the ship arrives, they have to be disposed of. The time trusted way, is to put them in an old paint drum, seal it with cement, and drop it overboard, preferably in very deep water.

It is however, much more fun just to fire them off. Plus, on a line throwing rocket, the 'line' is brilliant as a clothes line.

If you are not in too much of a hurry, then you can go fishing with the distress flares. Normally they are fired upwards, but if you want to go fishing, then fire them downwards. I'm not going to tell you what happens next, but you can get a lot of fish.

Well, the voyage is rapidly coming to an end, so the arrival telexes start going out. Well, they went out okay, but nobody was receiving them. Even Wijsmullers, with their worldwide contacts, couldn't get through, so it's back to basics. Forget about satellite communications, just use the VHF.

You can 'smell' India 100 miles out to sea, and as you get closer, you definitely know you are in the right place. The Gulf of Khambhat (pronounced cambay), is a very odd part of the world, the tides are ferocious, and don't seem to follow any logic. One minute they are with you, they next you are fighting them. The current is all over the place.

So, I anchor where I am told to anchor, and set about trying to get inward clearance. The port next to the scrap yard of Alang, is Bhavnagar, so their port control seemed a sensible place to start.

Hours later, I have it established that we have arrived, and hours after that, the agent agrees to come to the ship. Wow! This was hard going.

It was arranged that half of my crew were leaving in the anchorage, leaving me with only seven, myself included for beaching.

Next day, I started again with Bhavnagar Port Control, asking for permission to beach. Hours later again, I am informed that I need 'permission' from Alang Port Control, who is working on channel 12.

Ah ha! Now we are getting somewhere. But Alang Port Control, and Bhavnagar Port Control is the *same* person. Words cannot describe the incredulity of this.

So, we set off to beach, having been told that our 'position' was marked by flags, and our 'pilot' would talk us in by radio (he sat in an armchair on the beach). For beaching, read 'go hard aground'.

Having spent years trying to keep ships 'off' the beach, then putting one 'on' you would think would be easy. Well, it isn't.

The only advice I was given was to 'go as fast as possible'. It also helps if your ship is stable, which the *Shahzadelal* (ex-*Regent*) isn't. She also has virtually no flat bottom, for the technically minded, a Coefficient of Fineness of 0.61, so there was concern that when she finally stopped, then she might just fall over. It hasn't happened yet, but with my luck, is very possible. Everything then is tied down, and off we go. The Chief has every interlock on the main turbine 'linked out', every possible source of auxiliary steam shut down, and both boilers working up to maximum output plus. The burners in the boilers at full speed plus, use 1.5 tons of fuel per hour each, and there are eight of them, so 12 tons per hour, of pure gas oil, none of your normal rubbish here. We had also found 2.5 tons of aviation fuel in the helicopter tank, so that went in as well.

First thing? Find the flags.

Easy, it would be, if they were bigger flags, but we eventually see where they want her, swing out, off the beach, and start building the speed. She was lacking in stability that even 5 degrees of helm (rudder) gave 8 degrees of list.

The ships design speed was 20.5 knots, we had her up to 22 knots, and believe me, we knew she was moving. The plan was that as we hit the beach, the bow would dig a trench, and the rest of the ship would slide into it, and 'not' fall over. As soon as she hit, the engineers would pull the emergency stops, run out on deck, and grab something in case she fell over. Nice plan with 45 000 tons of ship. Pity it didn't work.

Oh she hit the beach all right, but the bow didn't dig in. No, she started sliding over the bottom. We estimated that she slid 500 metres, before coming to a stop, with a little shudder. It was a bit of an anti-climax really. Mainly as she didn't fall over. Pity.

There was great hilarity on the bridge, when the pilot came out with, "drop your port anchor captain, in case she slides off the beach on the next tide." As started at 22 feet draft, but were now at 14 feet, there was little likelihood of that.

The next problem, was getting off the ship, as the accommodation ladder wasn't long enough. It was after all, suitable for 'normal' operational use, but I don't think that beaching was in their mind when it was designed.

We were going ashore in a lifeboat, which was duly launched, and after tying a pilot ladder to the bottom of the gangway, I was able to use a phrase that every shipmaster dreads, only this time, in jest, "abandon ship". I'll tell you one thing, beaching a ship, is a whole lot easier than beaching a lifeboat. That is just plain dangerous.

Before we left Devonport, I was asked if I would send a telex with a bit of humour in it, to the RN, to celebrate another safe delivery, with a copy to Wijsmullers' office in Holland. Having worked for Gibsons as master for 3 years, where any sort of jocularity in telexes was frowned upon, this was rather a shock to the system. But who am I to miss such an opportunity, especially with the Grey Funnel Line? So QHM in Devonport it is!

"To Damage Control Officer, Devonport, cc QHM. Regret to advise sir, that *RFA Regent* aground in position------------ ---North; ----------- ---East. On going aground, vessel passed over beach, and main road, before stopping in paddy field. Question, do lifeboats float in 9 inches of water?"

I was told afterwards, that for a time, I was taken seriously!

What should be waiting for me on the beach? Only an Australian Film Crew making a documentary. Now you know what I am like at speaking in public, only this time, there was nowhere to run to. I'm told it was broadcast in the UK a few months later, but I missed that, I was away repairing a gas tanker.

I had promised that I would buy my crew a cold beer on arrival. It was then that I found out, that we were in an alcohol-free state.

Our flights to Bombay, were not for another 2 days. To pass the time? Well, let me put it this way, if you seek a holiday where you will be bored out of your skull, then go to Bhavnagar.

For dinner that night, all 14 of us together celebrated with lukewarm Coke. And a curry.

Everyone else had an easy time at Bombay airport, but I had all the ship's equipment to clear through. The flight didn't leave until 7 in the morning, but I was at the airport at midnight. They had never seen an Inmarsat 'C' in a suitcase before, or indeed a complete radio station in a box, and it *all* had to be examined in great detail. It wouldn't be so bad if it was coming in to the country, but this time it was going out. They might never see it again. Eventually it was cleared, then I had to pay the excess baggage. That came to £1300, which went onto my credit card, the agent was nowhere in sight.

It had to be Air India of course. Bad airline? Let's just say, that next time, I'll walk home.

When the agent says to you, "Air India is a f------ awful airline," and he is Indian, then you know it is going to be bad.

Would I do this again? Too right, especially if I could get my fellow pirates together for it. There are a few sequels to this tale that only came out later.

When the *Regent/Shahzadelal* was being cut up, one silly Indian cut into the aviation fuel tank, which immediately blew up. There was no loss of life, but it set fire to the ship. The fire burned out virtually everything, as there was no means of putting it out. The owner of the ship lost rather a lot of money, or put another way, just didn't make as much as expected. Ever known an Indian to lose out financially?

After beaching, we were invited to the owner's 'office' while awaiting transport to town, and we were invited to meet his family. It was put to me, in a rather sly way, that I might be interested in his daughter, as she would make a very good wife.

It was very tempting, as she was gorgeously beautiful, and had obviously had the very best in schools and so on. However, I was happily married at the time, so gracefully declined. There was another reason. It's an old Scots saying: if you want to know what a girl will turn out like, then look at her mother. Oh, was she ugly, rolls of fat, some hanging over her skirt. Yeuch!

I have a friend, who is also a shipmaster, but worked on tankers at the time. Angus was dead interested in the story of the *Shahzadelal*, just in case he had to do it. Well, he did, and on his next voyage too.

There is one thing that neither of us realized. Beaching a tanker is different from beaching a ship such as I had. Tankers are much lighter in the water for a start, but Angus, with it firmly in his mind, that the secret was 'as much speed as possible', set about getting his ship ready for that final stop. Only this was a VLCC with a loaded deadweight of 250 000 tons. A biggish boat indeed. Over 1100 feet long. I'm told it was hilarious, and from the way he tells it, I can imagine that it was.

They don't want ships of this size too far up the tidal beach, but Angus didn't know this. He is going for glory, just to see how far up he can get it.

The pilot was as usual, sitting in his chair on the beach, when he realized just how fast this ship was going, and decided that it would be prudent to be somewhere else, like, pretty damn quick!

As people scattered in all directions, his ship hit the beach, and just kept on going, taking out a wall, and digging a fair old trench across the road behind the wall. He eventually came to rest with the bow in a field, totally blocking the road. Oops a daisy Angus! Bit too much speed I would say. He had an even bigger difficulty getting off the ship.

When I eventually got home, there was a letter waiting for me, from Bergesen of Norway, inviting me to join their company, as 'chief officer'. This suited me perfectly, after the strain with the pilots, and I prefer the technical aspect of the job, to being in command.

There was one other reason, they didn't have the *Borthwick*!

But I spoke too soon, as she turned up like the proverbial bad penny. Before I left, CQ asked if I wanted to do another delivery?

"What ship Colin?"

"The *Matco Avon*, now just named as *Avon*".

"In the nicest possible way CQ, no way Hosea, I know a bit about this ship, *and* the oil company which ran it."

It was my chief mate from the *Shahzadelal* who took it, on his first job as master.

The ship was handed over in the Solent, just off Portsmouth, and her claim to fame was going aground here, *before* they set off to the breakers. How did this happen? She was a steam ship, with a novel type of main engine. A steam turbine, with *no* astern turbine, control being affected by including a variable pitch propeller.

To get her under way, the turbine is started up, and the propeller set to zero pitch. Only this ship has a history, of being set to zero pitch, but in fact going to full forward pitch. A lot of masters had been caught out.

As the anchor was being heaved in, no-one noticed that the ship was on the move, and was overhauling her anchor cable, heading for the beach, which it went straight up on.

Nice bit of beaching Peter, pity it's the wrong beach. Try India.

She wasn't damaged, and dropped a whole load of ballast, before being hauled off by a couple of tugs.

So try again!

She was not going out through Suez, but 'going round the Cape'. Hands up if you think the Cape of Good Hope is the most southerly point of Africa?

It isn't, Cape Agullus is. I just thought I would chuck that in. Well, the *Avon* didn't even get that far. She got as far as Dakar, in Senegal, and broke down. Usual problem with steam ships, the boilers started leaking. Plus her emergency diesel (remember the story of Devonport, with the *Shahzadelal*) wouldn't start, so a tug came out from Dakar, and gave her a jump start. Just as you would do with a car really, only on a much bigger scale.

So she sets off again, but broke down the next day. She ended up getting towed into Dakar, where one of the boilers was condemmed.

Now she sets off on one boiler, and got as far as Walvis Bay, where the other boiler was condemned. She was towed the rest of the way to India.

That could have been me, if it wasn't that was I going back to work on gas tankers, only this time, the big ones. No more *Borthwick*, that was for sure.

Whoever owns the *Borthwick* when it is time to go to the breakers, give me a call, and I'll do it for free.

Part 5

It was not my initial intention to include my experiences in Bergesen of Oslo, as I had a private agreement with the senior management that certain details of events while I worked for them, would not be revealed by either them or me.

One of these is particularly distasteful, but I have since found that, while being used as a scapegoat for the fourth time, the incident was common knowledge with my chief engineer, who had also worked with the same group. We were at this time, working for Bibby Line.

It will therefore be detailed here, as well as a lot of other matters, which they may have preferred to remain confidential. Breach of trust can work both ways of course, and you will appreciate by the end of this chapter, that the degree of pollution this company are guilty of, is far beyond your imagination, and on a worldwide basis. My concerns for the atmosphere, which is finite, have been revised since working for this group. I feel sure that you will agree.

After delivering the *Shahzadelal* to Alang in India, and after my battle with Forth Ports plc, I decided to step back from sailing as master for a while.

It was not that there weren't any opportunities, there were, and one interesting one was with VShips Cyprus, but this would have meant sailing on the *Borthwick* again, and this I was not prepared to do.

They had, however, found a way round the tank calibration fraud and explained this to me over the 'phone. I just laughed at this, as they just could not have been serious, but unfortunately, they were.

All crude oil tankers have a thing known as 'the ship's experience factor'. This is a number which compares the ship's loaded figure with the shore's loaded figure, and is modified with each cargo.

It starts off at 1.0. Shore, divided by ship, and usually, as more cargoes are carried, increases towards 1.2ish, then drifts back towards 1, but never quite getting there.

Gas tankers, with their precise tank calibrations, *never* have an experience factor, as some of their cargoes are calculated to the nearest kilogram.

But now, the *Borthwick* has an 'experience factor'. Whoever dreamed this one up, either worked for Unigas International, had a vivid imagination, or was just plain drunk at the time.

I, therefore, went to work for Bergesen as chief mate, once again, a job that I still enjoy, as the technical aspects of the job are much more interesting than moving paper around.

One of the hardest things for a master, is getting a chief mate, who is supportive. When you get a good one, then as master, the job is a lot less difficult. I have always been known as a supportive chief mate.

The reason I was asked to join Bergesen, and at that time as their only British officer, was that the managing director of VShips Norway (re *Norgas Challenger*), had joined Bergesen as their technical manager. This man, while brilliantly clever, is also an absolute gentleman, someone who is always a pleasure to meet with, even if you are for a bollocking. Not that I got any.

My first port of call, so to speak, was to Oslo, to the 'Bergehus', which is their name for the office. It is an impressive place, as it is filled with ship models. They have an interesting, while superstitious fact that, when a ship is sold, they retain the model, but delete the latter part of the ship's name, which for example may have been Berge Anyship, and replace it with Berge ----------. Quite curious really.

My friend wasn't there that day, but I was introduced to the ship's superintendent for the ship I was joining, which was the *Berge Raghnild*. A gas tanker of course.

He said a very curious thing, which although I noted, didn't become clear until over a year later, when I was on the *Berge Racine*. There are three ships in this class, the other being the *Berge Rachel*.

"We are experiencing problems in the port side of these ships cargo tanks. They are cracking across the bottom transverse girders. If you get the chance to open up one of the ship's tanks, then give us your opinion." This is really quite a serious problem, but I'll explain what I found when I come to it. I do know that what I found was *not* passed back, so this will probably be 'news' to them as well, if they read this book.

Off to join her then, in Fos la Mer, the gas port next to Marseilles, France.

Immediately, there is one huge fundamental difference, in joining a *big* gas tanker, as opposed to a *small* one. Getting on board! The *Quentin* for example, you just step onto, on this one, it's a heck of a long climb up the side, especially with a suitcase.

The *Berge Raghnild* is 81 640 cubic metres, as opposed to the *Quentin* of 2204 cubic metres. The principles however, are almost exactly the same, just on a different scale.

It was a delight to see an old friend, that I was relieving, who to save him any embarrassment, we'll just refer to as JB. He and I often came across each other, when we were both masters trotting around the European coast, on our respective gas boats. Unfortunately, a little prang cost him his job with the company he was with, and like me, ended up in Bergesen. Sixteen metres of his ship's bow fell off, after tangling with another ship in a matter likely to ruin your whole day, a collision.

The only other notable on board, was the stewardess, Regina. A lady who was on her last voyage, and a right worthy at that. I'll tell you an interesting story about her right now.

She had an accident on board, and suffered burns to her arm, which I had to dress on a daily basis, until it healed. From then on, she was always trying to get me to go to her cabin for 'a beer'. Now I was a happily married man at the time with two kids, and rather worldly wise, so continuously found an excuse not to go, without wanting to hurt her feelings.

By the time she got to within a week of leaving in Singapore, she was getting desperate, and I was running out of excuses, when she came up with, "I have a whole case of beer in my cabin, which I cannot leave, please will you come to my cabin, and help me drink it tonight?" I agreed, but a whole case for two people! So I went to her cabin that night, and took the whole crew with me. She was livid.

Apart from discharging in Fos, we were also discharging in Cartagena, and Huelva, in Spain. There was not a problem with this, until we came to Cartagena. Not with us, but with another ship, What do you think came steaming in? None other than the bloody *Borthwick*. I'm sure that thing has a homing instinct on me, and this was only the first of many times, when while I thought I was safe from it, it kept turning up like the proverbial bad penny. It even found me in Ecuador!

JB left in Huelva, and has still not forgiven me for doing this, so I'll mention it here. I played one of the *sloe-eyed Mancunian*'s tricks on him, a tame one really, unless you are on the receiving end. But fun still the same. You'd think by this time, I would have grown up, but no.

He was through his third airport before realizing why everyone was smiling at him as he passed. It was then that he saw the un-rolled condom, superglued to the bottom of his briefcase.

Going alongside in Huelva, the last port of discharge was terrible, we couldn't hear each other on the bridge. The third mate's uncle was a pilot in the Norwegian air force, and was based in Huelva training Spanish pilots how to fly Sea King helicopters. During berthing, he brought his sister, the third mate's mother along for a ride in his paraffin budgie, and insisted on watching the berthing operation, about 100 feet off our starboard quarter. I'm afraid I do not know the Norwegian for f--- off! But I could still learn.

Here is something I'll bet you don't know. The third mate's first name was Tom. Big deal, but if you look it up in a Norwegian/English dictionary, the equivalent in English is 'empty'. From then on, he was known as 'empty,' which didn't go down too well at all, but then the Norwegian sense of humour is vastly different from ours. You only have to watch Norwegian TV to know why. It is dreadful, *dreadful*!

Now empty by name and empty up top, in a slow kind of way. One day he made the mistake of leaving his camera on the bridge. What a silly billy, did he not know that I'd worked in Gibson Liquid Gas? Obviously not, and this was too good an opportunity to miss, so I promptly shot off 15 photographs taken at various angles of the bridge toilet, carefully avoiding the mirror of course. Then didn't say a word. He finished the roll, and sent it off to his mother for processing. He came off the 'phone one day with a puzzled look, mumbling that his mother had commented on his choice of subject to photograph, "but I don't know what she means?" You soon will empty, you soon will! The best bit was that someone else got the blame, as I can keep a straight face. It was only on the *Berge Racine* later that he found out the truth, but too late, it was round the company by then. I never got another chance, with anyone. Can't understand why?

One day early on, I saw this European working alongside the crew, cleaning the deck. "Who was this?" I asked. "Oh, that is the Norwegian cadet." "Well he isn't going to learn anything doing that, send him up."

The attitude was that this was what they, being the other officers, did when they came to sea, and if it was okay for them, then it was good enough for him. A bit of dinosaur thinking here is there not? "Right John, let's see your record book, of tasks completed." There were five, after 2 months. "Right then, you'll now be on watch with me, not as lookout, but conning the ship. I'll supervise, and the rest of the time, you'll be in every corner of the ship learning how it works, and that includes the galley and engine room."

The logic? He was going to be a watch officer on a gas or oil tanker, in 8 months' time, and he'd better know what he is doing on the bridge, when there are ships coming the other way. Scrubbing decks, pah!

By the end of 3 months, he *knew* what he was doing, and was good at it too. This cookie will go far.

I don't know what it is about some people at sea, but a ship fitted with a lift draws some people like a magnet. They seem fascinated by them. Take them into a department store, and it just does not have the same appeal. But on a ship, they will wait at the bottom of the engine room for the lift to come down all the way from the bridge, get in, and then go up one floor. It is much quicker just to run up a ladder.

Then there are the *really* lazy types, who will do it backwards.

They will happily wait for a lift to come down, all the way from the top, get in, and then go *down* one deck.

I heard a really good story about one third engineer recently, who had this penchance for lifts. Seemingly, he had to move a three-piece suite, a couch and two chairs, down two decks, from his cabin to the dayroom, as his furniture was being replaced. Rather than manoeuvre it through the stairwell, he worked out that it could fit in the lift, so promptly with the help of the crew, did so. Press the call button two decks down, and the lift duly arrived. Ah! Problem. It went into the lift okay, but they couldn't get it out again. No matter what they tried, it was jammed solid.

One would think that there might have been some sympathy from certain quarters, like the captain, but no! The attitude was, "well, you'll have to go up and down the stairs now, like the rest of us."

No concern at all about getting the three-piece suite out.

Seemingly, this particular third engineer went home on leave, worked on another ship, had his leave, and then went back for a second tour on this ship about a year later. The three-piece suite was still jammed in the lift. It was still there when he left. The mind boggles.

On the *Berge Raghnild*, however, we have the really lazy type, the ones who use it for going down. Rune, the Chief Steward.

I hadn't seen a Chief Steward on a ship in years, the last I can recall, was in Mobil, in 1976, and if you had met that one, you would know why they were phased out.

On a Sunday, before lunch, the senior staff would gather in the captain's cabin for a dram. Not the Scottish type, that virtually every country in the world is familiar with, but the Norwegian variety, which I can tell you tastes like a cross between petrol and turpentine. But they love it. A bit like 'Acquavit' crossed with 'Dutch Genever'. Only one mind. This is expensive stuff you know at $2.50 per litre. Apart from the expense, one is all the body can take. Rough takes on new meaning, but they all seem to thrive on it.

Now to get Rune out of using the lift is really quite easy, you have got to convince him that it has a fault, and is not *that* much quicker than walking.

So, heading off for lunch, as he waits for the lift, we use the stairs, but I'm legging it, and manage to press every call button on every deck on the way down. We are all sitting round the table when he eventually arrives, mumbling, "that lift stopped on every floor on the way down, but there was no-one there."

"Oh," says I, "it did that with me the other day, only it was going up from the bottom of the engine room to the bridge at the time. I think we should get the electrician to check it out."

Anybody who knows nothing about lifts should not fiddle with them, but then we have the company 'electrician' sailing with us. For 'electrician' sometimes known as 'sparky', read 'clown'. This guy could fuse a circuit that wasn't even live. How he managed to become the company's electrician is anybody's guess.

Oh, he checked it all right, only problem now was when the lift said 'arrived', it might be there, but then again, it might not. So we all used the stairs. *Much* safer, keep him away from the gas plant please!

When he was relieved, the new electrician had it fixed in about an hour, but then Rune had left by then anyway.

We were due to load in two ports, Yanbu, in Saudi Arabia, in the Red Sea, which is a right dump, and Ras Tanura, in the Persian Gulf, which is an even bigger dump. To get there of course meant a transit through the Suez Canal, and Bergesen's boys like it as much as anyone else. Not at all! Needless to say, I was recognized by the first pilot, who was still puzzling over his 'present', a helicopter rotor blade bolt.

Our captain had to have this explained to him of course, but declined to depart from the obligatory carton of Marlboro. A wise move Harald, you might have to come back. I wish I didn't.

It was the usual, middle of the night affair, and routinely boring, except for one small incident. A boatman sidled up to me, and very surreptitiously whispered, "would you like some Spanish Fly sir? I have a little here, only $20."

Now I thought this stuff was extinct long ago. It is a form of aphrodisiac akin to smoking cannabis, or so I am reliably informed.

I politely declined, before relieving him of it, by dropping it over the side. He refrained from protesting, at that most magical of phrases, "let's just go and see the captain." Works every time. Don't know why.

There is one thing that has died out in the Suez Canal though, the queue of hypochondriacs. I may have had something to do with this. This was when I was chief mate, on the *Traquair*, about 8 years before, and as usual, was up to my eyes in work, so pestering Egyptians, I could do well without. This one though was not for giving up, and complained all day long about his sore foot. There was absolutely nothing wrong with it, as he even followed me up the foremast on it, as I re-wired in the new floodlights.

Eventually I could take no more of his whinging, and said, "right, up to the medical locker then." He followed with a huge grin on his face, further proving that he was just 'putting it on'.

"Okay then, lets have a look," and I started poking it with a pin.

"Right, you have to see a doctor when you get ashore, this looks serious, so for now, I'll just put on a bandage, and give you some pills."

He now had an even bigger grin, as he divested himself of his trousers. We'll soon change that grin though! Now, you know that really sticky bandage, the one that takes off all the hairs, which nurses delight in ripping off. I'm sure they queue up for this. And this was an extremely hairy man, like a Gorilla really.

Starting at his toes, I elected to see how far up I could get it. I was finishing the sixth roll, when I ran out of leg. And, he was really happy with it all. He won't be smiling when he comes to get that off!

A few splints just to make it awkward for him to move, and were we done? No chance, now he wanted tablets. I'm not going to argue with that, as my eye caught the very thing, Sennatabs. Normal dosage, a half to one tablet, he got six, with six more in a little tub, to take in 6 hours.

He had extreme trouble getting off the ship, and was last seen, with his backside hanging over the back of his boat, not looking so very pleased with himself now. I never saw him again, and have never been asked again since. It must have been agony getting that bandage off.

After clearing the canal, I had to prepare one cargo tank for loading, No 1 was under butane, but we were loading propane into it. The other three tanks were load ready, they just had to be cooled down.

Now I have a way of doing this, *without* blowing any gas into the atmosphere.

On the *Quentin* and *Borthwick*, gas freeing meant blowing off around 20 tons, but on the big boys, the amount is colossal. It can be as much as 185 tons, and on one occasion, it was 440 tons. This is serious atmospheric pollution, and this was just one ship, there are over 200 worldwide that still blow off massive quantities.

Now, consider this. If any oil gets into the sea, whether in port or not, then all hell breaks loose, with massive fines and so forth, plus, nowadays 'clean up costs'. Oil is referred to as a 'hydrocarbon'. But what are propane and butane? They are also hydrocarbons, the only difference is that when they are blown off you cannot see them. But they are still there. The atmosphere is after all, finite, just as the seas are.

In Flotta, and I only choose Flotta, as I know what goes on there, the crude oil is stabilized, that is the methane, ethane and propane are taken out, and shipped out separately. This effectively means that it doesn't evaporate when it is shipped out in crude oil tankers.

When I was a cadet in BP, I sailed on a ship of 112 000 tons, the *British Admiral*, and on a passage from the Gulf to NW Europe, 95 tons evaporated off, and that was with a heavy type of crude. On the lighter grades, the loss can be greater, hence, the reason why it is stabilised. It was the only time we measured it in BP, as I recall.

Now gas tankers blow it off willy nilly, as it suits them. Believe me, getting rid of 440 tons is *not easy*, but that was on the *Racine*, which we'll come to later, as there is a story that goes with it. It will really shock you!

So how is it possible to change a tank of 20 000 cubic metres from butane to propane, without losing any? The chief engineer at the time on board, was also a lecturer in the Nautical College in Norway, and took this one back with him, as he hadn't seen it before either.

It all depends on your knowledge of gases, and the difference in their molecular weights. Butane, C_4H_{10}, has a mol weight of 58.1 Propane, C_3H_8, has a mol weight of 44.1. The easy way of a rough ready reckoner is C x 12 + H. So, Butane is heavier. Their respective fully reliquefied temperatures also come into play, butane at about −1 deg C, propane at about −42 deg C.

A reliquefaction plant draws its vapour from the top of the tank, pretty obvious when you consider that a liquid cannot be compressed. In this case, however, we need to draw the butane from the bottom, and the only way to do this is to put in a flexible hose from the liquid manifold to the vapour manifold. The two are kept separate normally, for obvious reasons, although I have been on two ships where you could do just this. The gas is drawn up the cargo pumps, which are in sumps, as opposed to the loading line, which can be about 2 metres off the bottom.

The next thing, is to set up the reliquefaction plant for butane, which has a much higher condensing temperature. Still with me so far? Good.

When the vapour is being drawn off, propane vapour from the other tanks is spilling over, as on this size of ship, we cannot go into a vacuum. So how do you know when the butane vapour is out, and the propane vapour has taken its place? Simple, the plant stops, as the propane will not condense on butane settings. All the time, the butane is coming through, the now liquid, after reliquefaction can be sent to a butane tank, in this case No 3, or alternatively, to a deck tank if the ship has one. A lot do, but not all.

Now the *Berge Raghnild* just has to be cooled down, and she is load ready. Amount lost? Not a single gram. Atmospheric pollution? Nil.

As we drifted off Yanbu waiting to load, drifting, because there are no anchorages as the water is just too deep. It is the Red Sea after all, the weather is never really bad, just damn hot. The gas engineer and myself decided to go fishing, not ordinary fishing as you would normally do, but shark fishing where the equipment is somewhat unusual. You won't be able to try this at home. Grey sharks (big ones) swim around the ships all the time, so going for a swim over the side, is not recommended. Unless you have a death wish.

First of all, we need a hook, which in this case was made from a piece of stainless steel rod, about 10 mms thick, the line was a length of rope, breaking strain, about 2 tonnes. Bait? A few kilos of liver, which we seemed to have over-ordered. Bait the hook and off we go.

Got one, about 10 minutes later, and pulled it up against the transom, where it did its best to protest. Well it did have a big hook in its mouth after all. Now the 'unusual' piece of equipment. Overkill really, a 6.5 ton crane, where the rope was knotted on to the hook, and up she came. It immediately showed its displeasure, after landing on a hot deck, by snapping at anything nearby. Not us mind, we were well out of the way, but it did have a good go at a mooring wire.

The gas engineer decided to do a bit of dentistry on its bottom set of teeth; it could have done with a few fillings, but settled instead for a few extractions. Well it did have an old oar to chew on, not very appetising I know, but its just had a load of liver and a hook.

Then the captain and a few others appeared, before asking the obvious question, "just what are you going to do with it?"

Strangely enough, neither the gas engineer nor I had thought of that. There is one thing that you should know before you try shark fishing on this scale. They smell, oh boy, do they smell, and it was still alive. What was it going to be like if it was dead?

"Okay, only one thing for it," now that we have got a few souvenir teeth, and taken a few 'photos, which strangely enough, I never got a copy of, "we'll throw it back."

No doubt you'll be asking, how? Good question, easy answer. We'll lasso its tail, lift it up on the crane again, move it over the side, then cut the rope. This would of course answer the next obvious question, can sharks dive? Answer, not very well, but this was after all, its first attempt. How heavy was it? Estimated at 750 kilograms. Did it survive? No, within 2 minutes it had been eaten by the other sharks, as it was injured from the hook in its mouth.

It was now, however, that I was introduced to, which for me, just should not be allowed: 'The Ras Tanura Panel.' This is a second set of switches behind the instrument panel in the control room, which allows the chief mate to dial in any temperature he likes. The requirements for gas tankers arriving at Aramco (Arabian American Oil Company) ports, are that the top temperature should be at least –25 deg C, and bottoms at least –39 deg C. It is so easy to achieve with 100 tons of liquid in each tank, that one should not really have to 'flog it'. This for propane mind.

So why do they do it? A 400 ton heel is deducted from the total loaded figure, to give the Bill of Lading figure, upon which, freight is paid.

Do the ship's crew get any financial benefit from it? In a word. *No.* Do Bergesen? Yes, they get more freight paid, and no charges for losses. It is possible for some people to lose up to 200 tonnes.

Do Bergesen know about this? Officially no, but every one of their ships has it.

Who loses out then? The charterer who pays the freight.

Do they ever get caught? Oh yes, and how big time once, and guess who got the job of sorting it out? Yes, me. But that comes next on the *Berge Sisar*. It is sad that a lot of their officers think this is a good thing and rely on it, rather than just be up-front and honest. It is in fact, nothing other than maritime fraud on a huge scale.

I'm willing to lay odds that when marine cargo underwriters read this book, there will be a lot of questions asked. I hope so.

On this loading, it was not a big problem, as I showed them how to meet the requirements, without resorting to this underhand way of working, and this ship was presented meeting the port requirements. All you have to do is start the cargo pumps, and blast liquid through the top sprays, using the expansion to cool the vapour and tank walls, while at the same time, reliquefying like mad.

So propane in Yanbu, and butane at Ras Tanura, although we were at the Juaimah terminal next door. Then off to Japan.

These are lovely ships at sea, although a bit under powered with only 15 000 horse power. Any head sea, and the speed really comes off. It was a bit desperate going up The South China Sea at 8 to 9 knots. In ballast, however, there are a bit on the 'stiff' side, and roll big style. A GM of about 6 metres and no way of reducing it.

The accommodation is superb, which after the *Borthwick*, was like comparing a back street B & B in Bombay with The Ritz in London. Apart from one thing, the toilets. Here the *Borthwick* comes out better, as on this one they are all the same size.

Each is a composite unit, and the old saying, it was so small that I could S,S,&S all at the same time. I'll leave you to work out what it means. Think crudely!

It was only later on another ship that I realized why these ships are known as the 'Green Ships'. The outside, hull accommodation etc is pale green, but then the bedding and even the towels are as well. You can't even escape it at meal times, as the table cover is also pale green, even the crockery has a pale green stripe. You can't escape from it at all. *It has nothing at all to do with the environment.*

There is, however, a very ugly side to life at sea, no matter how big or fast the ship. Plus, it is becoming an increasingly serious problem. 'Piracy.'

On passage from the Persian Gulf to Japan/Korea, it is rife from entering the Malacca Straits, passing Singapore, and as far up as The Luzon Channel, between Taiwan and The Philippines.

I am often asked, are the ships armed? Answer. No, we are merchant ships and do not carry arms. The reasoning being, from my point of view at least, that if I can shoot them, then they *will* shoot at us. If we do find that they are on board, then all we can do is preserve life, by giving them what they want, and letting them go. We are after all, insured for this. A cowardly approach? No, as they have killed even those offering even a token resistance, and are ruthless.

What then are they after? Cash and drugs. It is a well-known fact that at sea ships carry rather a lot of cash in the ship's safe. Anything up to 60 or 70 000 US Dollars.

Why? To pay the crew, who, if they come from third-world countries, as most do, demand to be paid in cash, after their mandatory allotments are paid.

If the crew are Filipino, a minimum of 80% of their basic wage must be paid by allotment, a bank draft really. On this then, they pay tax. The balance they get monthly in cash.

Going back to the *Norgas Challenger*, for example, my wages bill at the end of the month was 28 000 dollars in cash. As you cannot get US Dollars in some countries, while in others, it is very expensive, ships have to order in advance, and it is not an easy task I can tell you. Plus, damaged bills with a slight tear or a pen mark are not accepted, as the 'money changers' back home will not accept them.

It occurred to me recently that there was a way round this problem, which shipping companies could enforce by contract quite easily, and virtually eliminate the need to carry a lot of cash at all.

There used to be a thing used on British ships long ago. Just before I came to sea in 1972, it was getting phased out. That was a paper known as a 'note on owners'. It should not be difficult to set up an office at any major international airport, where these notes could be 'cashed in' for a seaman on his way home. All it needs is a bit of trust from both parties, which I know will not be easy.

What else are pirates after? Drugs. Not the illegal ones you understand, but the contents of a ship's medical locker, which depending on the ship's flag, can be very extensive, as well as expensive. The power of these also tends to be in excess of what can be bought legitimately. It is not unknown, for the pirates to take the lot. Anything else? Whatever takes their fancy. A wife's ring or other jewellery, and they are not beneath chopping a finger or two off, if say, a ring won't come off. Even mooring ropes are fair game, or any spares they fancy. They have even been known to take the whole ship, the crew never being seen again.

You can see therefore, that if reasonable attempts are made to stop them from boarding in the first place, then this is a far more pragmatic approach than carrying weapons.

How then, do they get aboard without being seen? There are a number of ways, but the most common is the two small boats trick. Two craft, at about 30 feet long, lie in the path of a ship with a heavy rope between them. Polyprop usually, as it floats, and probably came from a ship in the first place. When the bow catches the rope, the two small boats are then swung up against the hull, where they are aboard in seconds. It only usually works if a ship has a bulbous bow, but most do anyway. They get off the same way, and leave by letting one end of the rope go. It is not unknown for them to have raided the safe, tied up the captain, with the bridge team never having seen or heard a thing. They can do this on container ships running at anything up to 40 knots. A sharp blade slicing through at the waterline is all that is needed here. I've never tried it though.

Another but less used way, is the 'over the stern method'.

When a ship is running through the water, there is a small area, just behind the transom, where a boat can sit, and get pulled along by the wake. It may be a bit bouncy, but that won't bother them.

How ships go about preventing them from boarding, range from 'why didn't I think of that,' to the, 'just plain daft.'

We can start with one of the daftest I ever saw, and this was on a Shell tanker, a VLCC, in The South China Sea. Apart from having all their stern lights on, they also had their *big* ballast pumps running, and had thousands of tons of water flowing out from the manifolds amidships, and pouring off the deck all the way down to the stern. Daft? What it must have cost in fuel?

One that I used a lot, was to tow old mooring ropes from the stern. These eventually fray, and are a powerful deterrent in keeping anyone away from the stern.

The most common, however, is two men, one on each bridge wing with a searchlight. Plus every light on around the stern, and the accommodation, plus every access secured from the inside. If they are spotted coming on board, seal the bridge doors, and hit every alarm that you can find.

On small ships, a few parachute distress flares going up is usually effective.

Some ships even have dummy crew leaning on the rails, or 'talking' in a group on the poop deck.

The *Berge Sisar*, however, had one of the most complicated imaginable, called the 'Pifos system'. This translates into 'Pirates F--- Off System.' It took most of the night, just to set it up, so was a deterrent in itself by not working, as there were so many people about testing it.

More crewmen received powerful electric shocks, than even one pirate.

I never used it though, as I wasn't in the Far East on the *Sisar*, but NW Europe. If you met the master, you would understand how it came into being. On the *Raghnild*, however, we had the perfect system for one voyage, *Regina*. She would scare 'em.

Now believe it or not, I had never been to Japan before arriving on the *Berge Raghnild*, but I can assure you, it is the most convoluted country in which to get anything done easily. If there is a hard way, they will do it that way. Are they efficient? Like heck they are. Organized yes, but efficient, *no*.

This was my first experience with 'The Schedule.' Even a week out, we were starting on the schedule, theirs of course, not ours, as deflecting from the schedule by a millisecond meant yet another schedule. It must cost them a fortune. And remember, they have no sense of humour at all!

Everything is timed to the minute, and if a pilot boarding time is 07 30, and if they are at the ship's gangway at 07 29, then they will wait that minute, before boarding. The other thing is that they cannot do more than one thing at a time. I tried to get round this when I was Marine Superintendent to Qatar Liquefied Gas Company, but just plain gave up in the end. They can be infuriating.

Here is something you'll like, and perhaps Forth Ports plc should try.

In Japan, pilotage is not compulsory. For any ship, or in any port. So, where is the drawback? Fishermen. Plus of course, being able to speak Japanese. Even the Japanese have trouble with this one.

There was a master who didn't take a pilot just to anchor in an anchorage, before the ship went in to work cargo. The bill was ten times what it would have cost to take a pilot, as the fishermen objected that where he had anchored, he was scaring all the fish. Even although he was in exactly the same place as he would have been, if he had taken a pilot. So, everybody takes a pilot.

This discharge of course was not the usual, 'put her alongside and pump it all out', but was to two separate berths. Gas tankers are not allowed to move at night, so 'the schedule' was a protracted affair.

Now here is a joke that you *should not* try on Norwegians, or the Japanese, not unless you prefer insanity in trying to explain it. Going alongside the second berth, it was numbered in big letters 'K9.' "Oh" says I, in a jocular tone, "the dog berth then for us." Give the captain his due, he got it about a week later. I don't think the pilot ever will.

After discharging, and it all came out without any heel, apart from about 2 tons that fill the pump columns, and you just cannot get out, we set off back to the Persian Gulf, but first we had to pass Singapore, which is where they usually stop and take stores, and effect crew changes and so forth. Where we had to say farewell to the lovely *Regina*.

There was a bit of competition between the captain and me, as to who would be driving the crane. This is normally an ABs job, so why the two most senior on the ship? Because whoever wasn't driving the crane had to kiss goodbye to *Regina*. Sad isn't it, really.

On the way back, our orders came in, to load a full cargo of propane for Brazil, so the butane tanks had to be prepared.

Butane is extremely difficult stuff to get rid off, as it condenses into a liquid so easily. It doesn't matter whether it is a fully refrigerated ship, or a semi-refrigerated ship, it is still difficult. Not impossible mind, just difficult. Later on *Sisar*, I'll explain this again, as the captain there has a unique way of doing it. Doesn't work mind, but still unique.

Propane going to Brazil is for commercial use only, so quality is not that great an issue. So we just add in the butane, of which we had about 90 tonnes, but mix this in with 43 500 tons of propane, and you would be hard pushed to find it. This is infinitely more responsible than blowing it off to the atmosphere.

Loading in Juaimah, I had no option but to use the Ras Tanura panel, which I got away with, but as I loaded a full cargo in under 24 hours, made it difficult for anyone to detect that I had. I was loading at over 2000 tons per hour, and that *is fast*. Even for me. I also, had the ship fully sussed out by now, but I must confess, did give the captain a bit of a fright, as getting the ballast out in 24 hours was always going to be an issue. I had it all out in under 12 hours, by using a tanker trick, of 'jacking up the bow'. Putting on a heck of a lot of trim, and dropping the bulk out by gravity. This is faster than pumping it out, but *you have to know what you are doing*, as bending moments and shear forces come seriously into play.

For reliquefaction, I had it all on, and fully loaded up on maximum superfeed. The generators in the engine room were putting out nearly full load, and these are big engines. Their total output exceeds that of the ship's main engine, and this is a common feature on most gas tankers. The *Berge Sisar* has five generators, but there is a reason for that which I'll explain later.

So off we trot round to Fujairah, for bunkers. Fujairah came into being during the Iran Iraq war, as tankers waited here before making the dash in, to load, or in most cases, transhipped from others brave enough to do it. Or daft enough. I have a friend in Istanbul, who is a ship-owner, and he lost two 450 000 ton tankers on the same day to Exocet missiles.

It had been many years since I had been round the Cape, so it was pleasant again to pass close to The Comores Islands, and to pick up The Agullas current in the Mozambique Channel.

This current can, if you get it right, increase the ship's speed by as much as 7 knots, and carries on into The Atlantic, but whether you go to the south for its maximum effect, or come closer to land for a shorter distance is always a matter for conjecture. We had to stop just after clearing Cape Town, to do a test on the main engine electronics, and as we lay wallowing in the swell, a whale was spotted. Not any old whale however, this was a Blue Whale. I had only ever seen one from a distance before, when I was a cadet, but this one came alongside and gave itself a good old rub on the hull.

You cannot even begin to appreciate the size, until you see them close up. They are huge and it is good to see their numbers gradually increasing. Long may it continue.

We had Filipino crew on this ship, and they are a lot better now, than they were at the start. Then they were just a liability. Sadly, their place has been taken up by Indians. Officers too. They are just plain dangerous, and should not be allowed on gas tankers. They are largely the reason, that I've given up going to sea. The Steven N, later, will explain why. (Part 7).

Now Filipinos have no idea of responsibility whatsoever when going ashore, and they can find women, even where there aren't any. So, I typed out a list of diseases, and how to protect oneself when seeking out the 'ladies of the night'. Or in their case 'the day'.

Then put a complete box of condoms in the duty mess. There was a riot of humour when they got them at coffee time, but later, next day, there was one of them, a guy called Ronnie, some of them have weird names, like the unbeatable 'Jesus Contransfiguration'. Beat that! Ronnie was hanging around but not coming up to see me, until I could take it no longer.

"Ronnie, for goodness sake, what do you want to see me about?"

"Well sir," as he went a pale shade of grey, as they do, with their sallow skin, "it's about these condoms, do you have any more?"

"Come off it mate, we're still at sea, we haven't reached port yet."

He squirmed a little more, and then came out with "it's just that they are too big!"

"Sorry, but only one size available," as I burst out laughing, and he fled.

Our discharging ports were confirmed, and we all groaned. The first was a ship to ship transfer in Recife, in the north, to an older gas tanker, the *World Rainbow*, that was being used as floating storage, *and* we were to be the first to try it. The balance was for Santos, further south. I seem to be a magnet for these firsts, but there was one consolation, the *Borthwick* was in Nigeria. Please stay there.

To say that this ship was old is an understatement. It may have been modelled on the Ark. But it all went off without a hitch, well after they got all their plant on line it did.

Apart from one thing. Mooring wires. As we pulled in our after spring, it broke. This is a 38 mm wire with a breaking strain of over 200 tonnes. Only it didn't break. The splice pulled out. Someone was trying to save money by re-splicing this wire, but forgot to put a locking tuck in. This happens a lot in Bergesen. The *Berge Racine* had 16 like this. OCIMF inspectors please note next time you inspect a gas tanker, check the mooring wires. They should have Talaurits.

The captain and I left for leave in Santos, and old JB was back with a vengeance, promising that I would rue the day for the practical joke. It was to be another 8 years before we met again, and if you read this mate, I think you look more like a troll every day. So do Tafigura!

If you are going to steal, then *don't get caught*. You have to be extremely good to do this *and* get away with it, and if you are *that* good, then you don't need to steal it in the first place.

I, unfortunately seem to have the misfortune of ending up sorting out other people's 'mistakes'.

How do you steal 175 tonnes of liquid propane? Even this is flawed, as by my calculations later it was only possible to 'steal' 160 tonnes. Actually, it's dead easy. It's getting rid of it that is the hardest part. Sometimes, you can get away with it, but invariably dishonesty never prevails, and it all goes wrong.

Did this go wrong? Oh yes, $11.5 million dollars worth of 'going wrong'. A major insurance claim! This was going to be a nightmare in sorting it all out, especially with a boozed up captain on the loose.

So let's start at the beginning.

After my leave from the *Berge Raghnild*, I was asked to go to the office in Oslo, where I was given a most unbelievable task to do. To write a technical and safety instruction manual, for a ship called the *Berge Troll*.

Difficult? Too right, as I had never even seen the ship, far less had any idea about how it operated.

All I had to go on was my own experience, a huge portfolio of books and ships drawings, and the 'existing' manual. No wonder they needed someone with experience to do this. The existing manual was a perfect lesson in how *not* to do something. The chances of the ship blowing itself up were all too evident. But here I am, so let's see if I can score some 'brownie' points.

I had a quiet office, a secretary who did the typing, which was just as well as my speed at that time would have meant that I would still be there, and access to any other parts of their office that I needed. The secretary and I soon became friends, as she actually shared a similar sense of humour to mine, so she had to be weird in some way.

It took a full week, and even if I say so myself, was in fact rather good. It became the model for all their other ships.

The ship itself is a floating production ship, working off Cabinda in Angola, taking raw gas from the field, processing it, storing it in her tanks, and then transhipping it out in other gas tankers. It is by all accounts a pretty decent operation.

On her stern is what must rank as the world's biggest and most powerful outboard motor. It has a generator all to itself, and is used to keep the ship lying in a direction irrespective of what the weather is trying to do with it.

The original ship that was there was the *Berge Sisar*, and I remember being impressed with the 'outboard' when she was working as a transhipment gas tanker in Flushing, the Netherlands, when I was loading from her into the *Melrose* not long after I was promoted to Chief mate. This is why the *Berge Sisar* ended up with five generators. So, having left the office happy, I was in fact sent off to the *Berge Sisar*, joining in good old Yanbu.

There was a delay until we could board, so were put up in a hotel for as I recall 3 days. Saudi Arabia TV must rank alongside Norwegian TV in the total boredom stakes.

Now, here is a good one, this takes some believing, but it is totally true.

Remember that Moslems will not eat or even touch any meat from a pig. That's their prerogative if they believe that way. So how can they still serve up bacon in a hotel for breakfast? Easy, it was beef bacon. Work that one out if you can. It tastes as bad as it sounds too.

So we get into a little boat and chug off to join the ship.

It became very apparent, almost immediately in fact, that the chief mate I was relieving had very little clue about what he was supposed to have been doing. After an hour with the captain, he also came across as someone of limited knowledge. How he became captain is interesting, so I'll put it in here.

You may recall in Part 3, that I said that, 'could other people's Navy's be as bad as our own?' Well, to the Portuguese, add the Norwegian (at least in this case).

Our captain, was sponsored by the chairman of Bergesen to sail a yacht in a round-the-world race, when an officer in the Navy. They, I believe, did rather well, so much so, that he came to work for Bergesen on a gas tanker. Fine training for a gas tanker captain eh? Being able to sail a yacht should come in real handy with liquid gas!

With virtually no handover, meant I had to find out for myself just what was going on, so with the, also new gas engineer, had a poke around, and decided that this ship was not 'load ready'.

There was more bad news. The captain had gone and tendered his 'Notice of Readiness' for the time we all came on board.

This is an official document, which declares that the ship is 'ready in all respects to load a full cargo of' in this case 'propane'.

So, we are not taking any coolant then captain? Seeing as your last cargo was a full cargo of butane!

"Oh no, we use the Ras Tanura Panel, I'll show you how it works." he says with an annoying superior air, common in any countries Navy. And, ex-Queen's Harbour Masters, such as 'good' old Tony.

"Don't bother, I already know," I said, despairingly.

The saddest thing here, is that they are now totally dependent on committing fraud, come what may, as the arrival calculation is false. They actually cheat themselves out of 25 tonnes of freight.

So the gas engineer and myself set about finding out just what we do have in the ship's tanks, which according to the brain at the top is 175 tonnes of propane.

"Right Jan, let's gather it all up, and put it into No 3 cargo tank, measure it, and see what we've got." So, off we go.

Two days later, we measured it. Surprise Surprise! It ain't propane! What we had was 375 tonnes of what can best be described as bupane, a mixture, plus the lowest temperature we could get it down to was -18 deg C before we ran out of vapour. Remember, we cannot go into a vacuum.

'Ras Tanura panel' it is going to have be then. I hated this thing, as you may have gathered. It is so easy to do the job properly, once you know what you are doing. Very few actually do.

However, how did they get 375 tonnes of bupane? This is *really* hard to believe, but I'll tell you anyway.

To get the ship in a load ready condition, 175 (160) tonnes in the deck tanks should have been enough to gas up one tank, and provide enough vapour to cool the tank to –42 deg C. Then take say 4000 tonnes of coolant in this tank, before readying the ship to load. Again, if you know what you are doing, then you will not lose any of it. Coolant taken is included in the Bill of Lading figure anyway, so you don't, or shouldn't lose.

When bringing down the liquid gas from the deck tanks, you must remember that it is under high pressure, and hot, anything up to +35 deg C, and 17 bar pressure. It is brought down slowly, passed through the vapouriser, and sent to the tanks as a vapour, before reliquefying to remove the heat from the tank.

Still with me? Good.

Doing it properly, and there is plenty of time on passage to do this, will take anything up to 36 hours, just to do one tank. The butane is not actually lost, but mixes in with the propane, again only showing as a trace, as it becomes super-cooled.

Ah, but our super skilled brain at the top, and his sidekick, my predecessor, have got their own unique way of changing butane into propane. Doesn't work, but who cares? *I do* actually.

They have developed the 'quick' method, which takes 20 minutes. This is how it goes. On chosen day, open tanks vent risers to atmosphere. When no more vapour seen coming out, assume tank liquid free (which it isn't, as there is not enough heat to vapourize the liquid). Open deck tanks (liquid propane, at 17 bars) to all main cargo tanks ignoring all the considerable banging noises, as pipelines contract. Assume the liquid propane when it arrives at the bottom of the tank will vapourize, and push all the butane vapour out of the riser.

Go and have a beer as job well done. Good eh!

This is what actually happens. The remaining butane will not boil off into a vapour, as no heat is being supplied to the sumps, where it is all lying. There is no more vapour seen coming out, as the liquid butane is stable. You need to be crazy to let the deck tanks go at this rate, mad, or just plain stupid. Idiotic, _____, _____, _____, _____, _____, _____, insert your own adjectives here please.

As soon as the pressure is released, the liquid cools extremely rapidly. Just by passing the valve on the deck tank, it will cool from +35 to –42 deg C, in fractions of a second, and only a good quality stainless steel could take that kind of thermal shock. It will not be a liquid which arrives initially, at the bottom of the tank, but an extremely fast moving vapour, also at -42 deg C. (1 cubic metre of liquid makes approximately 500 cubic metres of vapour.) Any butane vapour it hits will be immediately liquefied, and what goes out the riser is most likely to be propane, not butane as planned. Still with me? It's a wonder nobody was hurt.

When Jan, the gas engineer, and I heard this, we were both just lost for words, and just looked at each other shaking our heads. I can see that this captain and I are not going to get along. But remember captain, you could always be a Chief Harbour Master on the River Forth. No skills required here whatsoever, in anything. You should fit in well.

The day comes when we have to load, and I could see that we are going to need a vapour return to flare. This is normally connected, but not used, except in an emergency, as anything going through it is lost, and Aramco will reckon about five times as much as actually went through, did go through, and bill the ship accordingly.

"Okay then Jan, we'll use a small gas tanker trick at the start, 'throttling'." Do not attempt this unless you *really know* what you are doing. Few do.

The Ras Tanura panel has been set up and off we go, pulling the initial cargo into our heel in No 3 tank. All the reliquefaction plant wound right up from the very start. It is normal to start slowly, and then build up the rate, but I needed to get as much really cold liquid gas into this heel, to cool it, so started rather more quickly, at the same time, bleeding off as much as I could to the sprays.

After 30 minutes, the throttling had to be stopped, but it had already done its job.

The safety valves lift at 250 millibars, so I don't have a lot to play with here, and I very nearly got away with it, as by the time the pressure was up to 240 millibars, it was stabilizing.

We were just about to clap each other on the back, having very nearly succeeded when the 'phone rang. It was the engine room. They were going to have to shut down two generators as they were overheating. Damn. This meant shutting down one set of compressors, and we had lost.

160 tonnes of hot vapour had to be sent to the flare, there was no other way. Even sneaking it up our own riser was spotted.

The cargo did eventually stabilize after some 6 hours, and I eventually got it all in.

Getting the ballast out, even caused a problem, and I still had 10 000 tons in when we sailed for Stenungsund in Sweden.

The saddest thing was that this captain actually thought that he had done very well.

This was the only gas tanker in 25 years that I have blown a safety valve on, and I got a real fright. Why? Because I was sitting on it at the time! It went off 20 millibars early.

The Suez Canal was its usual pain in the butt, and the rest of the voyage was uneventful, apart from one thing, the captain wants the bridge front painted. Not a big job, but? The Brain of Bergen, wants it done the Norwegian Navy way?

What is so different? He wants the glass on all the windows taken out, "to make a neater job off it."

"You are joking," I said, "they can't even get these out in the breakers' yard. They shatter if you try, and getting spares will take months, if they are available at all!"

"Oh no, just take out all the screws, and push them in from outside." Nearly fifty feet up mind, from the main deck.

"I'm having nothing to do with this," says I walking away.

"You will do as you are told," says he, a touch annoyed I think.

"For the final time, no."

So he organized some of the crew to prove the mate wrong, and started on the port side 'bridge window".

Now, if you have a mad idea, and want to try it, you start with a wee one, in a corner, where nobody will see if it all goes wrong.

By this time the gas engineer and myself are watching from a safe distance, along with most of the engineers. Even the cook thought it was daft and joined us.

He is only starting with the biggest window on the whole bridge front, about 2 metres by 1 metre, armoured glass, 8 millimetres thick.

Ten screws out, six sheared, to be drilled out later, and four mangled heads, when *crash*, it shattered, frosted over completely.

"It will come out okay now captain, but getting the 50 000 bits back in might be tricky though."

If looks could kill, I'd be dead. But it didn't end there though, he had another go, on a porthole. Same thing. Then he gave up, and we just painted the bridge front in the usual way. The bridge now had its own air conditioning, hard to control though.

Now Stenungsund in Sweden, I had been to many times in the past, but not with something as big as this. You can get in alright, but getting out is much more difficult, as there is a bridge in the way. Actually, this bridge is not the original, as a Greek tanker came in one day, not long after it opened, and gave it a bit of a bump. Well, actually demolished one end of it, so it had to be rebuilt.

Getting the *Berge Sisar* out under it, means moving all the fuel to the after end, then loading more fuel aft to capacity, then trimming back by the stern to 14.5 metres with ballast. Normally the trim would be in the region of 1 to 2 metres by the stern.

It looks ridiculous, but it works, so what do looks matter?

Samples were taken from the cargo tanks here for analysis, which would be carried out, while we took fuel. It was just after this that I started to detect that something was very wrong, very wrong indeed. Waiting on the berth, was another load of sample bottles. To the educated in the gas trade, this means one of two things. The samples had failed, or there was not sufficient space in the tanks ashore, and this was a legitimate way of buying some time. It was in this case, the first, they had failed, so did the second set, as did the third set. All failed.

By this time, the captain was well into the gin (which he should not have been) and had arranged for all his pals from Bergen to come for a party. I was left to sort the mess out, as this was a massive problem. The contaminant, as I at first thought was hydrogen sulphide, not just traces, lots of it. We have a piece of equipment we use to detect trace elements of different gases, usually when changing grades, or gas freeing to open up the tanks. It is a beautifully simple thing by the Draeger Company. Stick in a tube and off you go.

Normal calibration of up to 100 ppm (parts per million) within three 'bellows full' went 'off the scale' after even a half. This had to be something other than hydrogen sulphide, or we were in deep s---.

With the captain out of the way, I 'phoned the *Berge Raghnild*, which had loaded at the same berth, 2 days before us, and asked for my old mate 'JB'. The ship was arriving in Houston, Texas, USA, at the time. It went like this,

"JB, when you get in, call in a second set of cargo surveyors, and get an independent analysis of your product on board. Plus make sure it all adds up."

"Why?" he asked.

"Because our cargo is off spec, *big style*, and I think yours may be too."

"Can you tell us what is wrong?"

"Nope, sorry pal, at this stage, we simply just do not know, but we need to maintain our independence, until we do."

The ships Radio Officer, was Indian, a race I have come to detest, asked who was paying for the call. "Put it down to owners," I said.

"But the only man who can do that is the captain!" he said.

I replied, "right, you go and tell that drunken bum, that his chief officer is trying to get his company out of an $11.5 million dollar hole, and has just used up $50 off his budget in doing so. See if you can get any sense out of Captain Larsen, because I'm buggered if I will try again." He put the call down to owner's account.

So what was wrong? The cargo tanks are showing hydrogen sulphide in the vapour, but the deck tanks aren't, which suggests that this ship wasn't responsible for the contamination.

So what exactly was the contaminant?

It wasn't hydrogen sulphide, but something far worse, Dimethylsulphide!

This is not a ship's problem, but a refineries *big* problem, as my next call to the *Berge Raghnild*, confirmed that they had the same contaminant, in their propane, which had been by now, declared 'off spec'.

So, the *Berge Sisar* should be in the clear. Well no, not really, as the charterers, Stargas in London, were getting curious, and sent a telex which went like this,

"Can you please explain how, you managed to load a full cargo of propane, after a full cargo of butane, *without* taking any coolant?"

Our dumb, thick idiot of a Radio Officer, took this straight to the captain, (by-passing me, who was handling the 'claim'), and replied in his stupor,

"The vessel cooled its tanks, by preparing them with propane held in the ship's deck tanks".

Then he went back to his 'party'.

When I saw this next morning, I was dumbstruck, and got a hold of the radio officer, and asked, "did you send this?" He was in an argumentative mood, but when lying flat on his back with my fist about to come down on his face, conceded that this was so.

Now we are all in deep s---! How are we going to get out of this?

I pondered for an hour or so, thinking through all the ramifications, then called the office in Oslo, going *very* high up. Technical Director.

"Mr Andersen, Doug Harvey, sorry to call you, but have you received the reply from the master re-Stargas of London."

"Yes, we have it, it is just about to be sent, is there a problem?"

I replied, "Get it stopped. Fast."

There was a brief period, before he came back with "It's stopped."

Now, can you explain please Doug? You would not have called me if there was not something amiss." He sent a superintendent, by air to help sort out the mess. Temporarily, at least, but it kicked back later.

So we are back to "how do you steal 175 (160) tonnes of propane?" Now, take a deep breath, and digest this slowly. It takes some believing, and I know, as I am writing this. The ship is on charter to Stargas of London. Easy enough, but go back one cargo, and the ship has been chartered (by another charterer) to take a full cargo of butane to Japan.

So far so good.

The cargo before this was to take a full cargo of propane to Stenungsund, on behalf of charterers. Who? Stargas!

Now, it gets interesting. The ship has to sail heavy by the stern, just to get under the bridge, so declares an out-turn figure of 248 tonnes (73 tonnes of liquid gas, and 175 tonnes of vapour).

Off this 248 tonnes, the captain makes a statement to consultants that he pumped 175(160) tonnes of liquid into the deck tanks. However, we know it takes 175 tonnes of vapour, just to gas up the ship, and with this type of tanks, he cannot go into vacuum, so there is an immediate shortfall of 102 tonnes. It doesn't add up!

It gets better, or worse, depending on your point of view. When the ship is in Ras Tanura, ready to load a full cargo of butane, the 'Ras Tanura Panel' comes into play again, only this time, not to show 'lower temperatures' than actually exist, but 'higher' ones. The calculation came out at 285 tonnes of declared propane. Ah! But even the calculation is phoney, as the computer will not accept a temperature of minus 6 for propane, so even that was changed. The calculation was made for butane, with an also forged liquid density but the answer was 'called' propane.

They even got an independent surveyor to sign it!

Plus. They even got away with it. Well nearly. I re-wrote the master's statement in a different style, and got it faxed off. All we can do now, is pray, and keep our fingers crossed. And everything else as well. We did, then, but now in 2004, well...we'll see.

Back to Di-methylsulphide then. The *Berge Raghnild* was fortunate, as she had coated cargo tanks, was diverted to Plaquemine, up the river Mississippi, so could pump it out for processing. It is the only plant in the USA that could do this. The *Berge Sisar* is going to have to be chemically washed, after discharging in Terneuzen, the Netherlands, the only plant that can process this in NW Europe.

Now it gets mind boggling, a solution of 3% caustic acid in solution with fresh water, then pumped under high pressure by oil tanker's tank washing machines (20 in all, made from stainless steel). Plus it all had to go through a 24-inch tank lid hole, the only way in, or out. We took 5000 tonnes of fresh water (industrial quality), and literally, miles of stainless steel wire to hang these from inside the tank. How much caustic? 75 tonnes of it, in 208 litre barrels. Then submersible pumps, and high pressure pumps for all the wee corners that the machines cannot get into.

You really have to be inside a 20 000 cubic metre tank, to appreciate how big they are. Take my word for it, this is going to be some job.

Extra crew had to be flown in, although I still think it could have been done by ship's staff, as it wasn't me who was going to do it. No, the captain wanted me off the ship, and a Norwegian mate instead. I had to go to Oslo to explain it all. And this after saving his ship from foundering, we were minutes from going seriously aground.

The second mate was frightened of him, so, when the ship started dragging its anchor, as the weather got worse, didn't know what to do. Fortunately, I got to the bridge on time, got the engine started, and the still boozed up captain up as well, then spent the next 40 minutes getting the anchor up, as the old man could hardly see where he was going, far less where his ship was.

When I met the new mate next day, I couldn't resist a good dig at our 'master', and said, as I left "watch out for that effing idiot in there, he hasn't been sober for weeks. They are bound to ask me about it in the office anyway. Well, why should he take the credit for all of my work. I even wrote his reports for him."

So, I went to Oslo, spent a night in a hotel, and explained it all to a very stunned office staff.

Then went home, as I was off to the *Berge Racine* in about a week.

Talk about out of the frying pan, and into the fire! It was worse. I could hardly believe my eyes when I saw it.

There was not a single safety system that was fully operational.

Now my going over Larsen's head had got around the company like wildfire, and the officers on the *Berge Racine* had decided only to talk in Norwegian. I was being sent to Coventry, so to speak. Childish lot. That is never going to work, as although I don't speak Norwegian, I understand a lot more than people think. I can swear in it too.

Right, in the office on the first day, as they are babbling away, I asked "okay, if you're all so brilliant, how come this ship is using the wrong cargo record book?" They didn't know, and that was the end of the Norwegian.

There are two types, one for noxious substances, such as acrylonitrile, the other for all other substances, which is all this ship would ever carry. Even anhydrous ammonia isn't Noxious.

How did the ship get into this state, as Bergesens are not a 'mean' company?

It is all to do with the regular master's desire to have the lowest budget in the company.

It might have been the lowest for the last 5 years, but it is soon going to be the highest! I started ordering up, such as 16 mooring wires, at £2500 each, for delivery in Singapore, plus 16 new 'Karat' tails (this is a length of rope usually about 8 metres to give a bit of 'spring') plus 16 new Tonsberg links, just so we could get the certificates, as this is now a requirement in Saudi Arabia.

In all, I had 38 tonnes of stores coming. That is a lot, but I made sure the wires were not returned, by throwing away all the old ones before they arrived.

We were discharging when I joined in Izmit, Turkey, which even before the earthquake which so tragically struck a few years back was a dirty filthy place. We were making bupane for them, loading straight into smaller gas tankers, before it was shipped out to other parts of the country. Making bupane is not easy, as it is made in the manifolds before going ashore, and it is tricky in getting the mix just right. Proper bupane, not any old mixture as on the *Sisar*. However, this was the last cargo before we went on to pentane, and the *Berge Rachel* was taking over. They don't know to make it at all, so I would have to explain it, as the ships passed each other in the Red Sea.

What really annoyed me here, was that the chartering department would not allow me to 'pump out the heel'. Seemingly, once before they had done this, but didn't get paid for it, so refused to allow it again. This is really petty politics, as I am going to have to blow off over 440 tonnes, when it could be used usefully. I'll bet you that if I blew it all over Oslo, they would think differently, but it's okay to blow it all over the Sudan, or Saudi Arabia. I was going to pump it out on the sly anyway, until the master found out and put his foot down. So we sailed with it, 180 tonnes of vapour, and 260 tonnes of liquid. We could discount the butane liquid, as I managed to get all that ashore, one dark night, so to speak.

So, off to the glorious Marlboro canal once more, who could we upset this time? Only one of the pilots, and *it was* a pure accident, but I thought it was hilarious.

At night, heading towards Ismailiah, the canal divides, you can use either side equally well, and the pilot came out with, "mister mate, it is time for me to go and pray," which prompted the remark, "why? Don't you know the way?" He had no sense of humour, but got down to pray on the port side of the wheelhouse, and I thought no more about it.

Unfortunately, the captain appeared, and promptly fell head over heels over him, muttering in Norwegian, "who left that lying there?" The pilot muttering in Arabic, "what the heck," or something like that.

Then I got the blame! "Get lost to that," in English, which should translate quite well into both Norwegian and Arabic.

Now 3 days south we get orders to tank clean, and prepare for pentane. This is a type of condensate that is also known as stabilized crude oil, and is mainly a by-product from LNG production. Liquefied Natural gas, which is carried at -158 to -162 degrees Celsius, depending on quality. The only problem with it is its volatility. We normally load LPG to 98% of the tank volume, but with Pentane we can go up to 99%. But first I've got 440 tonnes of propane to dispose of and this isn't easy.

Many years ago, Shell tried this on one of their gas carriers, and came to the same conclusion, just hope you never have to do it. I'm going to see if I can pump it out, but first of all I'm going to have to reset the cargo pumps low amp cut outs. With there being almost 19 metres for the cargo to have to fill up the pumps before the discharge valves, they will have to be set as low as possible. The electrician did it, while we got the flexible cargo hoses out, connected up to the manifold, with the other end supported on the crane, about 3 metres above the sea. That should help to vapourize off the liquid, which was going to come out rather fast. It was an 8-inch pipe after all.

Once the ship had slowed down, and everything was sealed up, I had a go, and did manage to get one pump going, but not for long, it was just a wee bit too high, before the thermal cut out jumped in. I tried with another pump, more success this time, as I got about 50 tonnes out. But oh! Was this risky! In all I managed to get about 120 tonnes out, but I really couldn't afford to damage a pump, so decided to boil off the rest with the sump heaters. It just takes longer. In the end it took a week to boil it all off, before I could go in with inert gas, and I was getting a bit sick of it by then. I certainly wouldn't like to try it again, even although I do enjoy the kudos of 'an expert'.

Let's try and put this into some kind of perspective, rather than the usual, 'let's just hush it all up. Okay.' 440 tonnes of combined liquid and vapour, the breakdown being, 180 tons of vapour, which equates to 81 600 cubic metres of vapour. One *empty* ship's volume (empty of liquid gas, this is vapour). 260 tonnes of liquid propane, which is 520 cubic metres of liquid approximately, as density is in range 0.500 to 0.510. We'll be generous here. We'll use 0.500. Allowing for a condensing ratio of 500 to 1, 520 cubic metres of liquid is 260 000 cubic metres of vapour and we add on the ship's volume to give 341 600 cubic metres of propane vapour. *However*, this is 100% pure vapour. It won't burn as it is too rich. The flammable range is 2.3% to 5.6% in air, so we'll take a mean of 4%, which is 1/25th of 100%. 341 600 x 25 = 8 million 540 thousand cubic metres. Now that *is* a lot. Let's equate this to double decker buses. 10 metres long, 3 metres wide, and 5 metres high. Total volume, 150 cubic metres. 8 540 000 / 150 = 56 733 buses, which if parked side by side would stretch for 170.2 kilometres. Now that is scary. Plus this is only one ship, getting rid of something that could have been used usefully.

Next time you are standing in the rain, waiting for a bus, remember, I've got them all.

But we'll take it one stage further, and you can check this for yourself, as I lifted this information off the Internet. Total number of gas carriers over 70 000 cubic metres = 30 Total capacity 2 369 445 cubic metres. Total number of gas carriers 50 to 70 000 cubic metres = 18 Total capacity 879 006 cubic metres. Total number of gas carriers 22 to 40 000 cubic metres = 9 Total capacity 227 149 cubic metres. Total number of gas carriers 8 to 15 000 cubic metres = 14 Total capacity 154 493 cubic metres. Assuming they will all go to dry dock twice every five years, then this adds up to an awful lot of gas being blown away needlessly. I started off just using propane, which is relatively light. Then consider butane, ammonia, ethylene, propylene, butylenes, isoprene, ethane, and the chemical gases, propylene oxide, vinyl chloride monomer, and 1-3 butadiene. The last two being known carcinogens.

I'm not even going to begin trying to work out serious tonnages for this, that would require a mathematical model, which is beyond me.

A rough figure then perhaps. I estimate it at between 8 000 and 12000 tonnes, which is anything around 5000 tonnes per year, blown away into the atmosphere. You'll need 600 000 buses, plus. *And* this is only *one* company, there are many more. Do you still wonder why the seasons are changing? I'm not trying to be alarmist, just trying to open debate, to see if this can be reduced in any way. Well it can.

Technology exists to build the 'first' diesel powered LNG carrier, they are normally steam turbines, as the 'boil off' gas is used in the burners as a fuel. This technology could then also be used to run a ships diesel generators, and all this 'blown off' gas used as fuel. Or at the very least, some of it.

A little history here. Remember in Part 1 when I spoke of the *Melrose*, built by Geo. Gibsons?

She was an experimental diesel-powered LNG tanker, built in 1972, but with a difference, she was also a pressurized LNG tanker. Tanks to −162 degrees Celsius, but also to 5 bar, rather than 250 millibars.

After setting fire to the engine room three times, the project was shelved, and she ran ethylene instead for most of her working life. Unfortunately, the technology wasn't available at the time, even although this company was years ahead of its time. The engineers are still around who can confirm this, and I know where a few of them still are.

If burning LPG works in a diesel generator, and there is no reason why it shouldn't, then the next generation of LNG tankers will be much more efficient than the current steam-powered ones. It might even be possible to burn LPG in an inert gas generator.

Perhaps I shouldn't mention it here, but the current 135 000 cubic metre LNG tankers for Qatargas, burn up to 195 tonnes of fuel, LNG plus fuel oil, per day at sea. There are ten of them. That amounts to a lot of fuel.

A diesel burns about a third for the same speed at sea.

In the early 1980s, and it was on the *Melrose* that I first got involved in this, we experimented with back loading nitrogen, at the same time as discharging. When you think about it, the logic is sound. If you bring up the tank pressure above the 'saturated vapour pressure', then the vapour will condense, the higher the pressure the better. This results in the tank atmosphere being changed from LPG to nitrogen, so the 'entire' cargo is discharged. I next came across this on the *Traquair*, where instead of nitrogen, we used methane, as it was possible to separate out the methane with our next grade, the result being nothing was lost.

Sadly, this seems to have fallen by the wayside, it being much 'easier' to just blow it away. Green parties please take note.

Blowing off 440 tonnes is the exception rather than the rule, as is getting caught, in the case of the *Berge Sisar*.

Is this problem confined to the large gas carriers? Oh no, nothing is that simple, even on the small ones, they are all at it. There, they just plain steal it to suit.

Why?

The oldest problem in the book. Vanity. Not to be seen as having lost any cargo. Indians are the worst for this. They don't want to 'take the blame'. That won't last much longer though. Read Part 7.

For me, as a marine investigator, this is just pure honey. All I need to build a case, is the smallest chink, just to get in, and it invariably starts when someone has slipped up in the cargo figures. More on this subject at the end of Part 5. Remember, I've been around this business a long time, and I know every dodge going.

My advice to my chief mates before I gave up sailing was always the same. Put down exactly what it says on the gauges, and *don't* cheat in any way. It takes a lot of pressure off them.

I'll illustrate this simply. I investigated a case which had been subrogated from an underwriter. It bounced around London for a year or so, before it came to my desk. One document, about four lines was 'phoney'. It had been written after the event, to cover someone's back. That was enough to 'get me in'. Three months later, the ship's owner was trying to explain away 31 counts of technical un-seaworthiness, two counts of cargo theft, and one fraud.

With the advent of the ISM Code, this is a marine investigators dream card. Even more ways to trip up a crew who wish to 'cheat'.

Next time you want to try it, just consider that it might end up on my desk, and I will find out. I have been known to go back 2 years in a ship's history, looking for a trend. *I always find it.*

On a semi-refrigerated ship, I also know how to check the trim (a lot is 'acquired' this way), and I can tell when a pressure gauge has been tampered with. Even from the paperwork. It's a clever mate indeed who can beat me, so save yourself some embarrassment, don't try. You'll for certain never beat the lawyers, especially after I brief them.

Just think, if someone had been a little bit more responsible in Oslo, then this would probably not have come out into the open. Maybe some good will come of that decision.

But it's not only cargo that is stolen. On the *Steven N* (Part 7), they steal the fuel as well! *And,* they have deck tanks!

But, back to the *Berge Racine*. Remember, we are going to load pentane.

The loading was to be done in two parcels, the first in Kuwait, where it is unbearably always hot, the balance by tanker, which was coming down from Iran, for transhipment in Fujairah.

This ship is fortunate that its cargo tank insulation is 'perlite', a ground-up type of volcanic rock, and very efficient. I loaded another time in Kuwait on a different ship, which had polystyrene blocks held on with 'mastic', a type of industrial glue, which when the cargo went in, melted and it all fell off. We were weeks down there putting in all back on. It is not a job for the claustrophobic. It's damned uncomfortable as well.

Have you ever worked with Iranians? They are awkward, and I was at college with some of them too, which was tricky, as there were Iraqis there too. This one who came on the tanker started telling me how to load my own ship. "Just go back to Kharg Island please, we are quite capable here."

Filled up to the brim, and quantities agreed, we set off for Japan, going to Oita, for the interested. Everything was fine until we came into the South China Sea. This is a very distasteful story, and very sad, even now, 10 years on. One night, the Navtex alarm went off at midnight, but was so low that the second mate didn't hear it. It was not in the chartroom, as it should have been, but in a corner at the back of the wheelhouse, so the message was missed. Another one came in at 04 00, when I arrived on the bridge for my watch, and always checked this before taking over. It read "tanker Cosmos A reports on fire in position ******** *******. All vessels please render immediate assistance. Hong Kong radio receiving information and handling distress."

This was a tanker under the Maltese flag of some 32 000 tonnes, with a full cargo of petrol, and 35 crew on board. It must have been a bad one, but fire on ships can burn undetected, sometimes for days, before breaking out, and they are often very difficult to put out. I had a very bad one in Wilhelmshaven in Germany on a tanker, in the cargo pump room, that took us 4 hours to extinguish, and we had *everything* going in, from foam, to carbon dioxide, even steam, before we got it out with Halon 1301, which unfortunately isn't used any more. We used masses of stuff, like 1500 gallons of foam. All the time we were standing on top of 80 000 tonnes of crude oil. The damage was colossal.

The second message at 04 00 was 'Crew now abandoning Cosmos Vessels Berge Enterprise, and a Burmese ship (whose name escapes me,) shown attending. Position now ******** ********." Which is only an hour away from us.' Ten minutes later the ship exploded. It was like a nuclear bomb going off, and the force of the explosion blew the bow over 3 miles away from the stern.

Why sad? Because our captain refused to go and assist, breaking the most fundamental law of the sea, you help each other, even in times of war.

Why did he refuse? I never did find out.

I could have taken over and done it myself, but I still had my ears ringing from the office after the *Berge Sisar* fiasco, about taking over.

One of the most poignant moments for me was hearing on the VHF, "we've rescued 26 from a lifeboat, another nine are in a life-raft which was last seen being drawn into flames. Crew were seen jumping out, but I think they may be lost."

Nine people died that night, and while I do not say that we could have saved them, we could at the very least have tried.

But it didn't end there.

Next day I discovered that our Navtex had been sabotaged. Who it was, was not hard to work out, but I already had all the messages in my briefcase, and they stayed there until I left the company. A new Navtex was ordered for Singapore, and when our captain left in Singapore, just said, "Bye chief'n." I did not reply.

For once in my life at sea, I did not know what to do, if anything, about this, until many months later when I left the company, reported the matter and one other to the technical manager. I never found out what the outcome of that meeting was, but I had been truly sickened by it, and did not really care if he was sacked or not.

For many years afterwards, my bridge standing orders contained this, "following a serious incident while I was on another ship, any incoming distress messages from any source, are to be brought to my immediate attention, even if they are on the other side of the world. I and only I, will decide if they are too far away."

I should imagine, that when this becomes public knowledge, that there may be serious ramifications.

Now, 10 years on, this incident still affects me from time to time, and badly. I no longer even discuss it. Even writing this was extremely difficult. I trust you, the reader, will understand.

To end this sorry tale, on our way back from Japan, we passed the bow section being guarded by a tug. It was hard to imagine how 32 000 tonnes of petrol could have burned out in little over an hour. Judging by the discolouration of the 'wreck', the fire was extremely intense.

To Oita, where we had to discharge, I was by this time getting really fed up with 'the schedule', especially when a request came through for the ship's calculated figures regarding quantities on board.

That was a new one, they were willing to accept ship's figures *without* checking them. You could have 2000 tonnes of water mixed in, and get away with it. But I don't cheat, well, I bend the rules occasionally. In my next book, I'll let you in to all the secrets of how to 'cheat', and not get caught. Some of the things we used to get up to are mind-boggling. Especially with the US Coast Guard!

Holding this ship alongside was going to be a problem, as some of our mooring wires were breaking as they came off the drums. You cannot mix ropes and wires on the same 'lead,' say, as springs, but you can use ropes paired up as springs. So that is the way it would have to be. Two wires did part during the discharge, just with their own weight on them, but my crew were primed up, and got ropes out without anyone noticing.

I was using eight cargo pumps to discharge here through two lines, and they were 'humming'. Don't do this unless you put in 'surge protection'.

Half way through, after 25 000 tonnes were out, we were asked to stop, while they changed shore tanks. In any other country, they can do this without stopping, but the schedule said we had to stop, so they want us to stop. We didn't, as it would take 30 minutes for the thermal trips to reset, before we could start again. It is much easier to open the bypasses back to the tanks, and close the manifolds.

This is one they did not know about, and boy were they impressed, as we were back on full rate within 5 minutes, so that is the schedule buggered up. Then came the best one. Could you please slow down so we can get in line with the schedule? In a word, no! Tough.

Remember I said that these types of tanks cannot go into a vacuum.

Well, all the time we are discharging, the inert gas generator is going flat out, filling up the ullage space, keeping the oxygen content about 3%.

There is another trick that some Bergesen ships use, and if their office ever found out about this one, there would be hell to pay. They just open the mast risers, and put air in. Highly dangerous, but like a lot of things in this company, have become the norm. Why?

In a word. Arrogance. All the cargo came out, as I had sussed out how to do this now, and we sailed with 3 tonnes. A record. But I'm not telling you how it's done. If I can do it, so can they. They can puzzle it out for themselves.

We sailed just before breakfast, and I can start preparing for the next cargo. So tank lids off, big fans on, and start sweeping through with air. I could have left it for a few days, but you never know what the weather is going to be like, or what might be around the corner. It kept me away from the 'captain' as well, which was equally important.

Now I am going to find out just why these tanks cross girders are cracking. In the end it took me 2 weeks, but I got it.

To get out the residue, in this case, about 3 tonnes, some will put on the ejector, and ditch it overboard. This is oil however, and that is pollution. By sheer chance, I found a use for it. We filled up every plastic drum we could find, and the rest evaporated. It is a brilliant degreaser, and as we are going to have to install 16 new wires, we are going to need a lot of degreaser, as it can be a right messy job. The grease acts a lubricant within the wire, and protects it from rusting. They should last up to 7 years if properly looked after.

Years later, when I worked for Qatar Liquefied Gas, some of the Japanese masters reckoned on changing them every 2 years in dry dock. Fat chance here boys, you can look after them like everybody else.

Putting on new wires may look easy, and I suppose it is really, when you get the hang of it. First of all, they are heavy, as it is 38 mm wire, and they are 200 metres long, so we're talking about a ton or so each. The first problem is getting them off the reel, or sometimes, a coil, which is harder. With a rope, you just pull it from the middle, and away you go. You can't do this with a wire though, as they 'kink', and if it kinks, then it is destroyed.

Indians are notoriously dangerous when handling wires. You watch them like a hawk. I don't know why, if it is something inherent, or they plainly just don't know. This isn't a racist remark, just a plain fact.

My crew are Filipino, and succeed in unrolling the first one, manage to get it full of potential kinks, and thought they could pull them out with a winch. Whew! Caught them just in time.

"You have to roll them out one at a time along the full length of the wire."

To give them their due, they soon caught on.

I had to leave them to get on with it then, as there's so much to fix, but they were putting on four a day, which is rather good going by anybody's standards.

This is of course after we have passed Singapore, which was eventful in only one way, a change of masters.

The regular master, was notorious, and a lot of people thought that he would 'soon sort him (me) out'. It was the other way round, and I was one of the few people who could 'handle him', which he only found out about in my handover notes, when I left. He was not pleased, and claimed that even his wife 'couldn't handle him'. Poor woman, some people just never get it right.

Into the cargo tanks then, the Iranian pentane was full of mud, which was left on board, not pumped out in Japan. It has to be cleaned off with rags, and every night, to 'save money' as I had ruined his budget, they had to be washed, and hung out to dry.

On any other ship, they are used once, and then incinerated. Who got the job? Not me, our Indian cadet, who was about as much use as a chocolate fireguard. (That is not a racist remark, but one of the few 'polite' ones that I know.)

He suffered terribly from the caste system prevalent in India, and thought this was beneath him. He had a lot to learn, especially after his foray on Christmas Eve.

I'll put it in here, as it is rather good. For some unknown reason, the bar, when we were in Izmit was open, when it should have been closed, then as soon as we left when it should have been opened, it was closed, and remained that way. Same master as the sad tale. Odd.

On Christmas Eve, half a dozen bottles of liqueurs were put in the bar, and 'free of charge'. To an Indian, this is manna from heaven, and our cadet took full advantage of it. I was on watch, so couldn't check on him, as he was supposed to be studying. I know, studying, but he was a bit thick, and needed all he could get. It was going down like billyho, Crème de Menthe, Drambuie, Glayva, Tia Maria, and so on. There can only be one outcome! He had it at 4 o'clock next morning, big style. Why 4 o'clock? Because he was on bridge watch with me. Cruel? Perhaps, but he has to learn, and I couldn't stand the wee bugger anyway.

He was desperate to be allowed to go back to bed, pleading in fact, but no, "you are the lookout, so out on the port bridge wing, and start 'looking out'." He was suffering, oh, was he suffering, but there was more to come, only he didn't know it yet.

At 8 o'clock, he asked if he could go down. "Yes, but into the restaurant for your breakfast, then you will write an essay, on 'why I should not drink', to be on my desk by 12 o'clock, 2000 words at least please. If it is not there, then you will be cleaning a ballast tank with a needle gun in the afternoon." Not good for the sensitive head.

"But it's Christmas Day," he moaned.

"Tough son, but ships don't stop just because it's Christmas Day. So get on with it!"

As he wandered off, I caught a very faint "I'm never going to drink again." He was learning, at last.

Norwegians do have strange tastes in food. As they celebrate Christmas Eve, I took all the bridge watches, and for dinner, up came the traditional 'dinner'. It was belly pork, and the more fat the better. I was chewing for hours. It was even worse when the 'backalouw' came, that is probably not how you spell it, but take my word for it, it's disgusting, made mostly from Cod heads. There are seemingly 365 different recipes, so even they cannot get it right. The strangest must be on Sunday mornings, baked beans with stones in it. Mind you, some of it is interesting, especially the herring. But back down in the cargo tanks.

There had been dozens of theories as to why these tanks were cracking, where they were cracking, and what to do about it. These are big girders, 40 cms wide, 2 metres deep, and 15 mms thick, in an H pattern, but on their side, and about 10 metres long, welded onto a web (like a triangle) that is attached to the tank walls. Heavy stuff indeed, and there are eight in each tank. On the starboard side, is a different set up, as all the load bearing beams are on the port side.

They were all cracking in the same place, where they met the web. In their respective dry dockings, they had all been welded up, and the welds were holding, without further cracking.

Even Det Norske Veritas, the classification society, at Hoyvik had been brought in, and all they could come up with was vibration damage.

Possible? But on all three ships and in the same place. No, there was something else that we were all missing.

I was lying on my bunk one afternoon, when I suddenly realized what we had not checked. The alignment, so jumped into a boilersuit, grabbed a few of the crew and went to check.

Perfect! They were all bent, and bent in the same way, forwards. I measured it, they were all out by between 40 and 50 millimetres.

Vibration *never* bent a beam, there were only two possible reasons. That the tanks had been cold shocked, or the welds had not been stressed relieved.

You get that one for free Mr Bergesen.

As I ploughed my way through several tonnes of spares fixing all the safety equipment, and everything else that had been neglected, a telex came in "the ship will be OCIMF inspected in Fujairah, probably by Shell or BP. Please ensure all systems are up and running."

Who do you think got the job? Right, me.

The problem here was the 'systems' didn't actually exist. They hadn't got round to it yet, even although it should have been done years before. That damn arrogance again.

Now I was keeping a watch while we were drifting, waiting for Orders. Drifting because we lay half way between a prospective Yanbu or Persian Gulf. 23 days we drifted. Gosh it can be boring. But I still had to work all morning, plus a couple of hours at night, designing their 'systems' before putting them in place, as well as the rest of my spares to fit. I was exhausted, but it was worth it, because the ship was accepted by Shell. Only one fault, part of the engine room needed to be cleaned, which didn't please the chief one bit. Tough fatty, you shouldn't play computer games so much then.

All the time we were drifting, there swam around us these most beautifully marked fish, silvery green heads, tapering off into a sleek silver body, and boy, could they move. But we couldn't catch them.

Until one day, a Filipino worked out why. He noticed that they ate flying fish, but they only ate them when the flying fish were flying. He noticed they would take off swimming like heck, from about 50 feet away, then come out off the water, turning on their sides as they did so, and swallowed the flying fish whole.

He fashioned an old fork into what looked like a flying fish, threw it out as far as it would go, then pulled it in quickly, imitating them.

It took a few goes, but he got one, then we discovered something else. From the second it realised it had been 'had', it fought furiously, right up to the time it expired on the deck. It was good sport, and we soon all had the knack. They were delicious, but like all warm water fish, were best eaten the same day. They do freeze down though, which was just as well, as we had loads of them.

Then I went home before joining the *Berge Spirit*, where I got really annoyed on day 1. It still annoys me.

All the systems I designed and put in place on the *Berge Racine* were now on *all* of their gas tankers. "Thanks to Captain Telstoe," who claimed that *he* had made them all. That is just plain technical plagiarism. Petty? Bloody infuriating, that's the last they'll get out of me for a long time.

Ever flown British Airways from London to Singapore, non-stop, with Norwegians? No? Well take my advice, sit at the back of the plane, preferably well behind them. They are not all bad though, just most of them.

You sit behind them so as you don't get trampled on when the crew open the cabin door. Let them get away in front, well in front. They are nicotine hungry by the end of 14 hours in the air. Sad really, isn't it.

It is not only nicotine though, on the *Berge Racine*, our ethanol tank in the compressor room was going down. (We use ethanol as an anti freeze, in the reliquefaction cycle, if we get ice jamming up the valves. We used to use methanol, but that is dangerous stuff, as it can be absorbed through the skin.) Ethanol going down? We are carrying pentane, not LPG.

They were either drinking it, or taking it home in Vodka bottles. It is 100% pure alcohol.

You wonder why they end up looking like trolls? It is a wonder they have any stomach left, even watering it down 10 to 1!

So after sitting at the back off the 'plane, and avoiding the stampede, we arrive in Singapore, straight down to the sea, get in a wee boat, and chug off to join the *Berge Spirit*. Now this is tiring, as you also go straight to work.

The Master on the *Berge Spirit* is not a nice man, well he's retired now, good idea mate before you got thumped. A former alcoholic, who can only stay off the booze by working all hours imaginable, driving everybody up the wall. But oh, did he cock up, and *big* style.

This is also a 75 000 cubic metre gas tanker, sister ship to the *Berge Sisar*.

Bergesen are, or at least were, very good at maintaining their ships, on the fabric at least, the mechanical side often left a lot to be desired.

Insulating pipelines was done properly on most ships, only this brain has got a cheaper alternative, ordered everything up, had it delivered, and then lost his nerve, at least until I arrived. Instead of cladding the pipelines in aluminium, on top of the insulation which is not only rather easy to do, but looks good when it is finished, he is going to use fibreglass!

This can be the most awkward stuff to work with, even by experts.

He has ordered enough glass cloth to build a luxury yacht. Even the boatyards don't have this much in stock. The releasing agent? We have 500 litres of it, and we don't even need it, at all!

But the gel, the main component. We have 9 x 208litre drums of it (that's 45 gallon drums in old money). *And it has all gone off.* It has set in the drums, a pickaxe we need now, just to get it out.

Of course, it's not *his* fault; it must have been a bad batch, after all, good stuff would not have 'gone off' in a paint store at 45 degrees Celsius now after 6 months would it? It would, and it did!

So that's one job we don't have to do. Cargo this time, I didn't load, so it can't be my fault that the cargo tank insulation has all fallen off, and it's a right pain in putting it all back on. Good luck captain, I suggest you wait till the cargo is pumped out before trying it again.

It was pentane, loaded in Kuwait, at 45 degrees plus.

It is Bergesens standing orders that this has to be kept under inert gas, so you will know how I found out that leaving the riser open was easier than running the inert gas plant. Yep, *Berge Spirit*. And there was nothing I could do about it either. Arrogance must be ingrained in these people, one spark, and next stop, the moon.

For a change we are going to Korea, to Yosu in fact, where we pumped out all but 13 tonnes, which for this type of ship isn't bad going at all.

Now remember, I am the Chief Officer, the cargo officer if you like, but the captain? He is just plain stupid, and thinks he can do both jobs.

After we sailed, I left the crew to secure the ship for sea, and after tidying my office, took time for a shower, before going back out to check up on my crew. This is just good plain old-fashioned seamanship.

Going onto the foredeck, I found the cover off one of the tank measuring gauges, and an ejector hose leading from it.

The 'captain' in his brilliance, has decided to start removing the ROB (remainder on board), ready for the next loading. The next port is over 2 weeks away yet.

I looked over the side to find a nice long oily trail, although coloured white due to being mixed with water, trailing off behind the ship. At the time, we are only 6 miles off the coast of Korea, and passing us, less than 3 miles away, was a Korean Navy Patrol Boat! I kid you not.

I immediately shut it all down, pulled in the overboard hose, and hoped for the best.

If the riser is left open, why not, they do it loaded, so empty should make no difference, then 13 tonnes will evaporate before we even get to Singapore. It won't even show on the gauges anyway, as the trim will have changed as the fuel is being burned off.

Willy Reistad was furious, a bit like Paranoid Pete in Gibsons.

"Who stopped the ejector," as he stormed into the office.

"I did," I said, "we are not pumping oil over the side now, or at any other time."

He was fit to burst, this was good entertainment, you could almost see the steam coming out of his ears.

You, the reader will have gathered that by this time, I had had enough.

"I'm the captain on this ship, not you..." He couldn't speak. He had lost the plot entirely.

"You may call yourself the captain, but you don't behave like one. You are not putting my master's certificate on the line by breaking the law. Pollution is pollution, no matter what you think, and as long as I am here, there will not be any. Got that?" And, before he could reply, "you are a disgrace to the good name of the Norwegian seaman, you are disgrace to this ship, and you are a disgrace to yourself." I was, as you may have gathered, on a roll. And as he digested that little morsel, decided to finish with, "I request a relief in Singapore, I will not go another mile with the likes of you. You are foolish, and because you are foolish, you are dangerous. When I get back to the UK, then Bergesens will have my resignation, and I will make sure that not only is this little incident mentioned, but one or two others as well."

Then he totally lost the plot, and started spluttering, as I turned my back and walked out.

"Come back here mate, now."

To finally wind him up. "Not mate, former mate, I just quit."

He nearly had apoplexy.

We never spoke again, but he was hauled into the office to explain why he was causing pollution. I think he may not have enjoyed the experience. I resigned, explained why, sent in all the stuff from the *Berge Racine*, and to their due, they refunded my airfare which had previously been deducted. There is a limit to what people can take, and I was way past mine.

Well, so much for controlled losses, how about un-controlled loses? These are really dangerous, and have potential for massive accidents, of which unfortunately there have been a few. The only one I ever had is the subject of this next story. It was my next ship after I left Bergesens.

A few days after I left the *Berge Spirit*, the 'phone rang. I won't mention the name of the company, as they did me no harm. They also supplied Bergesens crews, so this may have been 'arranged'. I agreed to fly off to Cyprus for an 'interview'.

You can always tell that you have got the job *before* the interview, when they ask you to bring all your sea-going gear with you.

I spent the next 2 days being thoroughly bored with their 'Quality Assurance' introductions, and all this for a 1-month relieving position. They needed a British master, as the ship was registered in Hong Kong.

The *Tycho Brahe*. Odd name for a ship I thought, until I was skimming through the Internet one day, while writing this book, and discovered he was an early astronomer at the same time as Copernicus. He laid out most of the ground work for Franz Kepler, who introduced 'Kepler's Laws of Planetary Motion', which as every master old enough will know, was their introduction to Celestial Navigation. That's doing it with a sextant and a load of tables.

This wasn't a bad old ship at 15 000 cubic metres, smaller than the 'big boys', but then, we are not going-world wide, we are back on my old tramping ground, the North Sea. This is also a semi-refrigerated ship, safety valve setting up to 5 bar, as opposed to 250 mb on the big boys.

I joined her, after a tortuous number of flights, in Scapa Flow, and met up with my old pal Lou. We were in VShips Norway together.

Now, I would have expected better of him, but he had been on board for 6 months, and was pretty tired.

For the chief mate, there was no excuse. But he was Filipino, and they take no responsibility, when it goes wrong, for anything.

This is what happens when familiarity breeds contempt, and complacency sets in. This, on a gas tanker, you must always guard against. The golden rule is check, and check again. Keep checking!

The ship been on ammonia, and was changing over to LPG, in this case propane. For reasons best known to themselves, they elected to remove the ammonia vapour with inert gas, and then keep purging with inert gas, until they were below the ammonia ppm specifications.

It is much quicker, and more economical to take out the residual ammonia with air, and then inert the ship.

In that they were not down to the specification of ppm on arrival in Scapa Flow, the terminal decided to take the ship straight alongside, and give her her coolant propane into the deck tank.

Oh the good old deck tanks again. When you fill them up, you have to calculate the volume to load into them, not on the temperature at the time, but the temperature they are liable to be at their maximum operating time.

For example, let's say they are filled in the UK, and the ship is going to the Persian Gulf before using them. The temperature in the UK is say 20 degrees. But the temperature in the Red Sea is 45 degrees, then you calculate the filling ratio on 45 degrees.

Similarly, as in this case, if they are filled at 15 degrees, then you have to assume that the propane is going to absorb heat continuously until you are ready to use it, and allow say 2 degrees per day. A lot depends on the size of the tank, but there are usually tables on board. They didn't, and filled it to 98% as if they were going to using it straight away!

I obtained the record, which still stands, for taking over command of a gas tanker, and having to call in the P & I Club (third-party insurers).

30 seconds!

The propane in the deck tank had expanded to the extent that the tank was 100% full, and had nowhere else to go, except through the safety valves. These are designed for vapour, not liquid.

This is what is known as an un-controlled loss. The only way to stop it, is to get the safety valve to re-seat. They don't always do. I'll include a tale about this at the end of this story. To make matters worse, the ship was in Grangemouth, but then it was in 1977.

Some ships have portable nitrogen bottles with connections to the safety valve, but they usually take too long to find, so I did it the old fashioned way. Be careful if you ever try this, it has to be accurate, and you only get *one* go.

So dodging the drops of liquid propane flying out the top of the riser, I got into a position where I could hit the top with a lump of wood. (If a drop hits you, remember, it is dry, and at –42 degrees C, you will get a cold burn, and that is extremely painful. The treatment is exactly the same, for a hot burn. Plenty of water. For a hot burn, this takes out the heat, for a cold burn, you have to put the heat in.)

Expecting something grander eh? One good thwack, and fingers crossed, it goes back down, and more importantly, seals the release. It sealed. Whew!!!

Meantime, other factors come into play, as the propane is now flowing out of the riser drains, as well as flying out of the top, and if this goes on, then the deck could fracture. Answer, lots of water, to build in the heat, *but* never point the hose jet at the riser base.

There was an accident on an ammonia tanker (an earlier ship) that had a premature lifting, and filled the riser. The jet was directed at the base of the riser, in an attempt to empty it. Oh it emptied all right, but the heat ingress vaporised the liquid at the base, which in turn blew all the liquid above it straight out of the top, which in turn landed on top of two of the crew. They were killed.

In this case however, Lou had them schooled, and they directed the water at the top, and worked their way down.

The Filipino mate started immediately.

"Did you see that captain, the safety valve blew prematurely at 3.5 bar. It is supposed to lift at 17 bar. That is what caused the problem."

I said to him, "do you think that I came up the Clyde on a banana boat?"

He gave me a puzzled look, "I don't understand sir."

"Rule No 1 with me, don't lie, okay!"

"But sir, it did."

I took him aside for a little tête-à-tête. "I write the reports, not you, but for this one, I'll call it premature lifting. Now go and work out how much we lost, and if we still have enough to cool down with."

We lost 24 tonnes, and we did not have enough left for a proper cool down, but I could at least cool one tank, with the others about 50% ready.

"Do you want me to adjust the gauges sir?" said the mate.

I replied, "you will adjust nothing. Fortunately, I used to trade out of here, and I taught most of the loading masters about gas tanker operations, so, I'll work a deal with them. We will present 'ready in all respects' and as the cargo comes on board at a slow rate, we will divert most of it in through the top sprays to the 'hot' tanks, then finish their cool down, as we bleed off the increasing rate to the cold tanks. Okay?" (I'm not having Ras Tanura Panels here.)

"Sir, I don't understand."

"Okay, I'll do it, it's quicker."

But first, I have to tell the office in Cyprus. Remember about scanners in Orkney? So I got a boat ashore, and went to the agent's office to 'phone from there.

Immediately, I saw that I was glad I was only here for a month, as I got the chartering manager for this company. He was extremely officious, gave me a right bollocking over the 'phone, and followed this up with a particularly nasty telex, inferring that this was my entire fault. I know I can be fast, but to do all this in 30 seconds after taking command was pushing it a bit.

So, I sent an equally nasty one back. After Gibsons, and Forth Ports, I take no stick from anybody.

I'll let you into a wee secret here. When I was a marine investigator, for the case I was working on at the time, I asked for a copy of the charter party. When it arrived, it was an *Asbatankvoy* charter party, which is mainly used for tankers. It can be used for gas tankers (this was a gas tanker case), but there are so many clauses to delete, and others to add in, that it is quicker using a *Shelltime* charter party.

In this case, one clause had not been deleted, I cannot tell you which, due to the Laws of Privilege, but by not deleting it, rendered the whole charter party void.

The company stood to lose just under $600 000 in freight, and then the lawyers got stuck in, trying to recover it.

Who was the chartering manager who made the mistake? Only the same Greek as who had sent me the nasty telex! He got his rear end 'kicked' big style.

Now, I believe in divine retribution. The old saying, 'people who dig holes for others, invariably fall in them themselves'! It's true. The last time I saw the *Tycho Brahe* was in July 2001. She was lying in the Gatun Lake, in the Panama Canal, and she still looked good, but registered in Oslo now.

Back a bit in time here now, to the summer of 1977 to Grangemouth. The ship was the *Pentland Brae*, the same company as built the *Pentland Moor*, sic *Quentin*.

This time it was an uncontrolled release of vapour, but this can be equally dangerous, as you cannot see where it is going, and as it disperses, it passes through the flammable zone, which if it hits a heat source is liable to ignite. It will then flash all the way back to the source of release, so not only then do you have an uncontrolled release, but a fire as well.

The ship was loading propane, and again unfortunately, familiarity breeds contempt, as the tank pressure was rising, but nobody was really keeping an eye on it.

Now, to be fair all round, although it was not admitted that there was a design fault on the safety valves (nobody will ever admit that in a thousand years, so don't bother trying), there did become available a modification to prevent a recurrence.

The safety valve lifted with such force, that it jammed open, and would not re-seat.

With 14 fire engines pumping water over the mast riser, the only thing that could be done was to wait until the tank pressure fell low enough, then unbolt the entire assembly from the tank and blank off the flange. Not nice, but not impossible.

The modification, which became available almost overnight, arrived in the yard where the *Pentland Moor* was being fitted out, to be fitted to her valves immediately. To all intents and purposes, it looked like a saucepan without a handle. The idea was that, when the valve lifted, this would crush preventing jamming.

It may seem an odd way of looking at it, but occurrences like these improve safety, as safety valve design was looked at from a different perspective, and modern systems, although employing much of the same fundamentals are now also protected by ball valves between the tank the valve, so that in the now unlikely event of something going wrong, the safety can be isolated.

Now here is something that I, and possibly only one or two others, also know about this incident. The humorous aspect to it. The owner of the company was sitting at the end of a boardroom table in the shipyard in Rotterdam where the *Pentland Moor* was being fitted out. We were all sitting round the sides. When the 'phone call came in about the *Brae*, he jumped to his feet, jumped onto the table to run towards the door, got as far as the end, slipped on a piece of paper, fell onto his backside, catching the other end, before bouncing onto the floor, landing face down, cursing. "Hire me a 'plane," he shouted as he picked himself up, and continued. If he had taken his time, then it would have been quicker walking round the side of the table.

He is quite a guy! But then, how many ship-owners do you know who enter the New York marathon? He came 8001st.

Now, no story would be complete, without a contribution from 'The Adventures of the *Borthwick*.' Most satisfyingly, was that it was also in Grangemouth.

'Slip tubes!'

Some years ago, these were supposed to be banned, but some ships still have them. If they do, then they are supposed to be isolated.

They were a back-up liquid level detection device. All it is, is a pipe, with a valve at the top end, which can slide up and down in a collar. By setting the height above the tank top, and opening the valve, allowing vapour to escape, as the liquid level rises, it meets the bottom of the tube, and instead of vapour coming out, it changes to liquid, so you know when to stop filling the tank. Ropey? To say the least.

The whole assembly is screwed into the tank on a left handed thread, and the cover, a tube with one end closed is screwed on with a right handed thread. Why? If the top seizes on, then, when a spanner is applied, as the top comes off, the assembly becomes tighter in the tank top.

Quite clever really, until an Indian comes along. It just happened to be an Indian this day, and the tank pressure was high at about 6 bar. He really should not have been fiddling at all, but you know some people. Bit like *Blunderman* really.

Putting the top back on, he decided, for reasons best known to himself, to tighten the top with a spanner. It is only a cover, so finger tight is enough. But, as he tightened it up, it started coming loose, and thinking it wasn't tight enough carried on 'tightening'.

You've guessed it; he is now unscrewing the whole assembly out of the tank. One turn should suggest that something is amiss, but this guy is *not* thinking. If he ever did, and he is only a few seconds away from a massive fright. Something he will *never* forget.

5, 4, 3, 2, 1, Blast off! And the whole lot shot clean out of the tank, and what goes up, must come down, the only small problem is exactly where?

More importantly, where is *Ten Knot Tony*? I'll bet you don't have an 'Operation Clean Air Forth' *TNT*. Did they not teach you about air in the RN, *TNT*? Probably not, as you seem to have got most of the hot stuff.

So where did it come down, after it reached its vertex? Well, in that it was never found, it's a pretty safe bet that it has now retired to the bottom of the dock. If a ship dredges it up on an anchor, then it is a stainless steel pipe about 5 metres long with a mild steel cover on one end over a valve assembly. Address to send it to:

MV Borthwick,
Guayaquil,
Ecuador.

Now our little Indian friend, who a few seconds ago was beside a hole of 30 mms in diameter, now whistling LPG, and out of control, is legging it, giving proof to that age-old answer to the question "what steps did you take to remedy the situation?"

Answer: Great big long ones sir!

So, how do you recover this situation? You cannot wait for the tank to blow down, as you would be waiting for the best part of a month.

You cannot screw anything into the hole as it is a left-hand thread.

You could always wait for *TNT* to come with his binoculars, but fortunately, the Police and Fire Brigade have added to their flowchart for Operation Clearwater Forth, 'advise Chief Harbour Master of major situation in 'Methil'. Roads all blocked, so please take pilot boat, listening for our calls on channels 1 through to 78. Please listen to all channels, and please do not call us, we'll call you.'

The only thing you can do is the obvious one. Bang something into the hole. Then secure it with something.

But what? The only thing that springs to mind is a 'fid'.

Now before you laugh, the dictionary defines a fid as 'a conical pin of hardwood used to open up the strands of a rope in splicing". And this ship just happens to have one. (Actually this ship should have more than one, as an order got cocked up in Gibson days, and instead of 1 being ordered, it was in fact ordered as 1 off, and we ended up with ten).

It takes a bit of courage to do this, as that vapour whistling out is really moving, and it is cold. Courage not being an Indian thing, the British Chief Engineer had a go. You have got to be quick, and it's better with two, one to hold the fid, and one on the opposite side with the big hammer.

After several attempts, it was sealed, then secured with a fancy selection of planks and wedges.

For some strange reason, the *Borthwick* never went back to Grangemouth. But what then is better, the *Borthwick* not liking Grangemouth, or Grangemouth not liking the *Borthwick*. Not much to choose between the two really.

Here is an interesting question.

"Would you be able to take a gas tanker of 30 000 cubic metres and 3 cargo tanks to bits, and be able to put it all back together again?"

Your answer would probably be either no, or, I wouldn't take it to bits in the first place.

Very sensible. How about if you "'thought' that you knew all about gas tankers?"

"Oh, well.... . I might have a go, but I might need someone to help me."

Now come on, let's try and still be sensible. So I'll modify the question.

"Your ship is in dry dock in Singapore, it is the wet season, and you might have to take the main engine to bits as well. The ship was carrying ammonia, and it has to be prepared for LPG. The captain is British and an idiot, and the crew are Polish, who although LPG certificated, have never carried LPG before?"

"That's not a fair question."

"Somehow, that is what I thought you would say, but then you have the advantage of the question in the first place."

I didn't, as I flew out to Singapore to join the 'David Gas' as chief mate.

In London Heathrow, I got rather chatty with the check-in girl, who promised to check the passenger list for me. It's okay she said, there are Norwegians on board, but they are all in front of you, we put them all near to the door now anyway, it's a matter of routine. I rather think they had been asked this question before.

Upon arrival in Singapore, I came out of the arrivals hall, and there was a man with a wee sign that said '*Mr Harvey*'. I didn't expect this, so said, "that's me."

Off we went, with this chap wheeling my suitcase. This was all rather jolly, air-conditioned car as well, eh. "Help yourself to drinks sir," as we left the car park. I had a cold beer. Delightful, as it was so humid.

But we didn't go to the shipyard. No, to a block of luxury apartments. How civilized, we must all be staying ashore.

"Good afternoon Mr Harvey," said this very attractive receptionist, "please Mr Brian, sign here and here."

"Brian? No my first name is Douglas, Doug for short."

"You are not Mr Brian Harvey?"

"No, I am if you like, Captain Douglas Harvey."

The penny dropped, wrong Mr Harvey at the airport! Oops, but the beer was nice. I think I better skedaddle quick.

So, I got into a taxi, and went to Sembawang Dry Dock, where there in dry dock, was the *David Gas*, and, we were staying on board. Typical. I think I'll change my name to Brian.

What a heap of junk, paint holding rust together, and by the smell, had been carrying ammonia for years.

Lugging my suitcase up the gangway, found my cabin, or should I say, elevated dungeon, and went to find the 'captain'.

Now for this story, every time you read the word 'captain', think idiot.

I found out the same night, after I met my old pal DJ, a shore-based electrician, who I knew from my Gibsons days, that the captain, was the cousin, of a certain master in Gibsons, the one who had the first collision, and the one I took over from on my last fateful trip on that heap of junk, the *Borthwick*.

You've guessed it. Both tarred with the same brush.

The mate I was relieving, had already legged it. What did he know I wonder?

Now, you will remember that I said that they had taken it all to bits?

Well they had nearly got it all in bits, the only problem was that they had lost rather a lot of the bits.

The big job on, was to replace the chain lockers, which hadn't so much as rusted away, rather more like gone on holiday, and hadn't come back yet. So getting the old ones out wasn't going to be that big a job, a brush, shovel and a bucket should suffice.

When there is virtually nothing to remove, it gives repair yards a golden opportunity to really screw things up, and remember, they are supposed to be experts at this. Just think what beginners must be like. No don't, forget I said that.

There was an awful lot of welding going on, as it was like watching a steam train puffing uphill, and an awful lot of bits of steel were constantly being lowered in through the hole.

Nobody really wanted to venture in, like a superintendent for example to check, as the scaffolding was to say the least, stringy, that's like ropey but worse.

Did I say superintendent? Oops, what was I thinking of, Jonathan may be called a superintendent, but even *Snow White* had more of a clue. More meaning 0.1% above zero.

It soon became apparent, that I was the only one there who seemed to know what they were doing, but you know how it is, if I said don't do this, then they did it, and if I said, do it this way, then they did it another way, or not at all. Infuriating? To say the least.

"How should we prepare the tanks Doug?"

"High pressure water wash, and we'll dry them with the steam heaters before we go to load, on passage."

The listened, they actually listened, but then they excelled themselves, they decided to degrease them as well. Why? Don't ask me, I'm only the expert.

If they had not been degreased, then the minute cracks would not have been found, especially on the night before the ship was due to leave. They had probably been there since the ship was built.

The surveyor wanted them welded up, all 600+ of them, and they were mostly at the top of the tanks, so loads of scaffolding had to be built, everything going in through a 24-inch cargo tank door. It took a week. Oh well, the nightlife in Sembawang just benefited all the more, my wallet didn't.

Now to the cargo pumps. These were the infamous *Carter* pumps from good old US of A.

Anybody who is anybody on gas tankers *hates* these things. They are the most unreliable things ever made. The only thing that comes close for unreliability was the Royal Navy's 'K' class submarines from WW1.

The idea is good enough. An electric motor driving an impellor, the whole thing in a trunking, but at the *bottom* of the tank, with electric cables going down to the motor through the same trunking. Start the motor, up comes the cargo in the trunking, through a valve and away ashore. The cargo providing the cooling for the motor.

That *is* the idea. Now here is the reality.

They are forever breaking down. They can even break down when they aren't running. Sometimes if you say the wrong words in front of them, they will break down.

If you forget to waggle your big toes on alternate Thursdays, they will break down. Got the idea?

Now that is just the pump itself. Then there is the cabling. If it is possible, this is worse. It breaks down if the cook makes soup.

The only saving grace, is that they can be lifted in and out of the tank, without gas freeing, for, as soon as you lift the pump, a foot valve underneath it closes, sealing the trunking from the tank itself.

Then of course you could use *TNT*'s binoculars, and look at them from afar, so providing a use at last for at least one item. Tony can stay at home though.

More time has been wasted achieving nothing on these than anything else at sea.

The reliquefaction plant? Well let's just say, it goes round. A bit of work needed here I think.

The double bottom tanks? Why, I here you cry, you've never mentioned those before on the other ships you've been on!

Because I had more fun down here than I would have thought possible.

Here is the conversation between Jonathan and me, and I think by now, you'll have appreciated that I don't suffer fools gladly.

"The surveyor wants to inspect the steel on the bottom of the double bottom tanks this afternoon," says old J.

"Well, all he has to do is walk around the bottom of the dry dock."

"No, the inside."

"Oh, right. How many tanks?"

"Until he is happy, okay?"

"That'll be one then."

Now, I should add, that this ship last ballasted in Kandla in India. This is up the Gulf of Kachchh, (pronounced 'kak') the next sort of lagoon up from Alang/Bhavnagar (scrapyard for *Shahzadelal*). Read 'lagoon' very loosely, very, very loosely. Forget all these romantic thoughts. Just think 'mud'. Really smelly mud.

Lying throughout the bottom of the ship is close on 2000 tonnes of mud, rather like runny icing sugar, but grey. Welly sucking-off stuff. Get the idea?

Jonathan again, "take a few shovels with you, and if he wants to see the bottom off a bay, then shovel it over into the next one, okay?"

"You *are* joking?"

"No, why?"

"Because as fast as we can shovel it out, it will run back in through the clearing holes from the bays round about."

"Well, take some rags, and block up the holes. Do I need to tell you *everything?*"

"Not everything no, but if you eventually come up with a sensible idea, about anything at all, then let us know, and we'll organize a party."

So, we took a few shovels, the crew, the surveyor, and a case of beer, and spent the afternoon telling jokes and funny stories, only once venturing out of No 4 starboard, and that was to get more beer. It was okay to pee down there, as we were in effect diluting the mud.

Later, Jonathan had another brainwave, and without telling anyone, ordered for me, 5000 litres of, wait for it, 'mud converter'. I kid you not.

The salesman must have seen him coming. If you think about it for more than 1 second, it prompts the question, 'just what can you convert mud into? Only more mud.

Now back to the chain lockers. They are finished, and I have to go and inspect them. Well...

"Can anyone tell me where they've hidden the bottom bit?"

"What do you mean?" Old J again.

"There is no bottom in the chain lockers, the bit that should be flat, appears to be exactly the same shape as the hull, in fact, it might just be the hull."

"Can't trust a mate to give you decent report, I'd be quicker going myself."

"Good idea, try staying there, you won't be missed." But he missed that bit.

"Well?" as he surfaced, "is your report any different from mine?"

It wasn't, but he is far too clever to say so. They had forgotten to put the bottom in. Plenty of sides, even a top, *but* no bottom. That's another week! Oh dearie me!

It gets better, the captain joined in the fun. It was decided late one night, that the ship would be getting a GMDSS station (Global Maritime Distress and Safety Systems).

So the captain decides to remove the old radio station, not the useful way, such as careful dismantling, but the quick way. Crowbars!

"Eh captain," says I, "what are you doing?"

"Removing the radio station, so we can put the new GMDSS station in its place. I would have thought that was obvious."

"It won't be going in here; it will have to go on the bridge."

"No, it will go in here, because if it is on the bridge, then there will be no secrecy."

"The rules state that, at sea, it must be situated in a place where it can be covered 24 hours a day. That is the bridge. Anyway, secrecy went out with the ark."

"It will go where I say it will go."

"I think the surveyor for the flag state may have other ideas about this," says I retiring away from increasing devastation. I can't wait till the morning.

Morning, with old J again.

"What have you done?" he says aghast.

"Getting ready for the new GMDSS station." Says the captain. I'm listening around the corner with DJ.

"We haven't even ordered it yet, and anyway, it will have to go on the bridge."

At last, Jonathan and I agree on something.

To conclude this episode, it was ordered that day, as we no longer had a radio station, and couldn't go to sea without one, and it was located on the bridge, although the captain wangled a Satcom 'C' station in the radio room, which he used exclusively. Why? Because the GMDSS station was too complicated for him. Secrecy? Everybody sneaked into the radio room during the night, and had a look through the memory anyway.

Apart from myself and the old man, who were British, the rest of the officers and crew were Polish, apart from one other. The gas engineer was Russian. He was next to useless.

His favourite phrase was 'sugar time'. I was more used to the abbreviation 'IBT', which means exactly the same thing. International Beer Time.

Not overly well endowed in the brains department, he goes ashore one night, and guess where he picks a fight in his none too sober condition?

The American Servicemen's Club, up the road. We only find out next morning, when the Police 'phoned, and I took the call. The policewoman I spoke to asked when we would come and collect him?

She asked for clarification when I suggested about a week to 10 days. Okay, the captain will come up later this morning. That would get the two most useless out of the way for a while at least.

When they got back, he sought me out.

"We have to go back tomorrow, Monday, what do you think that will be for?" he asked.

I couldn't resist it. "Well, they take behaviour very seriously indeed out here in Singapore, and if you don't behave, it is usually the big stick (the birch), foreigner or not. Minimum of six strokes I heard."

His face fell to his boots, *"Do they?"*

"Oh yes, sometimes more. Then a few days in a cell to let you think about it, no doctor either. But wear an extra shirt when you go, they let you keep that on, takes out some of the pain I'm told."

He wandered off, white as a sheet.

It was very apparent that this ship was not going to be a great feeder, as the captain was skimping on the budget. The choice for meals was, take it or leave it.

At lunchtimes, DJ and I used to go to the gate canteen, where he would have his liquid lunch, and I would sample the delights of the chef. Most days, it looked a bit rough, but was in fact very good. Dead cheap too.

In the evenings, we used to get the bus into town, and try a different back street café. If you are ever abroad, don't go where the tourists go, but go where the locals go. It is always better, and cheaper too.

Our favourite place was run by a wee Chinese, who had fashioned a barbecue out of a lorry wheel hub. It looked a bit rough, but his chicken satay was out of this world.

When Monday came, it was one of these extremely humid days, and you were soaked as soon as you stepped outdoors.

It was time for the gas engineer to go to the police station.

DJ came up to me and said, "what did you tell the gas engineer? He looks as white as a sheet, and seems to be wearing about six shirts, one on top of the other. He'll boil in that lot."

So I told him.

"Hells Bells," he said, "you've got worse since your Gibsons days."

He was back about 3 hours later, visibly relieved, but totally exhausted under six shirts. He got off with a warning, and told to remain on board until the ship sailed. He won't be so quick to pick a fight next time.

Having now found most of the bits that were mislaid, including the bits we did not want to find for the cargo pumps, we started rebuilding. For the pumps, an engineer came out from the UK by the name of Lionel, a super chap, who warned me not to accept a dinner invitation from Jonathan.

"Why?" I asked.

"Because his idea of a night out for a meal, is the nearest MacDonalds. Come with me instead."

So I did. We went to this restaurant on Valentine's Day, and it was lit for the occasion. It is the one and only time that I have ever had to ask a waiter for a torch, just to read the menu, and then again, to find my meal. Apart from that it was very good. We got some very queer looks from people arriving, as we left, until it dawned on us that they must think we were gay. Lionel should be an 'honorary' Filipino, as he can find women faster than the Filipinos can, and he wasn't even looking for them.

The day arrives when we have to flood the dock, and Happy Harry, the captain asks, "is she set for floating?" What a dumb question.

"Well if she doesn't float, we're out of a job."

"What I meant, clever clogs, is she trimmed the same way as she came in?"

"I wouldn't know, I wasn't here, and there were no handover notes. Just have to hope for the best I suppose. Bit late now anyway, they have just opened the sluices."

Actually I did know she was fine for floating, but I had discovered that this guy was a worrier, and we can have some fun with that.

So we came afloat, tugs on, and pulled out, and alongside to finish putting her all back together. Time for some fun. Time to search someone else's scrap box. The *sloe-eyed Mancunian* taught me this one.

"Does anybody know where this bit goes?" as I held up a box, with a few wires hanging out of it.

Of course no one did, as it came from another ship, but they automatically assumed that it came from this one. Talk about consternation. Panic more like. So I left them to it.

When I first joined, I found that the condition of some of the tools was dangerous, so I dumped them. No disrespect is intended to the Polish nation, but they have for years had to make do with second best, and have trouble letting go of the past. Worn-out tools are dangerous, as Bergesen know only too well, after rather a lot of accidents. Now it is time to replace the tools, but getting the captain to agree. He was worse than *Ivor the Engine* and that is saying something. You would think he was paying for it out of his own pocket.

Of course, not having any tools helped, so I got new ones.

Why do engineers try not to allow shipyards in to dismantle the main engine?

Because they never put it back together again properly, and it was just so in this case. Oh, it ran, but a gear wheel was in the wrong way round.

My old mate DJ was asked if he would sail with us to the Persian Gulf. He nearly choked, before telling the superintendent, "the only man I trust on there is the mate, and I wouldn't go across a duck pond with the rest, especially the old man." It didn't go down too well.

In this shipyard, they have a thing known as 'Sundowners' on a Friday night. It only lasts an hour or so, and it was DJ who introduced me to it. Well, he would know, he could smell a free beer at 20 miles, which is exactly what it is, a sort of happy hour for masters, chief engineers, and superintendents of the ships they have in at the time. There is also a small buffet. All very civilized.

Now I was the chief mate on board, but as Happy Harry has not been let in on the secret, and who would want to tell him anyway, why ruin a perfectly good party. Thus, I went in his place. In all, we were there about four times, but there was a spin-off to this.

The 'yard' invite the master and chief engineer out for a meal, just before we sail, and as I had been going to the 'Sundowners' in his place, unofficially of course, they had got the idea that I was the captain. Oh dear, how did this happen?

With the chief engineer, and DJ in tow, we were taken to this sea food restaurant. This type, everything is kept live in tanks, and you go round with your basket and select what you want, then they prepare it for you. Sounds a bit cruel, but, oh is it fresh, and with the heat of

Singapore, is the only practical way of doing it.

It was a great night out, and laugh? Never have I laughed so much, DJ was in his element, but he wasn't so happy when I related a few things that happened in Gibsons that he was involved in.

Next day, the real captain found out. You would think he had swallowed a bomb. What? Something for free and he had missed it? Too bad pal, you shouldn't be such an old grump.

Just before we sailed, the company safety officer came on board, all the way from the Isle of Man, a man by the name of Hugh, or if you are Scots, Shuggie! A more useless cretin than the gas engineer? No, they were both on a par. The gas engineer may have had a slight advantage though.

He says to me. "You are not wearing safety shoes. Get a pair and wear them."

"Pardon," says I, as I don't like them. It is like wearing a safety helmet, you go around banging your head on everything. If you don't wear one, you never bang your head.

"It is company policy to wear all safety equipment as supplied. You will comply."

"Well, I'll need to order some more gear then, for the rest of the crew as well."

"Give me the order, and I'll get it down here today."

This is too good a chance to miss, so gave him my order, which he passed on to the chandler, without reading it. The chandler came to me and said, "is this a joke or do you mean it?"

"He said we had to wear it, so we'll wear it. It is no joke." But it was.

It duly all arrives in a huge box, along with an even huger bill, and for the time being, was put to one side. Then Hugh or Shuggie excels himself with, "Chief Mate, I want you to write a Safety Manual for the company, as I heard from Bergesens that you are rather good at it."

"Write your own, I have enough to do, and you don't seem to have very much. You can rough it out on the 'plane on the way home." He then went and told the captain, to make sure that it was done, by me.

So, we sailed for the Persian Gulf, and I start drying the tanks with the steam heaters. The air is preheated before it goes into the tanks, and over the next few days the tank surfaces are brought up to about 60 degrees Celsius. This has the added bonus of drying the insulation in the void spaces, so we have rather a lot of water to pump out of here too.

Going up the Malacca Straits, we were overtaking a Shell tanker. When it comes to safety, Shell think they are the bees knees, but in reality, they have gone so far with it that people on board are no longer capable of thinking for themselves. Just so this day.

The Collision Rules are very clear on overtaking vessels. Basically, the ship being overtaken will maintain her course and speed until the overtaking ship is past and clear. Similarly, the overtaking ship will when past, keep clear, and not for example, cut across the other ship's bow. Nowhere does it mention a specific distance, just to keep clear.

Well, this Shell tanker calls me up on the VHF, and says,

"David Gas, do you think you are too close to me?"

"Nope, 'bout right I would say."

"Well, I don't. I think you are too close. Give me more room."

By this time we are abeam.

"Put the third mate on please, I don't speak to cadets." I said.

"This is the captain! Now I demand that you give me more room."

"F--- off." And went back to channel 16. Impertinent moron.

This was most probably filed as a 'near miss'.

A lot of companies have a procedure for reporting 'near misses', although nobody can exactly define just what a 'near miss' actually is. Passing a ship at 1 mile in the open sea could be regarded as a 'near miss'. However, in the Dover Strait, you may be passing at only a few hundred metres, and this is not a 'near miss'. Get the idea? Mobil have gone one better, and this came straight out of their 'Instructions to Masters'. They have decided to give up on reporting 'near misses'. Instead, Mobil refer to them as, get this, 'near hits'.

I'm willing to wager that some bored superintendent in their offices spent the better part of a week dreaming that one up.

If you like bullshit, go and work for Mobil. In my next book, I'll tell you a few amusing stories about the time I worked for Mobil. What they say, and what they do, are two completely different things.

Having successfully cleaned the ship from ammonia, inerted the cargo tanks and inerted the void spaces (believe it or not, I was the only one who knew how to do this), we receive our orders to load.

What do you think would be about the last thing you would expect to be loaded onto this ship. Ammonia perhaps? You would be right. We have to load a full cargo of ammonia from Ruwais (near Abu Dhabi) for discharge in Kandla. Then, prepare to load LPG.

What a waste of 5 weeks, plus, what a waste of fuel.

Gassing up with ammonia, is a nightmare, especially onto inert gas. I wanted to blow it out, but the captain, with his vast 'experience' said no. Oh well then matey, you can suffer like the rest, 'cos this ain't going to be nice.

It wasn't. Until I had the concentration up, I had it blasting here, there and everywhere. Just about everybody ended up on the fo'c'sle.

It was eventually loaded and we sailed for Kandla. I told the captain what to expect in India, regards paperwork. He had never been there, so he should really have listened. He didn't believe me, prepared what he thought it should be, and then was left wondering why he had incurred a $500 fine. For him to pay, not the company.

I just allowed myself to gloat, just a little mind, well, a lot really.

Oh Kandla! You need eyes in the back of your head here. It is not quite piracy, but they are aboard like lightning, and will steal anything not welded down. I elected not to ballast here, as we still had to use the mud converter. I couldn't wait to see that working.

When you are on ammonia, it is quite permissible to do hot work on deck, welding and so forth, as ammonia is non-flammable. We had a lot of oxygen and acetylene bottles on the starboard quarter, and were renewing a lot of the pipework on deck. Why not do it in dry dock? Because this way is cheaper, not as good mind, just cheaper. Happy Harry informed me that he proposed to carry on with this when the ship was on LPG. I told him, "in that case, I won't be here. You can blow yourself up if you wish, but you are not blowing me up as well."

After Kandla, we went drifting, where we had to tank clean, and prepare for LPG. The office suggestion to water wash was not adhered to; rather it was kicked into touch right away. I'll do it with air. It's easier. And quicker.

A telex came in, from our Hugh, or Shuggie. "How is the chief mate getting on with the Safety Manual, is it ready for me to inspect yet?"

Inspect? He wants me to write a Safety Manual so he can inspect it!

"How are you getting on with it?" asked the captain.

"Oh, it's coming along fine." I hadn't even thought any more about it.

So the telex went back. "Progress satisfactory on Safety Manual, expect to have first draft shortly."

I got this from the Satcom C at 4 in the morning one day. Someone is going to be disappointed. As in *very*.

Ah, the mud converter. Following the instructions, it said, "discharge ballast from selected tank, add in the ratio 50 litres per 100 tons, fill tank with ballast, leave for 24 hours for action to work, discharge ballast again. Inspect tank."

That seems straight forward enough. Let's see if it works then.

Answer 24 hours later. 1000 tonnes of water ballast discharged, 500 litres of 'mud converter' discharged with ballast, total amount of mud discharged ... *nil*.

Obviously, we are doing something wrong. Try again, only this time, we'll put twice the amount in. That should work, usually does.

It didn't.

Right, bung the rest of it in. It might just do something this time, and if it doesn't, then we won't have to do it again. Nice plan eh?

Did this work? Come on now, you've read nearly 100 000 words up to this point. Do I need to think up yet another sarcastic reason?

Let's see if we can get it out the old way. Fire hose, and blast it. I'll work the discharge valve on the ballast pump, and strip the tank, as the crew work the hose. That worked, but oh was it tiring? Coming up for lunch, I abandoned the idea. Why? Because the beautiful emerald green/blue sea now had a long tail of grey mud in it.

As far as I know, the mud might still be there.

Before the dry dock, some 80 tons of ammonia, had been 'acquired' and stored in the starboard deck tank. We had two of these things, but for some reason, probably age, had been down rated from 17 bar, to 13.5 bar.

Bergesens are not the only company that steals you know, they are *all* at it. Except yours truly. I won't do it.

Now, in the heat of the Indian Ocean, we start popping the safety valves.

I wanted to dump it, as the ship is going onto LPG, and the quantity stolen was not really much use for anything. The opinion of the office was sought. Our whiz kid, good old Jonathan, he's bound to have the solution, or at the very least, we are going to get a laugh.

Back comes his reply, by telex, "put the ammonia into the other deck tank."

Eh yes... but the safety valves are set at the same as the other tanks... won't they just start popping as well?

The captain, he had his own solution. Totally wrong, and hope you don't go to the USA, just jack up the settings on the safety valves. No seals left, but that is a minor matter, a sea must have washed them off! Jings, some sea!

This ship is getting more dangerous by the day. I'm not staying with this crowd on LPG, as I now had to start giving lectures on safety, and the carriage of LPG. Not easy, when one Pole could not speak English, and everything had to be translated for him as I spoke.

In came another telex. "Re subject; Safety Manual. Have arranged to have it finally approved by 30th April. Please fax me what you have asap. Regards Hugh."

That was 7 days hence. Oh dear, and then I had a brainwave. This was bound to work, but first I had to wait 5 days. Ho hum. You will of course have noted that I am not overly enchanted with this set-up. But then it is only a 3-month contract anyway, and I only have 3 weeks to go.

"Do you have the safety manual ready for Hugh yet?" asked the captain.

"Just the cover note to prepare and I can fax it off this afternoon. I'll do it on watch, okay?"

"I'll leave it to you then."

If only he knew that the only bit that had been prepared was the cover note, then he may not be so relaxed about it. But then he is a worrier, and had been giving me a hard time anyway.

So, cover note sent, with 25 blank sheets of paper. One Safety Manual that Hugh or Shuggie should have done himself. Now he has the paper to do it on.

In the meantime, another telex comes in.

"Re safety equipment ordered by safety officer, can you explain why you need 24 safety harnesses, 24 pairs of trainers, 24 pairs of steel toe-capped Wellington boots, and 24 sledge hammers?"

"Well," said Happy Harry, "can you *explain* this?"

"Of course," says I, "it's quite easy really. Hugh (Shuggie) said we had to wear safety equipment *all* the time, so I have a complete set for everyone on board. Safety harnesses we will wear all the time, just in case we have to go aloft, trainers, because they are steel toe capped, and a lot easier than boots, Wellies is obvious, and sledge hammers in case we have to smash our way out through a porthole, in the event of a fire. See."

"You don't honestly expect me to tell him that do you?" says the captain.

"Best thing to do captain, is to tell the truth, always, never fails."

What does he send? "Order got muddled, will return excess next time passing Singapore."

"You can't do that captain, it has all been used. They won't take it back if it has been used."

"What, all of it?"

"Yep, all of it." Worry about that for a while, you moron.

Back then to the Safety Manual. Yet another telex from Hugh (Shuggie).

"Re Safety Manual, cover note received, but unfortunately our printer broke down, as all we have is blank paper, please re-transmit."

This gets better and better. So it was all re-transmitted by fax. Same thing again, but the telex this time was, "please send Safety Manual by courier asap."

Perfect! Why? Because we now had to go to Fujairah and anchor and I was due off. Happy Harry still has not latched on about the safety manual.

At this point, I reminded him that I was due off in about a week, as my 3 months were up. Normally, I wouldn't have bothered that much, but this lot are dangerous, and they are going to load LPG. Not with me they're not. The telex is getting red hot by now, as another two came in.

"Re chief officer, we have not received his contract. Please forward same by courier asap." And

"Vessel to load full cargo of propane at Juaimah terminal for discharge in Chile, ports of discharge to be notified in due course."

I begin to smell a rat, so was on my guard.

I was given the contract and asked to sign it.

"Can I have the terms and conditions document please captain?"

"Oh, it's just a standard contract, just sign it."

"Nope."

Just as well, as there was a clause, No. 2B, which read, 'If the vessel is at an out port, or is proceeding to an out port, then the company shall have the right to extend the contract by up to 3 months.' Fujairah is an out port.

There is no way I am going to be shanghaied. So I signed the contract and endorsed beside my signature, "except clause 2B."

The brown stuff hit the fan 2 days later. The 'company' refused to accept my returned contract with this endorsement, and 'insisted' that I agree to its deletion. No chance, so it was agreed that I would be relieved after 3 months, but could I do them a favour, in return for them doing me one, by staying behind to do an OCIMF inspection? They were doing me no favour at all, just complying with an agreement at the outset.

OCIMF inspection? I burst out laughing, and told Happy Harry to forget it, this tub would never pass in a thousand years.

There then started a period where I was promised the Earth if I stayed, as they could not get a relief. Tough, not my problem. In the end, they had to get a superintendent out of the office to come as mate. This gives you some idea of how hard it is to get gas qualified officers. Not much has changed to this day.

Of all the oil companies chosen to conduct an OCIMF inspection, they had to choose the toughest, Chevron. This is going to be even better than I had hoped, as they note down a lot of information extra to the basic inspection.

The paperwork bit is done first, and then it's round the ship. As we came on deck, the inspector said to me, "is it me, or is your captain a bit weird?"

"Oh, it's definitely not you, and he's *not* a bit weird, he is totally weird. He's at that awkward stage in life, somewhere between fuddy and duddy. Now you know why I'm getting off."

"You're leaving? Well then, you won't mind showing me what is wrong on board this ship then."

"David (because that was his name), it is not so much as what is wrong, but what is actually right, and that is mostly what I have managed to fix since leaving dry dock. This tight lot just won't get me the spares."

The ship failed, as expected, and I left Happy Harry to explain it to the company.

But then yet another telex arrived on the same old subject, the Safety Manual.

"Re Safety Manual sent by courier, we have a cover note and 25 blank sheets of paper. Can you explain?"

"Well," says the captain, "can you explain?"

"Oh yes," says I, "but you are the captain, and you sent it. Anyway, I just signed off. It's your baby now."

I was, as you may have gathered, a little cheesed off with him. I could have run circles round him at any time, but he treated me like a first trip cadet, and remember, I hated his cousin.

However, David gave me a lift to Dubai, and we had dinner together, before I spent 3 relaxing days waiting for my flight details and ticket to come through, then went home, vowing never to work for that outfit again. I never did. But then, I wasn't asked either. The Safety Manual? It was eventually completed, about 3 months late. DJ told me all about the furore, as he was in the office when Happy Harry's explanation came in. I'm not telling you what it was. I'm keeping that for my next book, but I can tell you, it was a cracker.

So much for gas tankers, I think you deserve a rest from that subject, but don't worry, there are even more incredulous stories to come, with the *Balder Phoenix*, and the best of all, the *Steven N*, where it is not only cargo that they steal, but fuel as well, big style. In fact, they would steal anything, and probably did. They were so tight, that they even kept the soot from the main engine, by spreading it through the accommodation. Puzzled? Read on then.

These are of course gas tankers, there is also the Russian barge carrier to come.

How about a bit of ship delivery, just to maintain the interest. How about the story of the *Princess Royal*? Sounds very grand doesn't it. Well it ain't, but we'll start at the beginning. My old pal CQ had this job for me.

"Is that Captain Harvey?" says CQ one day to my *wife* on the 'phone. He can be a bit slow.

"No sorry, he's out just now, can I take a message?"

"I have a ferry that needs to be delivered, take about a week, can you get him to call me when he gets in if he is interested?"

"Oh, he'll be interested," she says, "just book him up for it." Do you ever get the impression at times, that your wife may not really want you at home? I did from time to time.

I had to 'phone back for the details anyway, which were, 'deliver a 35-year-old day passenger ferry from Flensburg (just on the Danish border on the Baltic side) to Liverpool (just west of Manchester), where it will be converted into a night club.

It is a Greek who is buying it. Say no more then. Six in total for crew, it is hand steered. Passage via the Kiel Canal, no pilot on the Elbe, it is under the minimum length, and pilot in Liverpool at your option. Meet you in the 'office' at Heathrow, to collect charts and so forth, plus the money and ship's stamp.

I should add at this time, that it is January, and cold. The 'office' at Heathrow is nothing as grand as you would imagine. It is in fact the upstairs bar in the check-in area of Terminal 1, and the 'money' is usually about £1000, which means that I have to go to the supermarket for the stores. Fortunately, you cannot get mince in Germany.

My crew? The two ABs I had had before, so I should get a new supply of jokes. My chief mate was a second mate from the North Sea, rig supply boats, and my Chief Engineer, was a second, also from rig supply boats, and my second engineer was a third, also from the North Sea. They fancied their chances of a bit of 'promotion'. But please don't enter this into their Discharge Books. No problem. They're working a flanker.

They should take every prospective deck officer, as soon as he comes out of college, and give him a job like this. Why? Because this is where you really learn to navigate, away from GPS and computers, all seat of the pants stuff, these jobs. But good fun, in a funny sort of way.

Unfortunately, the standard of deck officers being churned out of the Nautical Colleges is not good enough for today's Merchant Navy. They are fine with computers, but that is only a very small part of running a ship. Give them a bag of tools, and they are lost. It is a problem not confined to the UK, it is worldwide, and the worst of the lot, 'graduate' from the Nautical School in Bombay, or Mumbai as it is called nowadays.

One cannot just blame the Nautical Colleges however, it is a problem inherent with a lot of youth. Attitude, with a capital 'A'.

Off to Heathrow, and collect all the bits. I wish the English would import some Scottish beer, especially for the 'office'. Then off to Hamburg, where we get into a minibus for the trip to Flensburg. It was during this, that we all started to realize just how cold it was getting. In Flensburg, it was −24 deg C. I hope this tub has heating. It didn't.

We met the new owner, he was on board. Jannie was a charmer.

He took us out for dinner that night, just as well, as there was no food on board yet, and then we all slept in or around the galley, with the ranges on full power. It was comfortable, but not overly warm.

Next day, paint the new name on. I left it to the two ABs while the 'mate' drew up the charts, and the two ginger beers got busy in the hurdy gurdy room. I went shopping. It is not that easy storing for six for a week, especially when you can't get mince, but it was poured into a taxi, and stowed away on board. At least, we won't starve. In fact, we ate very well indeed.

The rest of the day was spent with various surveyors, but to his great credit, Jannie had most of it done anyway, it was just for me to sign everything. We will sail next morning for Kiel, where we will take fuel.

The regular German captain explained that the Decca Navigator did not work due to the proximity of the Naval Base, and like a clot I believed him. What he really meant, was that it didn't work *at all*. Not that it was ever used. For years, all this ferry had done was ply between Flensburg and Denmark, a voyage of at least 20 minutes, where the passengers could stock up on duty frees.

For a 35-year-old boat, she was in remarkable condition, twin screws and a bow thruster. I suppose being a passenger ship, she could carry 750, she would need to have been well looked after.

The name painted on? Each bridge wing and the stern? Well, if I thought that the port of registry on the *Shahzadelal* looked rough, the *Princess Royal* on each side was ten times worse, and it had taken him all day. Jannie didn't help much by shouting up, "that looks all right, keep it up."

I said, "Jannie, are you blind or something, that is absolutely the worst I have ever seen."

"Oh, I agree, but you have to encourage them you know."

I just hope that this guy can steer a hell of a lot better than he can paint.

We just Sellotaped the name and port of registry to the windows at the back.

Next day dawns still and overcast, but damn cold. Off we go then. She handles like a dream, no *Leirna* characteristics here then, as we make our way to Kiel to fuel. It isn't a lot, only 20 000 litres, but you know engineers, they all have a tendency to spill it. It is universal with them. No matter what their nationality, they *all* manage to spill it.

I have argued for years that deck officers should take fuel, on the basis that we can load millions of tons of anything, without hardly ever spilling a drop. I'm arguing with a brick wall here though.

Fortunately, our two engineers didn't spill it. If they had, it would have been nothing short of a miracle, as it was all going into 1 tank, and only half filling it anyway. But stranger things have happened with engineers. Paranoid Pete's on the *Quentin* was the best, but, yes, that's in my next book too.

I had brought the ship down to Kiel, and locked her in, the mate could take her through the canal. The Kiel Canal, is a pleasant journey, through the countryside, but the best bit about it is that the pilots are absolute gentlemen.

It is odd moments such as these that make seafaring a pleasure. If I could make a suggestion, would you mind teaching how you do it to the Suez Canal pilots? Better still, just replace them.

At the south end, at Brunsbuttel, it is by now, dark, with a lot of sea smoke. This is a type of fog that is just the start of serious fog, so please, let me get to the sea before it closes in. No pilot for this bit though, and although I had been up and down the Elbe hundreds of times, had never really paid much attention to how the pilots did it. I wish I had, as now, I have to do it. So, off we trot, only the bow thruster jammed on, in the lock, which is why the rails on the starboard bow were now on the port bow. Ho Hum!

Going down the Elbe, I just followed the channel. There was nothing else moving, only us, when Cuxhaven Signal Station came on with, "*Princess Royal*, you are in the wrong channel". There was only one on the chart, so I countered with,

"What's wrong with this one, there's nothing coming?"

"You should be in the north channel."

Okay Adolf, keep your hair on, "sorry, will know next time." And carried on. Give him a wee wave when we pass Cuxhaven. I wonder if this guy is related to Tony? No, there can't be two of them can there?

Here is a little aside. For some years, the only nuclear-powered merchant ship the *Savannah* lay in Cuxhaven. There is nothing more odd looking than a ship without a funnel. Mind you, Mobil have more than made up for that over the years. You should see some of their efforts. Like the Mobil Transporter (Part 6, you'll need a laugh by then).

It is time to hand over the watch, when we get into the Separation Scheme running along the north coasts of Germany and the Netherlands, and of course, this prompts the inevitable question from the 'mate'.

"If the Decca isn't working, and we don't have GPS, how do we navigate?"

"What did they teach you at Nautical College?"

"We'll do it the old way. Put the searchlight on the buoy, and read the number, mark it on the chart, and then set off for the next one, okay?"

"You are kidding me, right."

"Nope. Good night, call me if you have a problem." The AB on with him knew me from before, so I knew he would be all right.

Six hours later, after I relieved him, he was still looking worried, so I enquired why?

"What happens at the Texel when there are no more buoys?"

"I'll show you when we get there."

Again 6 hours later, we are at the Texel, when he comes to the bridge for his watch, still looking decidedly worried.

"So, what do we do now?" he says. A little imagination from him would help a great deal here.

"Easy. Steer South West, and remember, France on the left, England on the right, we go down the middle. Keep going until you can identify something, then modify the course. Okay?"

"I'm not so sure about this." Says he, looking pained.

"Look, you took this job, you are supposed to be qualified, so let's see you do it. We have done it this way on a 'scrapper', going to India, this is just a coastal hop."

Six hours later, he hasn't found anything, which didn't really surprise me, as I don't expect to see anything for another 3 hours at least yet. But if I can work that out, so can he.

Bang on time, the North Falls Buoy, a slight adjustment, and we are going through the Dover Strait. Fortunately, the weather was with us, and I could make the Greenwich Buoy, before coming closer inshore.

The Greenwich Buoy is on the Greenwich Meridian, and marks the end of the Separation Scheme. If the weather had been against us, I could have come in closer earlier, but technically you are breaking the rules, and it's better not to, if you can help it. So we 'bay hopped', that is going into every bay, getting advantage of the shelter.

Working for Gibsons was the best education. It was known that, if a captain went for shelter, then that was fine. If the weather was that bad, then seeking shelter was preferable to incurring damage. 'Big' shipmasters would do well to learn this approach. Then there would be a lot less pollution, re *MV Willy* last year for example. No point using up fuel and going nowhere, might as well anchor, and save the fuel.

A little aside here I think: Who are the only people who 'demand' that a ship keeps moving? Answer, accountants.

People who have no knowledge whatsoever about the *power* of the sea, should make *no* decisions concerning ships. To this add, they should not put shipmasters under pressure to comply with a schedule, in particular, with container ships, not only the feeder container ships, but the big boys, the world-wide container ships.

Containers fall off these ships faster than you think, which doesn't matter to them, they, even if they wanted to, couldn't stop and pick them up again anyway, but to every other ship, are a nightmare. Why? They don't show up on radar, but they will still take your bow off if you hit them, which leads onto my next grumble, 'keeping a lookout'. This is the oldest thing at sea, 'watching where you are going'.

Even the very best radar is no substitute for a pair of eyes, which can pick out things that radar cannot see. Like icebergs for example. Does ice show up on radar? No it doesn't.

I'll stray a little further off the story, by citing this example. I had command of a ship called the *Sargasso* and was taking her from Philadelphia, USA, to Dunkirk, in France. You'll get the full story in my next book.

I had in my standing orders, "Obtain from the engine room, the seawater temperature on an hourly basis. Log this, and if the seawater temperature drops dramatically, call me immediately."

Despite explaining to my officers as to why, they failed to call me, but my sixth sense kicked in, and I arrived on the bridge in time to alter course for an iceberg. We were that close to losing the ship.

What did I know that others didn't?

Easy, radar is only a back-up aid to navigation, icebergs *do not* show up on radar, apart from many other things, such as containers, just breaking the surface, with 40 tons of whatever underneath.

Plus, I use the currents, all of them, world-wide, and the dramatic drop in seawater temperature would mean we had entered the 'Labrador' current. Which just happens to be the current that all the icebergs come out on.

Keeping a look-out is the most important thing on the bridge of a ship, any ship. Single-handed yachtsmen and women pay particular attention to this. If you hit a container, someone has to put their life on line to divert and save you, and this is not as easy as it sounds. Succeed in getting that through young officers' heads, and you deserve a medal. I'll come back to this on the *Steven N.*

But back to the *Princess Royal*. We started pitching, and the doors along each side started sliding back and forwards. Despite our best efforts, we could not jam them shut. So, I ordered a welding set, which we could pick up from our sister company, Deep Sea Pilots in Tor Bay.

It was important to keep these doors shut, as if we took a beam sea, then the risk of losing the ship, was a real possibility. When we round Lands End, the sea is going to be on the beam.

Not being one to let an opportunity pass, the order was given for a welding set, plus, six fish suppers. Well, we have to eat.

Getting that on board was hairy, but first things first, get the fish 'n' chips. We carry on to Land's End. Only one, small, wee problem. We have the welding set, we have the wedges, but nobody has remembered to send the electrodes! Now what? Funnilily enough, the fish and chips solved the problem. Well, not so much as the fish and chips, they were devoured, but the wrappers. Perfect for jamming in the gaps.

There was no way we were going to get round Land's End, at least until the weather moderated, or I could jump a 'coll'. We anchored for the night in Mount's Bay, just off Penzance, while I applied 'Buys Ballots' law.

This sounds grand, but all it means is, 'when facing the wind, then the centre of low pressure is 90 degrees to your right.'

This has a spin-off though, try it with a cyclone in the Far East. I did, and it works a treat, but it is not for the faint hearted. Later, on the story of the 'PENG', I'll explain how it works, but only on small ships.

A 'coll' is the area between 2 low pressure centres. Get it right, and the area is usually dead calm, as one depression 'fights' the other.

We got it right, and jumped a 'coll' and went round Land's End, like a walk in the park. Until,

"Captain, now that there are no more buoys, or indeed lighthouses, how do you propose to navigate?" asked the mate.

To think my first thought was to bring this boat across the North Sea, and down the inside route, as with the *Leirna*. I was now glad that

I didn't. How he finds oil rigs in the North Sea is anybody's guess.

"We'll do the same as we did at the Texel. Okay?"

"What? Do you mean France on the left and England on the right, we go down the middle?"

"Sort of, only we'll modify it a bit. Like Ireland on the left, Wales on the right, we go up the middle. Okay?"

"Are you joking, as I have never seen anybody doing this before?"

"No joke son, and if you have a better solution, let me know." He didn't and that is what we did.

I picked up the lighthouse of Fishguard, altered on it. And made for Liverpool. I must admit, I was getting a little tetchy myself.

We round the corner at Anglesey, and head for the Mersey. Perfect timing, we should be 'locking in' about 11 in the morning. Did I take a pilot? What do you think? I was still smarting about being let down by the Forth Pilots. Anyway, CQ was waiting at the lock, and he assured me he had been here before, so he could be an 'honorary' pilot for the day. He's not getting to drive though. I've been in a car with him, and he could do a lot of damage with a ferry. All I have to do is find the right lock, but this should be easy enough, just look for one with a scruffy little guy on the end of the wall. Sorry CQ, but you really should buy yourself a new jacket, you looked as if you had crawled through a double bottom tank in that one.

Why were the dredgers going into the lock, stern first? I pondered to myself.

Well, I've not been here before, so I'm going in bow first.

The reception committee were the new owners and their pals, pleasant in their own way, but had a cunning look about them. Probably explained how this project was financed, which I'll tell you about.

They had been exporting used car tyres to Nigeria. As long as they had 'some' tread on them, and didn't have obvious holes in them, like a bit of steel sticking out the side, they were packed into a 20-foot container, and shipped out. The Nigerians even paid the freight.

You can get up to 2200 used tyres into a container, and they got them free from all the tyre shops anyway, who were only too glad to get rid of them. They were sold on at £1 each. That is infinite %. Up to ten containers a week were being shipped out. On top of this, they all owned nightclubs. Not exactly hard up these people.

So why do the dredgers go in stern first? Because all they have to do is back out, swing a little to port to clear the wall, then come ahead and they are pointing in the right direction. We weren't.

It was during the swing to starboard that the bow thruster caught fire, but only about a mile or so to go now, then it won't be used again. Ever. Well, it might be.

So through all these silly little entrances, or 'cuts' and we eventually tie her up. Job done and signed over. Time to go home?

I could have done, but Jannie invites us out for dinner, to 'discuss a Proposal'.

He was only thinking about taking her to Greece, and setting up a duty free service to Turkey. "Could you take her there if we did this?"

"Oh yes, no problem, but I'll need a GPS, and a mate who can navigate."

This idea never did get off the ground, and she was converted into a nightclub.

It only lasted a few years though, before the police had it shut down. Like all these things, the drug scene took over. She is no longer there, but one day I'll find out where she is. If not already in bits.

Jannie asked me quietly if I knew of any other ship that could be used if he decided to take this one to Greece.

There is one in Leith, but it would have to be brought out by road, as Forth Ports in their brilliance have built a concrete bridge over the entrance to her berth, so she is effectively captive, until she falls to bits.

I had a look around her and discovered that she still has her original triple expansion engine. I've been after it for years, as it is the last of only four ever built in this way, and should be in a museum. Maybe after this book is published, I'll have another go at getting it. I have no shortage of friends who are willing to help restore it. Who knows?

My last gas tanker before I set up as a marine investigator was one that I did not particularly want to join at all, but I had a few months before the CDI Inspectors' course, and I was owe this guy a favour anyway. The *Balder Phoenix*, which was about the roughest ship I had been on for years. Nothing about this ship looked right. Oh the gas plant was ultra-powerful, but complicated? It took me weeks to suss it.

This type of ship is quite popular around the coast of Japan. They utilize spherical tanks, but these are terribly wasteful in terms of free space within the ship's hull. It is only by the time that you get up to the biggest LNG tankers that this design makes some sense.

In the case of the *Balder Phoenix*, she had a gross tonnage of 4604, which is a lot for a cargo lift of about 2200 tons of LPG. It also gave the wrong impression as to the 'size' of the ship.

She was running between Portugal and the UK. The charterer was a reputable one, so will remain anonymous. All we had to do really, was keep the Portuguese topped up with gas. Most of it came from the Tees, although we were into Milford Haven and Grangemouth as well. This was the ship the Chief Harbour Master (*TNT*) banned me from bringing into the Forth, but you'll find out later that he had not improved since I was a pilot. In fact, if it were possible, he was worse, but then he was thick to start with.

Teesport you already know about, as *Ratters* is not coming anywhere near my ship. He had the blatant temerity to 'phone me up one afternoon, and get this,

"Hello Dougie, *Ratters* here, it's about you banning me from your ship. Can we discuss this?"

"In future *Ratters*, it's Captain Harvey to you, and if you come anywhere near any of my ships, you'll be flying straight over the bridgewing. No if's, no but's, just stay away."

He was in the Chief Harbour Master's office at the time. Now is that clear enough for you Teesport? No *Ratters*, ever!

Just before I joined the ship, two of the superintendents had flown across from Japan, and a Det Norsk Veritas surveyor had flown to Lisbon from Oslo. On passage northwards to Leixoes (near Opporto), they had granted the ship ISM Code approval.

The ISM Code, which is supposed to prevent accidents, has in fact contributed to more. The only people who like it (apart from marine investigators and lawyers) are captains (at sea and in the offices) who think they are doing well if they shift paper around all day.

Never mind if their ships are falling to bits, as long as they have a bit of paper which says it's not. Again, you'll hear more about this in Part 7, when we get to the *Steven N*. That will amaze you.

Why the significance on the *Balder Phoenix* then? Oh, it's just that the first trip Dutch captain, was steaming up the Inshore Traffic Zones off the Portuguese Coast at the time, in direct contravention of Rule 10 of the International Collision Regulations. Why, so he could talk to his girlfriend on the mobile 'phone.

If you do that anywhere other than in Portugal, you can kiss goodbye to your qualification. The heavy fine is enough to further ruin your whole day.

On this ship, we had something I had not seen for some years. An officer's wife!

Most of the time, wives at sea are not a problem, as long as they don't get involved in running the ship, which is really a sore point with a lot of people.

This one, the chief engineer's wife was just plain crude, disgusting really, and the chief's fourth wife. You'd think by number four he might just manage to get it right, but it would be hard to find one worse than this.

What she found funny, the crew (Filipino) were embarrassed with.

They were starting to lose face over it. She had to go. This, however, brings about divided loyalties, so the chief left as well. Too bad, but the crew come first before anyone's wife.

About a year later, there was a programme on television about Piracy in The South China Sea, and they were both interviewed, having just been 'turned over'. There obviously wasn't enough soap in South Shields for her to wash her mouth out with and she was as foul as ever. She complained that the Pirates were threatening to cut her fingers off to get her rings. If they had had any sense, they would have left the rings and taken her tongue.

During this voyage, I hit upon the perfect way to discipline Filipinos. This method involves no paperwork at all.

Discipline is not really a problem with them. You still get the odd troublemaker, but by far and large, the Filipino seaman, isn't all together too bad. Watch their logic though!

I'd had trouble on a previous voyage, and 'logged' two of them. One thought this unfair, and 'lost face'. He then lost the plot entirely and had to be subdued after arming himself with a big knife, and judging by his eyes, was going to use it.

Disarming someone like this on a ship is a relatively easy matter, as there are always things to hand. More readily available than ashore.

In this case, it was a dry powder extinguisher. Not to hit him with, but a quick burst straight in the face generally does the trick. By the time he'd got it out of his mouth and eyes, he was handcuffed to a toilet pipe, where he spent the next week, until we got into port. Carbon Dioxide works well too, but this is best kept for someone who has fallen asleep on duty. A good blast of that up the backside soon wakens them up. It takes ages I'm told for the 'tingling' to go away.

In Lisbon, one Saturday, we were due to sail at midnight. Unfortunately four of the crew were late back. What made it more difficult was that the second mate was one of them. One officer, three crew. This was going to be tricky.

They all knew they had crossed the narrow line, so were expecting something on the way back to the Tees, but I had telexed on ahead.

In Teesport, two of my 'friends' came aboard, and the problem was sorted. I sent the entire Filipino crew to Mass, where after hearing their confession, they all received a sermon of their morals, behaviour in port, drinking in brothels and so on. The priests left nothing out. I had also given them $50 from the 'welfare fund' for the mission. The Filipinos had to dig deeper, and a total of $450 went ashore with them.

To give them their due though, each of the 'guilty' came up and apologized, and promised never to do it again. They all saved face! It's easy when you know how.

Filipinos feel the cold in NW Europe, even in summer time. They won't use their cabin ventilation at all. I know, as I turned mine on one warm day, and got the entire force of the system, which 'cleared' my desk in 2 seconds flat. It took hours to sort out all my paperwork.

It wouldn't be so bad, but, and this happens to every captain, this was not the first time. One would think that the most experienced person on the ship would 'learn' to secure his office before going to sea. If you knew the number of times I have spent on hands and knees gathering up all my papers, it would surprise you. Plus, you get no sympathy from anyone, particularly chief engineers.

Very occasionally, a master finds himself in an awkward position with his owners. It usually starts off fairly innocuously, but before long, can be a major issue. This happens to me occasionally, but I have my own ways of sorting out problems, as you will be aware of by now.

On this time, an overboard valve below the waterline in the engine room fractured. It was temporarily re-secured with that good old stuff, 'Thistlebond,' and a few bits of steel bar. It would need replacing, and soon, but this requires the services of a diver. It is a fairly simple job of holding a plate over the hull, while the valve is changed.

But my owner in Japan, when it was put to him, declined with that famous phrase, "we have no money in the budget."

Fair enough. Good chance your ship will sink then.

I don't put up with owners like this. It gets fixed, as not only does my life rely on it being fixed, but more importantly, my crews lives.

The Maritime and Coastguard Agency (MCA) can and do inspect ships around the coasts of the UK, where they take the attitude, that they are 'looking after our safety'.

Instead of waiting for them to call, and 'find' this defect, I call them in. In this case in Teesport, where he is shown the defect, and I get that all important bit of paper, which says, 'to be repaired before sailing from this port'. Actually, I can have quite a bit of influence here, which owners hate, but then, they aren't here on board. Tough.

Within the hour of faxing this off to Japan with a covering letter, money had been 'found' in the budget, and the valve was changed that afternoon. The beauty of doing it this 'unusual' way, is that your owners can't really say anything, as it a master's right to do as required. All it takes is a bit of courage. Well, a lot actually.

It has one huge advantage though. It gets the MCA on your side, because there may come a time when you need an 'extension'. In my experience, the MCA are the most helpful group charged with safety of shipping, not because it is a government agency, but because if you cooperate with them, they will move heaven and earth to help you. Try it, it's worth it.

Arriving in the Forth to load at Grangemouth, I thought I would test Forth Ports' rules and regulations.

One would think they would be cautious here. After all, they knew what I was like. Were they? Good grief no, usual arrogance, both from *TNT* and the OM.

I thought, right, apply for a pilotage exemption. After all, I was an ex-pilot with an unlimited tonnage authorization. I only resigned as a pilot, I still have my authorization.

No! No special favours, seven trips in and out and you can do the exam like everybody else.

Get stuffed OM. I trained the three pilots on the exam board! Plus, do you think the exam would be fair? Of course not, this is Forth Ports.

First time in, I anchored in A10. Why? Because the pilot is supposed to board a ship which anchors here. Did they? No, just come up to the pilot station for your pilot Captain, but do not proceed west of No 5 buoy.

The pilots I have no time for, a gutless shower of wimps, but the pilot boat crews. Not a problem, so as the pilot came on board, down went the boat's crew's dinner. Fillet steaks, lobster tails, giant prawns, oysters and so forth. The pilot can get a sandwich.

Actually the pilot I had was one of the better ones and there was no animosity between us. He even offered me the radio at Grangemouth, so I could dock her myself if I wanted to. I would normally, but I was a wee bit out of practice, so declined.

For sailing, I got the moaner. Enough said.

Next time in, I was a wee bit more adventurous. Forth Navigation nearly had a fit when I said I would anchor in Granton Small Ships.

"At 4604 gross, you are far too big, we can't allow that. K9 is available."

"What are you going to do about it? Set up a roadblock. It's in the non-compulsory pilotage area, and I'll go there if I please."

Who should venture to come on the VHF then, but *TNT*.

"*Balder Phoenix*, Forth Navigation. You may not proceed to Granton Small Ships. You may anchor in K9."

A pause.

"*Balder Phoenix*, do you receive me?"

Another pause.

"*Balder Phoenix*, do you copy me, over."

Yet another pause. This'll wind him up.

"Forth Navigation, I'll take L6." One mile from his window.

"*Balder Phoenix*, this is the Chief Harbour Master, if you anchor in L6, I'll be coming out to see you in the pilot boat."

"You can go anywhere you like in the pilot boat *TNT*, but you do not have my permission to board my ship. L6 it is." That is where I went.

No sooner than we had the anchor down, than the telex went off. A change of orders, proceed to Teesport to load, leaving immediately.

Oh *TNT* came out in his boat, and tried to come alongside as the anchor cleared the water. Now what I should have done was let him board, and then put the handle down. Then I could have had him arrested as a stowaway. But you never think like that at the time. I had also been playing a very elaborate April Fool's Day Joke on him anyway, which he swallowed, and then banned me from the Forth. Can he do this? Of course not, but he just made up the rules as he went along anyway.

I was leaving in Lisbon, as it was time for the CDI Inspectors' Course, at the College of Advanced Maritime Studies in Edinburgh.

I've been back up to Grangemouth since then. Not a cheep was heard. I think they may have got the message.

I did not realize just how much the distress of the 'Cosmos A' affected me, after the *Berge Racine*. For this reason, I had to give up the sea for a while. I now understood how a master in Gibsons many years before gave up the sea entirely after going to a passenger ship distress in the Bay of Biscay. A lot of people lost their lives here as well. It is not a nice feeling.

The CDI Inspectors' course. Did I qualify? No. Theoretically perfect. Highly experienced certainly. Only one more trial inspection to do when Unigas International in Rotterdam, banned me from boarding any of their ships. Why?

Because they know full well that I would find anything that is wrong. Even BP in Hemel Hempstead had agreed to employ me as an inspector. But then again we all know the famous saying.

"People who dig holes for other people, invariably fall in them themselves."

I might just try again though, the system is way beyond Unigas now. My next book is mostly about what went on in Unigas, and one individual in particular is getting singled out for attention. I have a long memory sir, and a few of your antics are about to be published. Especially the embarrassing bits. Like the day you sent Gibsons a memo, billing them for 10 kilos of butter, totally forgetting that you yourself diverted the ship to take fuel.

I'll also introduce you to how some characters got their nicknames, like *Ivor the Engine, Paranoid Pete, Diesel Dan, Phoney Tony, Tony the Tank, Berry Gerry, Buckie Bill* and so forth. Plus how to fool the US Coast Guard, and many others. You'll love it.

Comment:

During your reading of this part of this book, you have been given an insight into how much gas (liquid and vapour) is blown off by gas tankers around the world. Remember the figures I quoted are conservative estimates, and were for gas tankers in one company only, going to dry dock. Coming out of dry dock and going back into trade also results in gas being lost into the atmosphere. It is possible to reduce the losses to under 1% of the amount of coolant taken, but there are very few people left who either know how to do this, or can be bothered to do it. About 5% of the quantity loaded will be lost to the atmosphere, or if the ship is fortunate enough to do this alongside, then to the flare stack. So for a 75 000 cubic metre gas tanker, this works out at about 50 tonnes (for 1000 tonnes of coolant).

How about smaller gas tankers then, and we'll forget about dry docks for now, let's just consider normal trading patterns.

If a ship is on a regular trading pattern, carrying the same product all the time, then after discharging, the tanks will be kept in the same condition, ready to load the next cargo, and some will carry a declared 'heel', a quantity of liquid gas in the bottom of the tanks. This is deducted from the final figure loaded, and the ship is paid freight on this quantity, dependent off course on how the charter party is agreed. But there is a way round this. Many gas tankers can keep a 'heel' that *doesn't* show in the figures, and so get paid more, without actually loading more. It is rather difficult to explain in a book, but believe me, this goes on a lot. *You* end up paying for it. It is possible to 'hide' 20 tons per tank, but it would take an expert to find it.

If a gas tanker is 'tramping' getting different cargoes each time, then the tanks are 'liquid freed', and then 'blown down', before each loading.

Remember 1 ton of liquid makes (for propane) 25 000 cubic metres of flammable gas, and dependent upon where the wind is in the North Sea, means that pollution is drifting over some poor person's country. There is a lot of this in the North Sea. A lot more than you think. I would conservatively estimate that at least 250 tons per month (of all gases) is blown off in NW Europe alone. Remember, you are downwind some of the time, and some of these gases are carcinogens. (Could cause cancer.)

Could this be stopped?

Of course. It is lost energy after all, and we all know how much that costs.

All it needs is someone with a 'bit of clout' to make a stand. Who? In the UK, the best would be the Customs & Excise, who could soon justify the expense of becoming more visible in the ports and marinas with extra officers. (Comment in Part 1.) It would not take long in training them in what to look for and hand out 'fines' for offenders accordingly. Big Fines! It would of course require a declaration to be made in the previous port, *before* the ship came to the UK, but the Customs work closely with other countries anyway, and they too would soon copy the UK's example, if it took the lead.

Now that the general populace is becoming aware of what is going on through this book, and can argue from a more knowledgeable perspective, we can wait and see if anything develops.

Finally:

Getting rid of hydrocarbon gases you have seen is easy, but tank-cleaning a ship which has been carrying ammonia? This actually happened to the David Gas before it went into dry dock. I wasn't there so can only relate this story, but I did see the telex sent to the ship.

The ship was 250 miles off the Southern Tip of India, to the west, and was tank cleaning, when two fighter aircraft flew past the ship several times, and then disappeared off to the east.

One hour later, a telex was received from the Sri Lankan Government, requesting that the ship tank cleaning ammonia, either cease operations, or move further out to sea, as 'the people of Colombo, could hardly breathe'.

That will give you some idea as to how long it takes a cloud of gas to disperse, although ammonia is nasty stuff, even in small quantities.

PART 6

Here is something that you may find interesting. You've heard me comment about the amount of time that has to be spent undergoing survey on a ship. This is something that you cannot get away from, it has to be done, but over the years, more certificates have been added, and there is now rather a lot of duplication, which in effect means doing the same thing twice sometimes only a few days or weeks apart. Everyone grumbles about this, it is an acknowledged problem, but no-one does anything about it. It is a complex subject, and change would have to come from Government level. So how about it? UK Government: you take the lead, and the others will soon follow. Use your advantage now that other countries are switching to the UK flag in the advent of the 'tonnage tax'. The UK is still highly respected as a merchant flag, let's try and keep it that way. Need a hand with it? Give me a call, I could soon put a team together to tackle the problem, and with the way I do things, could have it up and running very quickly, and thus prevent more accidents.

This is only the tip of the iceberg though, by far the most annoying, as they always seem to take priority, are the Oil Major's inspections, otherwise known as the OCIMF inspection.

Oil Companies International Marine Forum.

The system is good enough, *but* the system was set up for oil tankers, and adapted for gas tankers, which in some ways only are similar, but in other ways not.

Getting an oil major to approve your gas tanker is a matter of chance to some degree. A good chief officer who puts his mind to it, could get even the worst approved. I could get any approved and have done so, read about this in Part 7. I can also, as you have seen prevent the worst from being passed. But my morals are more refined than those from the third world.

It is the old adage, to beat the system, first of all you have to understand the system. It is high time the oil companies latched on to this. Especially Shell. I bet that will surprise a few, but it's true.

How many of the oil majors operate their own gas tankers? LPG, only one that I can think of. LNG, a few.

There is a massive difference between LPG and LNG. To explain here would be too technical. I went off to become Marine Superintendent to Qatar Liquefied Gas Company in 1997, taken on as a gas tanker specialist to sort their mess out, but that will have to be left over to my next book. I'll give you a small insight here though later. Back to the oil majors then. Why is it significant that none of them operates LPG tankers? Because, they have no-one who understands them. Their inspectors have all come from their oil tanker fleets, apart from a few independent ones that some of them call in from time to time.

The old attitude, 'liquid gas is just cold oil' prevails in many camps, the most notable being Mobil, where the shipping manager, my direct boss in Qatargas, was the leading advocate. A bit thick he was too.

There is nothing more frustrating for a gas tanker master than having his ship inspected by someone who just does not know who what he is looking at. Plus, he may have to undergo this 'ritual' in every port, and on occasion, perhaps with two or more being performed at the same time. Even the terminals join in.

Is it any wonder then, that ships go to sea and have accidents? *Mostly because the crews are so tired from their workload in port.*

It would be a very brave captain, who sent inspectors 'packing' just to allow his crew to rest, such is the pressure brought to bear from above, the same people who at the end of their own working day, just head home. Not on a ship though, it goes on until it is finished.

Many a time, a crew will bring their ship in at say 4 in the morning, 2 to 3 hours on pilotage, which is intensive navigation, where, if you get it wrong, you can end up in prison, then a docking, and by 8 am when more than half a normal person's day has been completed, this crew are just starting. Apart from cargo operations which use up all the officers, and a lot of the crew, there may be survey to attend to, then two or three OCIMF inspectors turn up, you may also get one from the terminal. Sometimes, on gas tankers, you may get a CDI inspector, which is everyone's absolute nightmare. The ship may be taking stores as well, crew changes possibly? It goes on and on.

By the time cargo is finished, say 16 hours later, you are normally away within 2 hours, with more intensive navigation, and this crew are exhausted before they even start the sea passage.

Exhaustion, can be defined in a number of ways, mentally or physically. Which is the more dangerous?

If there is any question of danger, then both are. Equally.

How is this rectified then?

First of all, only send an inspector to a gas tanker who knows gas tankers. If he is experienced in oil tankers, then keep him on oil tankers. An experienced eye takes in what it needs to know, and drops the unnecessary. It also takes the load off the master, who doesn't have to explain minor matters in detail.

Have some understanding in advance of the ship's trading pattern, if it is hectic, as it often is, schedule everything way in advance, go with the ship if necessary, but whatever you do, *let the crew rest*.

The ISM Code is supposed to help here, but all this has done, has imposed such a high workload, that everything it was designed to stop, has in fact contributed to worsening the problem.

There are a number of different types of ship masters. The only type the ISM Code appeals to are those who think they are doing a good job if they have masses of paperwork shuffling around their desk all day long. It looks good when they have an 'audit', as everything is 'just so'. Then they get a pat on the back. This type of master is the one whose ship is invariably falling to bits, as everyone is so busy running around after the paper that no maintenance gets done.

I am not that type. First of all the ship operates as it should, safely, then the paperwork comes along. If I get a 'bad' audit, then tough. I'd rather have a lifeboat that works if the ship sinks than a box of papers.

I sent a telex to Bibby Line in the Isle of Man 3 years ago, when I had command of the *Steven N*, stating that the paperwork would have to wait for a few days, as one of our tank sounding gauges had broken, and I was the only one who knew how to fix it.

Back came the reply. "No captain, the paperwork comes first, the gauge can wait."

Just how exactly then am I going to be able to load that tank with no gauge? You'll read all about this ship in Part 7. And Bibby Line? The worst in this country? Probably. In my Letter of Appointment, I was awarded the position of Chief Engineer! I was the captain.

The workload, and paperwork on board ships *has* to be reduced if accidents are to be avoided. Crew fatigue is a major issue, and those voicing it must be heard. Don't come to me and say, "I wish I had listened to you before," after the next tanker runs aground with all the resultant mess, if the crew were mentally exhausted, or the pilot was not fully trained, or the Competent Harbour Authority were incompetent. An alert mind has much more chance of reacting just that much more quickly than a tired one, and this interval is usually all it takes to make the difference between a near miss and an accident.

Remember: I speak from experience.

Now what happens when an Oil Company has an operation where apart from LNG (cold oil) and Condensate (warmer oil), they also have a bulk product that isn't oil? Or even, a liquid?

This is where it all comes unstuck.

This is a true story and one that I referred to earlier, from Qatargas, and involves Mobil and Total. By the end of this book, you will see the Oil Majors in a different light.

As an aside, *whoever* thought that an English Shipping Manager from one company could work with the other Managers, being French, from another? Did he work for Forth Ports perchance?

The bulk product? Granulated sulphur. (Bit like coarse sugar.)

Not a single person from either company had a clue about sulphur, and they are going to try and load 18 500 tonnes of it into a ship. What do they do? They do what they always do, delegate it onto someone else. Who? Yes, of course you knew, me.

Fortunately, I am fairly adaptable, and had read up on this. Sit back and relax, because this is just sad, expensive, but still sad. It was also hilarious.

1) Faced with this task as it landed on my desk, I decided that the first thing to do, was to establish two things, What was the angle of repose?

2) How much sulphur did we actually have?

For 1) I went to see the Shipping Manager, and asked him. He had been on secondment to Qatargas for 3 years, so should know. His answer. "What is an angle of repose? I've never heard of such a thing. What do you need it for anyway?"

No joy there then. Didn't really expect it mind you.

The angle of repose is the angle made with the horizontal to the slope of a free standing pile. You need it at the end of loading to work out how much cargo to move, known as 'trimming', such that when the ship is at sea, the cargo will not move, or topple.

For 2), there is a highly technical way of doing this and an easy way. Bearing in mind that I was taken on to sort out the mess they were in, I elected not to take the technical approach, but the easy way.

This involves getting my pal Chafik, who was looking as though he could do with getting out of the office, to come with me to the port. He jumped at the chance. Then climbing a long split staircase to the top of the silo, and having a look. I told you it was non-technical.

"I'll tell you something Chafik mate, our bright yellow sulphur, is everything but bright yellow! Not all granulated either, some powder."

"You're not kidding there Doug, I wonder what went wrong?"

"Oh, in this company mate, it could be anything, you know how often it breaks down, and it's not even up to full production yet."

It looked like a patchwork quilt. What should have been a nice pile in yellow, was green, grey, some bits of yellow, black, orange and even some brown. Getting a certificate for this is going to be a challenge, but then again, it could be easy, just get the French to do it.

"Well I'll tell you one thing for certain Chafik, we have not got 18 500 tonnes of sulphur, nothing like it."

"How do you work that out?" he said, somewhat aghast.

"Call it an educated guess, so let's take some measurements."

This silo was circular, more flat than high, and built from concrete. When the year 3000 comes around, that silo will still be there. The walls are 5 feet thick. Why it should be as heavy as that is not all that difficult to understand. It has nothing to do with the strength of the walls, more to do with a Qatari called Misnad al Misnad, who supplied all the concrete. A millionaire perhaps? More like a billionaire! He and I had a falling out when I ripped a cigarette out of his mouth as I was gassing up an LNG tanker. It was only then that I discovered that he had the German Ambassador to Qatar with him at the time. Oops.

Crawling around the perimeter of the silo with a tape measure, Chafik noted down the 'ullages'. We then worked out the density of the stuff with a pair of scales and a bucket, and decided that we had enough to work out a tonnage. Head back then.

"Where are we going, this isn't the way back to the office?" he said.

"No, we're going to Al Khor (where I lived), for a swim, to wash this sulphur out of our hair. Anything is better than listening to that Frog prattling on all afternoon."

"Good idea."

Next day, I came up with an answer. We did not have 18 500 tonnes, more like 11 500 to 12 000 tonnes.

Of course, I was wrong, had not only every delivery been over the weighbridge before being sent to the silo?

We'll have to see then won't we!

Now if you thought the silo was over-engineered, you haven't seen the loader!

Sulphur is carried in ships that even the scrap yards refuse. But this loader was designed for bulk carriers up to about 40 000 tonnes. Ships with flat hatches, that open up to reveal a big empty box. Minimum distance from the quayside of 8 metres, and outwards, up to 20 metres. It could track up the dock for 400 metres.

The product is supplied on conveyor belts from the silo to the head, known as the 'foot spreader'. All this is, is a pipe, with a plate on the end, that opens against springs as the rate increases to spread the sulphur out in a circle, to get it into the corners. Loading rate? 1000 tonnes per hour. Well, we'll see about that.

But first of all, we need a ship.

At one end of the port of Ras Laffan, we load LNG, at the other end, condensate, in the middle therefore goes the sulphur, so that no matter which direction the wind comes from, someone is going to get the dust.

A ship is nominated, the *MV Ocean Cruiser*.

Boy oh boy, was this ship f-----, and I mean, really f-----!

On top of this, it has derricks and hatches. Getting the boom end down in the middle of this lot is going to be fun. Where is that designer?

Now the harbour master is a bit out of his depth here. His previous job was harbour master at BP Hamble near Southampton, where if they had a tanker alongside, then his 'port' was full. Before we can start operations, the ship has to be 'inspected'.

"He 'phoned me up the day before and said, "Doug, do you think you could help us out here? No-one here knows the first thing about bulk cargoes." Join the club then.

I should add, that he once said to me, that he was emphasizing his name *Raymond Bell*, to be pronounced *Ray Bell*, and not raybel as Indians tended to do. From then on, every one knew him as raybel. "Now go easy here raybel, I'll help anyone out who is stuck, or needs a hand, but just remember what happened the last time I helped you out. I nearly lost my job."

"Oh that was all sorted out. It's forgotten about now."

"Maybe by you it is, but not by me."

They were short of pilots, and as I was a pilot, went out to bring in an LNG carrier. The s--- hit the fan when the captain sent a fax to the office, complimenting me on my ship-handling, and asked, "in future could they have the same pilot (me) all the time?"

"Okay raybel, this time as a favour, but with you with me all the time. If you disappear, then so will I."

"Oh I won't. Thanks Doug, and by the way, Jim will be with me as well."

Jim was one of the pilots. He didn't go out to ships on the pilot boat, he went out on his big head, powered by his ego. Great. That's all I needed. The worst thing about him was that he was also a Scot.

Eventually, the ship is tied up alongside. Obviously, no-one in the crew can splice ropes, as the eyes on some of their mooring ropes were formed by tying a bowline knot. Now that is rough.

Jim, puts his foot in it straight away. "Your mooring ropes Captain, are not laid up on the bits according to OCIMF recommendations. They will have to be changed."

Quietly I said to raybel, "this isn't a tanker, drop it."

He did.

"Do you have your crew certification please Captain?"

Raybel, was back, "Is this legal Doug? His master's qualification, is for second master, inland waterways of India."

"Depends what it says on his Safe Manning Certificate, but as he is under the St Vincent and the Grenadines flag, I'd say that just about anything would do. A bus ticket if it's got your name on it. I'd accept it, because if you don't, then you are going to have to explain why to Qatargas, and it's a Frog who is dealing with this."

Time for a visual inspection then, inside first. My chief engineer on the *Borthwick*, the ball on legs would have been completely at home here. Imagine the worst place you can think off, then the worst smell, and combine the two, put it on a ship and you have what we found. It didn't take long. Even less when I opened one door, to find that it went straight into space at the top of the engine room, nothing between you and the engine, 30 feet below. We'll have that secured for a start!

Raybel said to me later in the captains' office, "well, what do you think?"

"Oh, excellent ship, perfect for our purposes, ideal, let's get it loaded up."

It was anything but, but the smell was nauseatingly bad by now.

He gave me a strange look, the captain beamed from ear to ear, everyone else looked mystified, as I nodded at him vigorously.

"Ship approved captain, okay Doug, you are clear to load."

"Thanks Ray, we'll get started right away."

The sooner we get rid of this piece of junk the better.

This loader, although brand new had never been tested, and my protests fell on deaf ears, about a trial run first so this was going to be interesting.

Everything was pulled into position, and the belts started up. We played with these belts for the next 2 days, trying to keep them on the end rollers. If they went out of track, then they all stopped.

Considering that they paid $20 million for this equipment, one would have thought that they could have come up with a better arrangement for keeping the belts under tension, and running on track. Suspended beneath each end roller was a box filled with bricks. You kept the alignment by moving the bricks around inside the box.

Nobody thought about putting a lid on the box though, so as they filled up with sulphur, they had to be emptied out. After the belts stopped of course.

Comes the day when it is time to put sulphur on the belts. Mobil in charge, tanker men even. This should be fun. It was!

There were four doors around the base of the silo, each operated hydraulically, which fed a belt, which in turn fed another belt and so on, until it was all heading in the right direction. That was the theory anyway.

Common sense says, open one door slowly, until you see how it is going to flow, then slowly increase it. Oh no, nothing is simple here. The first door goes full back on its ram, there is a pause and then whoosh! It came out faster than the belt could take it away, and there was soon a huge pile, which stopped growing as the belt was now managing. It should have been stopped but wasn't, and the belt which fed the hopper for the next belt at right-angles to it, soon over-filled the hopper, spilling it down the sides, but no-one noticed as they were all behind the silo. At the next hopper, same thing, although this was the one that fed the ship.

The sulphur that couldn't get into the hopper flowed down and got caught on the spare bit of belt that went to the end roller before returning. It then arrived in the ship, and the whole lot stopped.

Just then, my mobile rang. It was the Shipping Manager.

"How are you getting on Doug?"

"Oh not bad, got about 150 tonnes out of the silo."

"Why do you sound so flat Doug?"

"In the ship we have 1, possibly 2 tonnes, the rest is piled up in places that it is not supposed to be. Know anyone who's got a spare shovel?"

"Oh, that good eh. Well keep me posted."

I was back and forwards to that ship for 14 days all told, and remember I had LNG and oil tankers to load as well. It was one thing after the other. There were so many links in, just to get it to work, that it no longer met its specification in any way. But we did eventually get more into the ship than there was on the dock. One day, the operator even missed the ship's hatch. That takes some doing!

Then we ran out of sulphur! By this time, the Port Manager has been reading up on something, and decided to make a directive that no-one was allowed to walk on the cargo in the ship.

"Okay clever clogs, how are they going to trim it? To make it safe for sea?"

It was just one more piece of interference from people who did not know what they were doing. A draft survey was carried out, and the tonnage loaded calculated. I remember the figure well, 11 462 tonnes of sulphur. There were about 500 tonnes left in the silo that wouldn't come out.

"I think you need to get the weighbridge checked guys." I was not popular, especially with the French, but so what, what do they matter?

Watching the Scheduling Manager from Total who was French, preparing the trial cargo documentation, I said to him, "Gabriel, you cannot put this down on a cargo document." Colour of cargo: Bright yellow.

"Why not?"

"What if the guy inspecting it is colour blind? Then puts down 'Blue.' How are you going to explain away bright yellow sulphur that's blue?"

"Well, what do you suggest?"

"Just leave it out, it's not required."

It took 4 months to sort out the demurrage claim. It would have been cheaper all round if we had just given the stuff away, but remember, this is the Middle East, and Arabs never gave anything away for nothing.

My predecessor said rather facetiously one day. "The Arabs are the chosen race, and you can bet that, after all this oil and gas runs out, someone will come along and build an engine that runs on sand."

The weighbridge? Oh, it was fine. They just forgot to deduct the weight of the truck each time. Not bad, only 6000 tonnes out.

There was a very sad sequel to this tale. The ship was lost in a cyclone about 6 months later. She went down with all hands.

Was this Mobil's only foray into something other than oil? Nope. Told you I had a long memory.

In the early 1970s, they ventured into the transportation of coal. To you and I, coal is black stuff that comes out of mines in lumps, gets delivered to the house in bags, and then is stored in a cellar.

Carrying coal on a ship, however, is a wholly different ball game, with all sorts of inherent dangers. Such as spontaneous combustion among other nasties. It's not nice stuff to carry.

Some bright naval architect had dreamed up the concept of the OBO, oil or bulk ore, and Mobil thought it would be a good idea to get one, after all, coal one way, oil the other. Should be profitable, especially if you already have half a ship to start with.

Armed with a suitable tanker, which had 'midships accommodation, they set about building a hull, minus an engine room, fitted out as an OBO. Then when that was ready, they cut the engine room off their tanker, and brought the whole lot together in dry dock for marrying up.

Remember when the *Traquair* was 4 inches out on one side? Well, this ship was now 12 inches out on both sides. It gets better though, or worse, depending on your point of view.

The situation was saved by pulling the aft section back about 2 feet, and building in 'a bit' to make it watertight. It will now have two bow waves though. The engine room was wider than the cargo hull.

Then the amidships accommodation was chopped off the old hull, and welded on to the aft accommodation above the engine room.

Amidships tankers had a 'centre castle', which was a space above the cargo tanks for access and storage and so forth. It was now three decks up, on the stern.

Was this beginning to look ridiculous? Yes, but they haven't finished yet, they now need to extend the funnel, by 60 feet!

Now, it looks ridiculous. Remember the old saying, 'if it looks right, then it probably is.' This didn't.

But did it work? Oh yes, hopelessly inefficient, but it worked. Just.

Not long after I started for Qatargas, it occurred to me that I had come across the Shipping Manager somewhere before, but I couldn't place him. It was only after a few months, and during a conversation one evening that it dawned on me where. I had not actually met him before, it was his sidekick I ran over, but the concept was his doing.

He made up the Mobil Safety Checklist for LPG Tankers in 1982.

HIS LPG experience? Absolutely less than Nil, zilch, naff all!

Once you met him, you won't forget him. His weight was perfect for someone about 8 feet 5! A pity he had a Scots name though. McLeod.

How I came across this was when I was mate on the *Traquair*, which was about 5 months old at the time, and was the most up-to-date, and fully certificated gas tanker in North West Europe, with worldwide trading ability. This was in 1983.

Unigas called us up and said we would have this 'inspection' to see if our ship was up to the high standards they demanded for their jetties. It was to be done in Flushing before we transhipped from a P & O gas carrier, the *Garala*. A 75 000 cubic metre gas tanker.

Now Flushing is cold at the best of times, and this was winter time.

Out comes this guy on the overnight ferry from London, and we start on his 'checklist' at 08 30 in the morning. What a plonker!

He wanted measurements from the bridge front to the access doors into the accommodation, to check to see 'if they met the gas code requirements'.

"Hold on a minute," we all said, "we are fully certificated. We wouldn't have got that if it wasn't right."

But no, his checklist said it had to be measured so we measured it. This went on for about 3 hours, by which time we were all pig sick of it.

In the afternoon, we just made up the answers. Even the captain joined in. That ship had pipes it didn't have, non-return valves in pipelines that didn't exist, inert gas systems that hadn't been invented yet. Anything that sprung to mind really, and this 'expert' from Mobil happily wrote it all down. Then...

He wanted to 'test' a few systems. We talked him out of most as we were in ballast, but he insisted on the Emergency Shut-down System on deck. What he didn't know was that we were experimenting with a modification to this system, linking in the deck spray water pumps, such that if it ever had to be activated, the ship would be protected under a water blanket. Pretty novel at the time, and useful.

On deck, he picked on me, and in a truly arrogant tone, said, "what is the next point to test?"

Out of sheer devilment, I said, "booster pumps".

To get to these, you had to climb over all sorts of pipes, duck under others, and watch out for the spray system diffuser heads, which were at chest level, mostly. So he clambers in.

Rule No. 1 on any ship. Do not press any buttons unless you know what is going to happen.

With me on the deck was the chairman of Unigas, we were on good terms, and he retired not long afterwards.

"Get ready to run like hell Herman. Don't ask why, just get ready."

"This button here?" asks our inspector."

"Yes but... ." Too late. Oh dearie me. How sad.

We were off, as two, 500 hundred ton per hour pumps came on instantaneously, and all sorts of alarms go off, as the deck starts shutting down. He wasn't, as spray heads started popping all around him. Oh, did he get wet, drowned more like. Cold? About 3 deg C.

Getting it all stopped and all the systems re-established, he came aft going, "you didn't tell me that would happen," in a jittery, teeth-rattling mode, as we grabbed him, and pushed him straight into a hot shower, clothes and all. Well, that sea water in Flushing is a bit murky.

As he stripped off, the steward attended to his clothes, after a few instructions, "a quick spin, and into the tumble dryer. He'll need them back fairly quickly, so wind it up to 14 kilowatts."

Well, how were we to know they would all shrink?

"I can't go back on the ferry like this," he said.

"Sorry, but we're going to load, and don't allow visitors on board during cargo operations." I don't know how much good their checklist ever did them, as we weren't the only ones who made up the answers, as I found out later, but it did prove one thing. By the time he got to be Shipping Manager in Qatargas, he still hadn't learnt anything. Even about oil tankers.

There is one type of ship that doesn't get inspections. Ships being delivered. Like the *RFA Regent*, for example. Not that they don't have their own problems though. Here are a few others I delivered.

Not long after I came back from the Middle East, my old pal CQ was back on the 'phone.

"Hello Doug, fancy delivering a ship for us?"

"Okay CQ, what have you got for me this time?"

"Russian military barge carrier. Lying in Karachi. Can you take it round to Manilla in the Philippines? Stop off at Singapore and get some fuel. 18 days, 3 weeks maximum. You'll have a British chief, the rest are from the Ukraine, with two Russians."

"Sounds fine, anything else I need to know?"

"Yes, Jaap is running this one, you'll be working through the Dutch office, but you know him anyway and, do you know anything about cranes? We need to fix this one."

"Cranes, not a problem, I've fixed dozens over the years, and it'll be nice to see Jaap again."

Now I should interject here, that Wijsmullers are a good company, although the ship delivery section has since been wound up after they were taken over by Maersk Line of Copenhagen. They did, however, have a rather unique way of getting round the survey problem on all their deliveries. I've never seen this anywhere else.

Almost everything was re-registered under the St Vincent & Grenadines flag. Not because it was a flag of convenience, but because all of their superintendents were also surveyors for the flag state. Any problems? Fixed on the spot, they just bent the rules to suit.

Flying out to Karachi. I met my new chief, and we climbed aboard this thing in the anchorage. It was then that I realized why they need a specialist master. Fix the crane? I discovered that the crane to be 'fixed' was a 500-ton gantry crane, which ran on rails along the entire length of the cargo area. The accommodation block was forwards of this. The drawings and instruction books for the crane, however, were in Russian or Finnish, where it was built. Never mind, I've got an electrician, but he doesn't speak English. This was going to be fun.

Ever been on board anything built for the Russian Military? If you get the chance, don't bother. Exocets would just bounce off this thing.

Most ships are built on slipways or in dry dock, and from the bottom up. Russian military ships aren't.

It would appear that they build a mould of about the right shape, pour in molten steel, and then burn off the bits they don't need, which aren't a lot.

I have never seen such heavy construction. Here a few facts.

This ship was about 50 000 tonnes, could carry 52 500 ton barges, in nine holds and 36 on deck. 88 in all.

On deck, four per hatch cover, which is 2000 tonnes. As such, each hatch cover was strengthened accordingly, and in itself, weighed 136 tonnes.

The gantry crane could lift one barge or one hatch cover at a time.

On top of this were two more 3-ton cranes, and there were five more 5-ton cranes around the ship.

Apart from barges, it could also carry 36 reefer containers (refrigerated) down each side of the main deck. There was also enough space, not cabins, but space for a full division of troops. With fresh water capacity as well.

One day, not long after joining, I armed myself with a torch and set off down into the bowels. It was amazing, I have never seen so much equipment, except later on the *Steven N.* I had a torch, as there were at least 30 different types of bulb holders, with no spare bulbs.

When built originally, she was named *Indira Ghandi*, and traded between the Black Sea port of Odessa, and India. She never entered port. Just anchored off, dropped the barges into the sea, where they were towed into port, and in the Ukraine, formed into trains to be pushed up the River Danube.

The concept was dreamed up about the same time as containerization. The Americans were keen on it, with the Llykes Company, but it didn't have the flexibility of containers, so died a slow death.

Two days into the contract, and the voyage to Manilla was cancelled, the sale had fallen through. A pity as the idea was good enough.

The intention was to sail around the islands in the Philippines, dropping off an empty barge and collecting full ones with garbage, for disposal at a purpose built facility. (Not boiling at least I hope!)

She was a bit heavy for that trade though. And un-economical.

So, we sat in the anchorage and awaited developments.

Normally I am very patient, and take what comes along, my chief wasn't though. He was new to the company and hadn't done this before, and was always harping on about not having any beer. This was going to be a trial.

The rest of the officers and crew were from the ex-Soviet Union, and did suffer from a bit of an inferiority complex, which was a pity, as most of them were good seamen, except for two, the 'chief officer,' and the fourth engineer.

The fourth first then. He wasn't really an engineer at all, but got the job through his previous position on board. He had been the 'commissar'. I found him, as a person, okay, but as an engineer, hopeless. The others just plain did not like him.

The 'chief officer' was the old ship's captain, who for the purposes of the crew agreement only was signed on as chief officer, a point which was very sore with him. He was of the old school, this was his last voyage before retiring, and that would be the best place for him in the future anyway. Away from it. As far as humanly possible.

Quan is an odd name for a Russian ship. Actually she had been registered in Cambodia, and it had been shortened from *Quan Yin*.

Tinkering with the crane, we had to be careful, as there were few spares, but slowly, we got it working. The hardest bit was equalizing the lifting cables on the spreader. The spreader sat on top of the barges to lift them. I eventually got the hydraulics working, then it was easy, as there were slack adjustments you could make with hydraulic rams. There were 46 lifting wires.

First of all though, we had to see if we could get it to move up and down the deck. Obviously, with these weights, it would be best if the ship was near even keel, but to calculate this, I had to use the 'chief officer', as the load computer was in Russian. I got a bit short with him, as apart from the trim, I also wanted to know the GM. All I kept getting was 'ahhhhh is plenty, plenty!'

Later, when I started playing around with beaching calculations, all I could get out of him was 'with music, with music!' I hadn't a clue what he meant. I found out though, about 10 minutes before an axe went through it. I finished off my calculations on the spare. Myself!

One morning early, about 2 am, I awoke to a terrible smell. Nothing I had ever smelt at sea, and that's a lot, smelt like this. I got up to investigate, opened my door, and along with the smell was smoke.

I traced it two decks down to the port side, and as I turned the corner, was just in time to see the bosun lug something over the side, which had a strangely familiar shape, although slightly different from the more traditional Scottish variety. The bosun and the rest of his little gang weren't quite quick enough in getting rid of the rest of the evidence though, but had disappeared for the remainder of the night. I'll sort this out in the morning.

"Right bosun, my office please." I said, next morning.

He was looking decidedly sheepish.

"What was that you threw over the side during the night?"

"I don't know captain, but it was making a terrible smell, and I thought it was better to get rid of it."

"It looked rather like a homemade still to me." I said.

Even Ukrainians blush!

"Sorry captain, but we let it boil dry."

Now I knew why we were getting through so many potatoes.

"I won't ask what else was in the brew, but don't do it again. Okay?"

"Yes captain."

If this had been an operating ship, then he would have been on his way. But, he knew how to drive the crane. And could read Russian.

All this time, the fuel situation is running down, and I get orders to set off for Bombay (Mumbai) on one engine. She was twin screw.

Then I sat in the anchorage off Bombay for a week. There are no fish there either. Plenty of Indians, but no fish.

Getting down to my reserve, I start to push hard for fuel, and to give Wijsmullers their due, it was ordered and in a barge, but we couldn't get clearance to go in for it. I wasn't going to run out in the anchorage. That is just plain irresponsible, so I start pushing as well.

Eventually I declared 'Port of Refuge'.

That fell onto deaf ears as well, so it is time to take the bull by the horns, so to speak. I am not what is termed a 'soft captain'. You can't be in this game of ship delivery.

Only one thing for it then. Up anchor, and I parked my 275 metre ship across the entrance channel to Bombay Harbour, and requested a pilot. If I couldn't get in, then nothing else was. Or out. The Indians were not pleased, but I was just invoking International Marine Law.

"*Quan*, you must immediately proceed 25 miles to the west and anchor. You must move immediately."

"Bombay port control, I have declared Port of Refuge, I have fuel for 4 hours, please send out a pilot, or I'll come in myself."

By this stage, it has gone seriously 'upstairs'.

Did the brown stuff hit the fan? Too true it did. We had a visit from the coastguard. This is the equivalent to the Indian Navy. To the list of other people's Navy's being as bad as ours, add India. Awful!

Up comes this officious young Indian officer, armed with a 'Sten gun'. Cleaning weapons is not a high point with Indians obviously, as the person firing this is liable to get hurt before any bullets came out of the barrel.

"Okay son, first things first, take your gun back to your boat."

I don't think he liked being called 'son', as he got a bit stroppy.

"Do you have a crew list captain?"

"Yes of course. Why."

"You will get me one Captain."

"Only if you say please!"

It wouldn't be so bad if he knew what he was looking at, but he now wants everyone to come to the bridge, just to identify themselves.

Then, "captain you must proceed 25 miles to the west. Immediately."

"I've got a better idea. I'll just anchor right here, until someone gets me a pilot.

I had my pilot 30 minutes later, but they weren't finished yet.

"As soon as your fuel is on board, you must leave."

"Nope. I'll leave when I have purified the fuel, and my chief engineer is happy with the quality."

In the end, I stayed 24 hours, and the chief did a bit of trading as well, in broken Russian TVs of all things. For beer.

I also got a case of Scotch, but the chief engineer didn't know this. I'd found out that another still was under construction.

Then we went back to Karachi, where it got really complicated. Even for me!

It was here that my chief engineer lost the plot.

He was an alcoholic, who it transpired spent most of every day drinking beer in the pub at home. He'd been dry for about 3 weeks, but 'acquired' a supply in Bombay. It drove him nuts when he ran out. One day sitting at my desk, he wandered in looking for news. It was apparent that the 3-week voyage was dragging out somewhat, and my comment, "still no news Mike," flipped a switch somewhere in him.

The next thing, I was flat on my back, as his face grew purple,

"if I'm not off this ship by 2 o'clock, your head is coming off!" With that he stormed off.

Never had I come across this before, particularly with a 'British Chief Engineer'.

Only one thing for it then. Get rid of him. Fast.

Ten minutes at the Satcom C to advise the office, and I set about getting the engine ready. The 36-millimetre spanner was in my back pocket from then on.

We were anchored 15 miles off Karachi, but my cook chose the same morning to pour boiling water on his foot, so I closed with the port, to spare him time sitting in a launch as well.

It didn't help being a Thursday. Pakistan is Moslem, and their Thursday is like our Saturday.

They were both in a boat by 1 pm, and no one was more pleased than me. No chief engineer now though, but what was new?

12 Ukrainians, 2 Russians and me. You must be very careful not to call a Ukrainian a Russian. Not if you don't want to start WW3 that is. It's akin to calling the Scots, English. Just as dangerous.

Nobody has yet decided just what to do with this ship, so after another 2 weeks, we are getting short of fuel again. Tricky this, as diplomatic relations between Pakistan and India are somewhat fragile.

Someone came up with the idea of getting fuel from this Russian tug. Even to the extent of paying for it through their operators in Dubai. We were just getting to the start of the South West Monsoon.

I discussed how we would transfer the fuel from the tug to the ship. It was then that I found out that his transfer hose was only 10 feet long, which was about 30 feet short. Okay, then we'll use fire hoses.

Absolute consternation from my first Engineer. How about pollution?

Not bad coming from him, for 4 months the engine room bilges had been pumped into the Aft Peak Ballast tank, and one barge for the heavy stuff. How do we empty the aft peak tank then?

But first of all, we have to get the tug alongside. This is easy enough, I just get under way, give him a lee, and he steams alongside me at about 2 knots. Nothing between us and Africa.

Well, that was the plan, but he made a hash of his manoeuvring and had an argument with my quarter, destroying a lifeboat and about 40 metres of bulwark in the process on his tug. We only scratched the paint.

After that, he wouldn't entertain giving us fuel. Nor could he go into port in this condition, as he would be detained.

Jaap, in Holland, after getting my report, asked if I would go aboard the tug, and tender a Letter of Protest?

"Ordinarily I would Jaap, but not in this case. They have got an enormous dog on board, and I'm not too sure about it. Especially its teeth bit."

He suggested I was being cowardly. Okay, fine by me. I'll be a coward then, better that than losing a chunk of leg.

By now, someone has made a decision about the ship.

Only about the most difficult thing possible politically, but a decision no less.

They would sell the barges to Pakistani breakers at Ghadani Beach, just round from Karachi, and the ship to Indian breakers at Alang. *But*, don't tell either party about the other, not even in a coded telex.

However, first of all we need more fuel. Into Karachi then, *but* don't let on that the ship has come from India! Fortunately I still had the outward clearance from the Suez Canal which was in Arabic. That should confuse enough. It gets harder still.

Getting short of fuel even more, we were delayed as some bulk carrier has gone aground in the channel. Over the next 2 days, as they lightened her, she just got washed more up the beach until she was subsequently lost.

I never thought twice about going into Karachi, until I remembered that this ship was not in the habit of going into port, so how good would the crew be? I'll tell you. Useless. Awful. It was a nightmare. My Flip Flops from the *Borthwick* were on a par.

On top of this they are putting me onto buoys, not alongside. Too big you see. Or perhaps, not just awkward enough.

But what is on the buoys ahead of me?

The Pakistan Coastguard. An ex-US destroyer of WW2 vintage. Their pride and joy. I'd already tangled with the Indian Coastguard, so might as well make a proper job of it.

When my crew heaved up on the bow ropes, all of their stern ropes broke, as the mooring buoy was lifted up out of the water by our windlass which gives you some idea of their quality of ropes.

Only one thing for it. Supply them with new ropes. Well, we were going to scrap anyway. Even then they weren't pleased. The Commander still wanted to fine me, until I pointed out that if he did, I'd ask for all of our ropes back. We compromised. No fine.

The initial plan was to off load the barges in the port, but this lot trained in Edinburgh, and would not give permission. Okay then, Plan B it is. This was going to be hairy. Remember, each barge empty is still 84 tonnes.

After clearing Karachi, I had to anchor between two small islands, where the current would sweep each barge clear of the stern and towards Ghadani beach, where they would be lassoed by the beaching pilot, before being allowed to wash up in the scrap yard. This place is smaller than Alang, and much more organised. The beaching pilot goes by the name of Captain Sidiqui. What makes this unusual?

Illicit alcohol distilled in Saudi Arabia is known as 'Sidiqui'.

Imagine living in a dry Moslem country (Pakistan), with a name that suggests illicit alcohol!

The operation worked surprisingly well. As each barge is lowered into the well around the stern, the spreader engages into a tramway, which stops it swinging about as the barge comes afloat. After the barge is released, and the spreader comes back up, the barge was away like a shot. This was fun.

In Alang, where the ship is going to be beached, they want all the hatch covers open. On an ordinary cargo ship, this is not a problem, but the only way I could comply here was to stack them all up, one on top of the other on No. 1 hatch. *But*, getting the chief mate to see this was hard work. Anything out of the ordinary, and he just could not accept it. Then I found out about, 'with music, with music'.

All this was, was a little jingle, which went off if shear stresses were getting critical, not that that is much to worry about if you are heading for scrap anyway. Hence the axe in his screen. No more 'music'.

We got 11 barges off on the first day. Then the crane packed in never to work again with the twelfth. Unfortunately, the weather was worsening as well, and I had to make a decision. Not a difficult one really as the twelfth barge with the spreader on top was bouncing around on the stern, and the crane would go neither up nor down. Cut the wires then, all 46 of them. How? With an arc welder. It was about all we had. Quicker too than a hammer and chisel.

By the time the last one was cut, it was dark and Captain Sidiqui was nowhere in sight. They'll just have to try and find this one in the morning, providing it doesn't capsize with all the extra weight on top.

We added a few lifebuoys with lights in case it did.

Anchor up then, and head on out, all that is left is the tramway holding the spreader and barge captive at the stern. "Engines on for this, the wash was bound to break it."

It gives a fair old testament to the yard who built this tub that I was up to 10 knots before it parted with a satisfying bang. This being a barge, flat sided being pulled sideways as well.

I never enquired if they found it in the morning or not, as I left for India, with a huge headache!

Not only do I have all the paperwork for the *Quan* to do, on a Russian photocopier, but as each barge has its own certification, that as well. I am going to have to clear in 45 ships. An entire fleet!

Oh, and my crew as well. Better get started then.

One thing that gave me the biggest problem was that, as this was former Russian Military, there was a lot of 'nuclear' equipment on board. I couldn't get any sense out of the chief mate as to what it was. Perhaps he was sworn to secrecy, or just plain thick. The latter I think.

I elected to seal it up and dump it. First off all were these phials of chemicals. No markings on them, and they were about the only thing on board that was well made. They were packed into old paint drums. There was enough to fill two. Each phial was about 3 inches long, by half an inch in diameter.

A few lumps of scrap, then filled up with cement, and the tops sealed back on. Left overnight to dry, and I selected a deep hole to chuck them into next day. I usually do this sort of thing myself.

Next day as we headed south at about 8 knots, I chucked both over the stern about 2 minutes apart, watched them sink, and headed off back up the deck, when there was an almighty bang, followed by another. I even saw the second shockwave go out, just before an enormous amount of water flew up into the air. Ever seen a depth charge go off? Well, this was a double one.

The engineers flew out on deck after the shock wave hit.

I don't know what was in those phials, but sea water had a most disagreeable effect on it. The drums crush as they sink.

The bosun said, as I arrived on the bridge and starting turning the ship round,

"What are you doing captain?"

"I'm going to get the fish, get a bucket or something ready."

At least we had a decent meal that night.

Twenty boxes of paper, and eight toner cartridges later, and I was ready for India. I set off all the pyrotechnics on the last night at sea. Downwards!

Indians ask for some of the most stupid information on the crew declaration, such as your height, colour of eyes, and get this, place of residence. What the heck do they need that for?

In Scotland, in Fife, there is a town known as Auchtermuchty, which is hard enough for the locals to pronounce, impossible for Indians, so I elected to live there. Just to confuse you understand.

Then the ex-commissar came to see me with an ultimatum.

"It has been decided that we are not leaving the ship until we are paid, captain. We do not know this name, 'Wijsmuller', and we do not trust it."

I could see their point in one way. Since the breakdown of the Soviet Union, a lot of their countrymen have been short changed, and they did not want to join them.

I countered with though:

"The wages bill for you all comes to just over $100 000, which I will pay in cash in Wijsmullers Agent's Office in Bombay, before you fly to Vienna, then Odessa. No-one can leave the ship before she is beached in Alang, and if any of you think that I am going to walk through a scrap yard, where the pay is 1 rupee per day (about 50 cents) for the 30 000 Indians who work there, where it will be widely known that you have that sort of money in your pockets, then they are very much mistaken."

Very grudgingly, they agreed, as the junior officers could at least see the sense in this.

Clearing in at Bhavnagar was a nightmare, and remember, I'd been there before. I'm willing to bet that some poor little clerk is still going through those 20 boxes of declarations.

Then they came up with something surprising.

"Captain, do you have any walkie talkie radios on board?"

"Well, ones that work no, ones that don't work, dozens."

"They must be destroyed. Please, where are they?"

Now remember, this ship is military, so everyone was turned out to find them.

Between us, we found 216 broken radios, which a wee Indian duly smashed to bits on the deck, under custom's supervision.

I asked them why this was necessary.

"It is for security Captain."

More like keeping a Customs Officer in a job.

The chief mate, I specifically told to go down in the lifeboat after beaching, as physically he just wasn't fit enough to tackle the extended pilot ladder. He didn't of course, and we nearly lost him.

For beaching, there were all briefed, and my first engineer was well set up for it. Later, he told me that he truly hated these engines, and would love to blow them up. He very nearly succeeded.

Hitting the beach. She was heavy, but not quite as heavy as the *Regent*, then the *Shazadelal*, plus there was more height of tide. Speed 19 knots. Design speed 17 knots.

Normal maximum exhaust temperatures on the main engines, 480 degrees Celsius. Ours?

Let's just say that there were no tops left on any of the thermometers, which were scaled up to 680 degrees. Yuri did well there.

You will recall that I said earlier in Part 4 that beaching a ship is easy, but beaching a lifeboat was just plain dangerous. It is worse in a Russian lifeboat. We had to do it with oars. Engine wouldn't go. As the lifeboat hit the beach, one of the crew, despite being told otherwise, jumped out, then got trapped under the boat as it broached on the surf. We had to dig him out. Pity it hadn't been the chief mate.

The chief mate had been a pain since day one, so went home with 'additional' gear. A set of dumbbells in his shoulder bag. Everyone was in on it, but he never noticed. Even on X-ray at the airport.

We were spending the night in Bhavnagar, but I knew my way around here, and stayed myself, in the Maharajah's Palace Hotel. The rest could stay in the seaman's hotel, but it means doubling up two to a room, and this has to be arranged in advance. I had a lot of fun pairing them up, the least compatible being paired up together. Well, some had become a pain by then.

Next day, before driving out, I had to represent the buyers at the Indian Customs, who were not at all happy that I had beached with 44 barges in the ship and required a statement.

This is one of these pieces of bureaucracy that requires infinite patience and requires the ability to spot the next question in advance. This was then typed out on a typewriter that brought new meaning to the term 'original'.

Then we were 'fined' $20 per man on board, total $300.

How then is this relevant to the barges still on board? It wasn't, this was just Indian Customs corruption. But at $300, cheaper than spending one more day in that awful place.

There were no flights available out of Bhavnagar, so it was a bus to Ahmadabad instead. The countryside was fascinating, especially going through the towns. Ever been in an Indian bus? I haven't either, I was on the roof, beside the luggage and a box of hens.

In Bombay I had to pay the crew, this was my last paperwork nightmare, but the agents helped me there. They dealt with the cash, as an Indian *never* makes a mistake when it comes to money. Of course, we didn't have enough cash, Wijsmullers forgot about the extra day, even although I had asked for more, so someone was going to be unhappy. The Chief Mate, why not? He was a right old grump anyway. It will catch him up later though. He won't lose out.

Even to this day, they still maintain their 'pecking order'. Top to the bottom in terms of 'importance'.

So, I did it the other way round, paying those at the bottom first, (who earned the least), and worked my way to the top.

Oh! The chief mate was not pleased. He was away with $15 500 cash, just short of some $900. I didn't stay to argue, just took some of the crew for a beer instead, as I had become friends with some of them by now. The commissar could buy his own.

Then they were away, last thing to do. Send off the ship's equipment. There was no way I was going through another 7 hour stint at Bombay International Airport, so sent it all air freight. It costs about a fifth of the price and gets delivered free of charge in Holland anyway. Much easier. Wish I'd thought of that before.

Three days holiday in Dubai on the way home, and then back to Scotland.

Remember CQ said, "18 days, 3 weeks maximum," to deliver the ship to Manilla?

I was there 11 weeks, and never saw Manilla, far less Singapore. 'Twas good fun most of the time though. I'll never be bored again, and I certainly won't be learning Russian, where a number '3' is a letter 'Z'.

About a month later, I was staying in Pitlochry, in the heart of Perthshire, when with nothing to do, on a lovely hot day, I climbed up Benvrackie, a mountain overlooking the town. The view from the top is breathtaking, and as I took it in, my mobile 'phone rang. It was CQ.

"Hello Doug, busy?" He always starts that way when he needs something moved, usually something awkward that doesn't want to be moved.

"Not particularly Colin, but right now, I'm about as far from the sea as it is possible to get. Why?"

"Ever heard of a port called 'Buchanan' in Liberia?"

"No, but I know roughly where Liberia is. They seem to be having a civil war there just now though."

"Oh that is over. I've got two tugs to deliver, one from Avonmouth, the other from Lisbon. Could you do the Lisbon one?"

"What's the catch CQ, why not the Avonmouth one for me?"

"Oh. Yes. Well, you see, you would be taking the crew out with you who will operate out there, and they need to be trained up. On passage."

Something should have told me that there was more to it than this, but I accepted, and 3 days later found myself in Lisbon, looking for a tug called the *Moiness*.

Having found her, we, the chief engineer and myself preferred every other tug in the place to this one.

She was to be re-named *Moin*. She had Hong Kong Chinese owners. The start of 4 trying days.

Re-naming took 2 minutes, just paint out *ess*.

Then, the owners made an inventory of everything. Everything!

Occasionally part of these contracts requires the 'ship' to be painted in owner's new colours on passage, and I didn't broach this subject until the last day. Very fortuitously too. The Chinese superintendent intended to exact every last cent out of this contract, and asked about painting her. "Oh, we can do that," I said, "as long as you supply the paint. What paint system have they been using?"

He gave me that queer look that says, "paint system?"

"Oh, we'll just paint her in marine paint!"

"Never heard of it. There are over 30 paint systems you know, and they are not all compatible with each other. Nor can you mix them. Get the wrong one from what they have been using, and it will probably just fall off."

This was alien to him, so we didn't paint her on passage.

The rest of my crew showed up. The mate was a Humber Pilot, and first time in the company. Just fancied a change in his summer break, Fair enough, but I just got landed with one of the weirdest pilots in the UK. Arrogant? He brought new meaning to it. The second engineer was pleasant, and my two crew, okay for a change. This could be a pleasingly jolly 10 day cruise.

Then, the tug crew showed up. Two Thais. A pleasant race of people, but, the new skipper had not so much as handled a tug before, he had never even been outside of Bangkok harbour before. He'd run a 500 ton bunker barge for 28 years. His chief, at least spoke English.

On the last day, I upset the Portuguese, which actually isn't hard to do, remember, I'd been fined in Lisbon for *not* doing something. Why were they all so upset?

If you can't laugh at yourself, then you shouldn't laugh at others! I'd only gone and hoisted the Portuguese Flag, up upside down! Oops.

When we sailed, there was a bit of consternation from the Thai skipper. He was worried that he couldn't see any land, and I mean really worried. I'm not going to coast-hop down the coast of Africa.

He was like that until we passed Gran Canaria, and then relaxed. He thought we had arrived in Buchanan. Next day, back to normal.

The mate said 2 days out,

"We can forget about training him. I spent 2 hours yesterday explaining the difference between latitude and longitude. In the end, he had me confused."

"Fair enough," I said, "I don't see how I can teach him how to handle a tug on a delivery voyage anyway."

When we had stored in Lisbon, something went wrong somewhere, and we ended up with 150 tins of sardines, along with 5 kgs of blue cheese, which had been ordered as 0.5 kgs of blue cheese.

Ever had sardines on a barbecue? Try it, and you'll soon get rid of your neighbours. But blue cheese stuffed into chicken breasts? We lived on it. The sardines came in handy later though, as currency. They also got used as 'presents' later in the Suez Canal. Read on.

An interesting telex arrived from the agents in Liberia. How to establish communications on arrival, call on 8635 MHz. It was years since I had used MF/HF communications, and the mate had no clue either. This was going to be interesting. In the end, we just couldn't get through. Not surprising really as the agents couldn't operate their set at all. Something to do with no aerial!

Buchanan hadn't been used as a port in years, there were ships up the beach everywhere. The place was wrecked. One more was very nearly added, as approaching the berth to tie up, the tug blacked out. Emergency use of an anchor saved the day, as the chief appeared rather sheepishly, and said, "sorry about that. Now I know what that button does."

Living conditions on board were not that great, and my Humber Pilot chappie, who was a pain by now, wanted to be transferred to a hotel before we flew out. Only problem was that there weren't any hotels, only he wouldn't be told this. We had another barbecue that night, as someone had managed to find a bar, and a lot of the locals joined us.

You know, Liberians are really nice people. It is often said that you should not judge a country by its ports, and if Buchanan was anything to go by, then this country has a future.

The tugs were required by a German concern based in Hamburg who were going to exploit the timber resources which cover a large part of the country. They had leased 120 000 hectares, about 25% of Liberia for this, and would carry the timber out in their own ships. It shouldn't take too much effort to haul it out as a lot of the infrastructure (railways) is still pretty much intact.

Two days before getting into port, a telex arrived from CQ. "Would you Doug, and Ian, the chief, fancy another Wijsmuller special? Two tugs to deliver, one from Korea to Italy, a new building to be named Millenium, the other Hong Kong to Grimsby, to be named Peng."

Why not, the SW Monsoon has gone back. Should be fun.

But first of all, we had to get out of Liberia, and this is a lot easier said than done. The civil war had destroyed the roads to mere pot holed tracks, and Buchanan to Monrovia was a marathon 5 hours in a minibus. Fortunately there were a few roadside bars, which were frequented as there was no air conditioning.

The airport is interesting. So was the airline. They only had one plane. I think Orville Wright had a hand in its design.

After checking in, which was a case of, put your suitcases over there, here are your boarding cards, one between six, with our names on it. The 'plane leaves in 2 hours.

"Righto, where can we wait?"

"Oh, most people sit on that log over there."

Behind it, by about 100 yards was a wee bar, and as we hadn't eaten, set off to grab a bite. 2 hours to kill after all.

Wrong!

No sooner than we had our breakfast, than the flight was called, and people started to board the 'plane'. Consternation, they were six short. Didn't take long to find us though.

"But we still have over an hour before departure," I said.

They replied, "Oh we don't bother with that, everyone is here, so we go." And they did.

Aircraft maintenance in this airline is not a high priority, On board service didn't exist. We were, however, only going 2 hours to Abidjan on the Ivory Coast before transferring to an Air France flight to Paris.

In Abidjan though, it was civilized, the flight doesn't go out until 9 pm, and we have the day to kill. In a hotel, where we could have lunch and use the pool and so on. Lovely crayfish tails.

Getting back to the UK, I had one day to re-pack before going off to London, to pick up the equipment for my next delivery.

Which tug I ended up delivering became somewhat political between the UK office and the Dutch Office. The *Millennium* being brand new was a high profile job, and as such they wanted a Dutch crew. Didn't bother me, and as it turned out, was just as well, as they made a complete hog's arse of it.

I was to deliver the *Peng*.

In Heathrow, I met my 'chief mate'. My chief I already knew, and he was as they say 'large'. Fat and overweight is a nearer description. But the 'chief mate?'

Good grief, where did they find him. He wasn't overweight, he was gross, and it was all out of proportion, as everything was up top sides. So much so, that there wasn't any place left for a brain, which I would have settled for. He was Welsh, but lived in Venezuela.

I'd been master for the best part of 14 years. He was the same age, and had only 6 months before managed to get his master's ticket. He must have been the black sheep of the family though, as his brother was a top barrister in London, and probably got more than his share of the family brains.

Checking in our gear, the British Airways girl announced that there would be excess baggage to pay. I couldn't resist it.

"You want me to pay excess with this pair in tow!"

When I went to put the cases on the scales, I put the lighter of the two metal boxes on twice. It works in reducing the bill. Well it would have if the mate had kept his big mouth shut.

"Hey capn, you put that one on twice." Idiot. By the time it came to board, I was getting tired, remember only 2 days before I was in Liberia. The flight is 13 hours to Hong Kong, I remember none of it. I don't even remember arriving in Hong Kong.

A night in a hotel, and down to the tug next day. Oh, was this thing small.

29 metres, 3 double cabins, a small mess room, one toilet/shower come laundry, and 1 cupboard for stores. And that was it. Freezer at the back of the bridge for stores, and a temporary chart table secured by G-clamps. For crew, I had three Indonesians. A lot better than British.

Two main engines driving 'Zed Pellers', with a power output of 6500 hp. Now that is a powerful tug, albeit, a small one.

Fortunately, she had already been certificated, and after a day storing, she was ready. Apart from one thing. There was a cyclone coming in. A bad one.

I elected to get immediate clearance and wait in the anchorage, until the time was right to jump out. The 'mate' did not agree. He was put in his place, and reminded of his one and only 'command' before joining me. It was a disaster.

Wijsmullers Amsterdam, had put him on a dredger called the *Resolution*, working out in Turkey.

What he knew about command was equivalent to what he knew about dredging. Nothing. He had sailed as second mate on P & O Ferries in the Dover Strait, and had been in the RNR for years. A bullshit merchant no end.

Three days after taking command of this dredger, he got himself and the ship arrested and detained. Why? They had *no* permission to dredge, and *no* Dredging Certificate. It took lawyers 6 weeks to sort it out, and now he was here trying to tell me what to do in the South China Sea, which of course he had never been through before.

I actually sailed as the 'eye' of the cyclone came through Hong Kong, because I was then sailing with the wind behind me, getting a good old kick in the process.

I then set off for the Vietnamese coast. He had trouble with this, until he saw how much I gained by picking up the currents that can be strong here. Plus, I was, 'nimbus jumping'.

Closing close to Vietnam, takes you away from the main shipping routes, and more importantly, away from where the pirates are.

Nimbus jumping only works on small craft, and this was about the maximum size to do it with.

In the cyclone season in this part of the world, the air can become very humid, and local 'depressions' set up vigorous rising currents, which carry lots of water with them, which condenses building into towering nimbus clouds, often going up to excess of 30 000 feet. You can see the cloud forming, it is that fast.

It also generates fierce swirling air masses and winds at the surface, which rotate anti-clockwise, and if you are brave enough, you can jump into, giving yourself a good push up the rear at the same time. If you are lucky, you can get up to three an hour, and this I did, pushing my average speed up by about 2 knots, for no extra fuel consumption. My intended fuel consumption was 3000 litres per day at 9 knots. I was averaging 10.9 knots.

With modern pollution laws, getting rid of garbage on a small tug such as this is a real big problem. Plastics have to be retained for disposal in port. If you don't have any, you get fined. As simple as that, and you cannot argue. Even old paint drums have to be kept, as most paints contain phenol, which must not be allowed to get into the sea. I'll come back to this later, as I nearly killed the mate over it.

Before leaving Hong Kong, I acquired two empty 45 gallon drums, for conversion, one to a sea water tank for flushing the toilets. We didn't carry enough fresh water. The other for a barbecue. First night out though, we lost both, washed over the stern in the cyclone. Now we had to look for two more. Normally, most ships will pass at least one barrel a day, but when you are looking for something, you never find them. It was a week before we spotted our first, and as it looked as though it had been in the water for some time, went fishing underneath it first. I had a little spare time in hand anyway. Got a few even, nice for the barbecue.

Anything such as this, which have been adrift for some time, create eco-systems underneath them. Logs are the best, especially in the Indian Ocean. One fishing boat took in 46 tonnes of yellow fin tuna from underneath a log one day.

Next day, we got one more barrel, so now had, a water store, and an incinerator. Yes, I know it's only a barrel with the top chopped off, but it was ideal for burning our garbage, with a little paint thinners to get it going.

In the meantime, the mate is building a barbecue. As the chief and I looked at this taking shape, we were filled with the same resolve. This was never going to work. It didn't as the AB came round the corner, picked it up and threw it overboard.

"What did you do that for Doezen? That was our barbecue."

The chief and I were in stitches.

"Nah chief, that wasn't a barbecue, that was just scrap."

Remember I said he was full of bullshit? He insisted on flying the ensign and company house flag at sea. Nobody in the merchant navies I'd sailed with *ever* did that at sea. They do in the RNR seemingly.

It doesn't happen quite so much nowadays, with the advent of GPS, which even the most inept navigator can operate, but in the past, this area was notorious for ships getting 'lost'. Particularly around the Luzon Strait, between the Philippines and Taiwan.

Not long after clearing Hong Kong, the VHF came alive with,

"ship on my port side, this is XXXXXXXX, can you tell me your position please?"

Straight off, he has no clue who might respond, and as such this night it was just so. Back came a reply from what sounded like a German mate.

"XXXXXXXX, please go to channel 6."

On channel 6 with,

"my position is --------- North; -----------West."

"Oh thank you sir, thank you."

I immediately thought, 'that's odd, it should at least be degrees East for longitude. Two minutes later, a reply on channel 16.

"You b------, that position you gave me is in the middle of Africa."

"Yeah I know," he said, "but I'm not the one who is lost."

In the meantime, on the *Millennium*, they have a problem. They left over a week before me, but have had to divert into Vietnam. They had run out of fuel.

The high-flying Dutch captain had only got caught in the same cyclone. The one he should have been sheltering from. The Dutch office was not impressed. The UK office rubbed their noses in it. Poor old Jaap.

I actually passed him in the Malacca Straits, only he was now going the other way. Back to Singapore on one engine. He'd only gone and broken a fuel line. Remember, this tug is brand new.

On the Peng, however, we had a problem of our own. There was an unusual noise coming from the starboard Z peller unit. It was reported in, and back came all sorts of suggestions as to what it might be. We simply didn't have the men or the tools to open this up for a look, but as it wasn't getting any worse, just left it alone, until one day…

"Doug, you know that funny noise…?"

"Yes chief."

"I've fixed it."

This indicates embarrassment.

"Well chief, what was it?"

"The maker's name plate had come loose and was vibrating. I tightened the screws and it's stopped."

"Let's say we put some more oil in, and then it stopped. Okay?"

"Yeah, that sounds a whole lot better." And left grinning.

On delivery voyages such as this, it is often left to master's discretion as to where to take fuel. Singapore is a good option, but this means taking fuel again at the Suez Canal, and the quality there is dubious to say the least. I elected from the start to make the first stop in Colombo in Sri Lanka. If I ever do this again, I'll go for Callao in the south, less of a detour, and easier to get into. By bouncing on currents and other tricks I'd been using, Colombo was going to be easily made.

Passing Singapore was just its usual hectic self. When I worked for Qatargas before this voyage, a recommendation had been made by the Japanese Shipping Bureau, advising Japanese ships that it was safer to transit the Singapore Strait during daylight hours. To the Japanese, this is taken as a directive. It is actually safer at night now, as the place is full of Japanese ships and other craft during the day. The sheer amount of fuel that the Japanese waste trying to pass during the day is frightening. It runs to tens of thousands of tons per year, along with CO_2 emissions, and all thanks to one dumb bureaucrat in Tokyo.

The long bit of this passage was from Rondo to Dondra Head. Every deep sea navigator knows these points. Rondo at the top of Indonesia, is an island. Dondra Head is the southernmost point of Sri Lanka. Every time I had come round Rondo, I wondered what it would be like to go inside of the island, so I took the chance. It was here that I found out that my mate would *never* be a navigator.

There are on the chart some rocks which lie just below the surface to one side. Common sense says keep clear of them by leaning more to the other side. Did he, no, he went up the middle, nearer to the rocks than was prudent.

From now to Colombo is just a long haul across the Indian Ocean, but at this speed, we can troll for fish, especially these Dorado that eat the flying fish. Got a few too, but the fork is more fun than a spinner.

When I first came to sea, we used to find a lot of flying fish on the decks every morning. Nowadays, it is a rare sight to even get one. That is a pity as they are delicious for breakfast. Why so few now? Pollution. Not so much from ships, but more of what pours out of rivers.

But you can still catch flying fish at night. All you need is a bright light over the side, and a net, but you have to be quick.

Off course, we make Colombo during the night. What's new, this is a ship after all, and we were alongside at 3 in the morning, and store straight away, so collapse exhausted to sleep by 7 in the morning, which was when the fuel arrived.

The mate actually thought of having a day off, so expressed surprise when I sailed in the afternoon. He had to be reminded that this was a delivery voyage, not a cruise. He was starting to get to be a nuisance, especially as we had to paint this boat, and he was getting behind schedule.

From Colombo, this part of the voyage is just a drag. Not that the distance is any different than the previous leg, or indeed the final leg. It is what lies at the end of it that makes it a drag. The Suez Canal.

What are we short off? Marlboro. What do we need? Marlboro.

However, some of the crew smoked, and I was not going to let them run out by giving away our meagre supply to some hairy lazy Arabs.

Time to adjust the cartons then. Apart from which, it gave me something to do.

Very gently, peel back the cellophane wrappers from a carton, and slide it out. Then remove the packets from the box, and replace them with something of the same weight. Left over pork chops, sealed in cling film if you can, then secured in toilet roll to stop them moving. Slide back on the cellophane wrapper, and superglue the end back on. One carton of Marlboro, for a 'present'. Eight cartons should be enough. My crew were amazed, they'd never seen this done before.

The mate was harping on at me to divert to Suheli Par and anchor for a day, to 'paint the hull to the waterline'. He still had not twigged that our first responsibility was to deliver the tug on time. He still thought of this as a wee jolly. We did not divert.

Inevitably, we arrive in Port Suez, and anchor, for 'clearance'.

This tug is only 29 metres long, less than some ships are wide, but we still need to have a Suez Canal Searchlight, with an electrician, and an inflatable boat, with three mooring men, and they all need a place to sleep.

It's about time someone in that place considered modifying their regulations.

Eventually after every bum and stiff in the place had been for their 'present', we set off through the canal. They are in for a shock when they open their presents.

The agent asked after he saw the size of the mate,

"Is he married?"

"I'm afraid so."

"What is his wife like?"

"Don't know, never met her, but from the size of him, I'd say, flat."

Of course, the mate, without thinking, sets off the 'incinerator'. Every Arab running with us was terrified, as flames shot out of this barrel. They nearly jumped overboard though when the aerosol can blew up. Oh, was it spectacular, as bits of burning rubbish flew out and disappeared overboard.

At the top end of the canal, as they appeared to leave, I had the usual.

"Do you have a present for me captain?"

"Sorry, no presents, none left."

I was positively hounded. They kept jumping in front of me, and shouting, "but I *must* have a present."

It was the mate who found out why 'presents' are demanded.

Everyone who works for the Suez Canal Company, has a house for them and their families. Their food and heating etc, is paid for them, even the children's schooling. They want for nothing. However, they are paid about $9 per week for pilots, and less so, down the scale. The reason for this is to control inflation in Egypt. Fair enough, if it works, which it appears to do. Cartons of Marlboro are sold on the black market for a bit more cash.

Even when the boat to take them off was alongside, they were still 'demanding' a present, so I relented, and gave them a tin of sardines each. They threw them back at me. I could have done with some helicopter rotor blade bolts. To throw back at them.

So, we settled down for the next leg, 4 days to Malta. It could not come soon enough. Docked at 8 at night, took fuel next morning, and got ready to sail, but where was the mate?

He fancied a day off, so took off without telling anyone. I was not pleased when he returned, and even less when he suggested we sort out our differences on the quayside. I've never resorted to fighting as a way of solving a problem. I was all for sailing without him, as the crew could take a watch if need be. Looking back on it, I wish I had. At least I could have got as far as Gibraltar without him.

The only event worthy of telling was when we cleared the Straits of Gibraltar, and the P & O cruise liner *Oriana* came past, and got himself into a tangle with a cargo ship heading into Huelva. Some people just should not be allowed loose on the bridge of ships. Especially with passengers. A sarcastic voice came on the VHF.

"Thanks for that idiotic manoeuvre, try reading the rules."

I replied, "that idiotic remark could only have come from the bridge of the *Oriana*, a report will be telexed from here to London with a complaint attached, especially in VHF procedures."

Towards the end of the voyage the mate asked why I had changed the course lines for the Dover Strait.

"Because I'm not trotting halfway round the North Sea, when I can cross the South West lane between the MPC Buoy and the Sandettie!"

"I think I know best, that is how the ferries do it, and you've not been on the ferries."

"Well, buddy, this ain't a ferry, and that is where we are going. Apart from which, I've been up and down here a lot more than you have. Boy, have you got a lot to learn, and not much more time to do it in."

Before we got there, however, we had a surprise caller. The French Customs. We were asked to stop, and be searched. Technically, I could refuse, but I like the customs, especially if they are fighting against drugs, which this lot were. That we were in the Dover Strait, one of the busiest stretches of sea way in the world was neither here nor there. They boarded, and tested all sorts of things. I've said it before, the equipment they have should be broadcast, as it is so advanced, anyone would think twice about smuggling drugs by sea.

A clean bill of health then, and we were on our way.

With this visit, it delayed us sufficiently for me to be on watch when we crossed the South West lane. I've said it before, this mate, cannot navigate.

Next morning, I said to the mate.

"Where are all the empty paint drums?"

"Oh I threw them over the side. We don't need to keep them."

"Right buddy, if we get fined, you're paying it. Idiot, we've been keeping them for 7 weeks, and you dump them in the English Channel, 1 day before we get in."

Next day, I got a call through to Wijsmullers with our ETA. My Satcom C had developed a fault passing Singapore, and we could only transmit, we could not receive. It was a bit disconcerting, but I managed.

Then we entered the Humber for Grimsby. For some reason, I was told to take a pilot. This was unusual, as I'd normally do it myself. It would have been better if I had, as the pilot hadn't been to Grimsby in over 6 years, and had to get his book out to find out where it was.

There was a lot to celebrate that night, as I was in 7 days ahead of schedule, and was 80 000 litres of fuel under projected consumption. The owners were delighted, even although the mate hadn't managed to get it all painted. We had a super dinner ashore that night with them.

Next day, it was time to head home, but before we did, the chief and I shared a thought. The mate was going to France to his sisters. To paint her house. The chief remarked. "After seeing him paint this tug, I think we can safely say that the end result there will be some mess." That sadly was my last delivery for Wijsmullers. Their ship delivery division was wound up shortly afterwards, and doesn't exist any more.

But if anyone out there wants a ship delivered, anywhere in the world, then give me a call. I can soon get a crew together. Delivering ships, apart from the headaches, is fun, and as I said before, every ship's officer coming out of college should do it. It is invaluable experience.

CQ? Oh we still keep in touch. He's a consultant now, and is itching to get his hands on a copy of this book. But then, he is privy to a few of my more humorous tales, that I cannot reproduce here. Sadly.

I'll wind up this part with a few tales about when I was mate, just before I went master. To let you see what we used to get up to, before the bullshit brigade introduced things like 'quality management' and the 'ISM Code'. The things that have changed the worlds merchant navies into death traps.

Part 7 is all about Bibby Line, a few crooks in the USA, Bergesen and the *Steven N.*

Get a good night's sleep before tackling Part 7, as you've had your eyes opened up till now, and you won't want them permanently open after reading that lot!

Let's conclude with a few amusing tales.

In the early 1980s, Gibsons ran out of chief mates. Not that they had left the company, but were up at college studying for their Master's tickets.

To get round this temporary problem, they obtained dispensations from the Department of Transport for some of their second mates to sail as mates. The senior surveyor for the DOT at the time was a good friend with Gibsons superintendents, and at the time, Gibsons was still an excellent little company.

'Berry Gerry' as he was known ended up as mate on the *Heriot*. At the same time, I was mate on the *Melrose*. He screwed me up no end.

How come, he was on another ship? Only he could manage to 'steal' 95 tons of ethylene, while at the same time, convince the Germans, that they had received the full cargo. He only had 1000 tons to start with.

It wasn't exactly 'stolen', there was no intent to steal. He just cocked it all up.

At the time, we loaded in Baglan Bay, Wales for Moerdijk, and occasionally Stade (near Hamburg) in Germany.

The tank-measuring gauges on both ships were 'Krone' gauges, which were French, and were quite excellent. Probably the best, as they were totally sealed from the cargo. A twin walled tube filled with nitrogen, ran to the tank bottom from the dial readout. Inside the tube was a set of magnets suspended on a stainless steel wire, which was self-tightening to take up any slack in the wire.

On the outside of the tube, in the tank and floating in the cargo, was a 'doughnut' which has a set of corresponding magnets. Lower the magnets on the wire, until both sets came into their magnetic fields and off you went. Fully automatic from then on.

They did, however, have two minor drawbacks, which was not a problem if you knew about them. Gerry did not.

The face was analogue, with 1 metre to each revolution.

The problem here was if it read as a clock would, 'a quarter to four,' or alternatively 3:45, the actual reading was 3.75 metres. The *Melrose* on one occasion overfilled its deck tank, after the mate made this elementary mistake. A huge commotion ensued.

The other problem was lowering the magnets too fast. You could go all the way through the 'doughnut'. That is what Gerry managed to do, as his gauge on No 1 port tank stuck at the 2 metre level.

The gauge indicated the tank was empty, so he stopped the pump. The ship however then started to take a list, but rather than find out why, he took ballast out the port side to keep her upright. It was only after they sailed that he 'found' the missing cargo.

Meanwhile, the Germans are trying to find their 'missing' cargo. Of course they never found it. It's still in the ship!

We were due in about 3 days after them. We were allowed by Unigas to 'blow off' 10 tons per cargo to reduce the temperature for discharge. I didn't always need to do this, as I'd worked out a way of getting it on board that wee bit colder than everybody else, so on arrival, I was dead on my loaded figure.

Why should you not blow off ethylene?

Put a banana and an un-ripe avocado in a bag, and 2 days later it will be ripe.

Above 56 degrees Fahrenheit, bananas give off ethylene. Keep the temperature just below this, and they are in 'suspended animation', which is how they are shipped by sea.

Let a cloud of ethylene drift over a field of unripe strawberries, and the whole lot will ripen in 2 days, and be rotten within 4.

Blow 10 tons off on a regular basis in the English Channel, and France gets it. One does sympathize with them occasionally.

Better not too blow it off at all then!

I however, 'caught for Gerry's mistake' as soon as we were alongside. Little Hitler came aboard.

"Vee is going to test the latest design of turbine flow-meter from the University of Hamburg as you discharge. Now vee find out where you British cheat us. No!"

"What you do with it after it goes ashore is up to you," I replied. Of course it wasn't as simple as that. We had to stop every hour, and re-calibrate the ship, then start up once again. By the eighth time, I was getting cheesed off with this, so my mentor, Captain Mitchell put his foot down. No more stops.

"Ese okay now. The turbine flow meter is very accurate, to the kg."

By now, it's 2 in the morning, and there was no way Gerry would beat that thing if he came back. Time therefore to get rid of the flow meter.

The liquid line safety valves lift at 17 bar, but on this ship, they can be 'sprung' if you need to empty a line for whatever reason. They can also be locked with a wedge.

Tie down the relief valves on a compressor, and pump up the cross-over line to 40 bar, then shut down the compressor. Nobody looking? Good. Swing the valve and send a huge belt of vapour up the line with the liquid. Shut the valve and look innocent.

The hard arm nearly jumped off the jetty. A few minutes later a man appeared, "Stop, stop, stop, quickly." So I shut down.

"Got a problem?" I enquired, innocently.

"You zend something up zee pipeline, zee flow meter control equipment is destroyed. Vee must find out what you do."

"Now hold on a minute buddy, all I send up the pipeline is ethylene."

Two hours later, they are back with.

"Vee put rest of cargo in another tank, then we empty and the clean the first tank, and we find out what you zend up zee line. Zer vill be big trouble after vee find zee truth."

"You get no more cargo until you apologize for that."

Very grudgingly they did.

Cargo figures at the end revealed they had received 25 kilograms too much. They only have 94.975 tonnes missing then!

They cleaned out their tank at great expense, and found nothing. The turbine flow meter was never mentioned again, which was just as well, because Gerry was back a week later, and diddled them out of 25 tons more. I'm damned if I know how, but he did.

A full year later, I was back for my final time, and they asked, "please just tell us how you did it. The University of Hamburg are going mad with all sorts of theories, and driving us nuts."

I told them. "The only thing sent up the line with the ethylene was the one thing that you cannot find in ethylene. More ethylene!"

They were still scratching their heads as we sailed.

The only thing that Gerry did well was eat, prompting his captain to remark. "It's a great pity the output doesn't match the input." He was also the target for the most complex practical joke ever devised later when he sailed with me on the *Traquair*. It lasted over 6 weeks.

The story is in my next book. Sometimes though it worked the other way. The ship got something that it didn't expect. It was embarrassing for the terminal, and as I still have friends there, won't say where it was or what ship it was, but we were waiting to load propane.

As it started gurgling down the line, I put my hand on the pipeline, to make sure it started cooling down. Strange, it didn't. The pressure gauge wasn't reading either. Stranger, so I called a halt while we went off to investigate.

The first 10 tonnes wasn't propane! No, it was drilling mud. They had forgotten to clean out their newly installed pipeline.

Ever tried to clean mud out of a gas tanker? Probably not, but then we'd never tried either. I'll tell you this though. Never again.

Then there was the time that the heavy fuel oil pipeline fell apart as we connected to discharge ethane/propane in Donges in France. This is a grubby smelly little backwater, just up the Loire behind St. Nazaire.

They had just installed two new gas hard arms, with fully automatic controls, designed for one man operation, but somewhere, had got the wiring crossed.

This poor Frenchman was being watched by about 40 others as he tried to connect the first to the manifold of the *Traquair*. He activated the clamping gear, and the end fell off this big rusty pipeline, missing him by about 6 inches, before smashing its way through the jetty and disappearing into the river below. Oops.

A little tale about *Ivor the Engine*. I've got so many about him, that my next book won't miss this one. It was again on the *Traquair*.

I copped for the first deadweight lift of VCM out of Rotterdam. Deadweight lifts in Gibsons were a sore point as we had another ship that sagged so much that she could never lift a calculated maximum without overloading.

Unigas nominated us to lift 6000 tonnes, min/max. In other words, no more or less.

Ivor was really nervous, but I squeezed in 5999.998 tonnes. Damn it, 2 kilograms short. Unigas were ecstatic, which sticks in the throat a bit as to how they have treated me since.

3500 tonnes was for discharge in Singapore and heated to ambient temperature, the balance for Melbourne in Australia, only that had to be delivered fully refrigerated.

We had a great bunch on board, and every day was fun, until I had to order paint for Singapore. Grudgingly, it was supplied.

Just before we got to Singapore, *Ivor*, who is the tightest, meanest most miserable being going when it comes to money, informed me that he was going ashore to buy a 'Cross' fountain pen, as he could get a good deal here. I had to stay on board and work cargo, but there was nothing new in that.

He disappears ashore, just as my paint arrived, which was checked off and stowed away. At the time we used Hempels for paint, and there was always a bag of freebies sent down, lighters, ashtrays, beer mats, that sort of thing. As I signed for it, I was given the box, and dropped it into my cabin, thinking no more about it.

Ivor duly returned, sought me out and showed me his purchase. He bought one pen for £48 which must have really hurt him, but he was happy with it. It struck me as rather a lot to pay for a pen, especially as his handwriting wasn't that great anyway. This didn't improve it.

About two nights later, the chief engineer, a Glaswegian with a great sense of humour came out with, as we all enjoyed a cold beer.

"Did you get any freebies with the paint Doug?"

"Oh yeah, I'd forgotten all about it. I'll go and get them."

Before I left my cabin, I had a preview, three identical Cross fountain pens to the one *Ivor* had bought, amongst other things. This was going to be fun.

In the lounge and starting at one end, I started dealing it out.

"A pen chief? A pen sparks? A pen second. Oh, you've already got a pen captain, you won't need another one then, have a corkscrew."

His face was fit to burst. He had the piss taken out of him for the rest of the voyage.

After I left the company, that ship was back in Singapore, and sunk a boat, not in the usual way of hitting it. Oh no, much simpler.

A bumboat man had parked alongside, and had set up shop in the mess room aft, when the mate started the pump for the cargo heater, and promptly filled the boat parked underneath the overboard discharge. At first it was thought it had broken free, until it surfaced on its bow line when the ship sailed. Glad I wasn't there.

In Bergesen, they flog the cargo temperatures at will, but what happens when you don't have any temperature gauges?

This happened to me on the *Melrose*, the one and only time I sailed with *Gale Force Gordon*. The ship was badly damaged by this time, and was going off to dry dock to have a new bottom put in.

Stability was critical, as the fuel was being burned off in readiness for docking, but the double bottom tank tops had fractured and ballast was free to flow into the void spaces. I had a hellava job keeping her stable. *GFG* did not help here at all.

Last cargo of ethylene pumped out and we went off to Zeebrugge to tank clean, when Unigas had a brainwave. A part cargo to warm up our tanks. Brilliant.

These tanks are 2 inches thick, so they arranged for 900 tons of Butadiene, loading in Port Jerome, where the *Melrose* was previously banned from, for discharge in Londonderry, or for some Derry. I don't understand the difference here, so if I upset anyone, please accept my apologies.

For ethylene, we used a thing called 'Costald Correlation'. The temperature equated to the saturated vapour pressure, so we didn't need temperature gauges. We do for butadiene though, and *GFG* got in a panic.

"What are we going to do?" he exclaimed.

"Relax" I said, "I've fitted some."

He gave me a puzzled look, so I showed him.

"But these probes aren't even in the tank, and there's no glycerine in the glasses."

"You know that, I know that, but the surveyors don't. Trust me, okay? All I have to do, is nip down on the jetty when it comes aboard, see what the line temperature is, drop it 2 degrees, and then set the gauges accordingly."

Which is what we did. It worked beautifully.

Two days later, he came out with, "How are you going to know the arrival temperature, to calculate the cargo?"

"Easy, I'll back calculate it, to see how much heat it has absorbed, and reset the gauges accordingly."

He gave me that 'I'm not so sure' look.

The surveyor said after we 'calculated' the cargo, which came out perfectly.

"I'll just take a note of the makers of these gauges, chief. They are the best I've seen, and really easy to read. We could do with some of them here."

"Better still," I said, as I didn't want him looking at them 'too' closely, "I've got a spare, and we're getting a new digital system fitted in dry dock. You can have that."

The things I've had to do for Unigas!

Next book? *Ivor the Engine* and, where not to buy a washing machine, when not to deal in the International Currency markets, when not to go into the scrap business, when not to buy cheap wine, when not to drink the local hooch and many more. Including how to upset *Paranoid Pete* with a tape measure and a big magnet. How to upset *Paranoid Pete* anyway. What happens if a director in BP leaves his camera lying around. Why senior staff in Unigas should not drink Brandy and then ride a bike. How to confuse just about anybody, and why ship's officers should not go home on a ferry. Plus many more. And, why you should not challenge the Kirkwall Ladies Hockey team to a match. Especially if none of you have never played hockey before.

Ivor and the story of the bike in the bus? End of Part 7, you'll need a few laughs after that.

All true of course.

PART 7

One would expect that, with all of my experience, it would be very difficult not to be able to sort out a ship, no matter how bad it was. Ordinarily no, but when the ship's owners have been up to no good, and the ship's managers are somewhat inept, plus when they start to realize that they are going to be found out, start looking for a scapegoat, then things take on a different complexion. This was the fourth time I was to be used as the scapegoat, but the managers did not get away with their racket any more than the owners did. It cost them millions but, more than that, they lost credibility in the industry.

I have no doubt they will take a different angle to this tale. I know I would if I was being exposed as they are about to be, but the difference between us, is that I don't lie, nor do I cheat. I don't need to, as I know what I am doing. So what you now read is absolutely true.

Sadly this also reflects badly on Bergesen, who even up until this time were still living on the name they generated in the 1970s, and kept going mainly through their arrogance, that you have heard me referring to before. Only now, they've been caught. Again.

The ship, the *Steven N.* The managers? Believe it or not, this ship had two sets of managers, and *they didn't get along with each other*.

The ship first then. She was what is referred to as a 53. That is, her cargo capacity was 53 000 cubic metres, all up, about 30 000 tonnes of LPG. Built in 1979, and *not* in very good condition.

Indian Officers and Filipino crew. For officers, read rubbish, the absolute worst that you could get, a product of the Bombay Nautical School. Very smart in white uniforms, and that is where 'smart' ended.

The managers? We'll start with the British end first. Bibby Line of Liverpool joined up with Harrison Line and created BHMS, Bibby

410

Harrison Management Services. Referred from now on as just BHMS.

Now it is one thing running your own ships, it is another matter entirely running or managing someone else's. They are about as alike as chalk and cheese, but for some reason, even very experienced people still have trouble recognizing this concept.

But BHMS in Liverpool wasn't the end of it. Oh no, this was just the beginning, as they then made it really complex. Liverpool was where the 'technical managers' were located. Each ship had what they referred to as 'a ship management team'. A technical superintendent, and a ship manager operations. An ex ship's captain to boot, but unfortunately, with no idea of gas tankers whatsoever.

Ever seen a company with two managing directors? They had!

Was I going to be employed by them? No. Who then? By BHMS Isle of Man perhaps? Which is where my CV went, and all the telephone calls. Nope. My contract was with BHMS Cayman Islands.

For many years the Isle of Man had no Employment Protection Act, and if an owner wanted to reduce their staff, they just didn't bother 'phoning you back after your leave, which meant going to look for another job. You could not claim 'unfair dismissal'. It didn't exist.

And shipping companies wondered why there was no such thing as 'company loyalty'.

After the IOM passed their own Act, contracts were issued from the Cayman Islands, where of course there is no Employment Protection Act. I mentioned earlier that on my 'Letter of Appointment', I was appointed to the ship as Chief Engineer, but the second page left me wondering just what I was getting involved with here, as it said, 'the following sub-paragraphs do not apply in your case'. I counted them, there were 17 of them, but there was no indication as to what they were, and more importantly, which ones *did* apply, and what *they* were!

This company have really got themselves screwed up, but there was more to come. Lots more to come!

The ship's officers were employed through BHMS Bombay, which was another cocked-up mess, but this time, 30 years behind the times. You'll hear more about this later.

The ship's crew were employed through BHMS Manilla, who no matter how hard you tried to prevent it, took great delight in sending everything you needed from them, to the port you had just sailed from.

The second set of managers? This was just plain weird.

The ship is owned by a company in the USA, General Ore Corporation, which could be anything, but this company is owned by a mega-rich, fourth generation naturalized Indian, who is also of questionable integrity. His name? Not for me to say here, but he has it painted on both sides of his ship's funnels if you care to take a look.

His side-kick, or right-hand man as he is also known, looks after his 'interests', and is also a naturalized Indian in Los Angeles. His name, oh it means happy and rhymes with Holly, and this guy is anything but. He's a wildcard. He is also a crook, but in a sneaky way.

They are both Sikh, but drink like fish. The side-kick loves Laphroaig Scotch Whisky. I'll tell you how I found that out later.

So far so good. The ship is entered with Bergesens 'pool' of gas tankers, as ships operated by them, but owned by others.

The 'pool' was started as Bergesen wanted to control the 'freight rates' for their own ends, rather than be controlled by the market forces. It is not popular in the industry, but there is little alternative.

My interview, which I had to travel to Liverpool for was a farce. It lasted all of 10 minutes as something had 'come up' requiring all their personnel to sort it out. That was on a Monday.

I was back for pre-joining briefing on the Thursday, to continue on the Friday, and fly out to Panama City on the Saturday.

It was then that I found out that this was not going to be as easy as it first looked, and over these 2 days, I was told the biggest load of junk imaginable, apart from a colossal load of lies.

BHMS had the management of two of this guy's gas tankers, and were expecting to get a third. They didn't and it was entirely their own fault, although they tried to blame me, and probably still do.

There was a problem on board this ship between the master, the chief engineer and the chief officer. They didn't talk to each other.
At all!

The problem was entirely BHMS's own making, only they couldn't see this. Probably still can't. Indian Officers, and in particular Indian Captains follow the traditional British way of running a ship, where the captain is seen as a 'god'.

Over the years as shipping companies, and this started in the UK, reduced costs, the role of marine superintendents vanished, and engineering superintendents took over, which subsequently led to engineers being considered 'superior' to the captain.

On this ship, with its satellite communications systems, two separate lines were put in, one for the ship, and one for the chief engineer. This may sound sensible, and it does have its uses, but what it also does, and is not appreciated by engineering superintendents, is it usurps the position of the master on board.

Traditionally, all communications to the office were through the master. He *had* to know what was going on, on board his ship. Indeed many companies would not accept correspondence from anyone on board, unless it was countersigned by the master. Now, the chief engineer can go behind the captain's back, and did so. Furthermore, the superintendents, or in this case 'ship managers operations and technical' also bypassed the master. This destroyed the command structure on board, as with everything going through a GMDSS station could be read by any of the junior officers, who did so. Ships are not run by consensus of opinion.

The end result was that the four on board who needed to communicate all the time were not doing so, and the junior officers were out of control, doing as they pleased.

To further complicate the issue, the American manager was carrying out secret communications by Satcom C, which were not being copied to Liverpool, but it was his unexpected ship visits which were doing the most damage.

I drew this out of one of the officers after I became suspicious about something else.

It was being suggested that, if certain individuals on board wished to 'retain' employment, then it would be good if they could 'show their willingness' by cooperating with him. In other words here is what you will do, if you don't, find another job, which in India, is not all that easy. I'll come back to this as it involves 'theft'. Big-style theft!

But, back to Liverpool, I was told that within 2 days of joining I had to be ready for an OCIMF inspection, as Bergesens were pressing for this. I just laughed, and told them to get serious.

Two days after joining! One of the primary requirements is that the senior officers must be fully familiar with the ship, and that is just not possible in 2 days.

Then I found out that not only were they changing the master, but also the chief engineer, the chief officer and third engineer, *all* on the same day, *but* the chief engineer was also new to the company and this was going to be his first trip as chief engineer. The chief officer was also new, and had not been on board a gas tanker bigger than 7000 cubic metres. This was to be a major headache for me.

On top of this, all the paperwork systems on board had been, in their own words, 'screwed up', and had to be sorted out as well.

Then came a cracker. "We need you to re-write the Gas Form-C. We want this done in the same style as the *Hugo N*," a sister ship.

Alarm bells started to ring with me here, as this ship was 22 years old, and 're-writing' a Gas Form-C. Why?

The Gas Form-C is a document which goes out to prospective charterers giving the ships cargo performance, how long to change grades, various tonnages, former name(s), etc. It is an important document, as this assesses how much a charterer will pay for a ship. In this case $23 000 per day.

Re-write it? Why? Is someone up to no good perhaps? It was the latter, they were on the fiddle, big style. Again, I'll come back to this, as this is more easily understood in chronological order.

It didn't end here though, they also wanted me to give them a hand in re-writing their Company Instruction Manual. Again a throwback to my days in Bergesen. Their CIM it appeared referred to Noah's Ark!

Plus, 2 days after joining, I had to perform an STS transfer, (cargo ship-to-ship transfer to another gas tanker), only in this case, the other ship is anchored in a tidal river that I'd never been to before, Guayaquil in Ecuador, plus there were no tugs available. Wonderful. Not many masters could do this.

Then they started on about Legionnaire's disease. I nearly fell off my chair until I realized that they were serious. They wanted us to take off all the shower heads, and disinfect them once a month, to prevent an outbreak. Where they got this load of old rubbish from, goodness knows, as I've never heard of a single case of this disease coming from a cabin shower head. I thought it lived in air-conditioning systems.

Finally, both the chief and myself had to meet the 'Fleet Safety Manager'.

I do not think in 30 years at sea, have I met a more obnoxious man, a complete contradiction in terms. In short, just plain dangerous. The last I saw of him was when he moved a ship he was not qualified for! I kid you not. Pillock, just does not seem enough here! His Name? Why? It's not even worth remembering, but if you're looking for him, try the sewer, under M for Mighty big idiot.

His first words to me were,

"I am the DPA, do you know what that means?"

Remember, I am an experienced master amongst other things.

"Of course. What's this then? Master's orals exam?"

"What does it mean then?"

"Designated Person Ashore. A requirement under the ISM Code."

"In any event of anything, you contact me first. Understood."

"Let's just cut the crap here. I know my business, but if I have to contact you, it will be because I don't know what to do next, and that has only happened once," says I.

"What was that?"

"None of your business, it was in another company."

"I have a right to know."

"*No you don't,* and if you continue to treat me like this, then I'll walk out the front door, and you can get someone else." (Not easy to do.)

I said to my new chief after he had been in.

"What do you make of *him*?"

"I was going to ask you if we were on the same planet?"

Enough said.

Friday night, we trotted off to Manchester Airport for a flight to Miami, and then Panama.

Americans in the main are extremely pleasant and hospitable. Only they keep all their nerds to work in immigration at their airports. In any other country in the world, if you are in transit to another country, you do not go through immigration. Even Saudi Arabia, which is by and large still in the twelfth century, manages this. But the USA? And remember, I'm not going to the USA.

The Immigration Officer said to me.

"You do not have a US visa."

"Yes I know, I don't need one, as I'm not going to the USA. I'm in transit to Panama City."

"Go and wait in that line there." Pointing to one which is about a mile long. I just dug in my heels.

"Nope. I'm in transit, here is my ticket, and by the time that 'line' goes down, I'll miss my flight."

"Do as you're told, or I'll call security."

"Call them then."

When they arrived, I explained the 'problem' to them. I was through in less than 2 minutes, but little Adolf wasn't pleased.

415

Arriving in Panama City, we TWO are now four with all our luggage, but only one small taxi. We were tired and still had to get to a hotel in Cristobal, at the Caribbean side of the Panama Canal. The driver was adamant we would all fit into his taxi. We didn't even try, so he ordered another one, by threat of being chased.

The hotel was basic, I was dead thirsty and all was shut.

Next morning we went out to the ship.

Stepping on board, I now knew why I could not get any technical information about the ship from the office in Liverpool. What a wreck! She had just arrived from Bethouia in Algeria with a full cargo of propane, having just before this, spent a month in a repair yard in Malta. Before that she had discharged ammonia in Dakar. This is relevant as you'll find out as we go along. The off-signing captain? He'd been treated very badly, and had every right to be bitter. He'd caught the wrong side of everyone in BHMS, who just would not listen to him. 'They knew best' syndrome prevailing. Not for much longer though.

I didn't get a handover as such. I just counted the money in the safe, and listened to his moaning till I'd had enough. Then I had a good look around. I can get more out of a look around than most people think, and what I saw did not impress, either with the crew or the company.

This was going to be a massive job sorting this lot out. There was enough here for three captains, not just one.

The junior officers just came across as plain bolshy. We'll see about them later. But the crew?

In the main, I like Filipinos, but this lot had their heads down, and that is unusual. I soon found out why.

Next morning, early about 4 am, we set off through the Panama Canal. Neither the ship nor I had been through before, which created some problems, as this ship was going to be inspected for at least the next five transits. A headache we could well do without.

We agreed that I would take over from the captain in the Miraflores Locks, the last set before the Pacific. He would leave by boat one hour later, along with the others. We were at this stage still amicable, but that didn't last. He wanted me to sign his discharge book. Why? I'd no idea either. I'd never been asked this before, so refused. He wasn't pleased but he had already taken his revenge. Whether this was against me or BHMS, I wasn't sure, but I rather suspect it was against the company who had treated him so very badly.

He erased everything from the master's computer, leaving me with nothing. Even the back-up discs disappeared. Thank you very much! Call yourself a seaman!

By this time, I had prepared my Master's Additional Standing Orders and had all the deck officers sign them.

I had also noticed something odd, and was ready to check it out as soon as we were on passage. I also started to crack down hard on safety, within minutes of taking over. "Get the bosun up here now!"

"I've just watched you putting a derrick down. Do it that way again, and someone is going home early."

Rather than pull it sideways on the luffing tackles, and lower it into its seat, they had put the lifting runner on the stowage hook and were pulling it into position on a runner winch. All the forces are now working against each other, and this is highly dangerous. This can be enough to rip a winch out of the deck, or break the runner, which in the case of a wire, you do not want to be anywhere near, as this could easily kill you.

"Secondly, replace both pilot ladders. Start right now, and have it done by the time we arrive in our next port. Neither of them is safe, and neither of them complies with Solas." So much for BHMS Fleet Safety Manager, who had been on board in Malta.

Getting up to full speed, we set off for Guayaquil. I was looking at the 'Load Program' control computer, when I was told that it didn't work. I 'phoned the engine room.

"Chief, bring her up to full sea speed, and when you are clear I'd like a word with you and the mate."

"Right," I said 60 minutes later. "In the Gatun Lake, when we stopped, I did a draft check, and even allowing for it being Tropical Fresh, we seem to be lying 30 centimetres deeper in the water than she calculates out at. There is no indication of sag. That is about 800 tonnes that is unaccounted for."

By next day, we had found it, but why it was going on, took longer to find out.

She had rather a lot of 'sleeve oil'. Every ship has this. It is the amount a chief engineer keeps 'up his sleeve' in case he 'loses' any. Some just refer to it as 'un-pumpables', but it's the same thing. Most captains keep it in check though, but not in this case. We found, 365 tonnes of heavy fuel oil, 148 tonnes of diesel oil, 164 tonnes of ammonia in the deck tanks, and for some reason, 100 tonnes of propane that wasn't in the Bill of Lading. All told, 777 tonnes. Putting this correctly into the loading computer and she was now running correctly. This is above what is officially declared.

But why so much 'sleeve oil?'

The American Manager, remember 'rhymes with holly', had got the previous chief to 'siphon off' a few tonnes per day, and keep it in undeclared tanks, for 'the future'. Not only is this theft, it is fraud, international fraud. You pal, just got caught. Weasel out of this one! The ammonia, was 'acquired' in Dakar during discharge, in case the ship went back onto ammonia, saving the owner some $45 000. Only by cheating the previous charterers though. Caught again! But the cargo? This was a new one on me. To make the mate 'look good', as he could deliver more than he'd loaded. A few tonnes you can get away with, but 100 tonnes?

The ammonia though was the best. BHMS were in on this. One deck tank had 100 tonnes in it, the other 64. But how could this be verified? It couldn't, because it had started leaking in Malta, and if there is one thing that you cannot mistake, it's the smell of ammonia. But the deck tanks had been declared empty to the repair yard. To stop the leaks which were from the tank sounding gauges, spades were pushed into the lines, severing the tapes, and bolted up hard. The only way to measure this now, is to blow some off, cool down the liquid, wait to see where the condensation level appears on the outside of the tank, and then very roughly calculate how much you have. To further complicate it, there is no temperature gauge.

"Right boys, no more flogging, no matter how it calculates out, you put down what it says on the gauges. Okay."

"In the meantime chief, we'll build this extra fuel back in. It belongs to the charterers, they paid for it, so start writing it off. Sleeve oil maximum for this size of ship, 20 tonnes combined."

"But first of all, we'll have a set of cards."

Chief engineers don't like masters asking for this, they regard it as their exclusive domain, but I know how to work out a 'set of cards'.

"What are you looking for, captain?"

"It's Doug, Mike, and I want to know how much power this engine is developing, as we are only doing 12.5 knots."

A few hours later he was back.

"It's putting out between 12 500 and 13 000 horsepower. A bit low don't you think?"

It should be putting out 20 000 horsepower.

"Yep, let's see why it's under powering."

"We can start off by keeping the boiler room door to the accommodation shut for a start, and bring up the pressure to the turbo chargers," said the chief. This ship had two turbo chargers.

"I've already shut that this morning," I said.

"So have I, but it's open again."

"That probably explains why the accommodation is filthy, there is soot on everything."

I winkled it out of the crew. They opened the door because they were cold, and kept warm by the heat from the engine room. The fact that the expansion bellows on one turbocharger is cracked doesn't seem to matter. Never mind that an engine room fire would wipe out the accommodation, or that the carbon monoxide levels were already dangerously high, from the cracked expansion bellows.

I said earlier that the crew had their heads down. A practice which had been going on for nearly 2 years was that each officer had a crew member assigned to him, as his servant. That was stopped immediately. The 'officers' hated me for this, but things had to change and change fast. They resented this till I left, harbouring a grudge.

Most of the next week was spent cleaning the accommodation, it was that filthy, and the company were worried about Legionnaire's disease from shower heads? Half the cabins didn't even have shower heads, some just had an end of a pipe!

In Cristobal, two new dipole aerials were being fitted to the Satcom C system. This is mainly telex, and the aerial is about 6 inches high, looks like a cone with the top flattened off and sits on a base like a flat disc. They are plastic coated.

Our records showed that this was the fourth time they had been replaced in a year, but nobody bothered to find out why. At $1000 each, this was getting expensive.

It didn't take me long to work it out.

They were only 6 feet away from the main engine exhaust, pumping exhaust gases out at 480 degrees Celsius.

During the first night, I heard the whistle going, so got up and went to the bridge. The navigating second mate, I had two second mates and one third mate, was in restricted visibility, but hadn't called me.

"Did you not sign my additional standing orders less than 12 hours ago, which said I was to be called immediately in the event of the visibility falling below 2 miles?"

"Yes sir, but there is nothing around."

"That is not the point, you call me in future, understand? Now switch that whistle off."

"But sir, the rules say it should be sounded in restricted visibility."

"Switch it off, and don't argue with me again. Got it?" Next day, I tried the main ship's whistle. During the night he was using the forward one. The third mate said.

"No need to use that one sir, we only use the forward one."

He got that look that translated into, go and turn the air on.

"But sir, there is no need."

"Right sonny, I've been here 2 days, and what I am finding is a whole load of crap. Now go and get the air turned on to that whistle." "*Now!*"

That explains why it didn't work, a section of pipe had rotted away, but nobody bothered to fix it. It took the chief and me less than an hour.

On the second night before we arrived in Guayaquil, the third mate and I had serious words. Very serious words. It would have been in the logbook, had it and the crew agreement not expired some 3 months before. So much for BHMS's 'quality control'. Wait till we get to the ISM Code. That'll stun you. Fleet Safety Manager's fault too.

Remember how I said I was very strict about keeping a lookout. I'd already drummed this into my three watch keepers on the first night.

I came to the bridge at 10 pm, to find him on the satellite 'phone talking to his fiancée in India, looking out a side window, but not really seeing anything. I pushed my finger on the receiver holder and cut him off. Then I discovered that he had no lookout, and there was a ship passing that he hadn't seen.

"Did you see that ship there?"

"Oh yes sir, I saw him come up on the port bow."

"Really! So how come he is passing us to starboard?"

"It is okay sir, I have the guard zones set on the radar."

"No, it f…ing well is not okay. If I catch you doing anything again on watch apart from keeping watch, then you will be sacked. Got it?"

"But sir."

"No, but sirs! No arguing, *Do as you are told, right*!"

"Yes sir."

"Now, where is the lookout?"

"He has gone for coffee."

"Why? There is a kettle on the bridge."

"But sir, that is the officers' kettle." Where had I heard this before?

"My instructions state that the lookout is maintained at all times, from sunset to sunrise. In future, if I come up here and find no lookout, then a report will be sent to the Maritime Authorities in Bombay, instructing them to investigate your negligence. Your certificates will be forwarded separately. A kettle is a kettle, anyone can use it. Right? Any more of this nonsense, and the kettle goes for a swim. Make sure the 12–4 second mate understands this as well. *Got it?*"

"Yes sir, but."

"Don't push your luck son."

This, however, wasn't the end of it. I caught the 4–8 second mate doing the same thing 2 days later.

I had him in the office next day, and asked him to account for it. He stood there and denied that there had been a ship passing, and that I was wrong. Okay Mr Chakraborty, I'm going to watch you. I could have called the lookout in and cross-examined him, but I don't need friction between the officers and crew.

All Indian officers lie!

Whenever I join a ship, one of the first things I do is to contact my charterer. In this case it was a huge multi-national trading company, based in London, Lucerne and Athens, apart from other offices around the world. My primary contact was with a lady in London.

It is not unusual to find women in chartering, although shipping is mostly male orientated, but I can tell you one thing, women are invariably much more 'switched on' than men, tend to be a lot sharper, and in the main, easier to work with. Good manners always prevail.

This particular lady, turned out to be one of the best, and we still keep in touch. She is also itching for a copy of this book, having read some of the early stuff. It's on its way Janet!

I make a point of keeping charterers informed as to what is going on, rather than having them find out later, which never goes down well. BHMS do not like this approach, but as before, I'll come back to that. You'll like it.

The receiving gas tanker was also chartered by the same group. The *Berge Eagle*. One of Bergesen's 75s. Not a bad ship either, pity about the dumbo they had on board as captain though. But like others before him, he'd picked the wrong guy to argue with.

Guyaquil, Ecuador. Sounds romantic? It's not, trust me.

At least where the *Berge Eagle* was wasn't, but I believe the city was 'acceptable'.

I elected to lie off and drift when we arrived, as I knew nothing about this river or its' currents. I'd already cleared this with Janet so there wasn't a problem.

I started heading in about 3 in the morning, getting my pilot at 07 00, and then put her alongside the *Berge Eagle*, slowly. The operation looks haphazard and amateurish, but it isn't really although the mooring boats were just dug out canoes with big outboards. Being a 53, the *Steven N* has all rope moorings, just under the minimum size for wires which was fortunate. I'd hate to do this with wires, not because of any other reason, than Indians and wires *do not go together*. Plus, ropes float, wires don't.

My first greeting after getting alongside, was not from the captain, but from none other than my old pal, JB. He shouted up from the deck.

"Hey Dougie, where did you find that piece of shite?"

This was going to be trial!

After connecting up the transfer hoses, I started to find out just how good my chief mate was going to be. He was on day work, so there was no excuse for his errors. He had ample time available daily.

In Malta, four new cargo pumps had been fitted. Previously they had had 'Carter' pumps. Someone somewhere had at last woken up to just how useless these things are, and replaced them. Actually as I found out later, they were not replaced because they were useless, another reason entirely, and yes, I'll come to that in due course.

There were eight pumps in all, only although they were the same make, Svanehoj from Denmark, and about the very best, they were two different types. The first four had been used before, but the four new ones had not yet been tested, and I also had to get 'Class' approval for them. Not in Ecuador I won't! It's not known as the 'Land of Bananas' for nothing. No surveyors here, so that can wait.

We had two flexible stainless steel hoses for the transfer, and after four pumps were on line, the cargo was only going through one of them.

Although this was the mate's responsibility, he was rather clueless, so I was called to find out what was wrong.

"Easier Mate, if you open the cross-over valve, that helps!"

He wasn't even embarrassed. This is basic tanker work, setting up your lines correctly before starting cargo. I'm going to have to watch him as well as the junior officers.

To help matters along, the *Berge Eagle* didn't have enough spare capacity to take our full cargo, we were going to have to sail part loaded. Then, disaster.

The chief officer came to me and said,

"I think the tank measuring gauge on No. 2 tank has broken."

Sure enough, it had. Normally a tank will have a back-up system, but the Nos. 2 and 3 tanks on this ship had no central bulkhead, so only had one 'Whessoe' gauge. This type is British and are normally very reliable.

"Right," I said, as he was a bit lost, "shut in the other six pumps, and pump this tank dry. You'll need to watch the discharge pressure gauges all the time as we don't want the pumps running dry. When it is empty, we'll refill it when we've finished."

He was lost, so I explained further.

"On completion, No. 2 is empty, so we can calculate how much is left in the other tanks. Then we know how much this holds to 98%, so we can recalculate the soundings to reduce the other tanks to, as we fill it up."

He was still lost.

"Never mind, I'll do it."

During the discharge, the master on the *Berge Eagle* announced that he had been asked by Bergesen to come over and do a ship visit, and prepare a report for them. Technically, I could refuse, as I knew from Bergesens Standing Orders to Masters (part of which I wrote), that during an STS transfer, the master had to remain on board his own vessel. I had enough to do without another letter, so agreed. Oh boy! Did they have a witch hunt. He and I are not going to get along too well. Charterers had little time for him either I found.

The *Steven N* on deck was a disgrace, rust I can tolerate, but dirty I cannot. Liquid Gas if it gets spilt, cleans itself up, so there is no reason for a gas tanker to be anything other than pristine. If the accommodation was filthy, it at least was getting cleaned up. The engine room was 20 times worse, and the LPG compressor rooms 20 times worse than the engine room. Getting an idea of the magnitude of my task?

Then there were the glory holes!

Spare parts for gas tankers tend to be expensive, mostly because everything is of a very high standard. It needs to be as it can take a hell of a battering, especially in the gas plant, or generators.

Outside the ship's central office, which I also had to resurrect, was the first 'glory hole'. This was mostly junk, but Indians never throw anything away. That was going to change. This is *very* hard to do!

One deck down was the expensive 'glory hole'. I estimated in this one room alone, were spares with a value in excess of 1 million US dollars, *but* it was just thrown in, no logic, organization or care given to what was, delicate equipment.

Then we had three electrical lockers, value of spares, well in excess of 4 million US dollars.

Then there were the LPG spares. You could have run a fleet of gas tankers with what we had in here. I was told by one of the managing directors in Liverpool, that this ship had five spare crankshafts for the LPG compressors. *Five*!

Gas tanker seamen reading this would use the word *incredible,* or *unbelievable*, are you sure? As they would never have seen as much as one spare crankshaft in their time. I'd never seen a spare in 25 years on gas tankers.

Sadly, not one of them had been looked after, and were rusty. They were of questionable use.

Type of LPG compressor? Sulzers.

Only the best type of oil-free compressor ever made!

In 20 years with this type of compressor, I have only ever seen the cylinder block off one once for re-skimming, and that was on the *Melrose* in dry dock. These compressors are akin to Allen Diesels. They can run with bits hanging off them. They are that well made.

Most modern gas carriers use screw compressors now, as they are smaller and much more efficient.

The best are made by Howden, a Scottish Company based in Glasgow. But the idea for this type actually came from another process which started over a hundred years before. In the Jute Industry. You can see an example of this in 'The City Mills' in Dundee. It's also a fascinating day out.

I'll stay on this subject, as apart from crankshafts, we had more, lots more. Each of our four compressors has 12 valves, six on the inlet side, six on the discharge side. These valves are stainless steel, highly machined, and expensive. Roughly $4500 each. It is normal to carry one spare set, six of each. Plus a big bag of their little springs, which generally go '*boing*' when you dismantle one, then disappear, hence lots of spares.

In the store, I lost count as I passed 700. All brand new.

Pistons? A mere 25. Connecting rods? Only 20.

Then there were the padlocked lockers.

I hate padlocks on ships. You can never find the damn key. They are useful for the Suez Canal, and West Africa but that is about it.

In Gibsons it was a matter of pride that nothing was ever locked. Nothing ever went missing either.

For padlocks, I keep the master key. Bolt cutters! Big bolt cutters!

When they were 'un-locked', in behind the doors we found spares for other ships, and then in every corner, junk. Nothing other than plain junk.

The master from the *Berge Eagle* of course photographed this, and a few other things and sent the pictures off by satellite to Oslo, along with a few derogatory comments, which I thought was not only unfair, but unprofessional. We'd inherited this mess only 3 days before, so weren't to blame. There started a witch hunt from Oslo.

There was one very interesting photo though, which he took as we came alongside. There was a white trail on the hull from the hawse pipe under the port anchor, and all along the side. On boarding, we'd come up the starboard side. What could that be? I had a closer look.

This I had not seen in years. It was ammonium nitrate. From 2 inches thick to a trace. Where did this come from then?

I weaseled the truth out of one of the second mates. It took some doing but I got it. They just do not like telling the truth, in case they get the blame for something, or, anything at all really. That is why you should never employ an Indian as master. Personally, I would restrict all Indian officers to live sheep carriers. Or, better still, India.

One thing I have said to my crews for years, is this, 'if something breaks or if you break something, or if you just plain cock-up, then tell me. Then we can get it fixed or sorted. But if I find that you are covering something up, then I will get annoyed, and I will always get the truth in the end. Better to tell me the truth at the start.'

It transpired that after discharge in Dakar, before going to Malta, there was a residual amount of liquid ammonia in No. 1 tank, so they stuck the eductor hose down into the cargo tank. Normally LPG cannot be drawn out in this way, as, as soon as a vacuum is created above the liquid, it will vapourize. But not with ammonia. It can be pumped out this way, but for another reason. It is anhydrous and has a terrific affinity for water. As soon as it smells water, it jumps at it. But, after the venturi in an eductor, is also cavitation, air, so ammonium nitrate is produced, which after leaving the discharge hose sticks to anything it comes into contact with.

Why were they doing this? Because they didn't like the smell. Aw dearie me!

Of course, the 'photos end up in Los Angeles, where I am asked to comment. You know me by now, tell the truth. With a copy of course to Liverpool. Then the brown stuff hit the fan.

The technical superintendent, the one with gas tanker knowledge exclaimed, "ammonium nitrate, where the hell did that come from? I told Captain -------- (rhymes with Holly) that it was salt!"

Not a lot you can say about that really, other than. What a silly billy! Of the 30 000 tonnes of cargo we arrived with, we discharged some 17 000 tonnes, and then hit a snag. If we weren't finished and ready to sail by 14 00, we were delayed to the next day. Fair enough but why? Oh it has nothing to do with the ship. The pilot. He has to get home afterwards, and doesn't like travelling in the dark. Bandits!

We spent the evening filling up No. 2 tank, the mate now having sussed out what to do. Then he came up with a cracker. Now bear in mind this is his first time on a fully refrigerated gas tanker.

"Do you think we could just lift the top off and lift up the float on a hook?" (On the Whessoe tank sounding gauge.)

"*You are joking aren't you?*"

There was 7000 tonnes of propane in this tank by now. He wasn't joking, he was quite serious about it.

"We'll fix this gauge on an empty tank, not a full one, and as I'm the only one who has does this before, I'll do it, and you can assist."

I'd already informed charterers about this, because if I couldn't hook it up from topsides, then I was going to have to gas free the tank, and go inside. Losing about 40 tonnes of propane, and using about 30 tonnes of diesel, making inert gas, all told, the better part of a week, for something I could normally fix in an hour.

Having filled up No. 2 and re-calculating once more, we settled down for the night.

Down aft, they were letting their hair down. The Filipinos that is.

Ordinarily I wouldn't allow this, especially in Brazil, where it is strictly taboo, but after the abuse the officers had given the crew, I relented. I allowed the girls on board. They needed to relax a bit.

Actually it had great spin-offs which we all benefited from, but that came later. The mate was aghast. He came bursting in.

"Captain. There are girls on board. That is not allowed. They must leave, and you must tell them!" Just who does *he* think he is?

"Now look mate, first of all, I know, because I sanctioned it. It is better that I allow it, as if I don't they'll sneak aboard anyway. This way, they are limited to a small part of the ship, and the crew need to let their hair down. Trust me, I know Filipinos and after tonight, We'll get twice the work out of them."

He was another who suffered from the caste system in India.

Here is a tip for shipping personnel managers. If you employ Indian Officers, *never* mix creeds. If you have a Sikh, ensure they are all Sikhs. If Moslem, all Moslem and so on. It saves oodles of aggravation and work. Secondly, never agree to an extension of a contract. When they first come on board, they work their contract at half speed, if extended, that goes down to quarter speed. If you have the option, don't employ them at all.

The girls were *never* a problem, they behaved impeccably, and were good fun. We fed them, but that was nothing to us. It was probably the only chance they had of a decent meal anyway. Yes, they were all on the game, but their boss kept a good eye on them. The crew on the *Berge Eagle* were jealous though, as most of them on our ship were their girlfriends.

Apart from the mate, the only other who objected were the two second mates, and it was only afterwards that I discovered that they were homosexuals. If I'd known at the time, they would have been on the first plane back. That can cause no end of trouble on a ship.

Before we sailed I said to the mate.

"We have to get the ship's speed up, I noticed on the way down that she's making too much wake, for ballast passages, pull her back to 3 metres by the stern, that should help." It did, improved the speed by 2 knots. Now to get to work on the engine. But I had to go more by the stern in the end.

That night, a horrible problem arose, one we never really got solved.

'Crickets.'

These are not the European type, the little green ones that you can hear, but never find. Oh no, these are the rain forest type, that live in families of 20 billion plus. Plus they can fly, at near sonic speed and usually, all at once.

They are about 4 cms long, 1 wide, and black. They must have been attracted by our lights, because in the morning we couldn't move for them. They were everywhere. They may only live for about 7 days, but they are damn quick learners, especially where to get into a ship's accommodation. Just cleaning the bridge, we emptied the Hoover 37 times, and that filled a black bin liner.

They were impervious to fly spray. Eventually I got something in Venezuela that got rid of them, and that was after I tried Malathion and Pyrethrum, two insecticides used to fumigate ships. I ended up with Cetremitum, which I remembered from my college days. They didn't like that at all. Oh, did it make them hop! Usually dead as well.

We had the deck sprays on, we hosed down, and we were still at it 3 days later going through the Panama Canal, where even Port Health came down, with a view to detaining us. It was the pilot who told him.

"Look drop it, they've been fighting this for 3 days, and are sick of it too, they nearly have it cracked."

The *Berge Eagle* was delighted every time we came alongside, as all of theirs just hopped over as well. Obviously they don't like the colour green then.

When you start increasing the power of an engine back up to its design output, you can expect a few bits to fall off. On the way back up to Panama, the chief called up with,

"Doug, we are starting to show water in the crankcase."

"Okay Mike, shut it down, that sounds like a telescopic leaking."

Sure enough, it was, but not in a normal place.

A telescopic is a pipe which supplies cooling water to the piston crown. Where they pass through the engine block is a small collar which acts as a guide and a seal. This one had come loose. He said about an hour later.

"How did you know that?"

"Easy Mike, I've been with this type of engine before."

To get it back in though, meant pulling out the piston, which is no mean job. Ordinarily, a ship would have hydraulic jacking gear to take off the cylinder head. Not this ship, though, she just had a big impact spanner, which is far from ideal. Taking it all to bits and putting it all back together again took 18 hours, to replace the collar took the best part of 10 minutes. These are big weights as well, and you have to be careful, as the ship is rolling on the swell, and there is nothing you can do about it. A piston, complete with connecting rod, is 3 tons, a liner 5 tons, a cylinder head 1.5 tons.

We just drift around waiting until it can get started again. In the meantime, the mate and I had a good look around and out came the order book.

"Right mate, get two new fire wires. These are done."

"It would be cheaper to get a coil of wire and make our own sir."

"So how are we going to get certificates for them?" I said.

"Get a complete new set of wires for the derricks, and specify *non-rotating wire*."

"But sir, there is nothing wrong with these. They are okay."

"These wires are kinked, flattened, and rusted. The safe working load of these derricks is 5 tons, I just down rated them to 2 tons. While we are at it, see if you can find the Chain Register, I've not come across it yet."

Why is it that Indians will put up with cheap inferior junk, at great risk to themselves and others? I'll tell you, because they just don't care. Alang beach, being the perfect example.

"Now, the accommodation, get all these welds on the doors painted, and leave out some paint for the deck heads. I'll get the galley crew to paint them in the evenings."

"Oh no sir (wobbling his head as they do), that is a job we keep for wet days."

"Now look here mate. If the inside of the accommodation is dirty and badly maintained, then the outside follows suit, because nobody is taking a pride in their ship, or in their own personal hygiene. You may be happy going around in a hovel, but I am not. We'll have cabin inspection tomorrow morning to find out what needs attending to while we are at it. Oh, and another thing, order up a complete set of shower mats, the rubber sucker type. Okay?"

"No sir, we don't need shower mats. They only get dirty underneath."

Give me strength, please!

"Well, if they get dirty underneath, then you clean them. Okay?"

More head wobbling.

Now the Panama Canal should be easy. In the main, it is, but we have to be inspected for the next four transits, and they have their own paperwork, which means writing out a crew list in longhand, they will not accept a prepared crew list that all ships have, to be attached.

Oh, and they have a Panama Canal Tonnage as well, but I'm not even going to try to explain how that is worked out. Judging by the standards of their surveyors, they don't know either.

The Panama Canal is the most fascinating place I've ever been to.

To build this place in the first place showed remarkable foresight, considering it was finished in 1914. The locks are 33 metres wide and 300 metres long, and in 1914, nothing was that big.

33 metres equates to just over 108 feet which was fortunate as the *Steven N* was 107 feet in beam, which left me 6 inches on either side, plenty really. I wouldn't trust a Forth Pilot here though or a Suez one!

The place is well run, but us being LPG could only transit during the day, and I can tell you that that makes a long day.

One day I will take a holiday there, not for the Canal, but for another reason. On joining I met a lady from Chicago, who was a naturalist, and she told me that there were something like 974 different species of birds in Panama. The ones that fly around the ships, and the neighbouring jungle are absolutely beautiful. Gorgeous colours.

There is another reason though. I got on great with all the pilots, and on one day alone, both the agents and the pilots came out with the same thing.

"As you are a single man, captain, you should come out here and get yourself a Panamanian wife, then get a job as a pilot."

I'm not as much as going looking for a wife, but they have all invited me to their farms. Forget their names? Not possible, the best was called Jimmy Hendrix. I kid you not. He even looked like him. Crew problems though were never very far away, and my electrician was forever at the doctor, this time being no exception. When I had the full story, he was 3 months over his contract, and had suffered in the same way as the crew. When he came back, I collared him. He was Filipino, an officer ostracized by the Indians.

"Right, I've arranged for you to be repatriated today, go and pack your gear, and I'll sign you off now. I don't need the doctor's report but

I'll take it anyway."

Was a man more relieved, a full year on a ship, is more than enough for anyone, but with Indians? BHMS in the Isle of Man weren't pleased though. Seemingly I required their permission. Tough girls, I don't work that way. An electrician was available and had been on the ship before, so would join in our loading ports, along with a new second engineer.

This was where personnel and I had a serious difference of opinion, which to give them their due, they (she) later apologized for.

The second engineer who was joining had been sacked from the *Hugo N*, and was transferring to us, to 'finish his contract'. One of Los Angeles' little nerds, who was 'in'. Had I known this at the time, I would have sent him packing, as he was responsible for a serious incident that nearly cost the ship. Our loading ports were to be La Salina and Puerto Jose, both in Venezuela. Our charterers had the contract to export all the LPG from Venezuela to the Pacific seaboard countries of South America.

La Salina is a devil of a place to get to, as it is in Lake Maracaibo, and the pilot station is 80 miles to the east of the entrance to the Lake. On the way there, I sent a request to Liverpool. It went something like this.

"Re cocked-up filing systems and paperwork, you were not joking. This is in such a mess that we are going to need some help here in sorting it out. Please consider having two secretaries fly out to sail with us for about 3 months who can overhaul this system and then teach us all how to use it properly. My trading pattern just isn't going to allow us the time to do this as well as operate this ship."

Oh, it was considered at board room level in Bibby Line, then turfed out. They regretted this decision later, it cost them dearly. They suggested sending out the quality assurance boy to do an audit, which would do nothing other on board, than irritate and annoy. We needed it sorted out, not made worse with 'discrepancy reports'.

To further complicate an already unbelievable system, BHMS were trying in conjunction with the Panamanian Flag that the ship was under, of operating the ship with British Legislation as well, because, 'they liked it that way'. What a load of dinosaurs! That lot went for a swim, which reduced the number of files by 20. Totally and unnecessarily, a complete waste of time.

Then I had to find the rest of the files. There were loads missing, but I found 16 when I had my first cabin inspection. Why were they in cabins? Oh they just liked having them there. Indians? Yep.

Going into La Salina, I said to the mate.

"As soon as we are alongside, get a fresh water hose on and keep it on until we sail. We are down to 30 tons, and there is no telling how long we may have to wait for our next parcel in Puerto Jose."

Two hours after getting alongside, it is still not on, so I asked why.

"The crew wanted to go ashore Sir, and now there is no-one to do it."

"Oh yes there is. You. You let the crew go ashore without attending to their duties first, so get it on now."

"But sir. *I am an officer.*"

"If you don't get it on right now, you will soon be an unemployed officer."

He never did improve, he just got worse, which pushed up my workload no end. In the end I was putting in 120 hours a week.

I'll say one thing about Venezuela, they are dead easy to work with.

We loaded butane in La Salina, this being our intended pattern for the next few voyages, Nos. 1,2 and 4 in propane, No. 3 in butane. All up, 22 200 tonnes of propane, 8006 tonnes of butane. Unfortunately, this was not what was termed the vessels 'normal segregation'. More modern gas tankers can cope with this, but for this ship, the reliquefaction plant was split into two units, one for each grade. Normal segregation would have been Nos. 1 and 3 tanks, and Nos. 2 and 4 tanks.

But we managed until it went bang!

The master's computer, apart from being erased, was about as slow as a snail, so I ordered a laptop, eventually for myself, but until we had this mess sorted out, we would use it in the ship. To speed up the masses of repetitive paperwork, of which about only 10% was necessary, I had my technical superintendent bring out 'Via Voice' software, as he was joining us in the Panama Canal, and leaving after the OCIMF inspection was completed during the next STS transfer in Guayaquil.

Actually, he was a pleasant guy, and I got along with him okay, apart from his desire to buy the cheapest of anything, which invariably fell to bits after a few days.

His problem was that he just didn't have a big enough budget to work with.

The 'crook' in Los Angeles (rhymes with Holly, but from now on, we'll refer to as em em) was trying to run a gas tanker as you would run a bulk carrier, which is obviously much cheaper to run.

A ship of this size needs a budget of about 12 to 14 000 US dollars per day, roughly half of its earnings. We had half of that.

There is a company in Norway, but they are worldwide, called 'Unitor'. Anyone who knows anything about ships has a contract with them. They are slightly more expensive, but you are guaranteed quality, and on a ship that is important in the middle of the ocean. You can also get anything, almost anywhere, anytime, and that is precious. I talked my superintendent into getting a contract.

My laptop computer eventually arrived after 2 months, but was useless. I'd arranged for it to be bought through the Isle of Man office, but they forgot to register the software before sending it out. I could have done it by satellite 'phone, but not at an additional cost of $300 plus.

Before arriving back at Panama, my chief wandered in with.

"Come and see what you think of this. See if you think the engine room fans are going in the right direction."

With me, any chance of getting away from my desk was welcome.

Sure enough, one of the fans was going backwards.

"You know Mike, that's 50% of the air that's not going to the engine room. These drive belts look a bit slack as well, got any spares?"

"I've got more spares for things I don't need, and none for things I do." He was getting exasperated, but then again, he was first trip Chief Engineer, so could be excused.

"Right, get a part or reference number, and I'll get a full set in Cristobal."

"We need to go through the office for this you know."

"Look Mike, that'll take months. We need them now."

I got a set, and after they were fitted, blew a proper amount of air into the engine room. It was a heck of a struggle getting a door open to get in though, with the over pressure. Ships speed went up again. At the end of each month, it is time to work out the wages on board. This is always a heck of a lot of work that should really be done in the office, but it is 'cheaper' for them just to dump it on the ship, and do. BHMS don't help much here though, as in their instructions to masters it says, 'we will be happy to accept ship-generated forms.'

In other words, we have to design and produce the forms as well.

Remember this is a convoluted set-up, and nobody tells you in advance how it works. Oh no! They leave you to find that out for yourself.

Now, here is how it goes, see if you could do this, at the same time as operating a ship and going through the Panama Canal and watching out for just about every dangerous practice imaginable with fourth rate officers and engineers.

Filipino crew, after allotments and deductions for sales from the ship's bond and slop chests are paid the balance in cash at the end of each month. Cash has to be ordered in advance, usually $25 to 30 000. No matter how much you tell them, they send it to the wrong port. The one you have just left and are not going back to.

Indian officers will allot most of their wages, after deductions on board to their bank accounts in India, but the remainder is carried over to next month, which accrues until they leave the ship, in which case they take it as cash, unless of course, they take it at the end of the month without giving you any notice. You draw cash for Indians from the Isle of Man.

For British Officers, you notify the Isle of Man at the end of the month of deductions to be made for sales from the bond and slop chest or cash advances etc.

So far so good. Now it gets complicated.

Charterers' representation from the bond locker and slop chest?

Charged to charterers through the Isle of Man. Then there is radio traffic for all three different groups on board, which is notified to Bombay and Manila, but routed through Liverpool.

Now when someone sends flowers? It really causes chaos.

I don't profess to be good at accounts. I manage, but it causes some severe headaches, which I and just about every other master at sea could well do without.

But what really causes the greatest offence, is when you receive a snotty message from an accountant, asking where such and such a thing is, about 2 months later, by which time you are totally confused.

In Gibsons there was a woman who did this. Her nickname? *Nit picking Nan*! *And could she nit pick*!

Virtually every master has a column, miscellaneous! Just not to waste any more time, to get it all to balance.

When you think you have it worked out, along comes one of the crew, with a 'special remittance'. Or worse, getting rid of junk, and selling it to a scrap merchant for example, means putting the money back in. Is it any wonder then that this just 'disappears?' It is better to get it in somehow, because this causes utter chaos in the office. Why not? They created this mess in the first place.

Having finally got it all together, you pay everybody. Only I have Indians, and they have everything worked out to the last lakh, and to hell with your exchange rates. The obvious thing is to carry any 'mistake' over to the next month, but will they agree to this? Like heck, but I'm not starting over again for one who cannot keep himself at least clean.

Now, to further complicate matters, the third mate had a negative balance from the previous month. This is against most company's standing instructions and BHMS were no exception. Normally there is no allotment in the first month. This is retained on board in case he is a naughty boy and requires to be flown home at his own expense. If this guy had had that, he would already have been on his way.

I put my foot down. No allotment next month, and none until you have at least $1500 on board. He tried everything to get me to change my mind. Tough. Then he did something very stupid. He went behind my back and complained to the company. They replied in his favour, and he read the message which came in on the e-mail before me, so smugly came and said so.

I said to him.

"Have you ever seen a Sikh with no hair?"

"Because that is what you are going to have if you pull a stunt like that again. Now f--- off."

I was as you may have gathered, none too pleased. The company? Oh they were well and truly put in their place, prompting yet another profound apology from the Isle of Man.

Trying to bring this ship up, and maintain discipline was being made impossible by the very people who should have been supporting me.

To finish off, getting rid of ship's garbage, has for some time now been stopped from just 'chucking it over the side'. And rightly so. Our incinerator wasn't working, just like a lot of other things, and this garbage just had to be landed ashore, but we have to pay to get someone to take it away, generating yet more paper, and another two files, one for receipts, one for messages requesting disposal.

But where does the money come from, Manila, Bombay, Isle of Man, or Liverpool?

See what I mean about lack of foresight. It will be a clever accountant who works that lot out, but nobody's fault except their own. Try getting them to see that though.

Now, before I get too cross, here is a thing that a few people in Government and other places may like to consider, as I am sure that this was never thought of at the time.

GMDSS equipment is on the bridge. Okay, at sea, this is manned 24 hours a day. Not in port though.

But, and it's a big *but*. How do you get through to officers from third-world countries, and these make up the majority of ship's officers nowadays, that the navigation of the ship is more important than answering the 'phone?

I have seen this time and time again in a lot of companies.

On my bridge, no one on watch may make a telephone call while on duty. Penalty. Instant dismissal. No ifs, no buts, just plain sacked.

But what about incoming calls?

The only two people on watch at night are the Officer on Watch and the lookout.

To answer the 'phone, either the lookout is suspended, or the officer of the watch is distracted. It is invariably a family member calling in from the other side of the world with little regard for time differences, so the recipient has to be tracked down, further distracting the watch from looking after the navigation of the ship.

Could we therefore have a GMDSS unit designed with an answering service, preferably a selective one, so that when the captain is asleep, the office can't waken him?

If you could get a computer for the e-mails that you can't play games on, then that would be a big help. The first person I caught doing that is still waiting for his coccyx bone to re-attach to the rest of his skeleton.

The non-marine reader may be surprised to learn that there have been collisions between ships, as the officer of the watch has been on the 'phone. A particularly bad one in the North Sea when a man was killed. The ship was carrying acrylonitrile. Remember Part 3?

I wonder if any of the three ships that 'ran aground' on the *Tricolour* in the southern North Sea, had officers on the 'phone at the time. I'm willing to bet that at least one of them was.

Our transits of the Panama Canal were almost always pre-booked. This costs the charterer more, but means they get their ship through with the minimum of delay.

I still have to anchor until we are cleared though, only on this occasion, I went straight into the inner anchorage. The pilot station, in keeping with every other pilot station in the world, is nowhere near where it says on the chart, so I get my pilot inside the breakwaters, where the only thing left to do is stop and throw the pick (anchor) out.

Oh by the way. Would the person who sent in to the Admiralty, the Hydrographic Note, showing a 3.6 metre patch across the entrance, please note that, you had the wrong port!

I referred to my chartering manager earlier as a very switched-on lady. I do not wish to be derogatory to the female gender, but there are some jobs in shipping that they should not get involved in, especially when they do not know what they are doing. At the same time though there are some jobs that men should not get involved in either, in this case, Panama Canal Surveyors.

Now this particular female was rather pleasing to the eye, spoke impeccable English, and that with Filipinos is somewhat fatal. Lecherous race! She said to me during inward clearance.

"Captain, our computer shows that this ship is a 'Combined Timber/ LPG carrier.' We have never heard of this before. Could you comment please?"

"Certainly. It's about time you bought a new computer!"

"It is wrong then?"

"I'd say so, I think."

"Thanks captain, I thought so too." Liar, very pretty, but still a liar.

Then we get the male variety. Obnoxious? He'd put *TNT* to shame.

"I am here for your safety captain, so I want to test a few systems. We will start with the emergency shut downs on the generators, and then as you clear the locks at Miraflores, I will test the emergency shut down on the main engine."

"You can just forget it mate. We are not doing any of that."

Then he got awkward.

"I can detain your ship if you do not do as instructed, captain."

"For a start, my generators are on line, because my LPG refrigeration plant is on line. Stop a generator, and that shuts down the reliquefaction, and before you know, propane will be bubbling out and drifting towards town. Do you think that is responsible? No? Nor do I.

Secondly, if you think I am going to allow a 30 000 ton gas tanker to go NUC in a channel, just to satisfy you, then you are wrong. Now, I want your name, as I am going to 'phone your boss."

We did not test anything, but next week received a lovely letter from his 'boss' complimenting us on such a fine ship. Little did *he* know!

Next morning at 3 am, is time to heave up the anchor and set off. Like anything, the first time is interesting, by the third time it's just a drag, as it is going to be another long day. No rest until clear at about 17 00, and even then there are all the messages to send.

My superintendent though has decided that we don't quite have enough to do. What did I know about hydro blasters? Had I ever used one? I could see what was coming.

What did I estimate was required to bring the deck fabric up to scratch?

At a very rough estimate Alan, I'd say, 4 months, six specialist cleaners, and an increase in the budget of $250 000.

He did some figures, and they didn't match mine. Lower of course.

My second mate (navigating), the queer one, and in more ways than one, did not take kindly to having me re-draw his course lines.

"But captain, I am the navigating officer. We go where I say we go."

"No, Mr Goldie Arora, *I am the captain*. We go where *I say we go*. Right now, by going my way means we reduce the distance to Guayaquil by 8 miles, which is 30 minutes' steaming time. On top of this, take that useless piece of information out of your passage plan. The one where you give advice about submarines on the Clyde."

"But sir, this is a Submarine Exercise Area."

"I know that Goldie, but the Clyde is in Scotland, we, are in Columbia. How many submarines do you think the Columbian navy have? Or indeed, do they even have a navy?"

Then I was put under severe pressure. The charterers had decided to extend the charter party by 30 days with an option of extending it again, by 30 days.

"How long will you be on board Captain?"

"Probably till the end of November, why?"

"Oh, we'll probably extend it further, as long as you are on board, as we have seen a vast improvement in performance." See what I mean about being put under severe pressure.

So it's back to the *Berge Eagle*, not only for an OCIMF inspection, nor only to discharge, but to get a new load of crickets!

The OCIMF inspection was performed by an independent consultant who had flown out from the UK, on behalf of Shell in London. Fortunately he was an ex-tanker man, so we ran circles round him and got the ship approved. Bergesen in Oslo, just couldn't believe it. You just have to be economical with the truth.

It was only a part discharge, but it ran over 2 days, so plenty of time for the crickets to join us. A double load this time!

But what else showed up? Nothing other than the *Borthwick*, and we were loading him, after going through the *Berge Eagle*'s pipework.

However, at 2 o'clock in the morning, we had a big problem.

Our Automatic Voltage Regulators (AVRs) started acting strangely on the generators, then we blacked out completely. Then the new electrician showed unbelievable incompetency.

To get the ship up and running again, we had to use the emergency generator, but to get the breakers in and held in until the main generators came on, was powered by batteries. I'd never seen this before. *But,* what has the electrician gone and done? Only the previous day? He's topped up the batteries with fresh water.

Why?

Because he was too lazy to go down to the engine room for some sulphuric acid.

Why?

Because he no longer had his 'servant' from his previous voyage.

And actually said so too!

All the cells were as flat as a pancake. Dead. Goosed. Forever!

Fortunately, we got two sets from the *Berge Eagle*, and were up and running again, only some 5 hours later.

Not back to Panama though, no, too easy, we're off to Callao in Peru. We're off to visit the pirates. Fortunately, we didn't enter port, but went to a submerged pipeline about 2 miles off. A bigger fiasco would be harder to organize. To hold position, we have two anchors out, then two long headlines to buoys, and slackened until the pipeline was beside to manifold.

But down aft, the four stern lines were precisely 5 metres too short to reach the buoys. Ever seen an Indian trying to marry two mooring lines together? Take it from me, you don't want to. My hair was black when I joined at the start of the voyage. It was grey by now. And shorter!

The pilot reckoned to take 40 minutes to moor. It took us 5 hours.

Of course, it couldn't be a normal discharge, we had to use the cargo heater, and it hadn't been used in years. Plus guess who had done no maintenance on it. None other than super-mate. It had a big crack in it. One new booster pump had been fitted in Malta. Straight on to the old mountings, which when you looked underneath had rotted away. But we got it all to work, after a fashion. Just as well we weren't in port.

The amount of representation I got through was incredible, akin to Brazil.

But we're now empty, and could fix the Whessoe on No. 2 tank. Could I find any spare tapes? They are about 10 mms wide, with holes every 10 cms. You cannot use them for anything else.

You don't automatically think of looking for Whessoe gauge tapes in a biscuit tin, and if it hadn't slipped off the shelf as we explored the glory hole, and sprung open, might never have been found.

Doing this sort of job when you are still fully gassed up can be risky, and I've no doubt that if our 'Fleet Safety Manager', the pillock, found out, then it just wouldn't have been allowed, so we just didn't tell him.

It is actually quite easy, and requires a bit of luck. BHMS had faxed us out instructions as to how to do it with a magnet, but they were binned straight away. Stainless steel is *not* magnetic.

All you need is a biggish hook, a bit of angle iron, and a length of rope. No finesse here, it is all home made. The hook is tied onto the angle iron which is then clipped onto the guide wires and lowered on the rope. All the time propane vapour is spilling out, as we don't want any air in the tank. Then a bit of jiggling to try and catch the float. I actually got it first try, but it fell off. About 10 minutes later though we did get it up and secured with another rope. Now for the nasty bit. Putting on the new tape, as propane vapour is cold and you've got your head, hands and arms in it. That blooming split pin just would not come out. It did eventually, and we were up and running again after putting it all back together.

The mate wanted to do this with a full tank? Idiotic to even think it, far less consider it.

That night at dinner, the chief told me a funny story which I woke up with, laughing at 2 in the morning. I'll tell it here, as it is rather good.

This ship had originally been owned by the Mexicans, who are hilarious to work with, as when common sense was handed out, they were having a day off.

Now my chief was working on a Mexican container ship and on passage to Mexico, when they noticed that one of the reefer (refrigerated) containers was warming up, and no matter what they tried, couldn't reverse the rising temperature.

After consulting with the company, the manifest declared that it was full of Tiger Prawns, which are very expensive. So, hunt around for another one of the same size that has something less valuable. They found one. Diced vegetables.

Right, dump the vegetables overboard, and transfer the Tiger Prawns. A big job, and there are 10 tons of each. They had every fridge on the ship full of vegetables, before the balance went over the side. This is okay to do, as the fish will get a free meal. As long as you retain the plastic bags.

Eventually the container is empty, time to start transferring the prawns, so they opened the doors, *but* there weren't any prawns! What there was, was the Mexican Ambassador's brand new Mercedes! In a block of ice to boot. Not a Prawn in sight.

We also at this time started having problems with the deck tanks, they were starting to leak. I wanted to dump them, but my 'ship manager operations' who incidentally knew precious little about gas tankers, said no. Most forcefully. It wouldn't have been so bad if it had been possible to stop the leaks, but there was no way of isolating them. By this time, the ammonia in them is up to 13 bars pressure, and I reckoned the starboard one was now 100% full, but no way of checking though. I warned him that if a control pipe fractured, we may not have been able to seal it, and if it went in the Panama Canal, then we would most certainly be detained.

To no avail. I'll come back to this.

Now back in Balboa for the canal again, we are up for survey, one of which was load line. This is going to be fun, as this ship's steel work was iffy to say the least. Not the hull as such but all the attachments such as ventilators.

About halfway through, the surveyor, who it turned out was Indian, but a naturalized US citizen, and very pleasant with it, and I were standing on the poop deck catching our breath and having a cold drink, when I just leaned onto a ventilator, and kept on going as this thing folded up beneath me releasing a big cloud of crickets.

He thought it was funny, but not when another two went the same way. Okay, I'll get the shipyard in, which I did, only BHMS didn't agree, and wanted me to take 6 months on a visa. I took 30 days. I'm not mucking around with my or my crew's safety.

There were a few other things that cropped up, but nothing major, until there was a bit of a rumble, then a bang. An LPG compressor motor had collapsed. These things weigh 2 tons each, and are the most cussed things to get out, involving a lot of heaving and grunting.

This is where it all started to go wrong.

I 'phoned in to the office in Liverpool, but the only person who was there was one of the managing directors.

Where is the DPA then? The obnoxious one? So much for the ISM code then eh! Even they (he) can't get it right, but then they couldn't get much else right anyway.

I agreed with the MD, that the motor would be landed while transiting the canal, and flown immediately to New Orleans, where I knew of a company who could do a rush job on it, and then fly it to Jose where it could be back in before we went to load.

This is also where I fell out with the 'mate'.

After clearing the Gatun locks, all he has to do is land the motor into a launch, and *make sure everything is ready beforehand*, so as we're not delayed.

He didn't and he was so slow lowering it that the wire runner started unwinding, and then he got it stuck about 2 feet above the boat. Remember what I said about Indians and wires? Fortunately, the bosun saved the day, as he didn't like the mate overly much either.

Now remember the second engineer, the one who was sacked on another ship and transferred to us? He nearly had us up the beach. As I came up to full power for going through the entrance, the engine suddenly stopped, with the most hideous noises coming up from down below. I missed losing that ship by seconds, and got through the entrance with only feet to spare. There is a current that sets across the entrance.

The chief engineer was absolutely livid with him. He hadn't bothered to drain the water out of the fuel tanks. The most basic engineering principle in the world. A first trip cadet knows this.

I didn't bother to sack him, although the Fleet Safety Manager demanded that I did. I couldn't as the crew agreement was out of date, and had no disciplinary code attached to it anyway. Even Indians can claim for unfair dismissal, and I had enough to do as it was. It seemed pointless as he was leaving in Jose, 2 days away. The company should have supported my decision, but were treating me as a third mate by now. Well, two can play at this game.

In José, we could only load one grade at a time, which went down like a lead balloon.

The electric motor, which should have been back from New Orleans, and fitted before loading was still in Panama. The superintendent gave the contract to the dry dock company there, 'to save money'.

If this motor had been from the butane plant, they would have got away with it, but remember what happens to those who cheat, *they are always found out.*

At the end of loading which took twice as long as it could have done, I had a 'phone call from the charterers in Caracas, who were suspicious to say the very least. It went like this.

"Tell me captain, how old is the *Steven N*?"

"Built in 1979 sir, makes her just over 22."

"We have no record of a ship that old called the *Steven N*. Has she been re-named? There is nothing on our copy of the Gas Form C."

"Yes to that, her previous name was *Monterey*."

There was a massive groan on the 'phone. Alarm bells start ringing with me, as this is starting to make some sense.

"*Captain, that ship is black listed in Venezuela.* She was banned for life." Why? Carter pumps!

Now I know why BHMS want me to re-write the Gas Form C, they knew, and so did Bergesen. They deleted the previous name and hoped to get away with it, but the real responsibility lies in Los Angeles, with em em."

However, we are finished loading, so sign Bills of Lading and sailed. We will see if we can sort something out on passage, or at the very least, the others can, I'm not carrying the can for this one.

There was a crew change in José. I now have a British gas engineer, who had been here before, so we were in with a fighting chance now. The new second engineer was the old gas engineer. I wasn't keen on this idea, as he is first trip, and we need experience. My chief was quite happy though, but again showed lack of experience in judgement, as he proved to be 'in over his head'.

The deck tanks are leaking again, and I once more requested permission to empty them. No chance and they were getting annoyed in Liverpool. But then, they weren't smelling it. *Or running the risk.*

The *Berge Eagle* had a new crew, and the replacement master I knew from my Bergesen days. He immediately asked if we could pick up 250 tonnes of fresh water for him, plus all his spares, which were in Panama.

No problem here Sven. A pleasure. Our fresh water tanks were aft, so any additional stern trim, would keep the speed up. We were now running at just over 15 knots loaded, 16 in ballast, and Bergesens were puzzled as to how the same ship could be running 2.5 knots faster than before, but using less fuel. Sleeve oil has now been used up, only em em doesn't know it yet, and Bergesens could work it out for themselves.

Back through the canal again, and I now know why no-one swims in the Gatun Lake, apart from it being a little muddy. The place is full of enormous crocodiles, or is it alligators? Never mind, they both have lots of big teeth.

Carrying on with trying to sort out the paperwork systems, was proving to be an enormous headache. It was all over the place, with little way of checking as to what was missing. My desk is now in the central office, but the mate wants to move his to the control room. Why? Because he is building up a little cohort of Sikhs, of which we had three, and he was the most senior. Remember what I said about mixing Indians. He'll stay put in the central office.

So I started on the paperwork according to the ISM Code. This Code is really the biggest waste of time ever dreamed up, as most of it is flogged. Here is a perfect example, which also shows up the incompetency of the 'Fleet Safety Manager' in Liverpool.

Everyone joining has to have instruction in how to use the engine room stores crane. Why? Goodness knows, because we had to do that at college before we could get our 'tickets'. In this case it had fallen to one of the second mates, a certain Mr Chakraborty, who I was keeping an eye on. This all happened before I joined.

According to the file, everyone has had instruction, so I asked him how he managed it, only this time with the Chief as a witness. He explained how he had done it, and "sir, it is all in the file, one separate page for each person. See, I show you."

And did. *It is time for some serious head wobbling.*

"How exactly can you train someone how to use a crane when there is *no* motor on the winch drum, the wire is *condemned*, the top sheave is *seized* as is the *swivel* above the hook as well as the hook *mouse*. When the jib is raised, the hydraulic rams *leak oil* faster than the header tank can refill the system, and now that I have found the Chain Register, it is *2 years* out of survey?"

Lots of head wobbling, lots and lots of it as he wriggled.

"Plus, do not lie to me, I've had enough of lying on this ship."

He had to confess that it was all flogged. So much for BHMS's auditors as well then! Really pretty poor eh?

The problem with the system is that auditors only check to see if the correct paperwork is in place, *not* if the correct paperwork actually relates to the task.

An auditor checking the system would have been satisfied that all was well. This is why the ISM code will *never* be of any use.

"Any more lying, flogging of documents, or hiding files, and the airlines are going to be busy between here and Bombay. Right?"

"Yes sir." With more head wobbling. "Now, all the missing files to be brought here immediately. Within an hour, I had 16 more files. My big mouth!

The chief then came up with an interesting comment.

"Try getting an Indian to say 'desiccated coconut' without wobbling his head."

"Why? Can't they?"

"Nope, they just can't do it."

During this period, I'd had three pipe fitters flown in, and we were starting to re-pipe the deck. To give you some idea of the magnitude of this problem, we had bought up all the available pipes in Panama, and were still short. More is coming in for us. Another 3000+ metres.

Before we had started, I'd said to the chief.

"You know Mike, we have a pipe on deck that doesn't go anywhere, and more to the point, doesn't seem to start anywhere, where it might be of some use."

"Oh, the blue one?" he said, "yes I came to the same conclusion."

"Well, we'll have that one out for a start."

It was also about this time that the mate 'lost it' with the Filipino crew, who were sick of him, and all came to see me. He did not understand 'losing face'.

To save the situation, I ran the crew from then on, while he set down to work with the new gas engineer. My workload was now getting rather heavy, but we had to try. The crew were very happy.

With the pipe fitters, we had a system, simple, but it worked beautifully. When a length of pipe was removed, the area was marked with a spot of red paint, then anyone with a needle gun would come along and scale it, then add a coat of primer. It looked as though we were working all over the place with no coordination, but it came together in the end. In the meantime, a new length of pipe was made, and then fitted, then the whole thing given another coat of paint. There was a lot of head scratching going on, as just how to get some bits of pipe out.

I had a very puzzling problem, with the fourth engineer, who incidentally, was worse than useless. He had a British Class 4 Steam and Motor 'Certificate of Competency', and a Panamanian Chief Engineers one. But he had never been on a steam ship. It also looked as though he had altered his Class 4, allowing him to sail as second engineer, at 3500 kW by handwriting it in, it's normally printed. It didn't comply with STCW 95 either (the regulations).

When I asked him about it, he went quiet, and said, "Indian Navy". And that was it. I tried again.

"According to your discharge book, you started off as Chief Engineer, and have worked your way back *down* to fourth engineer. A bit odd to say the least? Most people do it the other way."

"I do it to get more money sir," very quietly. He *was* lying.

"Right then, I'll see what the MCA in the UK have to say about it." I posted the whole lot off to the MCA standards branch in Southampton with a covering letter, querying its validity.

I make this point here, and I will come back to it, as the Fleet Safety Manager and I had a right ding donger of an argument about this the day I left the ship. There were repercussions too.

An old friend joined to sail with us in Panama, I'll just refer to him as IP. He runs a marine electrics company with DJ and BD. He is one of the most patient people I've known but he was having a hard time with the ship's electrician.

Back alongside the *Berge Eagle* then. Got the hang of the going alongside a swinging ship now. But there was a problem. I'd complained about the cargo transfer hoses before. They had holes in them.

One was even marked damaged, but still in use. I refused to use it, which really went down like the proverbial lead balloon. The 'ship manager operations' tried to give me a rocket on the 'phone. Now I am not stupid, and I knew he was out of his depth here, as he was trying to get me to use a damaged hose. Plus, I'm getting rather fed up being told what to do, when I already know a lot better than they did, so I sent a telex to the managing director in Liverpool.

"Please confirm by return if I am expected to use damaged equipment to transfer this cargo to the *Berge Eagle*."

Now that it is in writing they have to agree with me *not* to use them, but I got more of this in the next loading port when the 'ship manager operations' came out. For all he did, he might as well have gone to Butlin's.

Unfortunately for him, another 25 000 cubic metre gas tanker went alongside the *Berge Eagle* a few days after us, and the master there refused to use it either, and complained in the same way. I was totally vindicated. Even BHMS had to concede that it was correct, although somewhat reluctantly. They were being pressurized by Bergesen.

Transferring fresh water to the *Berge Eagle* proved to be rather more difficult than expected, as the Chief 'forgot' that when it was being pumped across, meant that we had no pressure for our own systems. Time for a little joke on old Sven then. Remember, Norwegians have a different 'sense of humour'.

After about 6 hours pumping, when they received about 60 tons, I called him up and said,

"Okay Sven, that's your lot of fresh water, we reckon you've got 250 tons, so are shutting down the transfer."

We didn't, we just needed a shower.

They were frantic on the *Berge Eagle*, running around trying to 'find out where it has all gone, as there is only 60 tons in their tank.' It took them ages to twig. Score: UK 1, Norway Nil.

The Ecuadorian who ran the 'girls', was also quite a wheeler dealer, and had agreed the previous trip to take all of our junk, including old ropes. I left the mate to 'work the deal', as Indians are at least reasonable in making a bargain. I do not wish to insult all Indians, but our prize crew. I also said to him.

"Get rid of *everything* that is of no use, we can use the *Eagle*'s crane. Okay?

When I asked him if it was all away, and a lot of it was plastic, he replied,

"I kept one old mooring rope in case it came in useful."

Now you will understand why I don't like him, they were hell bent on keeping junk.

Sven and his chief engineer came over later, when there were no cargo operations. We stopped while the *Borthwick* loaded on the other side. Wise precaution mate, very wise! They understood the magnitude of my problems, even if BHMS didn't. They were amazed at the amount of spares.

Joining us here was a Filipino who was reckoned to be the company's computer whiz kid. BHMS were going to install the software for a spare parts control system. Only the software mind, and instruction on how to use it. Filling in all the details, such as number, part number and location would be down to ship's staff!

This brought home to me that BHMS are totally out of touch with reality. They have seen the state of the spare parts system, but gave no account as to the reality of the task. Or, where we were going to find the time. All this to be done in conjunction with our extremely busy schedule, bringing the ship up, running a maintenance team, and keeping the 'officers' in line, all at the same time. I ran more ports in 1 month, than the ship had been to in the previous 6 months. Just to enter the spare parts would take the combined efforts of everyone on board, the best part of 3 months. He stayed with us for 3 days, and then left, the software was not installed. I'll guarantee that it never will be, as the owner insists on Indian Officers, and they just don't care.

So, we set off once more to José to load, even although we are black listed in Venezuela. I've got the job of trying to get her 'Off the Black List'. This is not easy, believe me.

We are to have a thorough OCIMF inspection, *but* I have to be able to load two grades simultaneously. I had a decent gas engineer, so he and the chief and I sat down to work out if we could modify the gas plant. We modified it. We *could* load two grades simultaneously, so put it in place. All it was, was a valve that went in between two blanked sections of loading line, which could be swung after loading the butane, to allow us to increase the rate of the propane. It worked too, leaked a bit, but this was just the start.

I had more serious words with the third mate during the loading. As I walked up the deck, he was walking down it, and passed the leak, which by this time was propane. I said to him.

"Without turning round, tell me what you have just seen?"

"Nothing sir," with that vacant look that he always had.

"Did you not notice a liquid gas leak, dropping propane onto the deck?"

"No sir."

"Well turn round, and tell me what that is," pointing at it.

"Oh it's been like that for ages."

"Aren't you going to do anything about it then," I said.

"Like what sir, the bolts are as tight as they will go."

"Like putting some water on the deck, just in case it cracks."

"Okay, I'll tell the bosun."

"Oh no you won't," I said, getting rather exasperated, "do it yourself. All you have to do, is move that hose from there to here. Then open the hydrant. Okay?"

Very reluctantly, he did so, but hated me for telling him to do it himself. They must be the laziest race on Earth.

Back to getting off the blacklist then.

And, to help us get off the blacklist, BHMS are sending the 'ship manager operations' out from Liverpool. This just gets worse. Not only has he never been on the ship before, he knows next to damn all about gas tankers! Plus, he's going to the charterers in Caracas first. Talk about out of your depth! *But* then, you are appreciating by now that BHMS will *never* be good ship managers. *In fact, they'll NEVER be ship managers!*

One night on the way to Panama, however, I decided to go for a wander around the ship. I often did this, as it lets the crew know that you are interested, and keeps them on their toes, only this night, the fourth engineer on watch in the engine control room wasn't on his toes. Oh no, he was fast asleep in a chair. I woke him up, with the greeting, "be in my office at 9 o'clock tomorrow morning, and bring a witness." Now technically I cannot sack him, as my new set of articles and log books are in transit from the Isle of Man. At last, someone there has woken up. But BHMS said I had to, 'sleeping on watch is a dismissible offence.'

Just forget all about the legal procedures then? Leave him with a case against the company? That be all right will it?

Believe it or not, *yes*!

I eventually worked out what was wrong in BHMS.

Bibby Line's ships were under the British Flag, so the Disciplinary Code was utilized. But the *Steven N* was under the Panamanian Flag, so for it to be effective, it has to be attached to the crew agreement, *and* stated in everybody's contracts. They had not done so, but just blustered through regardless. There are far too many people in the Liverpool office, who are hiding behind titles, their experience being distant memories, and if anyone argues, just 'put them down'.

Next morning, he comes in. The chief had already been briefed. He had no witness. I started off with,

"Last night when I came to the engine room control room, I found you asleep on duty. Were you or were you not asleep?"

He replied, "Yes sir, I was asleep."

That makes it nice and easy then, "you are dismissed from the ship, and will leave in Panama."

Then the trouble started. BHMS backed him up later, after all, by then, they had their scapegoat.

"I cannot leave the ship without my certification." He said.

It had already been explained to him that his certification was in the UK being checked. It would be forwarded to his home in India, if found to be in order. He had a copy of the letter sent to the MCA.

He just kept repeating the same thing over and over.

Now remember, I'm putting in over 120 hours a week, and was getting truly p-----d off with him, so ordered him out. I've to try and get off a black list, and I still had the Panama Canal to get through.

"You can stay until I get a new logbook and crew articles, then I'll get you off the ship properly."

(As an aside, he was still there 4 months after I left, and I'll explain how I found that out later. It was more ineptitude from BHMS.) Just then we had a serious problem, the deck tanks started leaking again. Badly, from the tops or saddles of many valves.

"Okay Rod (Gas Engineer), get the blast pipe on, we're going to let it go. I suspect the starboard tank is now 100% full."

"Are you going to 'phone Liverpool?"

"No, anyway it's the middle of the night, and I'm captain here, not them. This is a 'Safety of the Ship' decision. We'll dump it, and hydrate the tanks crossing the Gatun Lake. We cannot afford to be detained in The Panama Canal with leaking deck tanks, which have been filled with 'stolen' cargo anyway."

We'd been chasing these leaks for weeks, and as it got hotter, it just got worse.

A blast pipe is just a length of pipe, the longer the better that goes on the manifold and sticks as far out as you can get it to go. Too short and the gas swirls back into the ship's wind eddies.

Four hours later it was all gone. 164 tons of *stolen* ammonia.

We filled them with fresh water crossing the Lake. Ammonia being anhydrous hydrates as the water is being pumped in, but you must keep the tank open to atmosphere as it generates a lot of heat and can go seriously into vacuum.

Now the 'ship manager operations' goes to Caracas, while we anchor in Jose bay, and meets the charterers. Meanwhile, I'm getting ready for a delegation from PDVSA (State oil company of Venezuela).

You will recall from Part 2 that I know how to promote a ship.

His first comments when he came on board was,

"I took them out for lunch and it came to over £150."

"Then you got off cheap mate, I've just spent over $1000 just getting the ship ready."

I said to the gas engineer one day.

"Say Rod, how are you getting on with training up the mate with the gas plant?" (It wasn't a complicated gas plant).

"Let's just say it's like dealing with dumb, dumber, and dumber still. He is just not interested. He wants someone else to do everything for him."

"Oh that good then, a bit of promise perhaps?"

By reply, he just rolled his eyes.

Now when everything goes well, it goes very well, but when things start going wrong, they go very wrong, and did.

A gas analyser alarm came up on No. 3 void space. This is full of inert gas, and about 2% oxygen. This is the space between the cargo tank and the ship's structure. The tank is effectively just a big box, covered in insulation.

"Nothing for it Rod, we're going to have to open it up."

As if we didn't have enough to do!

Of course, just as we are ready to go in, it takes a long time to get them gas free, as the insulation holds a lot of the CO_2, we get orders to go and load, so up anchor, and set off for the berth.

Apart from the Gas Engineer, I'm the only one who knew what he was doing down there, you have to be careful, as there have been too many fatalities in enclosed spaces. The Chief had enough to do, and didn't like long ladders anyway. I can't trust the mate.

Even berthing was a trial, as I had the 'ship manager operations' on the bridge with me. As a person, he was quite pleasant, but I could have done without someone from the office breathing down my neck.

Especially when one of the tugs ripped off his bow fendering, by getting his lines crossed. They were operating on a 'bridle'.

Fortunately, I saw it happening, and told the pilot that "we are not being held responsible for that!"

It's a vagary of marine insurance that we would get the bill anyway, probably after 6 months or so, when memories were getting a little jaded.

I tried to get the void space out of the way, before we started cargo operations, and the 'ship manager operations', decided he would accompany me down, as he, 'had never been in a void space'. It was at this point that I discovered that not only had he not been in a void space, he had never even been on a gas tanker before, and this was the guy who was telling me what to do all the time! I was dumbstruck, and said to him,

"Is this your first gas tanker Paul?"

"Yes, is that a problem?"

I elected to say nothing, but I'll tell you this, BHMS fully deserved what ultimately happened to them.

Going into a void space, or any such space is not something that is taken lightly, and apart from the extreme care taken, there is also a load of paperwork to be done first, although on this ship, you could do it 2 years in advance and nobody would be any the wiser, except me that is.

I warned the SMO not to proceed away from where I was until I'd either found the LPG source, or had tested the atmosphere. I test the atmosphere continuously. If this ship had had what is known as an OX82 meter, then life would have been much simpler. This meter sits in your top pocket, and samples continuously. If the oxygen content falls to 18% (air is 21%), then it sets off an alarm, and you just simply get out, no arguments, just plain, out.

Crawling underneath the cargo tank, which is not a pleasant experience, as there is only about 40 cms of height to move in, I set about trying to find the LPG. I found it, in the inert gas line, indicating that the valve on deck was passing, and reported this back to the gas engineer by VHF, which we also carry. Time to get out then, no need to waste any more time down here, apart from the fact, that by this time, you are filthy dirty, very sweaty, and starting to bruise in odd places.

But where is the 'ship manager operations?' He was told to wait at the foot of the ladder, until I was finished, so I called the deck by VHF.

"Rod, have you got Paul up there?"

"No Doug, nobody has come out yet."

Where the heck is he then?

Looking under the tank, I spot a loom of a light at the other end of the void space. He has only gone to inspect the rest of the void space with an AB. Why the big deal? Because that bit that he is in has not been tested yet, and he hasn't got a radio.

When we were back on deck I said to him.

"I told you to wait until I was finished then I would go round the void with you, but you went off on your own. *Why*?"

"What's the problem?"

So I said, "what is the point of having safety procedures in this company for 'entry into enclosed spaces' if the ship managers themselves will not observe them?"

"Plus, do you know what sort of example this sets to the crew? I have enough trouble with the officers on this ship without you coming along and making it worse."

"Oh now wait a minute, I was perfectly okay down there." He replied.

"That is not the point, you broke the cardinal rules, and that is just not good enough."

Of course, who should be waiting for us but the inspector from PDVSA ready for the inspection to get us off the blacklist. The SMO offered to help.

"Look Paul, just stay out of the way, say nothing, and leave this to us. With your knowledge of gas tankers, it will be better this way."

So, we start yet another OCIMF inspection, only this time, this inspector knows his stuff. By the end of the first day, we are doing rather well, and have struck up a good accord with him. He would complete the inspection next day, in the meantime, we carry on loading.

Next day, he is back, and starts with an apology.

"Captain, I have an apology to make. I've forgotten my glasses."

"No problem, I have a reading pair in my cabin, I'll get them for you."

I had a pair of these disposable ones, that come in a little tube, and cost about $3. The type you buy in airports or just about anywhere really.

"Try these," as I passed them over.

"These are perfect Captain. Is it okay for me to borrow them?"

"Oh just keep them, then if they get dropped, it won't matter."

That is day 2 off to a good start then. So it continued, but in the end, we failed. Why? Penny pinching largely, by em em.

The only thing he could pick up on, on the deck, apart from its fabric, was a leaking expansion valve underneath the port side cargo condensers. Rod, the gas engineer told me later that that job had been on the dry dock list, when he was here before, but not done, as em em thought it unnecessary. Typical, people with no relevant knowledge, making decisions without understanding the implications. How often do we see this? Just once is far too often.

The main thing in the engine room was that there was no auto-start on the generators. This is a requirement, such that if one trips, another will start up automatically, and share the load. I was surprised to learn that the *Steven N* didn't have this, because virtually every other ship does.

However, what upset PDVSA the most was that instead of coming clean from the start, the owners had tried to sneak the ship back in, by the back door so to speak. Plus Paul had to open his big mouth and put his foot in it. After being told to keep out of it.

Left to my own devices, I could have had that ship off the black list, as I had just received an e-mail from London, informing us, that after the next discharge, we could 'look forward to 18 days well-earned rest, before the next scheduled loading.' Two weeks would have been ample time to have an auto-start system fitted, and the expansion valve we could do ourselves. A right pain getting it out, as we would need to lift the condenser, hence the dry dock preference, and the fabric was well under way, as my next three Indian cleaners were standing by ready to fly out and join us. During a relatively quiet period, I brought up the subject of the chief officer and his performance. I was told quite categorically that I just could not get rid of him, I was not allowed to sack him, as they could not get chief officers. Now is that 'could not', or knowing BHMS by now, 'would not even try?' The latter as it turned out, was the more accurate, but what I didn't know at the time was that he was overheard, with disastrous consequences.

When you read this, Paul, just remember, it was *you* who said I could not get rid of him. You cannot pass the buck here. It stops at your desk. He reminds me of *Gonzales* from Part 1. Equally dangerous.

After we finished loading, and all the documentation was signed, Paul came out with a beauty. Remember, this is not a gas orientated man, but a bulk carrier captain. "You are not to issue as many Letters of Protest."

Letters of Protest, or LOPs as they are known, are about as much use as an ashtray on a motorbike, but they are one of these things, that you're damned if you do issue them, and you're damned if you don't. If in doubt, issue one.

"Yes Paul, point noted." Instantly forgotten, I'll do it the way I've done it for the last 15 years.

He then left to fly home, as I said, it would have been better if he had gone to Butlin's.

But.

Then Rod (the gas engineer) came to see me. I could tell by his expression that this was not good news.

"Doug, we have a problem, a big one."

"Go on Rod, everybody else has had a go at me today, you might as well join in."

"I think we have major damage in the port side LPG condensers." Fortunately, these are on the butane side, as opposed to the propane.

"How major?"

"I won't know until we get the end covers off, but I think serious. Is it okay to take them off?"

"Yeah, no problem, but we're sailing now, just take any crew you need to help you after we secure for sea."

Then we sailed for the Panama Canal, where the fun really started, well for me at least, and BHMS, who are really in for a shock. It could not have happened to a more deserving company, but we'll come to that, especially on the back of what Paul told me very quietly.

They had just been fined $50 million, yes that's $50 million, or put another way, $50 000 000.00 by the US Coastguard, as one of their bulk carries had been caught on video, during daylight hours, getting rid of its hold residues, by dumping it over the side, in (wait for it) the Caribbean! You daren't as much as drop fag ash over the side in this

455

ecologically sensitive area.

But the crew? Guess where they came from?

It would be indulgent of me to tell you, but they came from a country that fits in between Pakistan, Bangladesh, and Sri Lanka. Need any more clues? I don't think so.

Then I received a very strange e-mail from BHMS in Liverpool. It said, "In future, all correspondence between the master and the charterer is to be sent through the Liverpool office for verification purposes. It will then be forwarded to charterers."

Over my dead body it would, so I contacted the charterer and got a hold of Janet, who replied when I read this one out, and somewhat angrily.

"That is absolutely ridiculous. You are the only master who gives us feedback. What are they trying to do? What do they have to hide?"

It is a shipmaster's primary responsibility to safeguard his charterer, and to keep them informed. This was totally new to me this one.

BHMS have just gone and shot themselves in both feet. You could not obtain a bigger hole if you'd used a Blunderbuss.

BHMS realized that their little game was falling apart around them, and were frantically trying to save a situation that was all of their own making in the first place. Too late for that now.

You should not have been acting fraudulently in the first place.

What they were up to, I will not disclose here, but there is now a very real danger that the charter party will be cancelled, as the ship is technically unseaworthy, and had been on leaving Malta. Furthermore, and I checked up on this, Bergesen were kept in the dark about it.

Technically unseaworthy, is when part of the equipment is either damaged, or missing, or doesn't operate and so on. It can be just a minor thing, but not in this case.

The first and most fundamental rule in a charter party is that the ship must be *seaworthy* at all times.

This is of course in addition to the fuel that was stolen, as well as the ammonia, both of which they knew about, and did nothing.

When Rod had the covers off No. 4 condenser, we went testing. Now these covers are big affairs, weigh about 250 kg, and are held on by about 50 bolts through a heavy flange. There are close on to

800 tubes in each condenser. Each is tested in turn by inserting the explosimeter sample tube, and waiting to see if we get any deflection. There are other ways of doing it, but this is by far the easiest and most accurate.

I said to Rod, as we progressed.

"You know, I've seen the odd tube go in one of these from time to time, but never this many, and there seems to be no pattern to it, which rather rules out vibration damage."

He replied, "you've been reading my mind. I was just wondering just what could have caused this." I found out 5 months after I left the ship, when I received the most disgusting e-mail from a group calling themselves the 'Steven team.' By this time the ship had been taken over by Bergesens, so I sent a copy to Bergesens' Fleet Safety Manager, who I've known for many years, with a complaint. It must have worked because that was the last e-mail I received, but it didn't take me long to cross-reference my retained crew list with the Bergesens 'where are our people now' list. I'll get them one day, there is absolutely no doubt about that. But to the condensers? They let it slip, by trying to blame the gas engineer, when in fact it was the chief officer who did it, that methanol had been injected into the R22 reliquefaction gas, as opposed to the LPG line.

Occasionally, the expansion valve will freeze up, as butane is notorious for carrying water vapour, which freezes in the valve. We inject methanol, or if you can get it, as it is much preferred due to the dangers in using methanol, we use ethanol. Basically, it melts the ice.

In all my years on gas tankers, I've never heard of anyone doing this, so I simply don't know what effect mixing methanol, and R22 would be, but I think judging by the damage to this condenser, it must be bad, or it builds up the pressure inside the condenser, such that the tubes just break at their weakest point. As I say, I don't know for certain. I doubt if anyone does.

Now at sea, I wandered up to the bridge, as was my bent in the evening, and found, lying on the chart table, a new book. What was this I asked myself?

'Chief Officer's Instructions to Bridge Watch Keeping Officers.'

I was furious. It had taken me nearly 3 months to get them by fear of death to keep a lookout, and his first instruction was,

"During quiet periods, the lookout can be called to the chartroom, where he can be employed making stencils etc."

Just who does this prick think he is!

That was immediately photocopied, the book went into my safe, and a covering letter with the photocopy faxed off to BHMS, with a request for a new chief officer.

It was only after I calmed down, that I remembered what Paul had said. Now it made sense. The officers were going to do exactly as they pleased and to hell with the captain. See what you've done Paul!

3 months' work down the drain.

Try explaining that one to the MCA. You just might have to!

This is the standard that you can expect from BHMS. The Lowest. I had it out with him next morning, and he replied.

"I thought it would be okay, captain."

"Well it f…ing well is not okay, since when did a chief officer who has no bridge role whatsoever go over the captains head?"

But there was more to this than meets the eye, as I went through the 'deleted box' on the e-mail, and took a print. Oh that got the reaction that the 'Steven team' wanted, but it all back-fired on them.

Who is coming to pay us a visit?

None other than the Fleet Safety Manager, Mr Trouble himself. This is another from Liverpool who hides behind titles. In this case, they have Captain in front and MNI after.

Do you know what MNI means? Properly, it means, 'Member of the Nautical Institute'. *TNT* on the Forth had it, but then anyone in the country could have it too. A secretary could row a boat across a pond, and then join the MNI as an honorary member, by filling in the form, and posting off the requisite fee.

'Miss Susan Antonsen MNI.' Typist. Sounds good, eh? What do they do?

They confuse you on already well-understood principles of navigation, by exploring some obscure point that even they themselves don't understand. Oh, and they have formal dinners occasionally too. Now MNI also has other meanings. For Paul, we could have: memory needs investigation (entry to enclosed spaces). Or mostly normal inside. Or many new Indians.

Now we are getting a visit from The Brain. FNI. (Fellow of the Nautical Institute). Or in this case: f…ing nutter indeed!

I pre-guessed just what he was coming out for, as I had the e-mail from the deleted box. Let's see if he starts off telling the truth.

In the meantime, I advise the charterers that I think I may end up getting sacked. They badly need a scapegoat.

The reply, "That's not fair, not after all the work you've done."

By this time, I was past caring, as I was about exhausted, having done my own job, and most of the mates as well, plus the junior officers were deliberately being obstructive. By the 15th of the month, the second mate on crew wages still had not finished them even although I was pressing him for them. They must think I'm daft.

We anchored outside the breakwaters in Cristobal, ready for the Panama Canal.

The first thing anyone does on boarding a ship, is to present himself to the master. Apart from good manners, it is safety. Did this idiot? Oh no, straight to see his little cohort, then came to see me, and this is someone who calls himself 'Captain'.

Now I didn't like the way I was treated by him first time round, and I'm still annoyed at the mate, when he comes out with,

"What have you done with the fourth engineer's certification?"

My reply, "how do you know about that? Because I didn't tell you."

Him, "that doesn't matter, what have you done with it?"

Me, "oh it matters a great deal pal, because it means someone is going behind my back, and I want to know who!"

I don't think he was used to people standing up to him. So I said, "it's been posted off to the MCA for checking, right."

"What you should have done," he said, "was to photocopy it, and send off the photocopies, and retained the originals."

"If I do that and it turns out they have been tampered with, as I suspect, then by the time the reply gets back here, he may be long gone, which gives another master the problem. I have a responsibility to the MCA to report such matters. Doing it this way, means that if they are to be cancelled, then they will be cancelled, and as far as he is concerned, he should not have been so stupid in the first place. *You* are the one who is wrong, and not for the first time either."

It was quite apparent that if I said it was white, he said it was black. The sheer barefaced arrogance of this man borders on the idiotic. I continued, "that is a minor point, most important now, is getting this ship off the black list, which I very nearly had, *and* keeping the charter party."

Him, "we are all working very hard on that (keeping the charter party), it would be very embarrassing if it was cancelled."

I just laughed in his face, "working hard on it? I've been at it for 3 months, and I keep getting f...ed up at every turn by either BHMS in Liverpool, or the Isle of Man, or Bombay, or Manila. You've only been bothering for the last week, and that is only since it dawned on someone in Liverpool that they may soon be up to their neck in alligators, that they realize the implications."

"Now you are the 'Fleet Safety Manager', work this one out. Here is the Chain Register, it is 2 years since an entry was made. Why?"

He couldn't answer, which for someone high up in a shipping company is nothing other than disgraceful, there being no excuse for this. Obviously, *he has not been doing his job properly.*

We did not start off well, and it steadily degenerated. He was hell bent on causing as much trouble as possible, which the Indian Officers thought was okay. They may just get their servants back.

Next morning as we sat in the office, he came out with,

"I'll just sit in on your morning meeting. There is concern in Liverpool that the management of this ship is not up to standard." If that's BHMS's standards, we were *way* above it. *Way above it!*

"Well you'll be sitting in on nothing then, as we don't have morning meetings, we just get on with the job."

However that day we did, and the chief officer was very subdued.

He was the one who was stirring up the trouble. Oh, I knew all about it from the e-mail he sent to BHMS, behind my back. He'll keep his job, and to hell with anyone else. He may even have gone Captain if he'd played his cards right. He didn't.

Afterwards, The Brain of Liverpool said.

"Well that seems to be alright, you will no doubt have further discussions at coffee time."

I said, "as I've already said, we don't waste our time having meetings on this ship. We just get on with it."

He then excelled himself.

"Right then Captain, let's see if we can get your office sorted out."

The chief was horrified as I told him.

"I asked for two secretaries 2 months ago, and was turned down. What I don't need now is an arrogant, obstreperous, rude bastard to start telling me what to do. After the discharge, I have 18 days clear to finish this lot, something which anyone of you could have done in

Malta, but didn't. You just lumped the job onto me. Now, I've got a job on, on deck, and that is where I am going right now, and you *do not have* my permission to open any drawer or go through any file. Until you can start treating me as *a master* in your company, then you can just stay out of the way. Okay?"

With that I went to get changed, but he followed.

In my other office, we had it out. I cannot stand being spoken down to. I don't do it to others, and I won't take it myself.

It came to a head, when I said to him.

"Right then, you can't get fourth engineers, you can't or won't get me a chief mate, even although he is endangering the ship, a point you seem to agree with him on, which says everything there is to say about BHMS, so, can you get captains?"

He was purple with rage, and replied.

"Is that a threat Captain?"

"Oh," I said, "I don't threaten, but I'll *ask* again, can you get captains?"

He replied, "if we had to, I dare say we could."

"Right then," I said, "get one, as I will take no more of this disgusting treatment from you, or any more crap from BHMS. I've done more here in 3 months than any of you have done in 2 years, and I guarantee that, within 24 hours, you will have notification of cancellation of the charter party. If you want to blame someone, go and look in a mirror. Now, *get out of my office*!"

He gave me 2 hours to get off the ship, confirming that he came out from Liverpool looking for a scapegoat, and had found it. He probably had a 'captain' waiting in the wings.

That was the fourth time I was to be used as the scapegoat.

Then he did something incredibly stupid. He moved the ship to the Inner Anchorage!

Why stupid? Because he does not have a Panamanian Master's Certificate, and his British Certificate was no longer valid. He isn't qualified for anything. In the airline industry, this is called hi-jacking. I doubt if he even had a gas endorsement, but it wouldn't make any difference if he did or not. But then, his incredible arrogance has taken over from common sense, which he had in miniscule supply in the first place.

Just as I left the office for the final time, he whispered in my ear, further confirming that he was looking for a scapegoat.

"You have let a lot of people down very badly."

He was lucky he didn't end up flat on his back, as I replied.

"Because I won't join in with your fraudulent practices? Or steal from and deceive the charterers? Or run a third rate ship with rubbish Indian Officers? I still have my standards, it is a pity that you've lost yours. 24 hours mind, and you've lost the charter. *Guaranteed.*"

I was correct. As soon as they notified charterers that there had been a change of master, notification was declared. Now they are in deep trouble, and they have brought it completely upon themselves.

When people get to be as arrogant as this, it is usually because they have something to hide, something they are trying to cover up from long ago. It was something I was told by the technical superintendent, that I shouldn't have been told, that I pitched in with purely out of curiosity that really hit a nerve with this idiot. My intuition is seldom wrong, and then I knew that this guy knows something about the loss of the *MV Derbyshire*, that hasn't come out yet. This was a bulk carrier which went down in The South China Sea with the loss of all on board, and the subject of an on-going investigation.

Something really very serious that will explain a lot of unanswered questions. Just like Forth Ports, he has a lot of explaining to do, and it will not be at all pleasurable for him.

I flew home, at my own expense, still seething, but what they did not know was that I had been invited to London by the charterers, who I travelled down to see on the second of September 2001, and went to stay overnight in the Merchant Navy Hotel in Lancaster Gate, London.

By sheer coincidence, em em just happened to staying there as well. I had just come in from a walk in Hyde Park, and was sitting in the reception area reading a magazine, when the lift doors opened, and this guy in a Turban walked out. As he passed reception, he was greeted with, "good evening Captain ------------." My ears pricked up.

I said to the receptionist, "Is that Captain ----------, from Los Angeles?" She confirmed that this was so. Time for a change of location then, time to move through to the bar. He didn't know me, but I was soon to know a great deal about him, such as his love for Scotch Whisky. This guy is on a par with 'unbelievable', in Part 1. I do not wish to insult the distilleries on Islay, but Laphroaig was never a favourite of mine before I gave up Scotch some time ago, but it was for him. He had the best part of half a bottle before disappearing up to his room with a full glass, about four doubles.

After he had gone, I said to the barman, "boy, he can get through it."

"Oh he's always like that." He said.

"That probably explains his temper tantrums then."

"Yes, he was asked to leave last time he threw one of them."

Isn't it amazing what you find out about people?

You get that one for free BHMS. Now you know.

Next morning, I was off to see the charterers, and meet Janet. We hit it off straight away. I had also been invited to lunch.

We discussed the ship and its problems, and they accepted that it had a very poor set of officers on board, and expressed great surprise at BHMS for not supporting their master. They were also appraised about the fuel situation and were somewhat relieved that they had got it all back. In fact, they may have come out on top, as some of the 'sleeve oil' may have come from the previous charterer.

Then I was asked who 'The Brain' was. I told them he was the 'Fleet Safety Manager', a complete contradiction in terms.

It transpired that he had been seeking a meeting with the charterers, but was being fobbed off until they had met with me. They obviously do not trust BHMS then. He never did get his appointment.

We had a super lunch in this little restaurant, not far from their offices. You don't have to go far off the main thoroughfares in London to find these wee places, which always tend to be on the good side.

Then I went home.

Will I take command of a gas tanker again? No.

Will I take a mate's job on a gas tanker again? No.

My gas tanker sailing days are over. I've had enough. I probably have more gas tanker knowledge than anyone, but it is now reserved for cargo underwriters who need expert opinion, or charterers who need either a ship inspection, or someone to check if they are being cheated or not. I would hope that this book will send a shock-wave through the industry, as there is now in place someone who will expose all these nefarious practices, which in the end of the day will result in less LPG being blown off to the already polluted atmosphere. I intend to re-start my company as a Marine Investigator. As I said before, if it is going on, I can find it, and you will be surprised just what I can get out of the paperwork.

Will I go to sea again? Oh yes, and that is where you, the reader come in. You may have noticed that this is no 'normal' book. You have been educated in things you knew nothing of, but more importantly, you have learnt how things are done other than in an obvious way. You'll need this knowledge and more from the next entitled *An Alternative A to Z*, to unravel the third, *The Golden Sextant?* and subsequent titles, all different from anything you might have already read. Then you will also have the opportunity to sail with me. Because I'm going back to sea, as well as being a writer.

Ever heard of 'Mercy Ships?' This is a global charity, although mainly based in Houston, Texas, USA, with offices in other countries around the world. They are, as the name suggests, a charity which runs ships to third-world countries, where they provide medical care to those who would not normally have access to such facilities. The things that you and I generally take for granted. Colour, race, war situations, different religions are of no importance to them, if there is a need, then they show mercy.

They are a Christian-based organization, but you should not be put off by this, as whether you are a Christian or not, then you will also be welcome to join in. In fact, you already have done so, as part of the Royalties of this book are being donated to them.

What of their ships then? There are currently two in operation and a third being converted in the UK. They are hospital ships, with operating theatres and wards and so forth. The *Africa Mercy* nearing completion in Newcastle will have six operating theatres and will be able to carry a crew of over 400. This is a major project.

To staff so many theatres obviously needs a lot of committed people, as on these ships you do not get paid. In fact, you pay for the privilege that is getting there and back, plus all your food etc.

If a surgeon, a doctor or a nurse can give up their time and earnings to help someone from the third-world, then so can you and I. There are far more qualified doctors and nurses than there are Master Mariners, and so it is time for me to 'give something back'.

But you say, I'm not a Master Mariner, or a medical specialist, what can I do?

First of all, read up all about this charity from the Internet, their site is very good, and you'll find that, no matter what you can do, there will be a need for it. Or, I or others will just plain teach you.

Secondly, remember and never forget that each cog in a wheel is as important as the next cog, a surgeon cannot operate if there are no lights to see by, so an engineer provides the power, but if the fuel is not cleaned before use by the motorman in the engine room, then the engine driving the generator won't run. If the navigator has no charts to navigate by, then the captain doesn't know where he is going, and if there are no communications, can't tell anyone when he will arrive. The list is endless. There is a job that everyone can do.

The two highest costs in running a ship are crew wages and fuel. The first is taken care of, so why not raise money to buy fuel. Doesn't sound very glamorous? One ton of fuel, about $250 at current prices will keep six operating theatres going for many hours. Just think how many people that will help. Or raise money in any way. There will never be enough, but at least they can keep operating.

The obvious thing is that, if the ship is at sea, then what do the medical staff do? They get ready, or if the ship is heading to re-store, re-fuel etc, get ready to change crews. The *Anastasis* is currently operating in West Africa, but pops up to Tenerife on a regular basis for re-supply. They get through rather a lot of things that their operating port just does not have. But in port, what do the ships crew do? Well, the engineering staff are kept busy keeping it all running, the crew look after the ship and the captain, his officers and others such as wives and children and support staff will do anything they can for the people locally. Build hospitals, schools and so forth.

While my bricklaying is a bit slow, I can mix concrete real fast, and I can labour for anyone as well as handle myself or represent Mercy Ships at the highest level. I am, after all, just another cog.

Try looking at it in this way. You will no doubt look forward to jetting off somewhere warm for your summer holiday, somewhere you have saved for to get 'away from it all'.

Why not join a Mercy Ship, and go somewhere really warm, somewhere no-one else can go as it isn't in a holiday brochure, where you can be rewarded by an experience that you will never forget by doing something worthwhile, and the family can all join in with? This sort of thing sets up kids for life. My son will be there with me. It takes a degree of commitment to do this, but I can assure you, that you will be enriched by it, far more than by lying in the sun, and your neighbours will not as much be jealous of you for doing so, but envious, if not more than just a little proud.

Thirdly, as I am going off to work for them, in-between my other jobs, I will unfortunately have to stop doing something worthwhile, something that people in the UK benefit from. I can no longer be a blood donor.

But you could, if you took my place.

I only need one, but The Blood Transfusion Service need a lot more than one, like Mercy Ships, they need all they can get.

It only takes about an hour, once every 3 months, and apart from being one of the few things you can usefully do lying on your back, also rewards you with meeting others working for others, that you would also receive with Mercy Ships.

I hope to see you there, as apart from other things, I need interesting characters to write about.

But, back to the *Steven N*. What happened to her, after the Brain of Bibby's took over? She transited the Panama Canal, and discharged into the *Berge Eagle*, then returned to Balboa, and anchored, initially undergoing repairs.

She was there, lying idle for 4 months. Nobody would touch her. Then she set off for Siros in Greece, where she was handed over to Bergesen Management, along with the Hugo N.BHMS never did get the *Harriet N*, which took over from the *Steven N*'s charter.

The fourth engineer was there until at least the 31st of December. Whether he got his certification back or not, I do not know, but in that it is Bibby policy to dismiss someone sleeping on watch, and that he was still there suggests that he didn't.

How do I know all of this?

Because Bibby Line 'forgot' to take me off their mailing list, so both Janet and I could keep up to date with the goings-on in BHMS. Inept of them eh? No, just normal.

That was the end of BHMS's foray into gas tanker management. It could all have been so very different if only they had listened, but as I said at the start, running your own ships and managing someone else's are two completely different things. It does make you wonder though just what their own ships must be like.

There is one thing that is certain. There will have to be a massive change of attitude before they take up their MOD contract, otherwise they will lose that as well. I'm not supposed to know about that, but now you all do. Here is a final example of why they need to change. When The Brain couldn't get an appointment with the charterers in

London, the two Managing Directors had a go. Both, mind, not one.

They arrived at reception unannounced, and asked to see the persons involved. That was as far as they got. They were turned away, because they did not have the common decency or good manners to make an appointment first. Oh, they had their scapegoat, they just couldn't exploit it. Tough boys.

The last I heard of the *Steven N* was that she was back on ammonia, you get a lot of this on clapped-out ships, and she was on passage to Houston USA. I was tempted to warn the US Coast Guard about her, but they'll make a big enough mess of it themselves, especially with the 'Steven team' on board.

What would I have done differently?

I would have changed one of the two deck officers who had just gained extensions to their contracts, the third mate, and the second mate I would have done away with, putting the mate on watch.

With hindsight, I would not have taken the second engineer off the *Hugo N*, and I would have booted off the fourth engineer under police escort if need be. Then I would have thumped The Brain. I know that is not a very Christian attitude, but he really does get under your skin.

Comment:

It may be construed by some that I am prejudiced towards Indians. Not so, as I have some friends in Bombay and Goa that I have sailed with and got on famously with. However, I have found that the general standard of Indian Officers is way below what would be considered as par. My initial experiences with Filipinos was detrimental to say the least, but I have trained many of them up to bridge watch-keeping standards, and produced some good officers.

Let me cite an example of other Indians, and the fact that in general, they just do not care.

In Qatar one day, a VLCC came in to load condensate, a ship by the name of *Eastern Fortune* of some 250 000 SDWT. It was in June, and it was hotting up in the Persian Gulf, getting to about 55 deg C each day 130 deg F. We went aboard at 8 o'clock in the morning. The temperature in the control room was 60 deg C. There was no air conditioning. The master, officers and crew were Indian. I asked why there was no air conditioning (A.C.).

"It is broken," said the captain.

"Well, can't you fix it?" I asked.

"Is no need, we don't mind the heat. India is a hot country."

"Right then captain, we'll come back when it is fixed. Here is my 'phone number, and until this control room is down to no more than 30 deg C, your ship is 'off-hire'."

"What is the problem, we don't mind the heat?" asked the captain.

I said, "Captain, it is not you or your crew that I am concerned about, it is your instrumentation and control equipment. We are not prepared to begin loading until it is safeguarded and operating within its design parameters. As I said, we'll come back when your A.C. is repaired."

It took him 12 hours, and he used the first 6 hours protesting. All to no avail. Next time he came back, it was all working properly. You'll understand now when I say, they just don't care.

The saddest thing about this is that there are an awful lot of them working around the coasts of North West Europe, with the potential for a massive accident, which will come one day.

We will never overcome the 'caste' system in India; all I would say to them is this, when you leave India, leave it there.

Finally: I quote this from a book I read recently, which sums up my life as a gas tanker captain, and as a Forth Pilot;

"Kennedy was right. Anyone who believes in fairness in this life has been seriously mis-informed."

Ivor and the bike in the bus.

Having just read the last bit, a little lighter reading is required as we wind down towards the end, *Ivor* first and one or two more tales about the *Borthwick*. Actually this tale is also about the *Borthwick*, but it all happened before he got on board, so doesn't really count.

When we joined either the *Quentin* or *Borthwick* in Scapa Flow, we would fly up from Edinburgh, usually direct with British Airways, or if the company had an economy drive on, then with Loganair, which meant landing at Wick first. It cost the same in the end anyway.

If the ships were in, then we just went aboard as soon as we got in. Often as not, in the early days, as there were no flights on a Sunday, we would fly up on the Saturday, and then spend a night in a hotel, for a Sunday boarding.

On this particular occasion, the ship was due in that evening, which meant hanging around Kirkwall for most of the day. No big deal, but doing the 'tourist bit' takes only half the time, and when you've done it once, you don't tend to do it again. So in keeping with tradition, tend to fall into a pub.

A pint can be nursed for several hours if you are careful, but how many people do you know are careful in a pub, if that is your wont?

Ivor was not one of them. He brought new meaning to the word 'spendthrift'. Even with help, you could not prise his wallet open, but this did not stop us trying. Some were actually more successful than others, until we discovered his secret, then it was a free for all.

Preferring not to inhabit the local watering hole, *Ivor* went for a walk, as it was a sunny, but windy day, from the North for a change too. Passing a shop, it was painted on the inside of the windows, 'Bicycle Hire. Only 50p per day.' Good deal eh? *Ivor* thought so, and was soon kitted out with a bike and a map. This'll be cheaper than the pub, bound to be!

Ivor plans his route to take in the Italian Chapel, the Churchill Barriers, and the village of St Margaret's Hope, which he had heard the loading masters talking about. 12 miles there, and wind behind, what could be easier.

It all goes swimmingly, until he is spotted in St Margaret's Hope, by a loading master.

"*Ivor*" (not his real name, but close enough), "fancy a pint. I'm paying."

To cut a long story short, he has more than one, as more loading masters start to arrive, and 'treat' him accordingly, knowing that he is on a bike, as they had all been 'phoning each other.

Seeing the ship steaming out of the Pentland Firth, *Ivor* decides it is time to pedal back to Kirkwall, so with due compliments paid for their 'hospitality', sets off back to Kirkwall, only this time, it is uphill, and *into* the wind.

After 300 yards, he fell off!

But salvation was at hand, there was a bus stop, and here came a bus. Perfect.

Having stowed the bike in the boot, and paid his fare he settled down for the journey to Kirkwall, but buses don't go the most direct route, oh no, this is Orkney, and the driver has a natter with every farmer on the way.

Ivor fell asleep.

The bus carried on, and on, and on, and then *Ivor* woke up.

In Stromness!

About as far away from Kirkwall as he started, but on the other side. He was then charged for his extra fare, but had lost so much time, that he had to take a taxi back to Kirkwall, where he was still late. Nice sleep though, pity about the crick in the neck.

It was only after loading, that he remembered about the bike. That was 4 days ago, so he's got a minimum of £2 to pay in excess hire, and it goes up by 50p per day, until they can find the right bus. The agents got the job of locating it. This was not in their job description, 'bike finders'.

Oh, they found it, or rather, what was left of it, as by now, it had been rattling around the back of the bus for the better part of a week. When they enquired after the driver, did you not hear it rattling around? He with the usual speed of an islander replied, "I wondered what that strange noise was, but when I stopped, it did as well, so I thought it was just the road."

In the end, *Ivor* got the bill, paid by the agents, until the *Borthwick* returned from Norway. £128. The cost of a new bike, as there was little left of the old one, which was second- or third-hand anyway. Taxi fare £15, extra hire £4.50. Total £147.50

Just to save him from spending a few hours in a pub like everyone else.

It nearly broke his heart, but it was round the company like wildfire.

That new bike is still offered for hire, and it's 20 years old now.

The outboard end of the sewage pipe.

You will recall from Part 1, that we had a length of pipe renewed in Karstoe, Norway, for the sewage tank overboard to sea.

In 1983, we managed to damage both main cargo pumps on the *Borthwick* at the same time, and rather than trot off to Zeebrugge as before, tank cleaned and pulled both pumps in Porsgrun. How we did it involved *Snow White*, and the story is in my next book.

We were berthed while they were being repaired round the corner from our usual berth, on a dry cargo ship berth, when the *Quentin* came chugging in with a request.

They had damaged a seal on a cargo compressor drive as it went through the bulkhead, and had 'lost' their blanking plate. When this lot is dismantled, a plate goes over the hole which is about 1 metre by 60 cms, such that the ship can still operate. The electric motor room is over pressurised. Could they borrow our blanking plate? Could we take it over in a lifeboat?

Snow White agreed, and despite my telling him that ours was a different size, and wouldn't fit, insisted that we 'try' anyway.

Geoff, of sexy Sue fame, who was second engineer, I was chief mate, suddenly remembered that it was the *Quentin*'s third engineers birthday.

Say no more, off we go, our 3rd came with us. It was one of those dead flat calm clear nights, where the smoke goes straight up, and it was also cold, by virtue of the fact that it was also in the middle of winter.

Of course, it is seen straight away, that I was right, it didn't fit, but *we all fitted* very nicely into the third engineer's cabin. Very snug in fact, and set about demolishing a case of beer. You wouldn't get away with this nowadays, but you did then. More's the pity.

Eventually it is time to head back, but with a few extra passengers, such that we could return the compliment. This was most fortuitous in the event.

Just off the corner of the cargo berth is a rock, which just breaks the surface, and if you don't know exactly where it is, can present a problem. We didn't know where it was, even roughly.

Soon did though, as the lifeboat is now balanced on top of it. Fortunately, the extra bods on board all came to the stern, and we managed to get off without having to jump into the very cold water to 'push'. Oh, did they take the mickey out of me. Deserved a bit, I suppose. Well, a little at least, very little?

All we have to do now, is re-secure the lifeboat.

Geoffrey decides to take the forward fall (the lowering/lifting block), while I hooked on the after one. Then stopped the engine, and the bosun pressed the hoist button. It was at this point that the sewage tank decided to pump itself out. It was an automatic level control. Unfortunately, the outlet was about 12 inches above *Geoff's* head, and he copped for the lot, head to toe. Laugh? We couldn't move for laughing. Strange that he didn't join in though. Could never quite understand why. Then the hoist broke down.

"Acht, come on," I said, "I've had enough for tonight. We'll fix it in the morning." It was clear of the water by then anyway.

After regaling the story to the rest, we turned in.

Next morning there was the most horrendous smell. We'd forgotten to take the plug out, and the sewage tank had most obligingly filled the lifeboat to a depth of about a foot.

Who should be looking for revenge, none other than our *Geoffrey*.

"You'll have to go in and take the plug out," he announces triumphantly.

Well, not quite, there is another way of doing this. The hoist was repaired, it had blown a fuse, so the lifeboat was hauled up to the boat deck level, as I sought a length of pipe.

Geoff is standing beside me, and in his usual sarcastic tone said, "How is this going to work?" as I bent it round a bollard to 90 degrees.

"Like this *Geoff*," as I poked the plug up from the bottom. The plug floated free, but I forgot it was a pipe, as this sewage flowed back down the pipe and shot out the other end, covering, none other than our *Geoffrey* once more.

He swears to this day that I did it deliberately, which I vigorously denied at the time, but if you read this *Geoff*, then yes, it was sort of deliberate, mildly so.

Where not to park a lifeboat.

Now before you get let loose on a gas tanker, or any ship really, you are required to display a degree of competency, and pass rather a lot of fairly complex exams in a wide variety of subjects, some of which will be useful to you, others which are not. For example, navigation is useful for a navigating officer, Merchant Navy Defence isn't. Personally, I'd rather have a gun. Seamanship is useful, Liberal Studies is not, as I still fail to see how learning about the life story of Franz Liszt can be utilized on a ship.

One thing you are not examined in is common sense. It would seem to me, just common sense really, to take a course in common sense, as the degree of common sense varies enormously between different people. Especially *Gale Force Gordon*, with lifeboats.

It wasn't only at Porsgrun that we launched our boats. If the weather was fair in Scapa Flow, we'd do it there as well, as we knew where all the good mussel beds were.

However, on this particular day, we were heading for spares. The launch was busy, and as both ships were in, decided to have a 'race' to Scapa Pier. I, as chief mate of the *Quentin*, tied our lifeboat up at the end of the pier.

GFG, as captain of the *Borthwick* tied his up at the other end, and we all set off for Kirkwall. It would have been fair I suppose to point out to him that as the tide was 'in', it would be 'out' when we got back, but then he is a 'captain' and they know everything don't they? Eh, no.

Being rather determined in our deliberations, and making sure we used up as much time as possible, just to make sure that more tide went 'out,' we spun out our short foray ashore into rather a long one, and as selecting fan belts is indeed very thirsty work, necessitated a shortish visit to a refreshment hostelry, which let even more tide 'out'.

Arriving back at Scapa Pier, *Gordons'* lifeboat from the *Borthwick* was indeed high and dry on the beach. Mine was very happily bobbing up and down on its' moorings.

But.

We had a little devilment up our sleeve, as my chief engineer had sneaked off to the agents and got them to pass on a dummy message. As he looked at his boat with a 'how did that happen?' look, the message arrived. He was to berth as soon as possible to load.

He actually got the pilot boat to drag his lifeboat back into the water.

Then we sent out a Lloyds Open Form for salvage. Oh, was he unhappy, which just goes to show, that even professional seamen get it wrong as well.

How to get Ivor to actually pay!

For this tale, I can extract no credit, other than to regale the story to you. Remember my Chief Engineer from Part 1, the 'ball on legs?'

He, and this was not because of his engineering prowess, ended up standing by a ship that Gibson's were managing for an Australian company, Broken Hill Proprieties no less.

The ship, the *Boral Gas*, was lying in Singapore and doing nothing at all except lying there which was fortuitous given his lack of engineering knowledge.

Who should join him? None other than *Ivor*. They were both staying in a hotel.

Now Singapore is rather a nice place, and unless you are in the know, can also be a rather expensive place. Given that both were taking their meals in the hotel, which the company were paying for, and that neither of them will spend as much as a penny that they don't need to, would you would think raise just a hint of suspicion if one was to invite the other out for dinner. In this case, the chief engineer is taking the captain, as it is, his, the chief's birthday. Just how gullible can some people be? Especially as they are going to The Raffles Hotel no less!

This is not cheap.

Having perused the menu and both ordered accordingly, the alcohol gaily flowing and the conversation indeed lively, *Ivor* has still not twigged as to just what is going on. Remember, this chief engineer is noted for his meanness.

Towards the end of the meal, Irish coffee time no less, it went like this:

Chief, "excuse me captain, I'm just popping out to the toilet."

Captain, "okay Jack, I'll go myself when you get back."

Only, Jack never got back, the toilet he was going to, wasn't in The Raffles Hotel, it was in his own hotel, 5 miles down the road.

How long did it take *Ivor* to twig? About half an hour, *and*, he hasn't brought his wallet with him either! He did confess to me some 5 years later, that this was the most embarrassing thing he has ever been involved in, as he had to contact the agents to bring him some money and pay the bill.

As far as I know, he is the only Ship's captain *ever* to be banned from The Raffles Hotel, not that he would ever be likely to return.

Jack had the story round the company before *Ivor* got home.

Life at sea nowadays isn't as much fun as it used to be, a lot of the mavericks have left and the up and coming officers don't really have much of a sense of humour, which if you are ever going to be successful at this job, you need in abundance. But I'm still going back to sea, and I look forward to sailing with you. One thing is certain, it will be immensely rewarding, and because everyone who is there, is there because they want to be there, then it will be that other great word often missing from our stressed lives, it will be fun. With a capital F of course!